CONTROLLING CREDIT

It is common wisdom that central banks in the postwar (1945–1970) period were passive bureaucracies constrained by fixed exchange rates and inflationist fiscal policies. This view is mostly retrospective and informed by US and UK experiences. This book tells a different story. Eric Monnet shows that the Banque de France was at the heart of the postwar financial system and economic planning, and contributed to economic growth by both stabilizing inflation and fostering direct lending to priority economic activities. Credit was institutionalized as a social and economic objective. Monetary policy and credit controls were conflated. He then broadens his analysis to other European countries and sheds light on the evolution of central banks and credit policy before the monetary union. This new understanding has important ramifications for today, since many emerging markets have central bank policies that are similar to Western Europe's in the decades of high growth.

Eric Monnet is a senior economist at the Banque de France, a professor in economic history at the Paris School of Economics and a research affiliate at the Centre for Economic Policy Research (CEPR). This book, combining archival-based institutionalist perspective and quantitative economic analysis, extends his PhD dissertation, which received the Gerschenkron prize from the Economic History Association and the twentieth-century prize from the International Economic History Association.

STUDIES IN MACROECONOMIC HISTORY

Series Editor
Michael D. Bordo, *Rutgers University*

Editors

Owen F. Humpage, *Federal Reserve Bank of Cleveland*
Christopher M. Meissner, *University of California, Davis*
Kris James Mitchener, *Santa Clara University*
David C. Wheelock, *Federal Reserve Bank of St. Louis*

The titles in this series investigate themes of interest to economists and economic historians in the rapidly developing field of macroeconomic history. The four areas covered include the application of monetary and finance theory, international economics, and quantitative methods to historical problems; the historical application of growth and development theory and theories of business fluctuations; the history of domestic and international monetary, financial and other macroeconomic institutions; and the history of international monetary and financial systems. The series amalgamates the former Cambridge University Press series Studies in Monetary and Financial History and Studies in Quantitative Economic History.

Other Books in the Series

(*continued after Index*)

Controlling Credit

*Central Banking and the Planned Economy
in Postwar France, 1948–1973*

ERIC MONNET

Banque de France and Paris School
of Economics

CAMBRIDGE
UNIVERSITY PRESS

CAMBRIDGE
UNIVERSITY PRESS

University Printing House, Cambridge CB2 8BS, United Kingdom

One Liberty Plaza, 20th Floor, New York, NY 10006, USA

477 Williamstown Road, Port Melbourne, VIC 3207, Australia

314-321, 3rd Floor, Plot 3, Splendor Forum, Jasola District Centre, New Delhi - 110025, India

79 Anson Road, #06-04/06, Singapore 079906

Cambridge University Press is part of the University of Cambridge.

It furthers the University's mission by disseminating knowledge in the pursuit of education, learning and research at the highest international levels of excellence.

www.cambridge.org
Information on this title: www.cambridge.org/9781108400084
DOI: 10.1017/9781108227322

First published 2018
First paperback edition 2019

A catalogue record for this publication is available from the British Library

Library of Congress Cataloging in Publication data
Names: Monnet, Eric, 1983– author.
Title: Controlling credit : central banking and the planned economy in postwar France, 1948–1973 / Eric Monnet.
Description: Cambridge, United Kingdom; New York, NY: Cambridge University Press, 2019. |
Series: Studies in macroeconomic history |
Includes bibliographical references and index.
Identifiers: LCCN 2018029894 | ISBN 9781108415019 (hardback)
Subjects: LCSH: Banque de France – History – 20th century. | Banks and banking, Central – France – History. | Credit control – France – History.
Classification: LCC HG3034.M66 2019 | DDC 332.1/1094409045–dc23
LC record available at https://lccn.loc.gov/2018029894

ISBN 978-1-108-41501-9 Hardback
ISBN 978-1-108-40008-4 Paperback

À *Sophie et Noé*

Contents

Figures

Tables

Preface

The project of this book was born nearly a decade ago, several months before the greatest financial and economic crisis since the 1930s struck. It was a context characterized by confident optimism in financial markets and the stabilizing role of central banks. Many publications in the field of economics and economic history celebrated a return to a level of financial openness and development comparable to that of the period before World War I. Even more traced the success of central banks, which had achieved independence and could confine themselves to focusing on price stability, through no other form of economic intervention than targeted announcements and gradual modifications of key interest rates. Central banks, like a discreet and skilled conductor, could step back from debates on broader economic policy and concentrate on inflation targets, leaving it to the market to determine the optimal level and allocation of credit and risk in the economy. Having come across these accounts during my study of economics, I decided to consider, from a historians' perspective, the period that preceded the emergence of such policies and offered a counter-model to them. The little historical work on central banks from the 1950s to the 1970s compared to those on the nineteenth century and the interwar years justifies an approach that is limited to a single country and a relatively brief period. My intention is not to rehabilitate past political virtues, but to consider the past without relying on economic and political frameworks that would not become dominant until a later period, to attempt to understand the postwar period in a manner that is free of the assumptions that gradually began to emerge in the 1980s. From the outset, I embraced the well-established conviction that the task of economic history should be to dispense with teleological and monolithic discourses about paths to economic development – a goal that requires radical empiricism and extensive use of a variety of sources, as well as methodological pluralism.

If this initial economic and political context provided crucial motivation for this book, my research was also deeply affected by the way in which this context rapidly evolved. The financial crisis not only altered public and political discourse – though perhaps to a lesser degree than many might have expected, based on historical experience – but also the discourse of economists. After more than a decade of a burgeoning literature on the positive consequences of credit expansion for growth and the detrimental burden of credit restrictions, analyses began to appear (often using the same methods and data as the previous studies) on credit's potentially negative consequences for the economy and the importance of knowing how to rein in its expansion. The growth of so-called "emerging" economies, which had not gone hand-in-hand with financial liberalization and a withdrawal of the state of the kind seen in Europe and the United States, also modified earlier discourses about paths to financial development and growth. The idea that there might be different kinds of capitalism resurfaced. The rupture was even sharper as it related to central banks. The latter returned to the center of the political and financial game. The extent of their intervention in the economy mushroomed and their policies were discussed not only from the standpoint of their macroeconomic effects but also from the perspective of their distributive effects on the economy and their impact on budget policies and inequality. They were given new legal powers to intervene in the banking and financial sector. The ways they intervened in the economy changed so abruptly that they spawned new words ("non-conventional," "macroprudential," "quantitative," and so on), which were invented to describe economic policies and tools that, all things considered, strongly resembled those that had prevailed in a vast majority of countries in the decades prior to the 1980s and were the subject of the historical studies I had undertaken. In the discourse of central banks as well as economists, it was now accepted that interest rates could not be the only monetary instrument and that "controlling credit" was necessary for financial stability and a legitimate goal for central banks. What I had begun studying and describing as a historical practice – and a heresy for contemporary central banks – had, in a sense, returned to center stage. This abrupt and unexpected change forced me to grapple with new questions in my history work and made it necessary, in particular, to explain the difference between credit policies of the 1950s and 1960s and those of the 2010s – questions to which this book's conclusion will return. Just as, several years earlier, it had struck me as ill-advised to use history to justify the teleological advent of a form of *fin de siècle* central banking, it appeared just as debatable to see new central bank policies as a return to older practices. The current conceptions of credit, the purpose of controlling it and the state's role in the economy in France and in Europe have little in common with the aftermath of World War II. Clinging to technical similarities erases the historical and ideological stakes of radically different projects and political choices.

The period following the 2008 crisis was no longer simply an existential crisis for central banks and a reconsideration of standard economic models. It also gave rise to renewed interest in economic history, and particularly for the history of credit and various forms of capital. Some even spoke of a reemergence of the concept of capitalism in economic history. This reappropriation of the history of credit by historians also informed the thinking in this book, even if the latter appeared in another context and using different methods. Thus, one will find in these pages the idea that the development of forms of credit in an economy – and their possible regulation – is deeply embedded in social structures and a particular ideological and legal framework. But unlike several studies that are symptomatic of this historiographical revival that study the history of financial capitalism and the ideology underlying credit expansion within a private market framework, particularly in the United States, this book presents the development – followed by the disappearance – of a conception of credit expansion and control in a framework characterized by ubiquitous state intervention in the financial system. The policies I have studied start with the principle that market mechanisms were incapable both of promoting sufficient credit growth to finance investment and of controlling credit growth to avoid overly high inflation and banking crises. The state, conceived as the framework for coordinating different economic interests and sectors, was thus responsible for controlling credit. In France, as in many other countries (the United States and United Kingdom being partly an exception), the heart of the system of control over credit and investment was the central bank. While it did not ignore the existence of private markets or limit itself to targeted policies, the state nevertheless intervened on all fronts, at different levels, thus erasing the boundary between public and private credit. While continuing to situate itself in a capitalist economic framework, French postwar monetary, industrial and financial policies rested on an institutional basis that was known, at the time, as "the nationalization of credit." Money and credit were seen as two sides of the same economic process. Monetary policy and credit policy were conflated. Most of the time, moreover, central bankers used the two terms synonymously.

Though new questions sprung up in the course of writing this book, its initial goal remained the same: to understand, on the one hand, the political and economic specificity of the postwar period and particularly the factors that made it possible, while, on the other, studying how the effects of central bank policies depend on the nature of its (political and economic) interactions with the banking and financial system. The attention it devotes to ideas, as well as to decision-making processes and the way they evolved, is not isolated from the analysis of economic mechanisms and effects. There is often a tendency, when talking about money and credit, to see it as an almost virtual realm, as a series of games played with words and symbols – a sphere of speculation and immaterial bonds of trust, disconnected from its opposite, the real economy. Most economic models, especially at present, prefer, consequently, to do away with money, which is still often seen as a veil. It is only quite recently that sociology and anthropology have fully considered the materiality of money as a phenomenon and of practices associated with credit relationships. Thus, one can always be struck by what often appears as a form of dualism, as if the sphere of "reality" and the monetary sphere coexisted independently and their interactions remained beyond our reach. Recalling what the philosopher Daniel Dennett said about Cartesian mind-body dualism, one senses, in relation to money, the paradox of Casper the Friendly Ghost, who can pass through walls yet still manages to hold objects ("How can Casper both glide through walls and grab a falling towel?"). Money is replete with symbols, credit is only ever a promise, "but anything that can move a physical thing is itself a physical thing (although perhaps a strange and heretofore unstudied kind of physical thing)" (Daniel Dennett, *Consciousness Explained*, 1991, p. 35).

Acknowledgments

I owe a debt of gratitude to Pierre-Cyrille Hautcoeur who supervised my doctoral thesis on which this book is partly based. I could not have found a better person to help me establish close contacts with both historians and economists and navigate between these two oceans, which rarely meet with calm weather. It was the necessary condition for everything else. I met Michael Bordo at the beginning of this project and his influence on the final result has grown steadily over time. I am extremely grateful to him and it is a great honor to see this book published in his series at Cambridge University Press. At the Press, I have been lucky to benefit from the help, advice and patience of Scott Paris, Stephen Acerra and especially Karen Maloney, Kristina Deusch, Penny Harper, Liz Davey and Bethany Johnson.

Pierre Sicsic's help with this book has taken too many different forms to list them here, and I have certainly not managed to answer all his challenging comments. The Banque de France funded the translation of the first part of this book, originally written in French. I am very grateful to Michael Behrent for the translation. His intimate knowledge of postwar France was a key asset. The views and interpretations in this book are my own and none of them should be attributed to the Banque de France or the Eurosystem.

I would like to thank the members of my thesis committee for their many comments, which undoubtedly made it possible to improve the various chapters over the many years it took for this thesis to become a book: Antoine d'Autumne, Michael Bordo, Benoit Mojon, Mary O'Sullivan, Romain Rancière and Gilles Saint-Paul.

My thesis won two international prizes in economic history that have allowed this narrow study on an obscure subject of French economic history to gain recognition. I am very grateful to Dan Bogart (EHA), Jan Luiten van Zanden, Pablo Martin-Acena and Catherine Schenk (IEHA) for rewarding my work and giving me new opportunities.

During the early stages of this project, I had the chance to frequently discuss parts of this work with Guillaume Bazot, Olivier Feiertag, Michel Margairaz, Gilles Postel-Vinay and Jean-Laurent Rosenthal. Their influence has not stopped over the years. The seminar organized with Clément Dherbécourt on methods in economic history was also a decisive training space. Frederik Grelard and Fabrice Reuze, archivists of the Banque de France, were so helpful and insightful that it is impossible to guess how much this book owes to them. During the same period, interminable discussions with Arnaud Fossier on institutions and history have been the source of my interest in law and norms that led to the approach developed in Part I. Eugene White welcomed me at Rutgers for six months where I finished writing my dissertation and, thanks to him, I then started to realize how little I knew about financial and monetary history. Juliette Roussin had the patience to read and comment on the first chapters several times, which owe her much.

Since then, I have had the chance to work on new projects related to this book with several coauthors: Jérémie Cohen-Setton, Vincent Duchaussoy, Anna Kelber, Vivien Lévy-Garboua, Alain Naef, Stefano Pagliari, Damien Puy, Blaise Truong-Loi, Shahin Vallée, Miklos Vari. What I learned from them is obvious in many pages. Jérémie, Vincent, Alain and Damien were also kind enough to comment on previous versions of some chapters.

I have been extraordinarily fortunate to discuss chapters of this book with audiences in many different academic venues and central banks. They are unfortunately too numerous to be listed here, which is just evidence that this research project took too many years to complete. I should nevertheless say that the seminar organized by Nicolas Barreyre and Nicolas Delalande on public debt was key to giving a new life to Chapter 5 of this book, which was originally an annex only. I thank Martin Daunton, the discussant, for his comments. Sections on European integration in Chapter 7 were originally written for a political science conference organized by Benjamin Lemoine and Vincent Gayon. Emmanuel Mourlon-Druol helped me to transform them into a full chapter. Archivists of the Banque de Belgique, Banca d'Italia, Bank of International of Settlements and Bank of England were very helpful for this research.

In addition to the above-mentioned persons, I would also like to thank the following for their advice, reading or criticisms at various stages of this project (with no particular order): Angelo Riva, Laure Quennouëlle-Corre, Laurent Warlouzet, Sabine Effosse, Patrice Baubeau, Pierrick Clerc, Yannick Kalantzis, Moritz Schularick, Jean-Pascal Bénassy, Xavier Ragot, Thomas Piketty, Benjamin Lemoine, Nicolas Delalande, Hervé Joly, Christina and

David Romer, Barry Eichengreen, Albrecht Ritschl, Jean-Yves Grenier, Guillaume Calafat, Perry Mehrling, Hugh Rockoff, François Velde, Chris Meissner, Oliver Bush, Duncan Needham, Chris Colvin, Claude Diebolt. They certainly disagree with some interpretations of this book, but I hope that I have managed to live up to the help they gave me.

I also thank my colleagues at PSE and Banque de France for their encouragements, my family and my friends for their ongoing support and Sophie for everything.

Abbreviations

BIS	Bank of International Settlements
CCB	Commission de contrôle des banques (Banking regulation committee)
CDC	Caisse des dépôts et consignations
CES	Conseil Economique et Social (Economic and Social Council)
CGP	Commissariat général du Plan (Planning office or General Planning Commissariat)
CNC	Conseil National du Crédit (National Credit Council)
CNR	Conseil National de la Résistance (National Resistance Council)
DASM	Direction des analyses statistiques et monétaires (Directorate of Statistical and Monetary Analysis)
DGC	Direction générale du crédit (General Directorate of Credit)
EC	European Communities
EEC	European Economic Community
FDES	Fonds de Développement Économique et Social (Economic and Social Development Fund)
IMF	International Monetary Fund
INSEE	Institut national de la statistique et des études économiques (National Institute for Statistics and Economic Studies)
OECD	(Organisation for Economic Co-operation and Development)
PVCG	Procès verbaux du Conseil Général (minutes of the General Council of the Banque)
SCR	Service central des risques (Central Risk Service)

Introduction

The period from the end of World War II until the first oil shock of 1973 is known in France and in Western Europe more generally as a golden age, economically speaking. In France, the period is still referred to as the *Trente Glorieuses* – the "Thirty Glorious Years" – in recognition of Jean Fourastié's book of the same title (1979), even if recent historical work has shown that one should not take for granted the unity of this period, and even less should one downplay its negative aspects, notably its ecological consequences, colonial wars and the persistence of poverty (Pessis et al. 2013). If one limits this period to the twenty-five years between 1948 and 1973, France experienced the highest average growth rate in its history, relatively moderate inflation, low unemployment and a significant expansion of credit without banking crises.

The usual explanations of this achievement, which are not specific to France, give little attention to the role of the central bank and monetary policy. It is usually considered enough to note that they were guaranteed by "catch-up" growth and the stability of the Bretton Woods system, on the implicit assumption that these two factors were independent of the actions of monetary authorities. Equally widespread is the idea that moderate inflation and growth occurred despite the Banque de France's activity, which, it is believed, consisted primarily in inflationary government financing through direct advances to the Treasury and additional constraints on the banking and financial system.[1] As this period is seen as the apotheosis

---

[1] The generally admitted view that monetary policy during the three decades following World War II was passive and consisted in tracking budget deficits has been particularly well expressed by Pierre Siklos, in his reference book on the evolution of central banks' role after 1945:

In an era where there was considerably more emphasis placed on the role of fiscal policy, monetary policy was viewed as passively supplying the ingredients required to guarantee aggregate economic

of what is sometimes called "financial repression," it is assumed that the expansion of credit was constrained by strict financial regulation and by low, government-mandated interest rates, that were needed to finance the public debt. This view, once again, attributes central banks a passive role, stuck in a relatively immobile financial system or pulled along by exogenous economic growth.

This vision, which is still the consensus view, of central banks' role during the three decades following World War II does not, however, resist closer scrutiny, as this book will show. But when one plunges into the archives, it quickly becomes apparent why it has persisted. During this period, central banks exhibited two traits, which are particularly evident in the case of the Banque de France, which made their policy difficult to grasp and surrounded their actions with a web of confusion. This difficulty is exacerbated when one views this period with assumptions shaped by the direction monetary policy took in the 1980s. The two traits are, first, that monetary policy belonged to a larger framework of "credit policy" and, second, that interest rates were not the leading policy instrument of the central bank.

MONETARY POLICY AND CREDIT POLICY

Monetary policy can be defined as the means that a central bank uses to affect variables of the short-term economic cycle such as inflation, production and employment. Monetary policy's goal is to act on price levels, exchange rates and the credit and money mass, but its primary goal is not to influence credit allocation or bank and non-bank assets. A credit policy, on the contrary, seeks to act on the way credit is allocated across

well-being. This was in large part due to the breakdown of the Gold Standard, the failure of international coordination among central banks, as well as the response of governments to the global slump triggered by the Great Depression of the 1930s. Nevertheless, with fiscal activism came inflation. (Siklos 2002, pp. 12–13)

This viewpoint also still prevails in French historiography on the French postwar economy. For example, a recent comprehensive book on the Vichy economy and postwar economic changes argues that the Banque de France after World War II had little power because it was reluctant to use the discount rate for monetary policy purpose and that, in a global Keynesian context, monetary authorities no longer gave priority to monetary stability (Grenard et al. 2017, p. 291). Chapter 4 of this book (based on Monnet [2014]) challenges the direction of such arguments and presents for the first time a quantitative analysis of the macroeconomic effects of Banque de France policy during this period, showing that the Banque was able to strongly influence inflation without using the discount rate.

the economy by favoring particular sectors and institutions. One of the postwar period's distinctive characteristics in France and many other countries is that credit policy encompassed monetary policy. When the term credit policy (*politique du crédit*) was used, it could, at times, be meant in the relatively limited sense of monetary policy, referring to measures a central bank takes to fight inflation or, on the contrary, to stimulate economic activity.[2] Yet, in most cases, the concept of "credit policy" had a much more extensive meaning, denoting the full array of interventions supported or elaborated by a central bank to encourage the development of credit and influence its allocation, thus replacing free-market mechanisms that were deemed insufficient, unfair or defective. The concept of credit control(s), whether in the singular or the plural, was also often used as a synonym for credit policy, in the restrictive as well as in the extensive sense.[3] Historians who undertake the task of studying central banks during this period thus encounter a multiplicity of uses, which are often a source of confusion, especially since certain national particularities can further complicate them, as we shall see in the case of France. Moreover, the goals of a policy of intervening in credit allocation were multiple, and uses of the term were, consequently, numerous and often vague and multivocal: it could be pursued for purposes of monetary policy (attempting to limit the credit level through better allocation), industrial or social policy (helping key economic sectors), budgetary policy (giving priority to government financing), trade policy (favoring credit for exporting sectors), capital controls (favoring domestic loans), financial stability (preventing an excess of credit that is potentially disconnected from real activity in particular sectors) and so on. The very nature of credit policy was thus to interact with many other policies by directing financing and rendering credit control's various tools consistent with the latter. The central bank was thus connected to many other institutions and bureaucracies involved in implementing government

---

[2] This was the case of discussions in the Banque de France's Conseil Général. Such uses are also found, notably, in international literature: EEC (1962, 1972), Katz (1969), de Kock (1974) and Hodgman (1974).

[3] This second sense is clearly evident, for instance, in the contributions, relating to France and abroad, of an issue of *Revue Economique* from 1951 (vol. 2, no. 5) and, as we shall see, in most of the French debates on the opportunity represented by state intervention in credit allocation. In international literature, one also finds this second usage – along with the term "credit control" – in numerous publications, often apposed with rather than substituting itself for the term "monetary policy." This is notably the case in Hodgman (1974) or in documents from the international community. See Chapter 7.

policy. Something that might resemble a relationship of dependence – and was subsequently often interpreted as such – can be seen, from a different point of view, as evidence of the bank's central role at the heart of the political and bureaucratic system.

A POLICY WITHOUT INTEREST RATES

Making monetary policy and credit policy compatible – acting on the level of credit as well as its allocation – was an essential question, and one crucial to central bank policy. In doing so, the same instruments and operating procedures were used to regulate the overall quantity of credit in the economy (since credit expansion was seen as necessary to economic expansion, but also as inflationary) and to act on its allocation. It could involve simple recommendations and incentives given to banks, as well as direct controls of the credit supply (such as credit ceilings), of bank liquidity (reserve or liquidity ratios) and of the access to central bank financing (rediscount ceilings, informal selection and the choice of various loan maturities).[4] Credit policy, in this way, combined quantitative and qualitative controls, direct constraints on credit expansion and indirect constraints aimed at the distribution of credit institutions' assets and liabilities and on the financing they received from the central bank. These various instruments could branch out into various sub-categories, making credit controls more precise, and evolve significantly over time to adapt to the banking system's characteristics. Of these multiple instruments, the central bank's interest rate generally played a minor and often merely psychological role, as was recognized at the Banque de France, where it was partially indexed on foreign rates (in particular the US Federal Reserve rate). The fact that the interest rate was not Banque de France's primary instrument of monetary policy did not mean that it was indifferent to interest rates: it intervened to keep treasury bond rates low, it cared about the spread with foreign rates, it participated in regulating debtor and creditor rates and so on. But the Banque de France's discount rate was

---

[4] Liquidity ratios were used so that credit creation would be lesser, beginning at a specific deposit level. The break with prewar practices was not absolute and the role of rediscounting notably goes back to the Banque de France's origins. Because different kinds of collateral were selected, the central bank practice of rediscounting already implied a degree of involvement in the allocation of credit. American economists described this practice as "credit policy" rather than "monetary policy" (Friedman 1969; Goodfriend & King 1988). Postwar practices took root in the discounting tradition, as we shall see, but they also introduced radical innovations, if only in the form of bank-specific rediscounting ceilings, and particularly rediscounting as a way of acting on the sectoral allocation of credit, and not simply as a way of managing risk and bank liquidity.

not modified to fight inflation or, on the contrary, to increase demand and production. It could remain relatively disconnected from other central bank instruments, as financial and bank markets were highly regulated and thus segmented. Debtor and creditor rates were themselves regulated for much of this period. Thus, it was possible that a credit restriction would not result in a general increase in the various interest rates that banks applied. Monetary policy was, consequently, transmitted by quantities rather by prices. The Banque de France, like other European central banks, embraced this disconnection between its quantitative tools and interest rates in order to affirm the autonomy of its monetary policy vis-à-vis other countries and to favor the financing of the public debt in periods when credit was restricted. Often, the interest rate level provided no information making it possible to determine whether domestic monetary policy was expansive or restrictive, except when it was deemed necessary to send a "psychological" signal. Not all these characteristics were fixed; they could evolve over time, in conjunction with changes in the banking system or the views of the central bank's decision-makers.[5]

This brief description of instruments and objectives suggests why it is so difficult to understand a central bank's policies during this period. This is all the more true given that we have become accustomed to the idea that monetary policy is pursued through interest rates or control of the money supply, that these variables are sufficient for expressing the central bank's goals and that monetary policy can be disconnected from credit allocation.[6]

---

[5] Chapters 3 and 4 will emphasize these issues.

[6] A concept regularly used to refer to the French economy of this period is that of "overdraft economy." A number of theories relating to this concept developed in France beginning in the late 1970s, notably at the Banque de France (hence the occasional reference to a "Banque de France school"). Its history has been told by Goux (1990), Loriaux (1991) and Feiertag (2006a, 2006b). We did not want to take this categorization for granted, for two reasons. First, the term has been used very politically and circumstantially: it reflects, in this way, the state of the debate in France in the early 1980s more than it tells us retrospectively about the policies of the *Trente Glorieuses*. Furthermore, it is a rather imprecise concept that, based on thinking about the connection between the central bank and other banks, was ultimately used to characterize the financial system as a whole. Its relevance for analyzing the French economy has been challenged (Cobham & Serre 2002). It is not my intent to join the debate, but I have observed that theories of the "overdraft economy" were inadequate for fully and precisely explaining the mechanisms of French monetary policy before the mid-1970s, particularly in a context in which interest rates did not play a role and in which various ratios for controlling liquidity and credit succeeded one another. It strikes me as more fair to speak of "credit policy" when one wants to characterize in general terms the role of the Banque de France during this period, while using more precise concepts when one considers more fine-grained levels of analysis, whether one is speaking about control of bank liquidity or credit allocation across the economy.

Chapter 4 will show that if one measures the Banque de France's monetary policy stance in terms of its interest rate, as standard economic works on monetary policy would suggest, one would mistakenly conclude that the latter had no effect. By elaborating, however, a way of measuring the direction of monetary policy that takes into account the range of instruments used by the Banque de France as well as its goals, I find that it had an important effect on credit, money, prices and production, explaining nearly half of these variables' volatility during the period being studied.

FOR A COMMON HISTORY OF CREDIT POLICY AND CENTRAL BANKING

The primary task for an economic history of the Banque de France during the *Trente Glorieuses* is thus to reach a comprehensive understanding of the various facets of credit policy – its medium- and long-term goals as they pertain to credit development and allocation, as well as its role in specific circumstances and its short-term effects on inflation and the economic cycle. This also requires institutional reflection on the way authorities perceived credit and the bases of legitimate state intervention in credit allocation, which, in Part I, I will call the "institutionalization of credit." Credit policy cannot exist unless credit is thought of as a political problem.[7]

---

[7]   A study of this kind was begun by Olivier Feiertag in his biography of the Banque de France governor, Wilfried Baumgartner. On numerous points, the current book follows this framework, while expanding the period and sources under consideration and, most importantly, by adding, on the one hand, an institutional analysis of policy and, on the other, quantitative analyses, an engagement with various contemporary and later economic theories and a detailed study of the various instruments used by central banks. Unlike Feiertag, we leave aside the history of the Banque de France as a company. This was done incidentally by Vincent Duchaussoy (2013). Before Feiertag's book, the now quite old work of Guillaumont-Jeanneney (1968, 1991), Koch (1983), Andrieu (1984) and Mélitz (1991) examined different aspects of the Banque de France's policy after World War II, though without undertaking a quantitative analysis of the impact of monetary policy and credit policy. Guillaumont-Jeanneney's and Mélitz's analyses are not based on archival work. Koch's book (1983) was a testimonial by a former Banque de France official presenting the main decisions relating to monetary policy through 1958. Andrieu (1984) only used the archives of the Conseil National du Crédit in the 1950s, and thus did not address short-term policy for controlling the currency and prices. In the case of France,. Andrieu (1984) was the first to mention the ambiguity of the concept of credit policy and his pioneering analysis remains a reference point for political history. Margairaz's (1991) and Quenouëlle-Corre's (2000) dissertations on the Finance Ministry also address the Banque de France's policy during this period and will be used on several occasions in the following pages.

Credit policy, understood in the broad sense of state intervention in credit allocation (or "Credit Activism in Interventionist States," to use Loriaux [1997]'s particularly explicit title) has been the subject of several major studies by American political scientists, in the wake of Zysman's seminal work (1983) dealing with France. These studies focused primarily on the end of these policies and the reasons for the retreat from state intervention. Loriaux (1991) notably studied financial liberalization and the end of industrial policies in France by linking these transformations to the end of the Bretton Woods system, which led him to describe French credit policy from the 1950s on, including the role played by the central bank. These analyses, which followed the theoretical framework known among political sciences as "international political economy" (IPO), were based on secondary sources and concentrated on the moral hazard induced by credit policy and the possibility of autonomous public policy in a period of increasing globalization (see, more generally, the essays gathered in Loriaux et al. 1997), rather than on a detailed analysis of political decision-making and its economic effects. As Michael Loriaux (1997, p. 7) also recognizes, the literature on financial liberalization is voluminous, "though the literature on credit activism in interventionist states is not extensive in English." Regrettably, almost the same statement can be made twenty years later, despite the fact that archives have since become available. Most importantly, these pioneering studies gave relatively little attention to central banks, and even less to the instruments through which they intervened, whether to fight inflation or to allocate credit. The fact that credit controls were used to contain inflation and limit balance of payment deficits – even before devaluations – has never been the subject of in-depth analysis. It follows that the consequences for central banks of the end of credit policy in the 1980s have never been fully considered and, as a result, that international scholarly literature on the history of central banking has remained on the sidelines of political science literature on interventionist credit policies. Thus, the main synthetic works on the history of central banks in the second half of the twentieth century (Siklos 2002; Singleton 2011) make no mention of this literature or of central banks' role in credit policy.[8] Nor in his history of European monetary integration from the 1970s to the 1990s does Harold James (2012) discuss the importance of the end of credit policy

---

[8]   Recent monographs on the Federal Reserve (Meltzer 2010) and the Bank of England (Capie 2010) take stock of the credit control instruments, notably those used to fight inflation and favor public debt, but do not study central banks through the prism of their credit policy.

for central banks that gradually joined the Eurosystem, even though the conversations he cites between central bank governors in the early 1970s explicitly use the term "credit policy" in a way that is different from "monetary policy" (James 2012, pp. 78–79, 127).

One of this book's goals is thus to reactivate and to incorporate, based on the French example, the main insights provided by political science on "activist credit policies" into the history of central banks and their effects on the economic cycle and, more generally, in the longer history of financial intermediation and credit regulation. Chapter 7 will show how credit policy was not specifically French, even if the ways of conducting it differed from country to country, and will discuss its consequences for the history of European monetary integration.[9]

Integrating credit policy into the history of central banks makes it necessary to combine a historical approach based on the study of new qualitative and quantitative primary sources, on the one hand, and a macroeconomic perspective on the other, while resorting, when necessary, to economic theory and econometrics to study the central bank's political and economic role in the economy. Such an approach will guide the historical study of the Banque de France's policy. I also blend into this approach an institutionalist perspective, in order to shed light on the emergence and evolution of credit policy and the ways in which this policy was embedded in a distinct social, ideological and legal context that it influenced, in turn.

AN INSTITUTIONALIST APPROACH TO CREDIT POLICY

The institutionalist perspective does not consist solely in "contextualizing" the Banque de France's postwar policy. It also makes it possible to understand the various elements on which this policy was based. In particular, the production of statistics and a new legal arsenal allowed bank regulations to be used to achieve short-term and sectoral policy goals. These legal aspects have not been studied in previous historical accounts of the Banque de France. Most importantly, the institutionalist perspective helps us to understand why the fight against inflation was, by the late 1940s, seen as a condition of possibility and of the stability of interventionist policies in credit allocation. Excessively high inflation, by reviving memories of 1947–1948, would render state interventionism illegitimate for business leaders as well as employees, as unions are always suspicious that moments of high inflation will lead to a decline in real salaries. Thus, there are no grounds for

---

[9]   Initial steps into this direction were taken by Hodgman (1974) and Feiertag (2003).

opposing the "monetary" side of credit policy to its "interventionism" in credit allocation. One must, rather, understand why the sustained inflation of the 1970s – that the *dirigiste* system did not know how to contain – ultimately delegitimated and spelled the end of credit policy. The process of delegitimating credit policy over the 1970s and 1980s must be distinguished from the much more widely known and discussed way in which inflation challenged traditional Keynesian theories, notably the use of the Phillips curve over the same period. There is no reason for believing that it was only due to the stability of the international Bretton Woods system that interventionist policy was possible and could preserve its legitimacy. The structure of the international system was not exogenous to national policy, but resulted, on the contrary, from a partial convergence of national norms and practices. It is mainly on this crucial point that my argument concerning Banque de France policy differs from that of Michael Loriaux (1991), for whom the Bretton Woods system and frequent devaluations allowed the Banque de France to support credit policy in the 1950s and 1960s at no cost, leading to moral hazard. Loriaux (1991, pp. 38–39) thus believes that the Banque de France's monetary restrictions increased during the 1970s, following the end of Bretton Woods, when the limits on bank credits (*encadrement du credit*, or credit ceilings) became permanent. On the contrary, I show that the permanent use of credit controls in the 1970s was accompanied by an anti-inflationary policy that was far less restrictive than it was over the previous two decades and that this reveals a reconsideration of the earlier principles guiding how credit policy functioned. The mechanisms and policies that were supposed to ensure the institution's domestic stability through relative price stability had, in this way, changed, partly due to emerging institutional changes in the late 1960s (the intellectual reassessment of credit policy, the first attempts to establish an open market, the government's growing role in the Banque de France's decision-making processes and so on). We shall see that the transformations that occurred in the mid-1970s should no longer be seen as the culmination of the previously existing policy, but, on the contrary, as evidence that it was being undermined and was off course.[10]

The study of credit policy from an institutionalist perspective will be the subject of the first part of this book. I will borrow frequently from various institutionalist theories (including from legal history, economics and political science), but the general framework primarily bears the influence of

---

[10] It is also for this reason that I refrain from using the concept of "overdraft economy," which was forged during the 1970s.

Karl Polanyi. From Polanyi, I have drawn two key ideas. First, the economy is viewed as an instituted process: "The study of the shifting place occupied by the economy in society is therefore no other than the study of the manner in which the economic process is instituted at different times and places"(Polanyi 1957, p. 250). In contrast to many recent studies in the field of economics and political science (which are often described as neo-institutionalist), the concept of institution is not defined here as a set of rules that are exogenous to the market economy and actors' behavior, but as a process through which a set of rules, behaviors and economic practices is constructed.[11] This is why I speak of institutionalization as well as institution, and use the term "institutionalization of credit" in studying the history of credit policy. One consequence of this stance is that I will not, from the outset, oppose the realm of the market to the realm of state intervention. Chapter 6 in particular will examine the difficulty of establishing a boundary between the state and the market if one wants to understand investment in France during the *Trente Glorieuses*. Second, I follow Polanyi when he says that "the instituting of the economic process vests that process with unity and stability; it produces a structure with a definite function in society ... A study of how empirical economies are instituted should start from the ways in which the economy acquires unity and stability, that is the interdependence and recurrence of its parts" (1957, pp. 249–250). Embracing this definition's implicit functionalism, Part I of this book will broadly examine how credit policy emerged, stabilized itself and was then challenged. Specifically, it will consider how economic thought, the legal framework and administrative and political adjustments contributed to this theory. It is from this perspective that one should understand the role of the fight against inflation, which is conceived as a safeguard for protecting the institution's stability. I will, consequently, speak of institutional coherence when describing the interdependence between the institution's different components. The unity of the institutionalization of credit can be grasped through the complexity and uniqueness of its distinctive political, economic and ideological interactions in the wake of World War II. This book is not able to propose a social history of credit, which would have required drawing on a much wider and more diverse body of sources, but it does try to show the political and social mechanisms – and not merely economic

---

[11] Neo-institutionalism in economics has developed in the wake of the work of Douglass North and Avner Greif. Applied to the study of central banks, this approach has mostly concerned itself with measuring how central bank independence affects the average inflation rate (see, for example, Acemoglu et al. 2008).

ones – that made the question of credit a priority in the postwar years, and to explain why the answer to this question meant a major role for the state and the central bank.

In Part I of the book, I define three components of this institutionalizing process that will serve as an analytical perspective for considering the development of credit policy from the end of World War II to the mid-1970s. The first component is legal: principles are anchored in law, which functions as the institution's "conditions of possibility." A second component consists of the social norms or beliefs that guide action: an institution can, in particular, exist only if actors share beliefs about the rules of the game. This is the ideological component of the institution. Finally, a third component of the institution relates to its capacity for "control" or "self-control," which is crucial to its preservation. Any institutionalizing process engenders a set of more or less formal constraints designed to avoid institutional breakdown. I interpret various approaches to fighting inflation as a form of control and self-control of credit policy. A large part of the analysis in Chapters 1, 2 and 3 is devoted to studying the evolutions of these three components and their interactions over time.

By taking these various paths, I have encountered the recent literature in economic history that studies how the question of credit and financial risk has become a political and social issue and the social and legal mechanisms through which forms of financial intermediation and economic practices are justified (Hoffman et al. 2000; Hyman 2011; Ott 2011; Levy 2012; Fontaine 2014; Yates 2015). What makes my approach original is to link the study of the political vision of credit with macroeconomic history and to highlight how state-organized credit policies have been a key driver of postwar capitalism. In contrast to what has been done for debt and capital (Dyson 2014; Piketty 2014), few recent works have attempted to connect macroeconomic history and the social history of credit, with the notable exception of Avner Offer (2014, 2017) on housing credits in England and Hoffman et al. (2018) on notarized credit in nineteenth-century France.[12] The institutional analysis of credit policy also overlaps with work in economics and political science that calls attention to how various institutional configurations can lead to the rise of different forms of capitalism (Hall & Soskice 2001; Amable 2003; Fioretos 2011). Chapter 7 revisits this question, by emphasizing the

---

[12] Whereas studies by economists have reconstructed long credit series and brought to light the macroeconomic importance of credit cycles (Schularick & Taylor 2012), it remains to be understood how credit was encouraged and regulated politically at different historical moments.

common denominators but also the divergences between credit policies in several countries. This is in fact a return to the pioneering study of the "varieties of capitalism" approach, Andrew Shonfield's book (1965), which compared different forms of planning in Western Europe and devoted a few pages to the "management of credit."

A NEW PERSPECTIVE ON THE POSTWAR ECONOMY

The type of credit policy described above could exist only in a legal and ideological framework that is very different from the one we are familiar with in present-day Europe. In the first place, the central bank needed the legal capacity to use certain types of bank regulation measures (relating to credit and liquidity control) as instruments of short-term monetary policy. Consequently, it not only needed power over banks, but also sufficient flexibility in exercising this authority to ensure that decisions pertaining to quantitative restriction could be taken quickly and independently, without parliamentary approval or a ministerial decree. Second, the central bank needed sufficient legitimacy to ensure that its decisions relating to the loan selection process, which amounted to giving priority to particular sectors or particular banks (and thus indirectly influencing competition) were seen as serving the general interest and economic growth. Such was the ideological framework that informed the origins of the law of December 2, 1945 relating to "the nationalization of the Banque de France, major deposit banks, and the organization of credit," which at the time was referred to as the "law for nationalizing credit." Though it is often remembered primarily for nationalizing the bank's capital, the law also granted the bank significant power to control other banks and to intervene in the allocation of credit. We will see in the following chapter how the origins of the 1945 law lay in socialist and economic planning movements of the 1930s, which the National Resistance Council took up again in 1944. But it must also be situated within two institutional traditions. First, it continued the Banque de France's practice of intervening directly in the banking sector through rediscounting, which had been common in France since the nineteenth century. Next, it involved a rediscovery of legal instruments, notably banking laws, established under the Vichy regime that allowed the state to establish its control over the banking sector and industry. The ideological break with the previous regime did not, in this instance, entail a significant institutional break: while modifying the way the institutions it borrowed from Vichy functioned, the new policies defined in 1945 shared Vichy's rejection of the interwar years, which stood accused of favoring French banks and financial markets as they pursued goals contrary to the general interest.

Contrary to the conventional wisdom about this period, the Banque de France's policy had little in common with Keynesianism, or in any case with the monetary theory of Keynes and his British disciples, who were eager to emphasize budgetary policy. Unless one is prepared to defend the idea that "Keynesianism" is a very general concept that covers any form of state intervention in the economy, it is impossible to understand the specificities of the connection between the Banque de France and the banking and financial system from the standpoint of traditional Keynesian theory. Conflating the Banque de France's policies with Keynesian principles prevents us, moreover, from making sense of the deep differences that characterized France's discussions with the United States and England about monetary issues, as we shall see in Chapters 2 and 7. Specific references to Keynesian monetary and budgetary ideas did not appear at the Banque de France until the late 1960s and these took, in part, the form of a plea for the liberalization of the banking and financial system and for a radical change in the Banque de France's means of intervention. From the French central bank's perspective, Keynes's ideas were conflated with English money markets operations, the opposite of credit controls. The Banque de France doctrine – a blend of interventionist convictions and monetary orthodoxy – which held that the money supply and inflation must be controlled through quantitative and selective credit controls was primarily the result of the unique characteristics of the French credit market during the period, as well as a legacy of peculiar French intellectual traditions and central banking practices. I see the developments in central banking taking place between 1930s and 1950s – namely the rise of interventionist credit policies – as a part of a "global New Deal" led by ideals of economic planification in capitalist (non-communist) economies (Patel 2016). The 1944 Bretton Woods conference was a defining moment in this history as it recognized the priority of domestic policies over international constraints and gave official recognition to developmental activist policies (Helleiner 2014). Referring to such ideas as "Keynesian" neglects the many national traditions which developed in parallel and were often very different from Keynes's vision of state intervention (especially about the role given to financial and money markets), as well as how the war economy shaped domestic economic and political institutions.[13]

---

[13] Keynes's proposals that resembled the most the credit control policies implemented in France during the war and postwar period are actually those laid down in his 1940 *How to Pay for the War: A Radical Plan for the Chancellor of the Exchequer*.

Finally, the conclusions of this study of credit policy calls into question the idea that growth during the *Trente Glorieuses* can be explained as a process of catching up that occurred, as it were, naturally, and in which financial factors played a minor role. On this point, I agree with the conclusions of Alexander Gerschenkron (1962), who has shown how, in the late nineteenth century, financial institutions were essential to catching up and how states played a key role in creating them ("substitution of prerequisites"). Similarly to what Gerschenkron had observed in the case of late nineteenth-century Europe, the state in post-1945 France asserted its new role with the help of a deeply national ideology and theory that served to justify these interventions. This is the conclusion informing the analysis of the chapters of Part I on the values and social norms that were the basis of the new credit policy pursued following World War II. As Gerschenkron also remarked, it is essential to understand how the challenge the market presents to allocation does not contradict policies seeking to develop capitalism and the banking sector. This argument is also perfectly consistent with Barry Eichengreen's 2006 study of "coordinated capitalism" in Western Europe after World War II, which showed how the various institutions established in these countries were all essential to growth. Whereas Eichengreen's analysis focuses on the labor market and industrial policy, I offer a complementary perspective on financial and monetary policy. I insist in particular on the robust institutional coordination required to pursue the goals of fighting inflation, allocating credit, regulating banks and providing the government with financing. It is very difficult to offer an exact account of the Banque de France's role in credit allocation as Chapters 5 and 6 argue: on the one hand, the Banque de France directed many of its recommendations to banks through multiple informal channels; on the other hand, coordination between the bank and the government, the Commissariat Général du Plan (CGP) and "specialized bodies" also occurred through various means of which only very incomplete traces can be found in the archives. The distinctive trait of an economy that is "*dirigiste*" or "*concertée*" (i.e., "organized"), to use the period's vocabulary, is that state intervention takes the form of the coordination of various private and public entities, rather than decrees issued by an all-powerful planner capable of defining in isolation the amount of credit and investment that each company and sector requires.

Understanding how certain policies produced positive results during the *Trente Glorieuses* also makes it possible to consider the French economy's subsequent development from a new standpoint. Contrary to what is sometimes thought, the Great Inflation of the 1970s was not the logical cul-mination of the *Trente Glorieuses*' inflationist policies. The archives used in this book show how, in the early 1970s, the Banque de France's policy changed profoundly (see Chapter 3 and the conclusion of Part I). As for monetary policy instruments, the extent and means of selective controls, central bank's financing of the government and the influence of economic theory, the 1970s appear as a very distinct period. Many of the conclusions in this book converge on the need to recognize the major institutional and political changes that occurred in the early 1970s and shaped a singular decade of transition. In particular, many developments of the 1970s were the results of early attempts to liberalize financial markets and reform credit policy and economic planning.

Recent studies have examined the evolution of the policies of the Federal Reserve and the Bank of England after 1945.[14] The approach of this book is different in two ways. First, the French system is so different from those of the United States and United Kingdom that it is crucial to situate the development of its beliefs and norms in the broader context of the Banque de France's intervention in credit allocation, rather than contenting one-self with connecting them to monetary theories established in very diverse contexts. As said previously, references to Keynesian and monetarist the-ories – built in the Anglo-American contexts and in reference to peculiar models of central banking – are misleading to understand the objectives of the Banque de France and the evolutions of its policy. My assumption is that a similar observation can be made for other European central banks as well as in Japan. Second, I refrain from explaining the outcomes of the policies in the 1950s and 1960s based on what happened in the 1970s. Whereas most studies have attempted to find the roots of the inflation of the 1970s in the

---

[14] Notably De Long (1997), Mayer (1999), Romer and Romer (2002), Bordo and Eichengreen (2008), Meltzer (2010) for the United States and Batini and Nelson (2005) and Capie (2010) for England. Some of these studies concentrate primarily on the question of the role of monetary policy in the Great Inflation of the 1970s. In the case of the United States, they agree that the Fed gradually turned, in the late 1960s, to a less aggressive anti-inflationary policy either due to the belief that that inflation's cause was non-monetary or to the notion that higher inflation would result in higher levels of employment and production (i.e., a underestimation of NAIRU). That said, these studies differ as to the reasons for these changes: some attribute them to governmental influence (Bordo & Eichengreen 2008; Meltzer 2010), others to the influence of theory (De Long 1997; Mayer 1999; Romer & Romer 2002), rational learning (Primiceri 2006) and so on. For a recent state of the literature on the Great Inflation and the role of central banks, see Bordo and Orphanides (2013), Eich and Tooze (2016) and Chélini and Warlouzet (2017).

policies of the preceding decades, I am more interested in understanding why inflation remained surprisingly contained in almost two decades after World War II and in emphasizing the institutional changes that took place in the early 1970s.

DOMESTIC CREDIT POLICY AND THE INTERNATIONAL MONETARY SYSTEM

Like catch-up growth, the stability of the Bretton Woods international monetary system is often cited as a mechanical explanation of Western countries' economic performance between 1945 and 1971. As its approach focuses on the Banque de France's internal policies, this book is not able to undertake an exhaustive analysis of France's place in the international monetary system. Exchange rate policy and the functioning of the European Payments Union would, in particular, require a different study. But the example of French monetary policy suggests that the stability of the international monetary system was preserved because these European countries took measures required to ensure the stability of their balance of payments. Once again, economic results are not the consequence of good fortune or natural adaptation, but of deliberate policies. The French example shows that devaluations, capital controls, credit controls and the disconnect between interest rates and quantitative controls could ensure that credit policy remained, within the Bretton Woods framework, highly autonomous. France regularly pursued a restrictive monetary policy to solve balance of payments problems or to combat imported inflation, such as during the Korean War, so that monetary policy cannot be seen as isolated from international constraints and shocks during this period. But the many instruments of credit policy allowed the central bank to make credit restrictions selective in the short term, and devaluations relaxed the medium-term constraints. Thus, the incompatibility between democratic demands at the national level and the system of fixed exchanges, which sealed the fate of the gold standard (Polanyi 1944; Eichengreen 1992; Mundell 2000), had very much disappeared under Bretton Woods.

I will explain, particularly in Chapters 4 and 7 and the Conclusion, why understanding central banks' credit policy during the postwar years is essential to the study of the operation of the Bretton Woods international monetary system. The analysis of the French case is, of course, too limited, but it offers clues for rethinking the history of Bretton Woods that are to be found in the study of national monetary policy. To avoid interpreting interest rates as monetary policy's primary instrument and to account for the central bank's interventionist role in the credit allocation helps us to better understand the historical role of capital controls, the degree to which central bank policy was autonomous and the social norms associated with the international monetary system. Consistent with the work of John Ruggie (1982) and Eric Helleiner (1996), the Bretton Woods system no longer appears as an exogenous constraint – dominated by American hegemony – bearing down on central banks, but as the result and the convergence of practices and norms that were (partially) developed and embedded at the national level. One cannot understand the Bretton Woods system solely by considering the principles decreed by international institutions or through theoretical frameworks defining the constraints imposed on national policies. It is necessary to consider what Ruggie called "the congruence of social purpose among the leading economic powers" (1982, p. 384). Even if France never stopped criticizing the United States' hegemony during the 1950s and 1960s (Gavin 2004; Bordo et al. 2017; Monnet 2013, 2017), the credit policy that it pursued was, in part, similar to that of its neighbors and trading partners and participated in a set of norms that valued the expansion of trade, adjustable exchange rates and state intervention to control credit.[15] If credit policies have survived the Bretton Woods system and have continued to be practiced by many emerging market economies, their nature and conditions of possibility have no doubt changed over time, due to the very fact that they had ceased to be recognized at the international level as a legitimate model of central banking.

---

[15] On several occasions, France denounced, on the international stage (notably before the International Monetary Fund and Bank for International Settlements) the fundamental instability of the Bretton Woods system and pleaded for stricter operating rules, yet without ever questioning national autonomy in matters of policy. As soon as it found itself in a position of strength, notably once it had brought lasting stability to its balance of payments in the early 1960s, France attempted to impose its views on its allies. French policymakers and top civil servants were convinced that a devaluation of the dollar, rigorous monetary policy and greater central bank cooperation were indispensable to the survival of the international system. France's position was not only influenced by the interwar experience, but also by its domestic monetary policy (Chapter 4). During the 1960s, France frontally opposed the monetary policies of the United States and England. It did, of course, seek in this way to profit from its allies' weaknesses to impose itself as the major diplomatic power it could no longer be, but these debates were also reflections of fundamental differences with Anglo-Americans concerning monetary policy and central bank coordination. Only an analysis of domestic policies can, in this way, shed light on the international monetary system's stability and the stakes of coordination between central banks.

CHRONOLOGY, SOURCES AND ARCHIVES

As will become evident to the reader, the timelines in this study are rather broad and fluctuating. Chapter 1 tracks the origins of credit policy before and during World War II. Chapters 3 and 7 extend their focus toward the end of the 1970s and early 1980s. 1948 and 1973 were, however, two clear and important milestones for postwar credit policy. Indeed, it was in 1948 that the Banque de France's major role in credit control was truly established, with the introduction of quantitative instruments to limit inflation and guide credit allocation. Credit policy evolved during the 1950s (Chapter 2) and 1960s (Chapter 3), but it really changed its modus operandi in 1973 with the introduction of permanent but not very restrictive credit ceilings and a greater role given to open market operations rather than to quantitative control. As we shall see, the nature of credit policy became hybrid from 1973 onwards. 1973 also marked a moment when the government increased its power over the central bank and, in particular, its decisions on monetary techniques. The unity of the 1948–1973 period is also strikingly evident in the method of financing the Treasury by the Banque de France, as shown in Chapter 5. In this area, 1973 marked a clear shift toward market financing of public debt. This chronology is of course determined by external events and the general course of history. 1948 is the year of political and economic stabilization in postwar France (marked by the Mayer stabilization plan; see Caron 1982; Casella & Eichengreen 1993) while 1973 is the year of the first oil shock and the beginning of stagflation.

The work in this thesis is based, for the most part, on the archives of the Banque de France (henceforth, ABF).[16] When it proved necessary to consult other sources in order to understand the Banque's internal debates or decisions, I used documents from the French Finance Ministry, the

---

[16] Procès verbaux du Conseil Général (PVCG).

  Rapports du Conseil National du Crédit.
  Fonds du Conseil National du Crédit, n°1427200301.
  Fonds de la Direction Générale du Crédit, sous Fonds Cabinet, n°1331200301.
  Fonds de la Direction Générale du Crédit, n°1331200807.
  Fonds de la Direction Générale de l'escompte, n°1360200701.
  Fonds de la Direction Générale des Etudes, Direction des analyses et statistiques monétaires, n°1417200405.
  Fonds de la Direction Générale des Etudes, n°1397200602.
  Fonds de la Commission bancaire, n°1740200701.
  Fonds du Service d'études économétriques et de recherche, n°1404200701.
  Fonds de la Direction du marché monétaire et Direction des Interventions monétaires, n°1332199101, n°1361198802.

Commissariat Général au Plan, the Conseil Économique et Social and various committees constituted at a ministry's or the National Assembly's request.[17] Archives of the Bank for International Settlements (BIS), of several other European central banks (Italy, Belgium) and of the committee of the governors of the central banks of the European Community, as well as some official publications and reports from international (OECD, EEC, BIS) and foreign institutions (central banks, US Congress) provided information for Chapter 7. All original quotations in French have been translated into English.[18]

The choice of sources thus emphasizes the Banque de France's perspective. This position is justified, as this book's primary goal has been, above all, to analyze the instruments as well as the motives of its interventions. Despite the Banque's lack of independence vis-à-vis the government, I believe the archives contain enough information to help us understand the goals of its monetary policy. Disagreements or agreements with the government, even when they were not made public, appear clearly in the archives and were notably expressed in the General Council. When ministers suggested or imposed policies, they were always the occasion of discussions at the Banque. We shall see how this situation changed, in part, at the beginning of the 1970s, when the government acquired more and more power over monetary policy. In late 1972, monetary policy measures were, for the first time, implemented at the government's command without triggering internal debate at the Banque de France. I also benefited from the fact that Finance Ministry archives from this period have been well studied (Margairaz 1991; Quennouëlle-Corre 2000; Effosse 2003) and an important body of secondary literature exists on the economic policies pursued by successive governments.

The transcripts of meetings of the General Council of the Banque de France (*procès-verbaux du Conseil Général*, or PVCG), which met every Thursday and where decisions were made affecting the entire range of the bank's activities, were one of my main sources. These minutes were never made public and members expressed themselves freely. They are, moreover, quite complete, as they include discussions in their entirety, the

---

[17] Sources external to the Banque de France that I used were primarily *littérature grise* – that is, official reports and publications, rather than working documents or internal discussions of these various bureaucracies.

[18] Original quotes from archives and some further references are available in French in Monnet (2012a) – for those presented in Part I – or in an online appendix (for those of Chapter 4). https://assets.aeaweb.org/assets/production/articles-attachments/aej/mac/app/0604/2012-0255_app.pdf. Monnet (2012a) is also available online.

numbers presented and the documents that were approved. The PVCG have the advantage of being regular and continuous, and are a good starting point for retracing the Banque de France's decisions. They make it possible in particular to follow the Banque's short-term policies. Sometimes, as Chapter 5 will show about the financing of public debt, quantitative information in the PVCG is more precise and consistent than in the published balance sheet of the Banque and in the studies of staff economists. But PVCG are very insufficient when it comes to understanding, on the one hand, the relationship between the central bank and other banks and, on the other, the origins of monetary and financial reforms during this period. The great reforms (for example, medium-term rediscounting, the money market, rediscount ceilings and reserve requirements) were conceived and prepared, often over several years, within different offices of the Banque de France. As with daily relationships with banks, I thus found most of the information needed for understanding these reforms in the archives of the various directorates of the organization. Generally speaking, the consultation of these various archives proved indispensable to understanding the functioning of the various instruments used by the bank in fighting inflation and influencing credit allocation. Such technical information is not found in the PVCG.

Not until 1970 did the Banque de France acquire an economic research office (the Service of Econometric Studies and Research, or *Service d'études économétriques et de recherche* [SEER]), which gradually made prediction forecasting a common practice and built important bridges with university research (in France and English-speaking countries). It really took off beginning in the mid-1970s. I was thus also able to use the archives of this office to analyze the end of the period. But for most of the *Trente Glorieuses*, economic forecasts on the part of the Banque's staff are not available. Economists of the Banque focused on producing and analyzing statistical series (including many credit statistics). The creation of this research office poses an additional problem for the historian, as it is difficult to know to what extent its work represented the opinions of the Banque de France as a whole and if it really influenced political decisions. When considering some of SEER's studies (notably on money supply targets), I do not assume that it reflects the opinion of the Banque de France's management, except when its arguments are also used by other offices or at the General Council.

One of the primary and paradoxical challenges of recent history is the abundance of sources. To attempt a systematic and exhaustive reading of the ABF's various offices, which notably includes its entire correspondence with banks as well as all of its transactions, is a vain and impossible task. I have concentrated on political choices, with the goal of understanding the purpose of short-term policies, reforms of the bank's instruments of intervention and credit policy's overall direction.

Sources that make it possible to understand the ins and outs of monetary policy are, of course, abundant, but the paucity of the information they offer can, at times, be striking. One should not expect to find in the Banque's archives complete and perfectly articulated justifications of decisions taken, nor is it always possible to determine an idea's or a reform's origin. Even less frequently does one fall upon a satisfying and sufficiently neutral assessment of the consequences of adopted reforms and policies. I have, for that reason, sought to combine quantitative analysis, economic theory and quantitative methods in formulating interpretations. Quantitative analyses were facilitated by the quality of the statistics put together by the Central Risks Service (*Service central des risques*) on behalf of the National Credit Council (*Conseil national du crédit*). The Banque de France's desire to control the overall volume of credit and money and credit allocation led it to gather data the precision and extent of which is absolutely remarkable.

This book is not a history of the Banque de France. The focus is credit policy and the effect of the Banque's decisions on the domestic economy. Many aspects and roles of the central banks are not studied, not even mentioned: banknote production, the role of the many branches of the Banque in regional economies, the relationships with the Banque d'Algérie, the management of real estate, the management of the staff as well as the pensions of the employees. All these topics were discussed widely during the weekly meetings of the General Council, at least as much as credit policy.[19] The management of gold reserves and the functioning of the Exchange stabilization fund are also outside the scope of this study, although I will speak about the relationships between credit policy and the balance of payments in Chapter 4.[20] This choice is justified by the fact that the goal of credit policy was also to isolate the French economy from external shocks and constraints and support the economic priorities defined by the government.

---

[19] The reader interested in these issues can refer to Koch (1983), Feiertag (2006a) and, most of all, the recent PhD dissertation of Duchaussoy (2013).

[20] I have written elsewhere on international issues, gold reserves and France's complex relations with the Bretton Woods system (Monnet 2013, 2017, 2018; Bordo et al. 2017). The international stakes of this era's French economic policy were addressed by Esposito (1991), Loriaux (1991), Bossuat (1992), Lynch (1997) and Warlouzet (2010).

TERMINOLOGY

Some of the vocabulary used by the Banque de France during the *Trente Glorieuses* is no longer used today and did not necessarily have equivalents in other countries. I have tried as much as possible to offer translations or equivalent words, while systematically referring to the French original term. Some terms that are still used today had, at the time, distinctive meanings that differ from their current meaning. Thus, it is useful to present, at the outset, the keywords of the Banque's vocabulary during this period. The more technical and contextually specific words, as well as the Banque's various offices and directorates, will be defined and presented in the chapters themselves.

The term "credit ceilings" (*encadrement du crédit*) refers to direct limitations of exposures, meaning that credit institutions could not increase their outstanding sums beyond a certain percentage for a given period of time. The term dates back to the mid-1960s, but it was then used to describe retroactively the measure introduced in France in 1958.

The term "credit control" (*contrôle du credit*) is a more general term that denotes the ability of the central bank to influence the stock and the allocation of credit in the economy, either in order to combat inflation or to channel funds to specific sectors. It is usually loosely defined, referring to all the instruments of the central banks and, during this period, is frequently used as synonymous to monetary policy, especially in the PVCG.

The term "credit selectivity" (*sélectivité du credit*) was narrower and referred to the ability of the central bank to intervene in the allocation of credit.

The concept of liquidity is, at times, used very generally to refer to money, credit and bank refinancing. Yet, in most cases, it does in fact refer to the capacity of an asset to be exchanged. Thus, the bank distinguishes between the controlling of credit, which directly affects the sums banks can lend, and liquidity controls, which seek to immediately freeze certain bank assets and thus to shape the composition of bank balance sheets.

The term "transformation," the cornerstone of most discussions of the French banking system, refers to banks' use of short-term deposits to grant long-term credits.

After 1945, the Banque de France made no distinction between the terms discounting (*escompte*) and rediscounting (*réescompte*) when referring to its repurchasing of (already discounted) commercial paper or Treasury bills held by banks before they reached maturity. Direct discounting (discounting commercial papers presented by companies rather than by banks), continued to be practiced by the Banque's branches, even if it was minor after the war. The term "rediscountable" (*réescomptable*) was also known as mobilizable (*mobilisable*). After 1945, the Banque expanded its rediscounting capacities to various medium-term loans known as mobilizable medium-term credit (*credit à moyen terme réescomptable*). The discount rate was the rate applied to discounting eligible paper. Rediscounting was the main refinancing operation of the Banque de France and the discount rate its leading interest rate from its origin until 1971.

Commercial bills were a claim of one party against another (say, a customer and a merchant). They could be discounted by a bank to provide cash to the holder of the bill before the due date. Once discounted by a bank, the bill carried three signatures and could then be rediscounted by the central bank (or another financial institution).[21]

The terms "money market" (*marché monétaire*) and "open market" were used indistinguishably even if the French money market was at this time different from the English open market. Banks and credit institutions could trade on this market, in which the Banque de France had, since 1938, been able to intervene by purchasing, selling or purchasing under a resale agreement government bills and certain kinds of private bills. The Banque de France calls the bills that it uses on the markets negotiable bills (*effets négociables*).

Finally, the Banque de France, like the rest of the French civil service, frequently uses the terms "directed," "organized" or "planned economy" (*économie dirigée, économie concertée* or *économie planifée*) to refer to the French economic system of this period, which was characterized by robust state intervention in the economy.

OUTLINE AND MAIN ARGUMENTS

The book is divided into two parts. The first part contains three chapters ordered in a chronological order. Chapter 1 studies the intellectual and institutional origins of French postwar credit policy. It focuses mainly on the 1930s and the war. Chapter 2 explains the institutionalization of credit policy after the war until the end of the Fourth Republic in 1958 while Chapter 3 investigates the evolution of credit policy in the 1960s and 1970s.

---

[21] Rediscounting, together with Lombard loans, had always been the main operation of central banks in Europe, contrary to the United States. It was still the case in the two decades after World War II, although some (prominently the Bank of England) had turned to open market operations with Treasury bills. On the history of discounting in France, see Roulleau (1914), Plessis (2001) and Baubeau (2004) (and Wilson [1957] for an English reference). On the European discount system in the nineteenth century, a useful reference written in English remains the study published by the US Monetary Commission (Warburg 1910).

Although most of the analysis of Banque de France policies ends in 1973, I provide some insights on how the criticisms of credit policies developed further in the second half of the 1970s. The implementation of money targets in 1976, following their unofficial use starting 1973, is also studied in this chapter. The main purpose of these reflections, which go beyond the 1973 chronological boundary, is to explain what can be drawn from previous analyses in order to understand the Great Inflation of the 1970s and the "neoliberal" turn that followed. These three chapters are organized around the institutionalist analysis mentioned above which is presented in more detail in the introduction of Part I and highlights three components of credit institutionalization which made it "stable" and "unique" (Polanyi): the legal aspect, the ideological aspect and the self-control of the institution (i.e., controlling credit to avoid inflation). Each chapter therefore includes a section devoted to the evolution of each component during the period studied. One of the main contributions of this historical analysis is to show, from an institutionalist point of view, first, that the fight against inflation in the 1950s and 1960s was seen as an essential dimension of government intervention in credit allocation, and second, that the institutional basis of credit policy in the 1970s was very different from that of the previous decade, which I call a process of deinstitutionalization.

The second part of the book is thematic. While the first part studies the historical evolution of the institution and focuses on the breakdowns and continuity of the French postwar credit policy, the second part focuses on a few specific subjects and highlights the unity of the economic issues associated with these subjects throughout the period 1948–1973. The four chapters of this second part allow for a deeper economic analysis – in particular from a quantitative and theoretical point of view – of historical subjects whose evolution has been discussed in Part I. They can be read independently, although many links are made between them and with Part I.

Chapter 4 examines in detail the instruments used by the Banque de France to combat inflation and proposes a quantitative estimate of the effects of monetary policy on the main macroeconomic variables. It also examines the interaction between credit and capital controls, and thus analyses the interactions between domestic and international objectives of the Banque de France. This chapter constitutes the book's primary contribution from the point of view of economic analysis. It bring several methodological novelties and theoretical insights that change the common view on postwar monetary policy under Bretton Woods and could be extended to historical analyses of other central banks. It shows that the only way to estimate properly the effects of postwar Banque de France's policy is to build a measure of the policy stance by quantifying the objectives of the Banque de France (a "narrative approach") rather than by looking at interest rates. Quantitative results from this method run counter to the notion that monetary policy during the *Trente Glorieuses* was passive and suggests, on the contrary, that it was the primary factor driving the economic cycle. Using interest rates as a measure of the policy stance provides misleading results because they were mostly disconnected from quantitative credit controls used to combat inflation and restore balance of payments equilibrium. Understanding the disconnect between interest rates and credit controls is also key to understand the functioning and rationale of capital controls and to fully appreciate the autonomy of monetary and credit policies (i.e. the *trilemma*).

Chapter 5 describes how the Banque de France financed the Treasury. Its main quantitative contribution is to provide, for the first time, statistics on the financing of public debt by the central bank, which include the hidden part of this financing, not included in the official statistics. From the mid-1950s to 1973, this hidden part was roughly equal to official loans. This system was reformed in 1973 to make the financing of public debt more transparent, simple and accountable. This chapter goes beyond the discovery of new statistical data. Against the traditional narrative that describes the monetary financing of public debt as a simple free lunch for the state, I try to contextualize central bank loans to the Treasury in the politics and economics of the postwar public debt. As with credit policy in general, the main objective was to exit the market, but there were institutional mechanisms of self-control (although not always fully working). The rediscovery of the market in the 1970s therefore profoundly altered these self-control mechanisms. In the 1950s and 1960s, the increase in loans to government was thwarted by disinflationary policies. The system offered great flexibility to the government, but there were constraints on the monetary financing of public debt and, in this way, on the general expansion of public debt. The year 1973 marked a turning point: the real value of the Banque de France's loans to the Treasury began to decline irremediably and, at the same time, the share of marketable public debt in French public debt began to rise. As a result, the disinflationary policies implemented by the central bank were no longer a brake on the expansion of public debt in subsequent years. As also argued about credit policy in Part I, a new political economy of public debt emerged as a consequence of the turn to the market in the 1970s.

Chapter 6 makes a link between credit policy and the exceptional rates of capital accumulation during the postwar era. The chapter pays attention to the means of Banque de France's intervention in credit allocation but is not restricted to the central bank. The *dirigiste* financial system focused on the development of medium- and long-term loans (named "investment credit") to firms. By contrast to short-term credit, "investment credit" was mainly granted by public credit institutions rather than commercial banks. The Banque de France and CNC monitored closely the allocation of these loans but often not in a direct way. Credit policy was not limited to directed credit. It is all the more misleading to describe such a financial system with ubiquitous state intervention as a bank-based system. Using a new database matching credit and corporate tax statistics in forty sectors from 1954 to 1974, I find evidence that the allocation of "investment credit" across sectors supported capital accumulation as well as capital reallocation. It was not the case for short-term credit. Hence commercial banks played almost no role in the postwar expansion of capital. The main result of this quantitative analysis is that, besides capital accumulation and financial deepening, the postwar Golden Age of growth is the story of reallocation of capital and credit. Growth of credit and capital was not concentrated in a few leading sectors. These results go against the belief that credit policy in the *dirigiste* system focused on specialization only at the expense of adaptability. However, this chapter is silent on the potential misallocations, especially those that may have spread in the 1970s, undermining the legitimacy of credit policy.

Chapter 7 has two main objectives. The first is to show that credit controls and policies were widespread in Europe after World War II, but that there were significant differences between countries in the way they were implemented. I provide some explanations of these differences in a "varieties of capitalism" approach, highlighting the importance of factors such as organization of the state (centralized versus federal), market ideologies, history and structure of the financial system. The second objective of this chapter is to take stock of both national differences and the general importance of credit policies in Western Europe to inform historiographical debates on the construction of the European monetary union. The decline of credit policies and the construction of the European monetary union appear as two parallel historical processes that converged in the late 1980s only. Hence, understanding the end of credit policies and the evolution of central banks toward market-based interventions is crucial to understand the form the European monetary integration finally took in the early 1990s. Based on an analysis of the discussions of the governors of European central banks in the 1970s and 1980s, I show that the end of credit policies was not a concerted process at European level. The end of credit policies has been a crucial historical development for shaping European monetary integration in a particular way, but it should not be concluded that European integration has been the driving force behind this major change in central banking. Like their birth, the end of credit policies was a deeply national process.

Finally, the general conclusion examines the main findings of the book from the perspective of understanding the economic and political changes that occurred in central banks, financial systems and the international monetary system during the 1970s and 1980s. It goes back to the main objective of this book, which was to study the Banque de France during the three decades following World War II, without applying a backward perspective shaped by the dominant model of central banking that subsequently developed. I submit that, in many ways, a better understanding of the 1950s and 1960s radically changes our perception of the reforms that took place in the following decades. In particular, I discuss how the emphasis on central bank independence in historical and economic literature has overshadowed the historical significance of credit policy, or how a vision of capital controls has been constructed forgetting how and why they were historically associated with credit controls. I will conclude with what can be drawn from this historical study for the current policies of central banks, in particular for those of emerging economies that are still attached to credit policy, and others which have rediscovered the importance of credit in the economy, with a benign neglect of their history.

PART I

INSTITUTIONALIZING CREDIT

What planning was really about was faith in the state. In many countries this reflected a well-founded awareness, enhanced by the experience of war, that in the absence of any other agency of regulation or distribution, only the state now stood between the individual and destitution. But contemporary enthusiasm for an interventionist state went beyond desperation or self-interest.

Tony Judt, *Postwar: A History of Europe Since 1945*, 2006, p. 69

Introduction to Part I
Chronology and Methodology

I THE DIFFERENT STAGES OF CREDIT POLICY

Postwar responsibilities of the central bank were laid out in the law pertaining to "the nationalization of the Banque de France and the organization of credit" of December 2, 1945, which was not significantly modified until 1984.[1] The intention of Part I is to study how the Banque de France's credit regulation policy can be understood in a distinct legal and ideological context, as well as how the "organization of credit" was established and developed from an institutional perspective.[2] It will attempt in particular to examine the legal basis of credit market intervention; social norms that defined the credit's economic role and the legitimacy of state intervention; and, finally, measures for controlling credit aimed at containing inflation. The latter category includes what is commonly referred to as monetary policy and corresponds, in France during the *Trente Glorieuses*, to the full array of self-controlling measures imposed by the government to ensure that the credit institution established in 1945 could survive without being threatened by price instability.[3] Building on the vast literature on institutional change, the three following chapters seek, furthermore, to show

---

[1] The original title of the law in French is *"Loi n° 45-15 du 2 décembre 1945 relative à la nationalisation de la Banque de France* et des grandes banques et à *l'organisation du crédit."*

[2] Part I of this book was chapter 2 of Monnet (2012a) and has been translated from French by Michael Behrent and then revised and updated by the author. Some sections of Part I, Chapter 3, were previously published in French in a short article on the 1970s neoliberal turn (Monnet 2015).

[3] From a game theory perspective, this means studying collectively the institution's formal and legal rules, norms or collective beliefs, and the full array of the strategies of control and "credible threat" that actors developed in order not to deviate from equilibrium. From a more sociological standpoint, this means studying the different ways in which credit was established and attached to various institutional procedures, be they legal or social.

how the foundational principles of an institution came to be questioned, resulting in deinstitutionalization and radical change.

In the first place, from 1945 to 1948, the major principles announced by the National Council of the Resistance and the planners became anchored in law and had to adjust to economic reality and constraints. This adjustment of norms led to robust state interventionism in the credit market, as well as consciousness of inflationary risks and the refusal to organize credit allocation in a purely authoritarian way. If some principles arose from socialist and planning movements of the 1940s that found expression in the program of the National Council of Resistance, the system being established did not represent a complete break with the Vichy regime: it drew notably on bank regulation policies adopted in 1941 and borrowed a number of measures that sought to elaborate credit policy within the framework of an investment and production policy that would make reconstruction possible. This compromise between continuity and new principles resulted in a major consensus around the principle of state intervention.

Between 1948 and the mid-1970s, two major periods should be distinguished, located on either side of the great rupture that was 1958 (the foundation of the Fifth Republic). Each can be divided, moreover, into two sub-periods. The first decade, until 1958, represented the fruition of these policies and notably a great commitment on that part of the Banque de France to financing of the economy in the wake of the Marshall Plan. Challenges to state interventionism in the realm of credit were rare: they primarily took the form of a reticence on the part of the government and some bankers toward inflation control. Beginning in late 1958, the policies of Charles de Gaulle advocated increased liberalization and "debudgetization," which was primarily evident, as it relates to credit, in a desire to give banks and financial markets a greater role in financing the economy. As far as the Banque de France was concerned, this reduction in volume led more than anything to a decline in bank and Treasury refinancing. But this decrease of the state's role in the direct financing of the economy did not, however, entail an immediate challenge to the legitimacy of public intervention in credit allocation, and even less in the Banque de France's ability to control credit in fighting inflation. Thus, credit policy was excluded from the so-called "liberal" reforms of the early Fifth Republic.

Beginning in the late 1960s, however, one sees a desire to disconnect the central bank's interventions in monetary control from credit selectivity. Several reforms and reports at the time called for "neutrality" in monetary policy by privileging direct instruments, such as the open market and obligatory reserves rather than treasury ratios and credit ceilings. This movement, which reached its peak in 1971 at the initiative of Governor Wormser, did not occur without difficulties and was never fully accomplished.

Because they were never fully accepted by the entire Banque and did not meet with consensus, these liberalizing proposals seemed poorly adapted to the French system. They led in the 1970s to an increasingly hybrid system of intervention, in which state intervention in credit selectivity paradoxically increased, notably through the proliferation of special arrangements. In conjunction with money supply targets and measures seeking to "liberalize savings," the share of preferential loans increased and recourse to the open market ultimately decreased. The term "credit selectivity," which originally referred to the state's ability to intervene judiciously to tend to the economy's needs and dismantle economic rents inherited from the past, now became synonymous with the creation of economic rents and inefficiency.

Chapter 3 ends, then, in the mid-1970s, when new tools for monetary policy were established and criticism emerged that would continue to be heard until the early 1980s, when the socialist government finally liberalized the system.[4] Even if I refer to future changes relating to particular laws and measures, the break that occurred in the early 1980s is not the focus of this essay and merits further analysis.

II INSTITUTIONAL ANALYSES OF CENTRAL BANKING

Submitting monetary policy to an institutional analysis is an approach that has already proven its relevance and fruitfulness, as it avoids the reduction of central bank action to the automatic management of the quantity of money in circulation or to a "reaction function." By adopting a condensed typology, three institutional approaches can be identified, each corresponding to often very different methods and tasks. The first seeks to show that the political impact of monetary policy depends on institutional characteristics that are exogenous to legitimate monetary authority and gives particular importance to the effects of central bank independence (Alesina & Summers

---

[4]   In less than four years, François Mitterrand was responsible for two departures in relation to previous policies and his reforms deserve special study, which we cannot offer here. The first departure immediately followed the socialist candidate's election and consisted of a new wave of nationalizations in the banking sector and a struggle with the Banque de France to force monetary policy to submit to budgetary policy (Feiertag 2001; Duchaussoy 2011). The second and more fundamental departures, the consequences of which were more lasting, occurred between 1984 and 1987 and culminated in an almost total reconsideration of the principles of credit policy pursued since 1945. Symbolically, the section on *direction du credit* of the 1945 law defining the Banque de France's was rescinded in January 1984 and the National Credit Council, a crucial organization within the bank, was dismantled.

1993; Hall & Franzese 1998; Iversen 1999; Acemoglu et al. 2008; Cukierman 2008). The second is concerned with the question of the emergence of monetary sovereignty as an institution (Aglietta 1992; Aglietta & Orléan 2002; Broz 1998, 2009). The third chooses, for its part, to study central banks as organizations, notably by drawing on neo-institutionalism or contract theory (McNamara 2002; Broz & Grossman 2004; Gersbach & Hahn 2004), business history (Hennessy 1992; Feiertag 2007; Duchaussoy 2013) or the sociology of organizations (Abolafia 2004, 2010).[5] These three occasionally complementary approaches offer different definitions of "institutions," but they share a willingness to understand monetary policy within the framework of organizations with well-defined contours – central banks – and, with the exception of the second approach,[6] they consider the question of what institutions "institute" to be of lesser importance. The second approach, by contrast, highlights the fact that monetary policy can institute national sovereignty, notably by unifying monetary practices.

The approach presented in this book considers "institutions" in the broadest sense as the act of instituting and defines what institutions institute through various legal and political procedures. I begin with the oldest and simplest definition of the very verb "to institute" (to establish something, to mark a beginning or to assign a function) in order to consider the different ways of instituting. A question follows: what meanings and what functions does society give to credit and how is it organized? Understanding the central bank's role during the *Trente Glorieuses* requires that one first answers this question and thus that one considers central banking as simply one element of the institutionalization of credit. As laid out in the general introduction of the book, this is very much in line with the method of Karl Polanyi who viewed the economy as an "instituted process."

Institutions, Law and Power

My approach is also in large part inspired by that of French legal historian Yan Thomas,[7] in that it seeks to show, in the first place, how law functions as one possible way of organizing the social world. I will pay particular attention to legal arrangement and to the solutions that actors find in the

---

[5]   For an overview of recent work, notably in political science, see Bernhard et al. (2003).

[6]   The second approach sets out to study how central banks and, more generally, monetary sovereignty are instituted.

[7]   In particular in Thomas (1991, 1993). The title of this Part – "Instituting Credit" – refers directly to the titles used by Thomas in his studies of Roman law: "Instituting Nature" and "Instituting the City." For a general presentation of this author's approach, see Thévenin

law, without assuming that law determines practice. The "law of December 2, 1945 relating to the nationalization of the Banque de France, major banks, and the organization of credit" (which is usually known as the "credit nationalization law") forms the matrix of my argument, in that it compels us, in practice, to reflect on the central bank's role within the broader context of the "organization of credit." Without defining credit, not even how it should be organized, the 1945 law gives the power to "organize credit" to the Banque de France. To paraphrase Yan Thomas, legal characterizations give form to political power and social life, rather than imposing laws on facts; hence the importance of a nominalist perspective on how credit was organized and regulated.

Thus my institutional analysis of monetary policy is not an analysis of the central bank as an organization, but a reconsideration of this policy within the broader framework of what this period called the "organization of credit." The emphasis on law does not assume that there are clearly defined and identifiable rules with exogenous effects on the economy. The law both establishes social norms and lends itself to reinterpretation by actors. Every social fact is a process instituted endogenously through constant interaction between rules and individual practices.[8] To say that something is "instituted" (such as "credit," in this essay) is to analyze the processes that make it socially meaningful. Thus, we will see how the principles and criteria guiding credit allocation were discussed within the Banque de France and how actors' conceptions of credit and credit control are dependent on different values relating to the role of the state and the nation, the nature of money, the concept of economic profitability and the role of banks in the economy.

Strategies of Actors and Dissenting Views

The literature on institutionalism is vast and the terms and concepts differ considerably across disciplines. The point here is not to undertake a theoretical

---

(2009) and Madero (2012). The approach to the history of law that Thomas advocates – which we have attempted to follow in this chapter – is perfectly summarized by the following extract:

> Legal operations do not consist in the unthinkable and impossible action of imposing laws on facts, but in the remodeling that makes the latter eligible for the practical value judgments that it requires. These operations can be analyzed from a nominalistic perspective: facts are not given the names most appropriate to their nature, but those appropriate to what one wants to do with them. But they can also be operated from the standpoint of the effectivity of legal operations, from the malleable standpoint of the forms they elicit, independently from the imposition of law as a form of constraint: legal characterizations give form to social life, it circumscribes and singularizes entities or relationships such as persons, goods, property, contracts, work, representations, and so on, all of which are forms necessary to the practical and changing operations of law, and which have, in this way, become reality. (Thomas, 2002, p. 1426)

[8]   This position has previously been defended by Fossier and Monnet (2009).

synthesis but to borrow certain concepts from institutional analysis in order to bring greater clarity to the specifics of credit policy. That said, my argument is closer to economic analyses that consider institutions to be a set of strategies (Aoki 1996, 2007; Greif 2006) than to those that see them as a series of rules (North 1990), as I attribute particular importance to the coordination of beliefs and actions. I do not presume however that actors – political actors in this case – have an a priori form of rationality, but I nonetheless see institutions as the outcome of actors pursuing their interests, including in the elaboration and interpretation of laws. In this respect, my approach is close to the literature known as "varieties of capitalism," sharing its "actor-centered" and "broadly rationalist" focus, as well as the idea that institutions are not only structures and rules that enable actions but are themselves the object and target of actions (Crouch 2005; Hall & Thelen 2009). This approach notably compelled us to find which social groups and which actors defend – or, on the contrary, criticize – the institution and to study the various forms credit policy assumed over time, as well as the situations of equilibrium that led certain interests to coincide. In particular, it is essential to see the way in which interests can align themselves while attributing different meanings to the institution. This is, in my view, a blind spot of institutional theories based on rational choice. Thus, credit policy during the *Trente Glorieuses* is marked by a permanent tension between those who see it as a necessary consequence of postwar reconstruction and those who see it as the realization of socialist ideals or an original and distinctly French form of capitalism. The former constantly call for an eventual return of market forces, while the latter want the institution to be based on a series of foundational principles that reforms must respect. In many respects, the common characteristics of credit policy throughout this period often seem based on overlapping economic and political interests rather than a coherent and unified theoretical outlook. The actors agreed primarily that credit policy must "serve the nation's interests." This statement of principles often left considerable room for interpretation, economically speaking, but demonstrates that the nation was credit policy's unifying factor.

Three Key Aspects of the Institutionalizing Process

What follows will bring forth three aspects – or three components – of this institutionalizing process that will serve as my analytical perspective for considering the development of credit policy from the end of World War II to the mid-1980s. The *first component is legal*: principles are anchored in law, which functions as the institution's "conditions of possibility." A *second component* consists of the social norms or beliefs that guide action: an institution can, in particular, exist only if actors share beliefs about the rules of the game.[9] The latter are not exogenous to individuals and evolve in relation to perceptions of other actors' behavior. The criteria of justice, economic efficiency and the nation are examples of this. Eichengreen and Temin (2000) and Mouré (2002) have also shown how the principles of the gold standard functioned as a norm and, even as an ideology, guiding the actions of the Banque de France during the interwar years. In the case of credit policy, we shall see that the primary norms are those that tend to define credit as a public good and that give it a social as well as an economic meaning; credit, in this way, is summoned to serve the nation, or perhaps the "community of workers." But a collective agreement can fully encompass disagreements while seeking to overcome them. Finally, a *third component* of the institution relates to its capacity for "control" or "self-control," which is crucial to its preservation. Indeed, any institutionalizing process engenders a set of more or less formal constraints designed to avoid institutional breakdown.[10] An institution's stakeholders identify a problem (such as moral hazard or informational asymmetries) that could undermine its continuity and decide to implement controls (bans, direct assistance and so on) that seek to find a solution to the problem. In this essay, I interpret various approaches to fighting inflation as a form of control and self-control within the credit institution. As early as 1944 and by 1948 in any case, it was recognized that the primary danger threatening the "organization of credit" implemented after the war was inflation and that this required the establishment of mechanisms limiting credit and monetary creation. The goal of credit policy was to ensure that companies did not lack financing; the Treasury and the Banque de France's decision to make number credit

---

[9]   It seems to us that, taken broadly, this second component has been explored by a number of approaches in the social sciences, even if they do not share the same methodological assumptions. Collective action can indeed be explained as much through an economic analysis grounded in rational choice and optimal response (Olson 1982; Aoki 2007) as through a sociology of public problems (how are public problems defined and how do they emerge? [Gusfield 1984]) or a holistic approach that is close to regulation theory (Bessis 2009). Aoki (2007) has, for his part, developed a game theory model in which institutions are defined as "patterns of social interactions, as represented by meaningful rules that every agent knows and incorporated as agents' shared beliefs about the ways how game is to be played" (p. 7).

[10] Once again, this capacity for control or self-control is found in numerous institutional analyses based on different methods or assumptions. From the standpoint of contract theory and based on a definition of institutions as a state of equilibrium, Avner Greif and David Laitin, for example, analyze the conditions for preserving institutions in terms of quasi-parameters (Greif & Laitin 2004). Michel Foucault's analyses of institutions such as prisons and, later, of biopolitics also emphasize institutions' capacity to create their own forms of control.

facilities available was thus contingent on the latter, resulting in real production, not uncontrolled price increases. The fight against inflation was
thus, in a sense, a form of self-limitation on the part of the institutionalization of credit. For this reason, it strikes me as particularly interesting to
study how the latter became inscribed into a legal framework and how it
obeyed – and even strengthened – the institution's social norms.

This approach makes it possible, in particular, to emphasize the fact
that the various meanings of "credit control" and "credit policy" were
deeply complementary, as restrictions implemented to fight inflation primarily took the form of modified bank regulation and sought to respect or
even strengthen credit selectivity measures. Due to this complementarity,
the Banque de France and the National Credit Council did not see inflation control as a threat to expanding credit and production, but as their
necessary condition. Limiting inflation made it possible to save postwar
dirigisme, and particularly the legitimacy of state intervention in credit allocation. This vision, which was particular to the Banque de France, was not,
however, always shared by the government, other banks or companies.

These three components did of course overlap, and their boundaries might
seem porous and superficial. Anti-inflationary instruments, for instance,
can at times be legal measures that also function as institutional conditions
of possibility. But what matters is that each of these components can the-
oretically be considered in isolation; articulations or intersections between
them can themselves become, in turn, objects of study. The interactions of
these three components produced an instituted process that is unique and
stable despite constantly evolving features (Polanyi 1957, 1963). This is how
I view the institutionalization of credit in postwar France.

Law, Social Norms and Institutional Change

The previous analysis intersects in particular with a problem that is often
neglected in economics and that is widely debated in political science and
sociology concerning law's function (Swedberg 2003; Edelman 2004): do
laws have merely a coercive function (Kelsen 1967; Posner 1974) or do
we also obey laws because they reflect principles to which we subscribe
or that can influence our preferences? Legal scholars such as Sunstein
(1996), Lessig (1998), Anderson and Pildes (2000) have thus spoken of "the
expressive function of law,"[11] that is, the law's ability to express principles.
Two economists, Bénabou and Tirole (2011), incorporate this function by

---

[11] For a critical assessment, see Adler (2000).

showing how law can function as a signal sent to society (i.e., actors with imperfect information) about common values and beliefs. Actors obey not only because they cannot escape from the law but also because it suggests principles that guide their action.[12]

Another issue in legal analysis concerns individuals' capacity to interpret law in several ways. Whereas one current of economic analysis conceives of the relationship between law and practices as direct and mono-causal (Djankov et al. 2003), numerous analyses in economic history have shown that law is constantly subject to controversy and interpretation and that the same body of laws – and even the same legal code – can give rise to different practices over time (Lamoreaux & Rosenthal 2005; Lemercier 2008; Musacchio 2008, 2010). These analyses should be connected to those on the law's expressive function: indeed, one may well ask if the adaptation of practices to the same body of laws can, for example, arise from changes in norms or the symbolic charge found in a particular law. In the following pages, I will be constantly asking whether the legal aspects of the "organization of credit" express or reflect social norms and how these interactions and the discrepancy between law and social practices evolve over time.

The legal framework defined the stakeholders and distributed power among them; thus the banking laws of 1941 and the law on the nationalization of credit of 1945 clearly established what banks are and who supervised them. The 1945 law created the conditions of possibility for the Banque de France to determine policy until 1984, but it was not the univocal expression of social norms, any more than it mechanically shaped practices. In order to call attention to the various interpretations of actors and the values motivating them, Part I of this book often uses a method that is distinct to pragmatic sociology, which seeks to study actors in "situations of tests" (Boltanski & Thévenot 2006), that is moments of conflict in which they invoke values, justifications which, they believe, must guide their practice. Thus, on several occasions I will use debates in assemblies and comments on reports in which contrary opinions are expressed (see, for example, the discussions of the Lutfalla and Marjolin–Sadrin–Wormser reports in Chapter 3, Section II). We will see how the meaning attributed to the 1945

---

[12] Roland Bénabou and Jean Tirole (2011) construct a model in which they also distinguish between three institutional components: personal and social values; explicit incentives (laws); and sanctions and rewards (norms). Though it is neither a test nor an application of their theory, which is based on a strong hypothesis of rationality, this book does nevertheless make it possible to imagine how this distinction could be fruitful for empirical analysis. What Bénabou and Tirole call "values" is what I call "norms" or "shared values," and what they call "norms" is what I call an institution's capacity for self-control or self-limitation.

law, as well as to the National Credit Council, which the law created, diverged significantly over time and in relation to specific actors. When proposals to reform the system appeared in the 1960s, the institution's opponents saw the 1945 law as nothing more than a set of legal rules that were sufficiently flexible to accommodate a different financial system, whereas the defenders of the Banque de France's role in credit allocation appealed to the important principles that, in their minds, underpinned the law and the National Credit Council. In their view, the 1945 law had a major symbolic or expressive function that largely exceeded the narrow legal framework.

Distinguishing the institutional components allows one finally, to analyze the coherence of an institution and institutional complementarities from a perspective similar to that found in the "varieties of capitalism" literature (Crouch 2005; Hall & Thelen 2009; Amable et al. 2012). In the typology proposed above, one particularly important question concerns whether anti-inflationary measures and the institution's collective values and norms are coherent. A second important question pertains to complementarities that can exist between an institution, such as a credit institution, and the other institutions with which it interacts, like budgetary and industrial policy.

In both cases, complementarity and coherence are defined as the fact that two components do not enter into conflict and that each compensates for the other's possible shortcomings.[13] A typical conflict would be if institutional control took place outside of a legal framework or in a way that was contrary to the values advocated by the institution. Another possibility would be that actors believe that the consequences of an institution's action conflicted with its principles or its norms, or some people's interests. Conflict is thus the engine of institutional change. We shall see how different types of conflict occurred in the 1970s relating to the organization of credit and thus led to a process of deinstitutionalization. From this point of view, my conclusions concerning the Banque de France's policies echo those proposed notably by John Zysman (1983), Peter Hall (1986), Michael Loriaux (1991) and Barry Eichengreen (2006),[14] who call attention, in other economic domains, to the high degree of institutional complementarity and coherence that existed during the 1950s and 1960s, before they gradually disappeared.

---

[13] See Aoki (2007) for a different definition of institutional complementarity.
[14] Analyzing primarily industrial policy and income policy, Peter Hall concludes that the French state appeared, in the late 1970s, as a "state divided against itself ... faced with multiple tasks and well-defined conflicts of interest among the social classes it governs, or among sub-groups within them" (1986, p. 176).

1

French Credit Policies before 1945

I THE "SOCIALIZATION OF CREDIT" BEFORE THE WAR AND THE POPULAR FRONT

While the means of instituting credit as well as the authorities responsible for its institutionalization changed profoundly after World War II, the premises of the new interventionist system were present before the war. As has been demonstrated by the work of Claire Andrieu (1996), Bertrand Blancheton (2001), Patrice Baubeau (2004), Olivier Feiertag (2006b) and Michel Margairaz (1991, 2009a),[1] state intervention on the credit market increased following World War I and took on new proportions with the Popular Front.

During the nineteenth century, the Banque de France gradually established itself as a crucial actor on the credit market. A credit system still largely founded on personal and decentralized relationships at the beginning of the nineteenth century gradually evolved into a more harmonized system, symbolized by discounting and Banque de France supervision, notably through the role of the branches (Nishimura 1995; Lescure & Plessis 1999; Baubeau 2004; Bazot 2014). The state's role also increased with the creation of public and semi-public credit institutions. World War I saw the birth of the *Crédit Populaire* (cooperative banks) in 1917, the *Crédit*

---

[1] Several important books have also studied the implementation of banking laws, norms, policies and techniques establishing credit in France during the eighteenth and nineteenth centuries: Bertrand Gille (1959) on credit in the first half of the nineteenth century; Laurence Fontaine (2014) on credit directed at individuals under the Old Regime; Philip Hoffman, Gilles Postel-Vinay and Jean-Laurent Rosenthal (2000, 2018) on notarized credit and landed credit; and Patrice Baubeau (2004) on the discounting system through to World War II. Baubeau's work in particular studies the closely intertwined relationship between monetary policy and the establishment of the discounting system.

National in 1919, which was responsible for ensuring medium-term financing for postwar reconstruction, and the *Caisse Nationale de Crédit Agricole* (cooperative banks for agricultural credit) in 1920, which now stood alongside the *Caisse des Dépôts et Consignations* (large depository institution lending long term) and *Crédit Foncier* (mortgage lending), created respectively in 1816 and 1852, thus constituting a group of non-banking credit establishments specialized in particular types of financing. The creation of the *Caisse Nationale des Marchés de l'État* (whose main goal is to facilitate payments on account of public contracts) on August 19, 1936 also participated in this move toward public intervention in the credit market, which always increasingly took the form of a segmentation of the market.[2] These new credit resources were established in a legal framework that gave them a clear and precise function: "popular," "landed," etc. The creation of these "public" or "semi-public" credit institutions,[3] in contrast to the emergence of new banks and individual lenders, resulted on every occasion in innovation or a legal and financial expansion of credit's possibilities: for instance, the original goal of the Caisse Nationale des Marchés de l'État was to accept or to clear on the state's behalf bills of exchange or promissory notes issued by or subscribed to by purchasers on the supplies or labor market, while the state was not authorized to accept bills of exchange. The Crédit Foncier was, for its part, the only institution authorized to issue "mortgage bonds." To distinguish them from banks, these various organizations are commonly called "credit institutions." Their name indicates their purpose: to give a precise function to the credit with which they are supposed to supply the economy.

It should be recalled that prior to 1936, the arguments informing the creation of these institutions and monopolies primarily referred to national economic efficiency – from a Bonapartist or even Saint-Simonian spirit in the nineteenth century, in the name of national reconstruction after World War I – and not socialist ideals seeking to remove finance from the hands of private interests. The goal was to allow the development of medium- and

---

[2] A very useful presentation of these organizations written in English in the 1950s is available in Wilson (1957, ch. VII). Further references (in French) on their history are provided in the following footnotes and in Chapter 6.

[3] The term semi-public is used to refer to private organizations that are placed under the state's tutelage. Crédit Foncier and Crédit National belong to this category: they can issue shares and bonds on the financial market, but their director is named by the Finance Ministry. The Caisse des Dépôts and the Caisse Nationales des Marchés de l'État are public. Crédit Populaire is, for its part, a cooperative organization, the original legal form of which was defined by the 1917 law. The state supported the development of popular credit funds by granting them interest-free *amortissables* advances.

long-term credit in situations where the banking system had trouble doing so. As with the Banque de France, which at the time was a private institution, state centralism and the monopolism characteristic of public and semi-public credit institutions was tied to the preservation of the interests of financial capitalism represented by what was known as the *Haute Banque* and the "two hundred families."[4] The meaning of the words "public" and "national" arose from the ideas of nineteenth-century bourgeois and conservative France, which was perpetuated in part by the "synthesis" that was the Third Republic (Hoffmann 1963).

In the 1930s, on the contrary, numerous projects developed to institutionalize credit in new ways, notably through its "socialization," thus giving a new meaning to "nationalization." The first idea was not to nationalize the banking system as a whole but to make credit a national priority, notably by giving a greater role to the government and the Banque de France in credit allocation and control and in the development of a legal arsenal that would make it possible to free the credit supply from particular interests. Even if the terms of the "socialization of credit" are still vague and the object of many debates within planner and socialist circles, the idea caught on in the economic thinking of reformist currents during the 1930s (Lefranc 1966). Thus, at the congress of the French Section of the Workers' International (SFIO) in May 1934, the final motion, presented by Léon Blum, called for the "socialization of credit and insurance." Christian Pineau, who in 1945 would be the sponsor in the National Assembly of the law on nationalizing credit (Franck 1953), wrote in 1938 that the necessary financial measures should be taken to give credit the "place that it should occupy in the modern economy," replacing "the concept of risk with that of usefulness for the nation" (Pineau 1938, p. 91).[5] In 1936, before Pineau, and even before the Popular Front, André Philip and Albert Monceau proposed a number of reforms the goal of which was "to create a harmonious banking system, which, while respecting the fundamental distinction between short-term and long-term credit and leaving a maximum amount of freedom and

---

[4]   These ties are made particularly evident and studied in detail in Michel Lescure's dissertation on the Crédit Foncier (1982). On the Caisse des Dépôts, see Aglan et al. (2003, 2011), and on the Crédit National, Baubeau et al. (1994). On the ties between the Banque de France, its private shareholders and the *Haute Banque*, see Plessis (1985), Stoskopf (2002) and Leclercq (2010) for the nineteenth century and Jeanneney (1976) for the interwar years.

[5]   The role of Pineau and of prewar avant-garde currents can be found in Margairaz (2009a).

initiative, would allow the central bank to pursue an efficient course and to put credit institutions in the service of the collectivity of workers" (Philip & Monceau 1936, p. 100).

The Popular Front brought no radical change in the distribution of credit, and this was notably true because it failed to introduce banking legislation.[6] Yet it undertook a quasi-nationalization of the Banque de France, which consisted of requiring, in the statutes of July 24, 1936 (article 4), representatives of the "Nation's collective interests" and "economic and social interests" in the bank's General Council, which had hitherto been dominated by shareholders. Representation of these interests by members of corporate organizations (labor, artisans, farmers and so on) and by the heads of public and semi-public credit institutions marked an important change and launched a vision of how the general interest could be represented that would later be found in the law nationalizing credit following the Liberation.[7] This vision of national representation stemmed from the movement known as "republican corporatism," which developed during the 1920s.[8]

---

[6] This point is a matter of consensus among historians; see Andrieu (1991, p. 61) and Margairaz (1991).

[7] The primary change concerns the composition of the General Council. The bank's capital remained private but the 1936 law required that only two members of the Council be selected from among the shareholders. The others were named by the government or various state bodies: "nine representatives of economic and social interests, nine representatives of the collective interests of the Nation" (Article 9). Among the first nine, one was designated by the National Economic Council from among its vice-presidents; one was designated by the High Commission of Saving Banks from among its members; one was elected by secret ballot by the Banque de France's employees; six were chosen by the finance minister from lists presented by each of the following organizations: the National Federation of Consumers' Cooperatives, the General Labor Confederation, the Permanent Assembly of the Chairmen of Chambers of Agriculture and the commercial professions section of the National Economic Council.
The nine representatives of the nation's collective interests included, for its part, three representatives of the Finance, National Economy and Colonies ministers and six regular members: the president of the Finance Section of the Council of State; the director of the General Movement of Funds (the Treasury's predecessor); the General Director of the Caisse des Dépôts et Consignations; the Governor of the Crédit Foncier; the General Director of the Crédit National; and the General Director of the Caisse Nationale du Crédit Agricole.

[8] Republican corporatism was theorized in particular by Joseph Paul Boncour and proved influential in the creation, in 1924, of the National Economic Council, the ancestor to the Economic and Social Council (Margairaz & Rousso 1992, note 4; Chatriot 2003). On the importance and representation of intermediary bodies in French democracy, see Rosanvallon (1998, 2000).

The socialist Jules Moch, in his preface to Philip and Monceau's book (1936) on the nationalization of credit, had anticipated the difficulties that the Popular Front would encounter when he wrote in August 1935:

the much-needed transformation of the banking system will occur at a time, which is perhaps not far away, but that we cannot predict precisely, and most import- antly under technical conditions fatally influenced by considerations lying outside the problem that has been posed. We know simply that no unity or concentrated government will attack the very foundations of the regime from which it eman- ates: such a structural reform – which in present circumstances is urgent – can only be the achievement of socialist power or a Popular Front. But we do not know what kind of capitalist reactions will be triggered by such a mistrial succession ... These reactions, as much as our own will, will determine our attitude. They can take such varied forms that a detailed nationalization plan risks addressing none of tomorrow's realities. (p. 13)

These declarations are important for understanding the postwar system, as Jules Moch and André Philip (as well as Christian Pineau), both of whom were convinced and influential planners, played a decisive role in the new economic and financial order that was established after the Liberation.[9] The former was Minister of Public Works and Transportation from 1945 to 1947, the latter, Minister of the National Economy and Finance from 1946 to 1947. The Liberation, even more than the Popular Front, finally gave these men the means to implement a program of nationalizing credit, which they had sought in the 1930s.

II THE BANKING LAWS OF 1941 AND THE VICHY TURNING-POINT

Yet it would be incomplete to suggest that the Liberation realized the Popular Front's ambitions without considering the important changes that the war and the Vichy regime brought to the banking system and the state's role. Though the Economic and Social Charter of the National Resistance Council (*Conseil National de la Résistance*, or CNR) of March 15, 1944, the Provisional Government of the French Republic (*Gouvernement provisoire de la République française*, or GPRF), which lasted from June 3, 1944 to October 27, 1946, and finally the Fourth Republic obviously wanted to break with the political legacy and organizing economic principles of the Vichy regime, it cannot be denied that the latter brought about significant

---

[9] "Placed on the desk of the Constitutional [Assembly] in November 1945, Philip's proposal to socialize credit borrowed word for word from the project that Christian Pineau had, in October 1938, published in the journal *Banque et Bourse*" (Andrieu 1991, p. 13).

administrative and legal changes in the realm of credit, which the new government did not abandon at the Liberation. Historical studies have shown that the CNR and then De Gaulle's political strategy sought, in the name of national reconciliation, to disconnect the "state" from "Vichy," rejecting the latter while basing itself on the former, notably by preserving much of the existing bureaucracy (Paxton 1972; Margairaz 2009b).

The "nationalization of credit," desired by the planners and widely supported by the National Resistance Council, acknowledged in practice the reform of the banking system undertaken by the Vichy regime during the Occupation. The new banking laws, conceived by the banker Henri Ardant[10] and adopted in June 1941, organized the banking profession, first by providing a legal definition of banks and creating the category of "financial institution," second by creating organizations for regulating and supervising banks. The first measure defined banks as "companies or institutions whose regular occupation it is to receive from the public, in the form of deposits or through other means, funds that they use for their own activities, for discounting operations, credit operations, or financial operations" (article 1) and distinguished them from financial institutions by forbidding "companies other than banks from receiving from the public deposits of funds withdrawable upon demand or in less than two years" (article 3), thus following the examples of Belgium, Italy and Germany in 1934. The second measure created the Professional Association of Banks, the Permanent Committee on Banks (*Comité permanent des banques*) and the Bank Control Commission (*Commission de contrôle des banques*), consisting of bankers representing their peers.

As the historian Claire Andrieu points out, "the measures adopted in 1941 had to a large extent been advocated by the Popular Front government. Moreover, the reform was, unprecedentedly, undertaken by the very people who had successfully fought it in 1936–1938" (Andrieu 1991, p. 11) – that is, by representatives of the primary banking institutions and particularly Henri Ardant. Yet, to grasp this paradox, it is first necessary to understand that the 1941 reform cannot be considered a genuine "application" of the program of the Popular Front as the principle guiding the new regulation is not that of the socialization of credit "in the service of the collectivity of workers" or the nation, but the organization of a corporatist approach to

---

[10] Former finance inspector, general director of the Société Générale from 1940 to 1944 and vice-president of the bankers' union, Ardant established himself by 1936 as representative of the banks and a defender of corporatism. He deeply opposed his brother, Gabriel Ardant, who was a planner and adviser to Pierre Mendès-France (Andrieu 1983, p. 387). Though he was not found guilty at the Liberation, he was forced to resign from his position. After the war, Ardant wrote textbooks on banking techniques (Ardant 1953, 1954).

credit management by the workers themselves. The goal of these laws was as much to prevent German occupation forces from completely reorganizing the French banking system as it was to protect to establish a corporatist system that would protect the profession' interests (Andrieu 1991, p. 231). This did not prevent French banks from being made to help finance the occupation and payments to Germany (Margairaz 2009a).

An abundant historical literature has already studied the continuity between Vichy's institutions and policies and those implemented at the Liberation (Paxton 1972; Kuisel 1981; Margairaz 1991, 2009b; Margairaz & Rousso 1992; Chapman 2018).[11] In many domains, as Philip Nord in particular has shown (2010) in the case of demography and education, the roots of these policies common to these radically different regimes can be found in the 1930s. This was also the case for the national statistical system, which was begun under Vichy with the National Statistics Service and resulted in the creation of the INSEE (*Institut national de la statistique et des études économiques,* or National Institute for Statistics and Economic Studies) in 1946 and, in the domain of banking statistics, the Central Risk Service (*Service central des risques*), which was created following the 1941 laws and became increasingly important after the Liberation. These two organizations became crucial for the CGP and credit policy.

While the continuity between the 1930s, the Vichy regime and the Liberation's policies cannot be denied, the differences between them need to be examined carefully, as Margairaz and Rousso (1992) do in the case of industrial policy. Specifically, we need to analyze how a single legal framework and economic policies that, at first blush, seem similar can acquire different meanings and objectives. In the context of banking legislation, we will see how the "nationalization of credit" in 1945, which established national and social economic priorities as allocation criteria, based itself on 1941 laws that had originally instituted credit in a purely corporatist manner as part of Vichy's "National Revolution."

---

[11] A recent and rather comprehensive literature review in French is provided in Grenard et al. (2017).

2

The Nationalization of Credit from 1945 to the Late 1950s

This chapter will examine the implementation of a new system of credit regulation and allocation after the war through 1958, based on the three components of the institution laid out in the introduction: the legal framework, social norms and anti-inflationary policies.

I THE LEGAL INSTITUTION OF CREDIT

The Credit Nationalization Law

The major changes concerning the credit system at the Liberation were written into the law of December 2, 1945, "relating to the nationalization of the Banque de France and the major banks and credit institutions," which contemporaries often dubbed "the credit nationalization law." Public and semi-public credit institutions (the Crédit National, the Crédit Foncier and so on) were, for their part, maintained without new ones being created; the 1936 Banque de France statutes were not changed; and the 1941 banking laws were not significantly modified. The categories of "banks" and "financial institutions" were preserved, as well as the Professional Association of Banks and the Bank Control Commission (*Commission de contrôle des banques*).

International historical literature on central banks (Capie et al. 1994; Elgie & Thompson 1998; Singleton 2011) has often called attention to the law nationalizing the Banque de France and to a lesser extent the nationalization of other banks. Yet, the emphasis on these measures, important though they may be, may lead one to miss the essential. When it comes to the Banque de France's role and state intervention in the economy, the key factor is the "organization of credit."[1]

---

[1] The law's title uses the term "organization of credit"; the law's content prefers the phrase "credit management" (*direction du credit*). See Part 5 (article 12–16).

Indeed, the nationalization of the Banque de France's capital simply ratified the 1936 measures, in order to shield the authority that determined monetary policy once and for all from private interests. The nationalization of the four largest banks was, for its part, largely symbolic and did not represent a socialization of the banking market. It is no exaggeration to say that it played no essential role in future credit policy. Whereas there existed a consensus among the different political forces around nationalizing the Banque de France, only the SFIO (or socialists) and the Communist Party sought, from the outset, to nationalize banks, consistent with the rather vague statements made in the program of the National Resistance Council (CNR).[2] Ultimately, a compromise was reached: only the major deposit banks would be nationalized,[3] with no deep changes to the way they operated (the only difference concerned the nomination of new directors). Ownership of other banks, notably the large investment banks, remained unchanged. The fruit of compromise and various arbitrary decisions, the scope of banking nationalizations remained limited and does not seem to have been a decisive and coherent factor in the general organization of credit laid out in the December 1945 law. The American historian Richard Kuisel states perfectly how these new ways of instituting credit were the result less of bank nationalizations than of legal constructs and the complex but well-coordinated bureaucratic network that was created subsequently:

Nationalization of the Bank of France and the major deposit banks was more form than substance. What proved more effective in disciplining the banking community was the new control network centered around the Treasury, the National Credit Council, the Bank of France, the Banking Control Commission, and the professional bankers' assoMciation. Together they carted and applied credit policy and restrained private banks from acting contrary to public economic policy. (Kuisel 1981, p. 214)

It is thus this "control network" that must be studied if one is not to confuse what contemporaries called the "nationalization of credit" with "bank

---

[2] Aimé Lepercq, the finance minister prior to René Pleven, was notoriously opposed to it. On this note, the CNR's program declares: "The return to the nation of major, monopolized means of production, the fruit of collective labor, of energy sources, of underground wealth, and of insurance companies and major banks."

[3] Deposits in the four banks represented 52% of total deposits in French banks in 1944, a figure that was close to the 50% of 1936 but greater than the 40% of 1929, before the financial crisis. These banks were: Crédit Lyonnais, Société Générale, Comptoir National d'Escompte (National Discounting Counter) and Banque Nationale pour le Commerce et l'Industrie (National Bank for Commerce and Industry). In 1966, the latter two became Banque Nationale de Paris (BNP).

nationalizations." At the heart of credit organization, the 1945 law placed the National Credit Council (CNC), which it created to this end and which was incorporated legally and administratively into the Banque de France. Its general secretary, Pierre Besse, very clearly stated in a publication from 1951 why the CNC's role was distinct from the management of the nationalized banks:

> The problem very naturally presented itself of determining how the credit apparatus would be managed ... This question itself consisted of two dimensions: the first was that of the distinct management of each of the nationalized institutions; the second was that of defining a general policy to be followed by the banking system in its entirety, whether or not it was nationalized. The solution to the first problem was found in the December 2 law: we shall not dwell on it. We shall simply say that the latter preserved the administrative autonomy of each of the nationalized institutions, that it carefully shielded daily management from state influence by assigning it to a board of directors consisting of representatives of various economic categories that are concerned by the policy of our major banking institutions. The second problem affects the existence of the National Credit Council more directly. (Besse 1951, p. 579)

The National Credit Council: A *Paritaire* Vision of Credit

In the bill that was the origin of the very distinctive organization that was the CNC lies the idea that credit needs cannot be

> met in a logical and coordinate manner, by respecting priorities determined by the sole criterion of national interest, if a preeminent institution is not created with the broadest competencies to examine the financial aspects of the nation's reconstruction [*rééquipement*] and modernization and to provide the government with a fully enlightened opinion on the conditions according to which the Plan can be financed.[4]

The creation of the CNC of the Banque de France was thus the foundation of the new system: not only did it replace the role of the Permanent Committee on Banks (CPB) – created by the 1941 law – in managing credit-related professions but it was also assigned numerous tasks – counseling, consulting, informing and proposal-making (the law named more than a dozen) – that had not been granted to the earlier committee. These tasks concerned everything pertaining to deposits, from savings to currency by way of banking and currency statistics. In this way, even if it was ultimately not the decision-making authority (which, depending

---

[4] Presentation of the intentions for the proposed government law, parliamentary document, annex 46, session of November 30, 1945, cited in Dupont (1952, p. 47).

on the domain, remained the preserve of the government and the Banque de France), the CNC acquired a direct grip on credit policy, as it was able to propose its guiding principles and it was obligatory that it be apprised of information "necessary to the accomplishment of its task" (article 13). While it could not, of course, issue decrees or orders,[5] the CNC inherited from the CPB the ability to exercise its authority by means of "decisions of a general nature" or "decisions of an individual nature." The object of the former was regulating credit techniques and perfecting the organization of the banking profession, while the latter applied to specifically designated companies and could prescribe measures "justified by general or local economic needs" (law of June 13, 1941, article 34). In order to clarify decisions of a general nature or to move them forward, the CNC also issued recommendations and instructions. In addition to these discretionary powers, the CNC also had jurisdictional powers that the CPB lacked, which was unusual for a body of this kind. Only rarely, however, did it use these powers.[6]

Thus from late 1945 until 1984, all decisions concerning monetary policy and bank regulation (notably setting ratios various bank liquidity ratios, maximum bank interest rates, credit limits and so on) had the status of "decisions of a general nature" (*décision de caractère général*) and shared a similar form: they referred first to the 1945 law, which gave the National Credit Council decision-making powers, then to the 1941 laws defining the nature of banking institutions; they also drew on previous decisions of a general nature that they either completed or upon which they based themselves.[7]

These unique legal (i.e., administrative) responsibilities gave the CNC and the Banque de France the flexibility they needed to transform bank regulations into short-term monetary policy. This legal framework was crucial for carrying out the Banque de France's interventions in subsequent decades: the central bank could guarantee the control of inflation as well as "credit selectivity" by altering bank regulations without necessitating

---

[5] In French law, decrees and orders (i.e., regulations) are placed above directives and memorandums (i.e., administrative decisions) in the legal hierarchy. Regulations are actions of executive power. The central bank and the CNC are administrative authorities.

[6] By virtue of article 11 of the December 2, it befell the CNC to adjudicate disputes that might occur between investment banks and their government commissioner, and by virtue of the law of May 17, 1946, a court of appeals was created to hear banks' challenges to the classification they received from the Bank Control Commission.

[7] A "decision of a general nature" is reproduced in Monnet (2012a, p. 170).

modifications of the law (by the parliament) or the publication of decrees or orders (by government ministries). The CNC's responsibilities thus completely transformed the means through which the Banque de France could intervene in the economy compared to the prewar situation.

The CNC's membership differed radically from the CPB's corporatist-bank organization: the CNC replaced its six members, who had been chosen from within the banking community by the State Secretary for the National Economy and Finances,[8] with a "a kind of little parliament,"[9] modeled on the National Economic Council (disbanded in 1939 [Chatriot 2003])[10] and the Banque de France's General Council, which was appointed in 1936 and consisted of seventeen representatives of the "country's active forces" (industrialists, retailers, farmers, union delegates and some cooperatives) and twenty-one representatives of economic professions: seven civil servants from the economics ministry, seven bankers and currency traders and seven representatives of public or semi-public credit institutions. Thus, the goal of this assembly, which was at once a court of appeal, a consultative and decision-making authority and a space for the exchange and engagement between the interests of the nation's various "bodies," was to ensure the management of French bank credit – that is, to institute credit in accordance with national priorities. Though the corporatism of bankers, as it existed under Vichy, was now a thing of the past, the philosophy guiding the operation of this assembly was that of a representation of "bodies," and the CNC drew its authority from the fact that banks were represented, as members, within the council. Because of its regulatory and jurisdictional functions, the CNC resembled the Council of the Order of Doctors or the equivalent organization for lawyers,[11] but its *paritaire* composition and its subaltern position vis-à-vis the Banque de France meant that, rather than a strictly corporatist organization affiliated with a profession, it was an organization representing

---

[8] There was also a government commissioner assisted by an assistant commissioner named by the same state secretary.

[9] The term is borrowed from a famous and influential economist of this period, Jean Marchal (Marchal 1967, p. 292). In books and discussions from this time, the CNC was often described as an "assembly."

[10] The National Economic Council consisted of forty-seven members. Its successor, the Economic Council, which became the Economic and Social Council, was not created until October 27, 1946.

[11] The CNC was the only organization that could issue "decisions of a general nature," but other councils were authorized to make "decisions" that applied to their members.

the nation's various intermediary bodies, in a way that was typical of the "republican corporatism" theorized between the wars.

Seeking to be a space of dialogue and negotiation, the CNC did not set out to organize credit allocation in an authoritarian manner. It was thus a symbol of the mixed and "organized" economy that was desired at the Liberation (Bloch-Lainé & Bouvier 1986). The CNC regularly recalled this initial position:

> Of course, the primary mission that the CNC was assigned is to ensure that the various economic sectors do not lack the credit that is necessary and sufficient to play in the supply, production, and circulation of goods. But it should by no means consider that it has been assigned the role of carrying out in an authoritarian manner a preconceived distribution of a pre-determined sum of bank credits ...[12]

In this respect, parallels with the Commissariat Général du Plan (General Planning Commissariat, or CGP), created on December 21, 1945 to provide "advisory" planning, is striking (Fourquet 1980; Andrieu 1984; Mioche 1987; Margairaz 1991; Nord 2010). But the major difference between the Commissariat Général du Plan and the CNC lies in the latter's ability to issue and implement its decisions. This is due to the fact that the CNC was tied directly to the organization of a particular activity, namely, bank credit. Yet, in practice, it was the Banque de France that regularly acted "on behalf of the National Credit Council." The Banque de France's legal and political appropriation of the CNC was due largely to the fact that the CNC's personnel belonged to the Banque de France and operated within the same walls. Specifically, the Central Risk Service and the General Direction of Credit, two offices of the Banque de France, created statistics and reports, respectively, for the CNC. The Banque de France's governor, moreover, presided over the CNC's meetings. Thus, it is safe to say, with Andrieu (1984), that the CNC was fully integrated into the Banque de France. Neither the legislature, politicians nor the organizations' leadership did anything to establish rigid administrative distinctions between the CNC and the bank during this period. If such a distinction seems superfluous, it is because the CNC was, by virtue of its responsibilities, directly involved in the management of monetary creation and the control of inflation, a fact to which we now turn.[13]

---

[12] 1949 CNC report, p. 21.
[13] Andrieu (1984) concludes that the porousness between the bank and the CNC suggests that credit policy lacked both ambition and resources. We think, on the contrary, that

The National Credit Council and Medium-Term Mobilizable Credit: A Monetary Vision of Credit

One part of the credit system eluded the CNC. Its powers gave it no regulatory authority over "specialized financial organizations," which included two categories of institutions. The first consisted essentially of "banks having a special legal status" – that is, Banques Populaires and Caisses du Crédit Agricole which were two cooperative banks; the second included all the public and semi-public institutions, such as Crédit National, Crédit Foncier and the Caisse des Dépôts et Consignations. It is understandable that the second category was placed directly under the tutelage of the Finance Ministry, as these institutions did not in principle participate directly in monetary creation but solely in credit allocation: they did not take deposits and their own funds came primarily from bond issues. Thus, the CNC did need to act directly on them to limit the creation of money. These institutions were involved in monetary creation only when the Banque de France rediscounted the effects of the medium-term credit (credit with midterm liquidity) that they offered. According to the official texts, the CNC could thus also give its opinions and recommendations on rediscounting. As for qualitative recommendations on credit allocation, the CNC could have indirect influence over these institutions through the advice it offered them or that it shared with the ministry. Though they were not under the CNC's direct authority, public and semi-public credit institutions were thus incorporated into an organized system of credit selectivity, though they did not fall under the realm of monetary policy based on banking regulation.

The cases of the Crédit Agricole and the Banques Populaires are, however, difficult to explain and correspond rather to a flaw in the 1945 legislation (Dupont 1952). In practice, one-off negotiations took place between the CNC, the Banque de France and the national leadership of these "banks with a special legal status" to ensure that they were subject to the same regime and controls as other banks.[14]

It is crucial to note that the different regulatory framework these various institutions followed dovetailed with a theoretical distinction at the monetary level (with the exception of the Crédit Agricole and the Banques Populaires): institutions whose credits participated in monetary creation (by

---

this is not the case once credit and monetary policy are seen as inextricably tied. But the rapprochement between these policies occurs at the expense of regular coordination with the Planning Commissariat, as Andrieu notes in the case of CNC.

[14] This situation was officially resolved in 1973.

the multiplier effect of deposits) were placed under the Banque de France's tutelage, while others were placed under the Finance Ministry. This fact had obvious consequences for monetary policy that will be studied below. Bank credit creation could be controlled either directly by constraining banking loans legally or through rationing at the discount window. Credit of specialized financial organizations could only be controlled by qualitative recommendations or through rationing at the discount window.

We have thus touched upon the inherent duality of the CNC, an organization charged both with advisory credit planning and with the conduct of monetary policy. If credit allocation was conceived independently of monetary policy, it could unquestionably have been one of the responsibilities of the Commissariat Général du Plan (or of the Treasury) and all the credit institutions would have been subject to the same authority. Credit would have been viewed solely through the lens of industrial policy. The 1945 law, on the contrary, contains a monetary approach to understanding and managing credit.

The Commissariat Général du Plan (Planning Office) was assigned the coordination of Marshall Plan funds whereas, starting with the 1948 Mayer Stabilization Plan, the Treasury was in charge of the Caisse autonome de Reconstruction and the Fonds de Modernisation et d'Equipement (FEM) which granted reconstruction loans and would become the Fonds de Développement Économique et Social (Economic and Social Development Fund, or FDES) in 1954 (Margairaz 1991, p. 1033; Lynch 1997, p. 89). It fell to the Banque de France and the CNC to intervene in the allocation and regulation of bank credit. Connections between the two institutions were desired when the bill was first written, but the only formal link expressed in the December 1945 law was the requirement that the "Economic Modernization Plan" hand over to the CNC information "needed to allow it to establish an investment plan" (article 14). When the Commissariat Général du Plan was set up and replaced the Economic Modernization Plan in 1946, no one bothered to change the law. In the absence of a legal framework for formalizing their cooperation, the Commissariat Général du Plan and the CNC thus operated autonomously for the entire duration of their existence (Andrieu 1984).

In addition to the new legal framework that made credit organization and policies possible, all due consideration must be given to the Banque de France's financial innovations, which were also based on legal innovations, and particularly on the possibility of rediscounting medium-term credit, the genesis of which has been studied by Olivier Feiertag (1995, 2006b). The possibility of rediscounting medium-term notes – up to five years – to the central bank was initiated as a practice in the late 1930s, modeled on policies implemented in Germany. In France, it is described as being "mobilizable in the medium term" (*crédit à moyen terme mobilisable*). "Mobilizable in the medium term" was developed by the Caisse des Dépôts and Crédit National in the late 1930s, and it was only in 1937 for the former and 1943 for the latter that the issuing institute accepted them for rediscounting. This instrument thus also arose from a monetization of the credit question, in the sense that Banque de France committed itself to place its money-creation powers at the service of the provision of long-term credit which, according to contemporary opinion, the economy sorely lacked. Previously, only commercial paper with three-month maturities (and three credit-worthy signees) could be rediscounted by the central banks. The inflationist danger of mobilizable medium-term credit was recognized and understood from the outset; hence the special attention that was given to controlling it.[15] The public and semi-public credit institutions – Crédit Foncier, Crédit National, Caisse des Dépôts, Caisse Nationale des Marchés de l'État[16] – were thus reintegrated into the circuit of monetary creation, as they were the ones who, beginning in 1945, were in charge of "mobilizing" credits before presenting them to the central bank. Four signatures were necessary for the bank to accept them: the industrialist's, the latter's bank and that of two of the public or semi-public credit institutions of the four mentioned. For the largest medium-term credits (this amount varied over time), the law required the meeting of a committee at the central bank. It consisted of two members of the Banque de France (the directors of the General Directorate of Credit and of the General Directorate of Discounting), the director of the Crédit National and representatives of the Commissariat Général du Plan and the Finance Ministry. The composition of this committee shows, once again, that credit lay at the crossroads between monetary policy, economic and industrial policy, and planning.

The institutionalization of credit at the end of the war entrenched three essential principles into the law. First, credit policy was elaborated by representative bodies of the nation in coordination with the general policies of the government; second, monetary policy and "credit selectivity" were tied and based on administrative-style tools of bank regulation that were

---

[15] This danger was clearly expressed as early as a note from February 1944: ABF (Archives of the Banque de France) 1331200301/493, "Note de Février 1944 sur la politique du crédit de la Banque de France." See, too, the overview by Pavès and Simon (1955).

[16] The Caisse Nationale des Marchés de l'État (National Fund for State Markets) acquired, after the war, a new role – that of reconstruction – and became specialized in credits for rebuilding companies (Zentz 1951).

assigned to the Banque de France by way of the CNC; finally, the Banque de France could rediscount and thus control medium-term commercial paper offered by some of the public credit institutions.

II CREDIT AS A PUBLIC GOOD, OR THE INSTITUTION'S "COLLECTIVE" DIMENSION

The Emergence of Consensus?

Previous sections have examined the general principles guiding the establishment of the new legal framework defined in 1945. The law reflected these norms, particularly since it allowed them to have a lasting influence on practice. What I must now study is how adherence to these norms is built and maintained. How and why do different actors come to agree on a *dirigiste* conception of credit? How does dissent express itself and is it incorporated into collective norms, leading practices to adapt to the legal framework?

Work in political science that is devoted to the study of central banks have emphasized that the latter were conceived as offering a public good in response to problems of coordination. The most symptomatic example is that of the United States' central bank, which was created following the 1907 crisis, when the banker J. P. Morgan played the role of lender of the last resort. Lawrence Broz (2009) notes that the Fed's creation was made possible by the fact that it did not threaten the individual interests of bankers and financiers but, on the contrary, offered them the protection of a lender of the last resort and the prospect of a stronger dollar internationally.[17] In Europe, it is customary to situate the transformation of issuing banks into central banks, in the current sense of the term, in the second half of the nineteenth century, when the latter assumed the role of lender of the last resort (Goodhart 1985; Capie et al. 1994), that is, when financial stability was deemed a public good.

This perspective can be extended to other functions besides that of lender of the last resort and help us to understand the emergence and evolution of monetary institutions. Why was the "organization of credit" conceived in post-1945 France as a public good? It is not simply the result of theories about the socialization of credit from the interwar period that I described earlier, but also of actors' strategies. To borrow Lawrence Broz's words

---

[17] See, too, Eichengreen and Flandreau (2009) on the Fed's role in the diffusion of the dollar as an international currency.

about the creation of central banks: "What then explains the incentives of self-interested and free-riding individuals to contribute to institutions that bind governments?" (1998, pp. 231–232). The issue is thus to determine how individual interests can coincide with shared values.

In the case of France, it is particularly important to ask why the same interest groups (particularly bankers' associations) which blocked the reforms launched by the Popular Front did not make the nationalization of credit fail in 1945. The most obvious answer, which should be compared to Mancur Olson's (1982) broader thesis, consists in recalling that interest groups, in the immediate postwar years, were relatively weak, when they had not been destroyed, as the result of the purging of the economic system as well as the influence of the socialists and communists in the Provisional Government and later in the parliament. But it is well known that purges in banking and financial circles were trivial (Chaurand et al. 2008); and as for the left's influence, it diminished quite quickly and most financial reforms were in fact led by centrist elected officials of the MRP or the UDSR,[18] particularly by René Pleven, who tended rather to represent the interests of small business, artisans and industry.[19] Within the civil service, at the Finance Ministry and Treasury (Margairaz 1991; Quennouëlle-Corre 2000) as well as at the Banque de France (Feiertag 2006b), the renewal of personnel was not extensive and cannot account for a profound ideological shift. Michel Margairaz (1991, 2009b) has demonstrated along these lines that what occurred was a "conversion" of top civil servants to *dirigiste* and interventionist policies rather than a renewal of the state apparatus.[20]

---

[18] The Mouvement Républicain Populaire (Popular Republican Movement, or MRP) was a Christian-Democratic party founded on November 26, 1944 by Georges Bidault. It quickly became of the country's three primary political forces, along with the PC (communists) and the SFIO (socialists). This system was known as "tripartism." After the communists left the government in 1947, the MRP, with the SFIO, the UDSR and the Radicals, formed the "Third Force" (*Troisième force*), which opposed the PC and the Gaullists in order to preserve the Fourth Republic. Under Robert Schuman's leadership, the MRP was at the forefront of European construction. The Union Démocratique et Socialiste de la Résistance (the Democratic and Socialist Union of the Resistance, or UDSR) was a party that is usually described as centrist or as liberal socialist: its key figures included René Pleven and François Mitterrand.

[19] For a radical thesis that demonstrates the conservative and "bourgeois" character of the policies pursued during this period, see Vinen (2002).

[20] "For financial and monetary authorities, this conversion took the form of a genuine 'cultural revolution.' Their orthodox obsession with deficits and inflation gave way to a novel concern with depression and underemployment, at the same time that they abandoned a passive conception of their role for a voluntarist attitude in the face of growth" (Margairaz 2009b, p. 120).

The relative consensus around credit nationalization was to a large extent a consequence of the fact that the war left many professions and industries without a source of finance. That the state should take responsibility for the distribution of finance thus appeared as a social necessity and, economically speaking, as an "optimal" response to the needs of companies. At the war's end, the opinion spread that, without a credit policy, notably a medium- and long-term credit policy, private banks would not be in a position to finance the French economy. This necessity overlapped with a deeper argument that was critical of the "Malthusian" characteristics of the French economy before the war.[21] The claim that French business executives and banks had failed to promote investment and were responsible for the economic and political failures of the 1930s became a cornerstone of the policies pursued after the Liberation (Nord 2010). Historians sometimes use the term "anti-Malthusian consensus" (Margairaz 2009b; Nord 2010) to refer to this rejection of the interwar period.[22]

Continuity between Vichy and Postwar Credit Policy

The historiography no longer obscures the continuities or even the convergences between some of Vichy's economic policies and those pursued at the Liberation. This is particularly true of industrial policy and planning (Mioche 1987; Margairaz & Rousso 1992) and of credit policy.[23] In 1986, acknowledging the work of Paxton (1972) and Kuisel (1981), the historian Jean Bouvier observed that a historiographical renewal had resulted in "the discovery of convergences that, while certainly partial, are no less certain, between the long-term economic projects pursued by certain Vichy technocrats and their Resistance emulators" (Bloch-Lainé & Bouvier 1986, p. 39). This partial convergence was very clear in the realm of credit policy.[24] It pertained to the necessary role of the state and of the Banque de France in

---

[21] This "anti-Malthusian consensus" can also be seen as continuing a number of positions that were influential under Vichy. See Margairaz (2009a). See, too, the many pages that Nord (2010) devotes to Alfred Sauvy and François Perroux.

[22] Alfred Sauvy's work, in economics as much as in demography, is, in this respect, symptomatic.

[23] Cohen (2012), for his part, sees a continuity between Vichy's industrial policies, notably their technocratic dimension, unconnected from any parliamentary oversight, and the Monnet-Schuman Plan of 1950, which led to the European Coal and Steel Community.

[24] The influence of the credit policy pursued by Hjalmar Schacht in Germany in the late 1920s and early 1930s weighed heavily on French civil servants' conception of the efficiency of state intervention. This influence was also considerable in Japan during and after

promoting productive investment by facilitating companies' access to credit in the name of reconstruction and the rejection of the flaws of the 1930s' banking system. It is particularly evident in the continuity of banking legislation, and the desire for coordination between credit and industrial policy and in the choice of the central bank's instruments, notably the rediscounting of medium-term credit. Such a convergence of opinion can explain the consensus that was established around interventionist credit policies despite the major ideological fractures between the partisans of the socialization of credit "in the name of the workers" that one finds with the CNR and the bankers favoring a corporatist approach to credit, who had prepared the 1941 laws.

Particularly illuminating evidence of this continuity in methods and goals can be found in a Banque de France document from February 1944 that sought to establish the contours of a "credit policy" needed to rebuild France once peace has been restored. This note, which, needless to say, conceived of economic reconstruction in the context of a political system governed by Pétain, consisted of two features that were also found in the policies established at the Liberation. First, the note assigns the Banque de France the task of establishing a credit policy consistent with the production plan that the Vichy regime issued in 1942.[25] Thus the note says that "the latest reports of the bank's government to the General Assembly informed the public that the Issuing Institute [*Institut d'Emission*] had the intention of playing an active role as soon as possible in reconstructing the nation's wealth by providing the country's productive forces with the support of a vigorous credit policy" (p. 1). Concerning the government's directives to promote production and sales, the note explains: "Will these official, 'planned' encouragements continue to develop after the war? This is what, in their desire to avoid disorder, the circles at the Production Ministry seem to think" (p. 6).

The 1944 note also gives special attention to the development of medium-term credit – one of the bank's priorities – by attempting to carefully define the economy's needs. But the inflationary dangers of this kind of credit were well known, so the note emphasizes the need of not making this practice a regular one:

It is in the realm of medium-term credit – construction, equipment, transportation, foreign trade – that the bank will both have to show the most restraint and the

World War II (Werner 2002a). On Schacht's financial policies and the Reichsbank, see notably Overy (1995, p. 171), Tooze (2006, pp. 54–65), Clavert (2009).

[25] The plan was created following the creation of the Délégation Générale à l'Équipement National (General Delegation for National Infrastructure, or DGEN) on February 23, 1941 and the decision in favor of the principle of a plan on April 6, 1941.

most new ideas. But whatever the means employed, and our services are prepared to implement them, it is important that our interventions be seen as undertaken by force of necessity, on the provisional basis of the need to trigger the desired recovery, not as a normal and permanent means of developing the nation's infrastructure.[26] (p. 5)

At the Liberation, the National Resistance Council's desire to "nationalize credit" thus encountered interventionist strategies that had already been conceived and established within the civil service, notably at the Banque de France. It would draw on the latter while formulating new ideals and a new rhetoric concerning the social and not merely national value of credit.

The CNC's deliberations, along with the many letter exchanged between the Banque de France and the Professional Association of Banks, which I consulted in the Banque's archives, clearly demonstrates that extensive consensus existed around credit policy across very different professional milieus. The desire to break with the policies of the interwar years and the need for reconstruction are what bound these groups, over and above partisan cleavages. Moreover, there was very little change in the staff of the Banque de France, nor was there in the other main public credit institutions. At the Banque, only the governor (Boisanger) and one deputy governor (Villard) who were in office under the Vichy regime were suspended just after the liberation in December 1944. The legal purge in 1945 did not lead to any significant change in the high management of the Banque (Duchaussoy 2013, pp. 165–190).[27]

The main dissent within the CNC concerning the degree of state intervention came in fact from labor representatives – the majority of whom were communists – who regretted that the nationalization process had not been more complete and did not result in a genuine "rationalization and nationalization" of the credit system.[28] If few voices were raised

---

[26] ABF, 1331200301/493, "Note sur la politique du crédit de la Banque de France" (February 1944).

[27] Villard even became honorary deputy governor in March. The other deputy governor under Vichy, Bletterie, faced no charge. In 1949, the new governor of the Banque de France, Wilfrid Baumgartner, had been the president of Crédit National from 1936 to 1949. The president of the Caisse des dépôts (CDC) under Vichy, Henri Deroy, became president of the Crédit Foncier after the war. As far as credit policy is concerned – as in other areas of French economic administration – the Liberation did not change the men of power (Margairaz 1991). Deroy became president of CDC in 1935, showing again the continuity from the mid-1930s to the postwar period.

[28] ABF, 1427200301/8. Deliberations of the CNC's meeting of September 29, 1948.

against the principles of the organization of the credit system and state interventionism, the desire to restrain credit to fight inflation did, however, face considerable opposition. Thinking in terms of interests and coordination also makes it possible to understand why the nationalization of credit was accompanied, until late 1948, by a lax monetary policy, despite the fact that (non-communist) planners and influential advocates of nationalization, such as André Philip and Pierre Mendès-France, were by late 1944 proponents of austerity, in order to restore the value of a franc that was threatened by very high inflation (Chélini 1998; Nord 2010, ch. 3[29]). Representatives of retail and industry were clearly opposed to Mendès-France's austerity plan. De Gaulle thus named Pleven as the Provisional Government's Finance Minister and the latter decided to devalue the franc by 60% after the ratification of the Bretton Woods accords on December 26, 1945. The stabilization of inflation in late 1948 thus came late to France, compared to Belgium and Italy (Casella & Eichengreen 1993), which created a genuine credibility problem for the government by limiting its ability to borrow (Saint-Paul 1994). French monetary transition seemed locked in a vicious circle (Dieterlen & Rist 1948; Dieterlen 1954). High inflation restricted the government's ability to finance itself and to lend directly to companies, as well as the Banque de France's willingness to engage in unlimited rediscounting. Companies also thus relied on (often short term) bank credit that they found inadequate; consequently, they refused any credit restrictions aimed at fighting inflation. The graphs in Chapter 6 (Figure 24 and Figure 25) show that, from 1945 to 1949, the credits of the Treasury and the Banque de France to the economy form a small share of the total. Public credit institutions (mainly CDC and Crédit National) and banks were the main lenders. This explains, as we shall see, why the Banque de France and the National Credit Council made inflation stabilization the precondition of all credit policies.

---

[29] Casella and Eichengreen (1993), Chélini (1998) and Vinen (2002) all conclude that the influence of small business and bankers was undoubtedly one of the reasons why inflation stabilization policies were introduced in France later than among its neighbors. The communists were also opposed to authoritarian measures for bringing prices down. The late 1948 stabilization did in fact come later than in other European countries, particularly Belgium, where the recovery undertaken by Camille Gutt was achieved by November 1944, and Italy, where Einaudi and de Gasperi's drastic measures were imposed in 1947.

Representatives of banks and business continued to oppose the restrictive policies implemented in late 1948 by Governor Emmanuel Monick.[30] In November 1951, during the second period of monetary restriction, the President of the Paris Chamber of Commerce also wrote Governor Wilfrid Baumgartner (who replaced Monick on January 19, 1949) to express his disapproval of restrictive measures.[31]

As for employers, Béatrice Touchelay (2007) has shown that the Conseil National du Patronat Français (the National Council for French Employers, or CNPF) supported, for its part, the Banque de France's anti-inflationary measures, unlike bankers and small businessmen. Inflation had a negative effect on long-term orders and exports, which the CNPF wanted to promote.[32] The terms of the debate thus had more to do with the extent of monetary control than with the principles of credit administration. Notably through the voice of its president, Georges Villiers, the CNPF advocated a rapid return to competition (particularly the end of price controls), but also favored Banque de France measures seeking to develop French exports by applying a special system to credit exports.[33] Thus the system of administered credit does not seem to have been criticized by most employers as long as inflation was under control. The fact that it made it possible to finance long-term investments and export credits was presumably not unrelated to this favorable reception. The relative consensus that was established around the new organization of credit extended long after the implementation of the system drawn from the CNR program and that was established with the 1945 law. It was not challenged by American assistance under the Marshall Plan, which focused primarily on the recovery of the steel industry and energy production (Lynch 1997, ch. 3). This can be seen in several publications or reports from the mid-1950s. Thus, in January 1954 the "Commission for the Study of Disparities between French and Foreign Prices" was created, presided over by the banker and liberal economist Roger Nathan, which submitted a very "anti-Malthusian" report that

[30] ABF, 1331200301/9, "Note de la direction générale du crédit à la direction de l'escompte" from November 1948, which makes notes of complaints that branches have received from farmers, bankers and merchants.

[31] ABF, 1427200301/15. The accusations levelled against the Banque de France's policies are of this nature: "We cannot call your attention enough to the fact that such measures are incompatible with the development of production and improving productivity, goals assigned by the government itself to reduce present troubles" (letter of November 30).

[32] This opposition once again appeared in the 1970s, when the banks were accused of favoring inflation and profiting from it at business' expense (Plessis 1996, pp. 90–91). On employers' adaptation to *dirigiste* measures, see, too, Denord (2012).

[33] See notably Belin (1951).

criticized the many "rent-seeking" situations that were slowing down the French economy's expansion – and to which the war had not brought an end – whereas the general credit policy was viewed favorably. According to Nathan, the goal of the latter and in particular of the development of medium-term credit, was indeed to favor "actions on investments, capital for our country, if it wants to be in a position to gradually make up its backwardness in relation to its competitors." The report concludes that credit policy has in fact sought "to reconcile, in recent years, both the concerns of monetary authorities and the demands of credit users."[34] Pierre Cauboue, another liberal banker and the author, like Nathan, of books about economics and banking during the interwar years, published an article the same year in the journal of the Italian central bank, *Moneta e Credito*, in which he also recalled the necessity of the political choices and the system established at the Liberation, even if he believed that the ultimate goal should be to return money and financial markets to an important role.[35] Finally, when the Commissariat Général à la Productivité (General Commissariat for Productivity) was created in March 1954, its goal was not only to increase productivity in particular industries by promoting technological progress but also to ensure that "the distribution of credit take account of criteria pertaining to productivity."[36]

Adjustments and Complementarities: The Emergence of Credit Selectivity and the Fight against Inflation

The period between 1946 and 1948 proved in many respects to be decisive. The great principles of the nationalization of credit, anchored in law, adapted to the test of reality. Two tendencies in particular emerged and determined the Banque de France's direction and forms of intervention: the need to fight inflation and the elaboration of the doctrine of "credit selectivity."

---

[34] ABF, 1331200301/493, "Note sur la politique française de crédit et ses liens avec les prix 1945–1953."

[35] ABF, 1331200301/493. "Le crédit à moyen terme dans les Banques de dépôts et d'affaires Françaises," *Moneta e credito*, 2nd trimester (1954), 210–229.

[36] The decree of March 6, 1954 creating a Commissariat Général à la Productivité notes that the general commissioner, besides responsibilities of a general nature to be exercised in credit matters for the Department of Economic Affairs, in its quality as successor to the former Directorate of Programs, is charged with "ensuring that credit distribution take into consideration criteria pertaining to productivity, notably as it relates to issuing loans and government guarantees." *Objectifs et réalisation. Commissariat général à la productivité, 1954–1956*, p. 55, ch. 5 ("Action through Credit").

In the first place, beginning in 1948, the inherently inflationary character of the Banque de France's measures supporting the development of credit was ultimately acknowledged. As Andrieu (1984) also observes, the fight against inflation became the leitmotiv of the CNC's reports as early as late 1947. Yet, this occurred not without difficulty, not only because credit restrictions elicited opposition from business and banking circles, but also because governments generally did not offer their support. Tools of the anti-inflationary policy will be studied in the following section, but it is important to mention right away how the Banque de France, governed by Emmanuel Monick, had to fight bitterly to raise consciousness about the dangers of inflation at a time when consumer price increases reached annual averages of 52%, 49% and 58% in 1946, 1947 and 1948 respectively. The restrictive measures adopted in late September 1948 (see Chapter 4) were the result of Monick's pressure on the government. On September 4, the governor had thus taken advantage of the lack of a government (the President of the Council – i.e., the prime minister – had changed but a new government had not yet been appointed) to increase the discount rate. The express purpose of this symbolic measure was to put pressure on the government, and it ultimately achieved its goal by exploiting the government's weakness.[37] The Banque de France had in fact observed that the measures of the Mayer's Stabilization Plan of January 1948, which ended most price controls (which had proved very inefficient), devalued the currency and withdrew 5,000 franc bills from circulation, were not enough to fight inflation without a genuine policy for control credit and currency.[38]

---

[37] To this end, Monick called for a special session of the General Council on September 4. This decision provoked the ire of Paul Reynaud, the finance minister, who wrote in a letter to the governor:

Such a decision falls exclusively under the competencies of the central bank [*Institut d'émission*]. It is not for me to take a position on this matter and to evaluate, in light of government policy, its justification and effects. I will mention that the Government of the bank deemed it necessary to propose to the General Council an important measure, the scope of which transcends the limits of monetary technicity and credit techniques, without first consulting the appointed President of the Council, M. Robert Schuman, and before the creation of the new government, it struck me that it would have been normal, at a time when all financial activities had been suspended for forty-eight hours, to postpone the General Council's deliberations. (ABF, PVCG, September 9, 1948)

[38] On the price controls extending from 1945 to 1949, see Chélini (1998, pp. 393ff.) and Grenard (2010). On the Mayer Plan, see Caron (1982). But Caron neglects to consider how the long-term success of the Mayer Plan was contingent on the Banque de France's policy in late 1948.

But in 1951, the Banque du France still had trouble imposing its views on this topic and it had to fight if it wanted to convince. In February 1952, the letter addressed (and published in the newspaper *Le Monde* on February 29th) to the President of the Council Edgar Faure by the bank's governor, Wilfrid Baumgartner, contributed to a marked political change – with the creation of a new government led by Antoine Pinay – and allowed the bank to continue its restrictive policy. In 1957, the struggle between the government and the Banque de France over inflation resumed: the bank yielded by granting direct supplementary advances to the Treasury in July, but the government, notably due to pressure from the International Monetary Fund (IMF), endorsed the restrictive approach in January 1958.[39] Whereas political constraints had prevented a restrictive monetary policy before late 1948, the Banque de France was subsequently able to partially impose its views, notably by taking advantage of the government's weakness and the Fourth Republic's instability. Over the course of these various episodes, one sees in each instance a conflict between competing values, in which the Banque de France was first accused of endangering the national economy (Feiertag 1993), to which it responded by stating that the policy of expansion and efficient credit allocation depended on moderate inflation.

Second, the way that the Banque de France could and would intervene in credit allocation became increasingly clear in 1947 and 1948. Much effort was spent on avoiding an "authoritarian" *dirigisme* that would be a threat to individual freedom. Direct public financing was still very high at the outset of the 1950s, but beyond this intervention, the state primarily used recommendations as part of a system of incentives, not as constraints for guiding investment (Chapter 6). The CNC's goals were not to determine in advance a sum of credits per sector and to distribute these credits between banks. The importance of coordination and information gradually prevailed, even as the concept of "advisory planning" triumphed at the CGP (Fourquet 1980). Only in the fight against inflation did one find purely coercive measures in the realm of credit policy.

They keyword that emerged in the 1940s to refer to credit policy as a whole was that of credit "discrimination" or "selectivity." These terms referred both to the segmentation of the financial market necessitated by the existence of public and semi-public credit institutions, selections made by the Banque de France and these institutions during rediscounting operations, as well as "qualitative" recommendations of various kinds made by the CNC to banks. These recommendations included, notably, for 1947, a list of forty products

---

[39] On these incidents, see Chapter 3 and Feiertag (2006b, pp. 370–373, 511–515).

the production and transportation of which deserved to be supported with bank credits.[40] In other words, credit "selectivity" came to characterize all of the state's interventions in the realm of credit allocation (see Chapter 6).

The idea of credit selectivity or discrimination emerged in 1947 in connection with the elaboration of the Plan and, like the latter, its recommendations were "advisory." Selectivity was in the first place authorized primarily by the legal measures described above, by the statistics of the Central Risk Service (SCR), the information network formed by Banque de France branches and ties to industrial policy and recommendations of the Plan. Next, when Marshall Plan funding began to dry up between 1951 and 1952, selectivity also rested on a significant increase in credits from the Banque de France and specialized institutions. The beginning of the 1950s did in fact constitute a break in the Banque de France's financial activity, in that its priority was no longer to lend directly to the Treasury, but to the French economy (Figure 1). At this date, selectivity's legal and informational means were supplemented by financial means. It became difficult to separate public credit from private credit (Aymard 1960, pp. 63–85), in the sense that it is difficult for a bank, even a private one, to do without the credit guarantees or facilities provided by specialized institutions or the Banque de France.[41] If one includes the nationalized banks, it would appear that 90% of the credits granted during the 1950s were – in various forms – under the state's tutelage (Chapter 6). The state's omnipresence in the financing of the economy can be explain in part why planning became far less ambitious at the beginning of the 1950s (when the Monnet Plan ended in 1952), as several studies have shown (Boff 1968; Andrieu 1984; Margairaz & Rousso 1992; Lynch 1997, ch. 4). The state's means of intervening at sectoral and microeconomic were such that they could appear sufficient to influence credit and investment without resorting to setting intangible macroeconomic goals and forcing the private sector to follow quotas. We are thus far from a picture of a centralized state in which all orders come from on high and are scrupulously applied by administrative bodies. The investment policy laid out by the Plan and the government was broad. This suggests that it was considered a priority to invest in a few great sectors that in fact represented French industry in its totality. Thus, interventions in credit allocation took place in a much more decentralized way, with ex ante

---

[40] Report of the National Credit Council, 1947.

[41] It is customary, when speaking of this refinancing, to refer to the sector situated on the boundary between public and private credit (see notably the governor's letter to the Finance Ministry, June 26, 1957, PVCG).

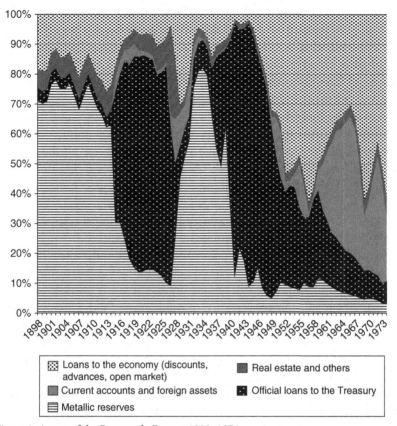

Figure 1 Assets of the Banque de France, 1898–1974

Note: These figures display official loans to the Treasury only. See Chapter 5 on how unofficial loans to the Treasury were included in the asset portfolio.

Source: Banque de France's weekly balance sheet (ANNHIS) and author's calculations. I annualized the data taking the annual average value. The ANNHIS database was constructed by Patrice Baubeau and is available online on the Banque's website.

coordination and, in particular, ex post adjustments in which the CNC and the Banque de France participated, unlike the CGP (see Chapter 6).

The institutionalization of credit after World War II can, from the standpoint of institutionalism in political sciences (Broz 1998; Bernhard et al. 2003), be considered as a response to a problem of collective action. The institutionalization of credit united individual interests and facilitated coordination between companies, banks and government authorities. It also seems symptomatic of what Barry Eichengreen (2006) has called the "coordinated capitalism" that was characteristic of postwar European societies. It is well known that the end of World War II marked a rupture in the history of the central banks of democratic countries, as they henceforth had to pursue what became known as the "general interest," which notably consisted of rising levels of employment and investment.[42] In France, the concept of "credit" became the focal point for defining the general interest that the central bank sought.

Among the goals that seemed to have met with consensus one finds the idea that state intervention makes it possible to end economic rents that had undermined prewar growth and the need to develop medium- and long-term growth that was indispensable to reconstruction. The state's ubiquitous intervention on the credit market aspired to respect individual liberty and be non-authoritarian. While the CNC supervised credit allocation, attempted to set objectives to be achieved and to identify shortcomings, in no instance was it actually responsible for allocation.

The consensus around credit policy that emerged in the late 1940s did, however, come at a cost, as the delayed stabilization of inflation was in part the result of the compromises that were necessary when establishing a new system. Above all, the convergence of opinion on short- and medium-term objectives could obscure potentially great disagreement on long-term goals: the 1945 law on credit nationalization incorporated the program of the Conseil National de la Résistance, which was close to the Popular Front's, which demanded the end to private monopolies and the management of credit in ways that would benefit the working class; but it also included the kind of authoritarian measures that were typical of Vichy for purposes of peacetime reconstruction and with the understanding that they were only temporary. One must thus be careful not to attribute the 1945 law on credit nationalization an "expressive function." It should not be seen as the expression of a set of clear and widely accepted principles concerning the legitimacy and goals of state intervention or the definition of the "general interest."[43] The institution's development during the 1960s, which is analyzed in the final part of this chapter, will bring to light the increasingly significant disagreement relating to various actors' interpretation of the principles underpinning the 1945 law.

---

[42] See, among others, Singleton (2011) for a recent synthesis.

[43] The well-known comment by Finance Minister René Mayer, a member of the Radical Socialist Party, suggests the kind of disagreements that existed: "a *dirigé* economy is not a good deed invented by Western democracies, it is a necessary evil that has been continued after the war" (quoted in Caron 1982, p. 427).

III CONTROLLING CREDIT AND INFLATION

In 1947, and particularly by September 1948, the fight against inflation had become an essential feature of the Banque de France's policy. Due to the strict constraints it imposed on banks and its desire to limit recourse to credit, an anti-inflationist policy would appear to contradict the general principles of credit policy, which emphasized the maximal development of credit and investment. But the Banque de France was conscious of the inflationary danger represented by the expansion of credit and thus of the need to adjudicate between inflation and production. It thus conceived of the fight against inflation as a way of defending the organization of credit implemented after 1945 against its own shortcomings and dangers. As explained in this chapter's theoretical introduction, the fight against inflation represented, in a sense, the self-limitation of the credit institution and is thus a full-fledged component of it. Consequently, anti-inflationary policies must respect the general principles of credit policy, notably the goals of selectivity. Any restriction on credits imposed by the Banque de France is thus selective and must compromise with the imperatives of credit allocation, the segmentation of the banking system, government financing and export support (in order to stabilize current accounts). In this way, institutional coherence took shape.

The 1945 law's emphasis on credit also placed credit at the heart of the Banque de France's doctrine concerning inflation control. But this control occurred neither through qualitative credit selection, as in the real bills doctrine (and discount operations of the Banque de France before 1945); nor through the money market's interest rates, as in Keynesian theory; nor through a "monetarist" approach to managing the monetary base. It was through direct and quantitative controls of credit and bank liquidity that inflation and money were controlled.

Control and Selectivity

The control of credit for anti-inflationist purposes was in the first place qualitative, in the sense that the CNC issues recommendations for banks about the types of credit that should be given priority in order to limit credit deemed purely inflationary. Thus, banks were encouraged from 1947 to 1948 to lend to key sectors and industries that produced urgently needed products (cereals, milk, meat and sugar).[44] This was not just a direction to

---

[44] ABF, 1331200301/9, DGC, preparatory documents for these measures and Letter of October, 1947 from the Banque de France governor and CNC vice-president

be taken but, beginning in October 1947, a means for fighting inflation by only granting loans that were particularly useful to the economy. The qualitative guidance of credit remained one of the CNC's roles in subsequent decades, but the governors soon realized that it was insufficient for fighting inflation. Thus, in September 1948, the Banque de France and the CNC put into place a series of measures seeking to control credit and liquidity quantitatively, particularly by imposing rediscount ceilings on banks and requiring them to hold a minimum portfolio of Treasury bills, called a "floor" (*plancher*).[45]

The imposition of rediscount ceilings by the bank participated in what Patrice Baubeau (2004, ch. 14) has called, in relation to the prewar situation, the "subversion of discounting." In a book on bank regulation and credit management written in 1952, the legal scholar Pierre Dupont had already taken note of the radical character of these changes:

The "self-liquidating" character of bills of exchange no longer suffices to justify the indefinite development of bank commitments of this kind. As soon as a bank hits its ceiling, it can no longer qualify for rediscounting, whatever the quality and maturity of the paper at its disposal. As some observers have noted, this marks a decisive break in the French banking tradition. (Dupont 1952, p. 328)

With rediscount ceilings, selection no longer occurred paper by paper, nor through the level of interest rates, but by a quota determined by each bank's characteristics and monetary policy's aims. Medium-term credit offered by public and semi-public organizations was not, for its part, capped until 1958, as it was considered a priority and was subject to additional selection. The date of September 30, 1948 and the shift to a policy based on quantitative restriction – rather than qualitative recommendations – also marked the end of a two-year experiment that had sought to apply two discount rates: one for paper issued by public companies and commercial paper representing sales, and another (higher) rate for all other loans. This discriminating approach based on dual discount rates, which was unprecedented in the bank's history, was abandoned in 1948, as it was

---

to Hottinguer (President of the Professional Association of Banks), Paul-Dauphin (Professional Association of Companies and Financial Institutions, Cramois (Crédit Agricole), Montfajon, (General Director of the Crédit Populaire de France).

[45] The level of Treasury bonds in one's assets was supposed to represent at least 95% of September 1948 levels and one-fifth of new acquisitions were expected to be in Treasury bonds. See Chapter 3.

unable to produce satisfying results in credit selection and the fight against inflation.[46]

September 1948 thus represents an important break: credit "selectivity" or "discrimination" was no longer considered a sufficient tool for fighting inflation, but simply a way of impacting credit allocation. Selectivity was subordinated to the quantitative control of credits during restrictive periods.

After the introduction of rediscount ceilings, credit selectivity as practiced by the Banque de France thus rested primarily on exemptions, or "special arrangements" (*regimes spéciaux*), as well as on cooperation between the CNC and the public credit institutions, which could issue medium-termed non-ceilinged bills available for rediscounting. Yet, each bank's rediscount ceiling vis-à-vis the Banque de France was different depending on the bank's commitments. The Banque de France has always described the way in which the ceiling level was set as "empirical" (see Chapter 6). Even so, during restrictive periods, the percentage by which ceilings were reduced was the same for all banks.[47]

The minimum requirement of Treasury bills (*plancher*) was aimed, for its part, at controlling banking liquidity. In other words, it ensured that the bank's resources were invested in existing liquid securities rather than being rediscounted by the central bank and then converted into new loans to firms. Hence, the goal of this measure was to make certain that the banks would not be able to expand credit by selling Government securities, directly or indirectly, to the Banque de France. But it also had an obvious dual function that illustrates once again how monetary policy participated in a broader context. First, its restrictive efficiency is tied to the fact that it prevents banks from increasing their liquid assets by acquiring, through the sale of Treasury bills, funds they could no longer acquire through discounting. It thus made rediscount ceilings more effective.[48] Second, its

---

[46] ABF, PVCG, September 30, 1948.

[47] Banks that exceeded their ceilings could also borrow from the central banks at a rate higher than the discount rate.

[48] This channel is particularly well explained by Hirschman and Roosa (1949) and in a document of the European Community:

> The fixing of rediscount ceilings would have lost its point if the banks, disposing as they did at the end of the war of a large portfolio of Treasury bills, had been left free to rediscount them with the central bank or not to renew them on their maturity. The banks were therefore called on at the same time to retain a minimum portfolio of Treasury bills. The imposition of "floors" ("planchers") for government paper, … is an automatic restraint on the volume of loans the banks can make to their customers. EEC 1962, p. 121)

budgetary efficacy was tied to the fact that it guaranteed the state financing in periods when policies were restrictive; this could, moreover, also
increase "monetary" efficacy by keeping the Banque de France from having
to increase direct advances made to the Treasury. As in other countries
where such tools were used by central banks, it was a way to reconcile
monetary policy and sovereign debt management (Goode & Thorne 1959;
Monnet & Vari 2017).[49]

These restrictive monetary policy measures were thus deeply incorporated
into what I have called the institutionalization of credit and depended on
significant coordination between the bank, other state entities and the
banking system. They depended, in other words, on the preservation of an
equilibrium that could only by guaranteed to the extent that actors did not
change their strategies. Thus, the *plancher de bons du Trésor* (Government
paper floor) sought to preserve bank indebtedness to the central bank to
ensure that rediscount ceilings remained effective. Coordination between
the government and the central bank was thus indispensable, not only on
the question of advances, but also on that of interest rates. Thus, the Banque
de France was constantly asking the Treasury not to raise its rates above the
discount rate, lest it render floors ineffective and limit bank credit in a period
of expansion by favoring budget deficits. Indeed, if bond rates were higher
than discount rates, banks would in any case hold a share of the former that
was greater than the lower limits set by the central bank, rendering credit
policy ineffective as a whole. The question of the differential between these
two rates was thus a subject of ongoing controversy between the Treasury
and the Banque de France during the 1950s: coordination was essential to
ensuring that the Treasury was satisfied with the floor of Treasury bills so
that Treasury bills rates remained below the discount rate of the Banque.[50]
An equilibrium was thus established, based on low rates and high Treasury

---

[49] So the *plancher* belongs to central bank policy instruments called securities-reserve
requirements, as opposed to cash-reserve requirements (Monnet & Vari 2017). Securities-
reserve requirements control liquidity by influencing the composition of banks' assets
while cash-reserve requirements control liquidity by forcing banks to deposit currency at
the central bank rather than to use it for granting loans. Both types of instruments can be
used to implement restrictive monetary policy to combat inflation or to sterilize capital
inflows. See also Chapter 4, Section I.

[50] An undated research note that is most likely from 1960 by the General Directorate of Credit
recapitulates the full array of policies and conflicts between the bank and the Treasury on
this topic over the course of the 1950s. ABF, 1331200301/10. See, too, a detailed explanation from the Treasury's standpoint in Quennouëlle-Corre (2000, pp. 261ff.). Treasury
bills rates were lower than the discount rate during the 1950s, with the exception of the
non-restrictive monetary policy period between 1954 and 1955.

rates floors, aimed at ensuring both government financing and the efficacy of the rediscounting system and monetary policy. The rise of the floor in July 1956 (see Chapter 4) fulfilled these criteria.[51]

The coordination between fighting inflation, credit selectivity and government support was still present in the decision of February 1958 to introduce a new instrument of monetary policy: the direct limitation of bank exposures (which subsequently became known as "credit ceilings" [*encadrement du crédit*]). This practice was also inspired by the policy of other European countries, notably the Netherlands, which introduced it in 1951. Its goal was to put ceilings on bank credit increases. In France, it first took the form of a requirement that banks should not increase their exposures in relation to their own average exposures of the last trimester of 1957. Next, exposure limits took the form of a percentage cap (common to all banks) on credit increases, set in relation to a fixed date.

During the 1958 plan, loans for construction, exports and nationalized companies were not subject to these limits. Later, during the 1960s, it was export and medium-term credits to which exemptions applied. Credit ceilings were of course a temporary restrictive measure that complemented rediscount ceilings, which were deemed less efficient given that banks were less indebted to the central bank and non-ceilinged credits were on the rise in the 1950s. The continuity with the principles considered earlier, notably selectivity, was clearly expressed by the governor when this measure was first introduced in February 1958:

The planned restrictions are a response to the idea of a certain selectivity of credit, or, more exactly – as this frequently used term is somewhat redundant [*pléonasme*] – of a certain way of managing credit. This is the position at which the Ministry of Finances has definitively arrived and to which, notably, M. Jacobsson [the director of the International Monetary Fund], after in-depth discussion with all the French experts, gave his consent a few weeks ago; it is perhaps not satisfying for us, but a better one was not found.[52]

The Banque de France Doctrine

Any attempt to understand the Banque de France's credit policy in terms of traditional monetary theories is condemned to misunderstanding its

---

[51] In the early 1960s, the *coefficient de trésorie*, which had replaced the *plancher*, would be used much more frequently in association with credit ceilings (see Chapter 4 and Monnet & Vari 2017).

[52] ABF, PVCG, February 6, 1958.

distinctive character. While it kept a firm hand when confronted with run-away inflation, French monetary policy was not *monetarist*, notably because the money supply was never the Banque de France's sole instrument, nor its sole goal.[53] Nor was its policy Keynesian: interest rates played no role, and the central bank's preoccupations were focused on inflation and balance of payments (what contemporaries called respectively the currency's "internal value" and "external value"). The central bank's primary goal was not to reduce the unemployment rate, but to favor credit. If the development of credit could contribute to greater employment, it was through investment, not through the nominal price illusion (i.e., the Phillips curve). References to Keynes are, moreover, absent from the reflections of contemporary Banque de France leaders and economists, as are, for that matter, any explicit references to theory. If one can speak of a Keynesian framework in reference to the consensus around state intervention that emerged notably within the civil service, particularly with the establishment of the Plan and creation of national accounting (Rosanvallon 1987), the men of the Banque de France during the 1950s in no way sought theoretical justification for their interventions in the writings of the British economist. In this respect, the fact that the CNC remained distinct from the Plan and that the Central Risk Service remained independent from the INSEE is also significant.

The leaders of the bank shared a culture forged in the crucible of French interwar liberalism and gold standard orthodoxy. For them, Keynes was the economist who had adopted violently anti-French positions on the question of German reparations in the 1920s (Crouzet 1972; Le Van-Lemesle 2004, p. 617).[54] Many of them had experience in banking or the civil service, but none were socialist theorists. Their conversion to the necessity of interventionism was not the result of an encounter with economic theory.[55] French economic culture remained largely national and differed notably from that of England and the United States, as did the definition of an "economist"

---

[53] Olivier Feiertag (2006b, p. 321) uses the expression "precocious monetarism" (*monétarisme avant l'heure*) to describe several restrictive measures of this period.

[54] A particularly virulent expression of the critique of Keynes in France came from the liberal economist Etienne Mantoux (1946). In an influential book with a preface by Raymond Aron, he undertook a theoretical critique of Keynes, followed by a political critique in which he reproached him notably for having weakened democratic governments by trying to discredit the Versailles Treaty.

[55] Emmanuel Monick and Wilfried Baumgartner were both finance inspectors. The former was the finance attaché in Washington and London in the interwar period; the latter was the director of the Mouvement Général des Fonds (the General Movement of Funds), i.e., the predecessor to the Treasury from 1935 to 1936, then director of the Crédit National between 1936 and 1949.

(Fourcade 2009, ch. 4). Faculties of law and economics were not yet separated, and engineers and financial inspectors were, in France, the primary embodiments of economic thinking (Le Van-Lemesle 2004; Fourcade 2009; Le Merrer 2012). The quantitative theory of money still formed the general framework of economic teaching, in the tradition of Charles Gide's *Cours d'économie politique* (1930, p. 322). The question of credit also played an important role, though the connection between money and credit had not necessarily been deeply theorized. During the interwar years, the distinction between credit and money was widespread among monetary theorists in France, notably Charles Rist, who in 1951 published a second edition of his major and influential book, *Histoire des doctrines relatives au crédit et à la monnaie*.[56] But Rist's metallic theory of money and his attachment to the gold standard provided little insight into monetary policy in a postwar, post-Bretton Woods context.[57]

Thus the discussions occurring in the General Council and the CNC's and the DGC's notes bring to light a simple rule: inflation is created by the growth of credit and the money supply. This rule was bolstered by the belief – against the grain of Keynesian theory – that a central bank can control credit directly in order to reduce the money supply and, by the same token, prices. Whereas for Keynes the infinite elasticity of the demand for money to interest rates meant a liquidity trap,[58] and thus an impotent monetary policy, for the Banque de France it meant, quite on the contrary, that the central bank could act directly on credit.[59]

Even if this was neither mentioned explicitly nor formalized, the Banque de France view about credit and inflation was in fact very close to the one defended and applied at the IMF in the 1960s and 1970s, which linked money, credit and the balance of payments (Polak & Argy, 1971; Polak 1997). In the IMF model, the main variable that the central bank could influence

---

[56] Translated into English in 1940 as *History of Monetary and Credit Theory from John Law to the Present Day*.

[57] His critique of Keynes' monetary theory, as well as his argument on the need for a devaluation of the dollar proved, for their part, more influential among economists and French politicians.

[58] Which can, in fact, be compatible with several possible "normal" levels of rates. See Leijonhufvud (1968, ch. 4).

[59] An alternative economic theory developed during this period which emphasized the power of credit controls when borrowers are insensitive to the interest rate was the "availability doctrine." This theory was built in the US in the late 1940s and was still discussed in the 1950s (see Miller 1956, among others, and Chapter 7 of this book). I have not found any mention to the availability doctrine in the discussions, studies or publications of the Banque de France.

was domestic credit creation. Credit booms worsened balance of payments deficits. Thus, restrictive credit policies (such as the ones imposed in France during times of balance of payments deficits, see Chapter 4) were seen as crucial to the correction of the balance of payments for which the IMF assistance had been invoked. In 1958 (when IMF assistance was invoked in France), there was a clear convergence between the IMF and the Banque to use credit ceilings as the main tool to combat inflation and restore the balance of payments equilibrium (Effosse 2003; Feiertag 2006b; Chapter 4).

Was the Banque de France Keynesian? French Perspectives on the Radcliffe Report

The term "Keynesianism" often lends itself to confusion, as it suggests both a theory – one that often postdates Keynes' writings and result from various reinterpretations – and a set of policies (Rosanvallon 1987; Booth 2001). Even so, it must be recognized that the Banque de France's principles corresponded neither to Keynes' writings on monetary demand and the preference for liquidity, nor to Hicks' synthesis (the IS-LM model) that completely dispenses with the question of credit, nor to post-Keynesian theories that maintain that money and credit are purely endogenous (Lavoie 1984). Unlike the Employment Policy White Paper in England (1944) and the Employment Act in the United States (1946), the French never produced a political or legislative document that argued for full employment on Keynesian grounds. Finally, the practices of the Banque de France diverged enormously from those of England's Radcliffe report of 1959, which clearly claimed a Keynesian affiliation and represented, at the time, the premier application of Keynes to monetary policy (Kaldor 1960) and is often considered as symptomatic of global monetary policies of the 1950s and 1960s (Meltzer 2010, p. 5; Singleton 2011, pp. 115–116). This report, which is both a retrospective validation of the Bank of England's policies during the 1950s and the matrix of those of the 1960s (Capie 2010, ch. 4), concludes that interest rates and the open market should be the preferred instruments of monetary policy, while asserting that the latter nevertheless has a limited effect – due to the endogeneity of supply and the instability of monetary demand – and must thus be subordinated to fiscal policy. It also makes a direct connection between management of the public debt (i.e., treasury bonds) and monetary policy, discussing at length the way the English money market functions. The report recommended, furthermore, the establishment of monetary and banking statistics, which the Bank of England lacked (Capie, 2010, ch. 4), whereas the Banque de France had built its entire quantitative policy on the exhaustive banking statistics of the Central Risk Service.

It is striking to note the extent to which nothing seems more alien to the Banque de France of this period than the Bank of England's practices and the theories announced in the Radcliffe report. The presentation of the Radcliffe report by Deputy Governor Jean Saltes to the General Council of the Banque de France naturally aroused interest but triggered no discussion. Saltes saw it above all as "the best and most thorough possible textbook on British financial and monetary instruments." Concerning the report's theoretical principles and general ideas, he claims that "it would seem that there is little that is worth remembering." Finally, Saltes concludes that:

The recommendations made by the [Radcliffe] Committee do not seem transposable here, not only because our mechanisms and institutions are very different from those that exist in England, but also because our statistical equipment, our knowledge of how credit is distributed, and our methods for controlling the banking system are at least as perfected and as efficient as all that is happening on the other side of the Channel, even if the committee's recommendations produce effects.[60]

Whereas the Bank of England's primary means of intervention in the economy were based on managing the public debt and intervening in the open market, the Banque de France sought, for its part, direct control over bank credit.

At the risk of sounding simplistic, one could describe the basic rule of French monetary policy of this period as combination of a simple version of the quantitative theory of money with the 1945 principles of the "nationalization of credit." The bank's General Council seems to have taken for granted that price levels and the money supply were correlated and that acting on money was the only way to lower inflation. This opinion was notably reflected in credit and money statistics that the CNC began to compile in 1947, and which were presented regularly to the General Council. These statistics clearly distinguish between bank credit, which was seen as a way of creating money through deposits, and non-bank credit. This statistical distinction thus also corresponded to the legal distinction defining the CNC's powers.

It was by directly controlling the bank credit supply, as well as bank liquidity, that the bank believed it could act on the money supply and prices. The goal of this restrictive policy was thus to reduce the credit

[60] ABF, PVCG, December 10, 1959.

supply while following the principles of the broader credit policy, in particular selectivity. Compared to Fisher's and then Friedman's versions of quantitative theory, the question of interest rates (notably the distinction between real and nominal rates), the money base, as well as the concept of velocity – and thus monetary demand – are missing. As it had before the war, the bank continued to adhere to the idea that money was created by banks through the discount mechanism. But it now believed that the priority given to credit in the postwar reconstruction required it to directly control its supply, rather than regulating demand through interest rates.

The Banque de France's theoretical conception of the need for credit regulation leads one to qualify Milton Friedman's distinction between credit policy and monetary policy in his 1969 book, *The Optimum Quantity of Money*. In his view, credit policy is adverse to any attempt to manage the money supply and is either Keynesian, or tied to the "real bills doctrine":

> The Keynesian analysis, emphasizing interest rates as opposed to the stock of money, is only the latest rationalization of that concentration. Its important earlier rationalization was the so-called real bills doctrine. The belief is still common among central bankers today that, if credit were somehow issues in relation to productive business activities, then the quantity of money could be left to itself. (Friedman 1969, p. 75)

The influence of the "real bills doctrine" was, of course, important to the prewar Banque de France, if only by way of the rediscounting tradition.[61] But the idea – implemented in 1947 and 1948 – that controlling credit through interest rates or through qualitative discrimination, would be sufficient to lower inflation resulted in failure. Confronted with this state of affairs, the Banque de France adopted a doctrine that maintained that the total credit supply creates inflation, not just a few poorly chosen loans. Hence the recourse to direct quantitative limits. Exemptions were made not because some loans were deemed less inflationary, but in the name of their primacy for economic growth. In this respect, it becomes more clear why the Banque de France governor described – and dismissed – the discount rate as a "qualitative" instrument, contrasting it to "quantitative" instruments for controlling credit.[62]

---

[61] Yet it lost some of its influence after World War I at the expense of quantitative theory. As Patrice Baubeau (2011, p. 229) explains: "the powerful parallel that appeared during the war between monetary issuance, higher prices, and declining unemployment partially destroyed the anti-quantitative posture on money adopted by the Banque de France before 1914."

[62] See notably the General Council meeting of October 11, 1951, ABF, PVCG.

Finally, despite a linguistic similarity, one must also reject the idea that the Banque de France's credit policy was a precedent for the "credit counterpart approach" elaborated in England in the 1960s and explicitly adopted by the Bank of England in the 1970s (Batini & Nelson 2005, pp. 29–34; Capie 2010, pp. 28–29). Stated synthetically, this theory posits that the growth of the money supply depends on the growth of its "counterparts" – that is, the totality of bank credit extended to the economy, loans to the government and public debt. The Banque de France's doctrine differed from this approach in two respects. First, it did not think exclusively in terms of credit outstanding (and thus of "counterparts"), as it also recognized the importance of liquidity ratios, which directly influence monetary creation by playing a role similar to that of reserve requirements (see Chapter 3 and the following section for the debate over reserve requirements in the 1960s). Second, it established a clear distinction between Treasury bonds on one hand, and loans or direct advances to the government on the other hand, as we have seen previously.[63] Thus the bank did not see the budget deficit as a whole as contributing to monetary creation, and did not confuse Treasury bonds with central bank loans to the government, a practice denounced by Friedman and Schwartz (1963, p. 566) and Batini and Nelson (2005, p. 30).

Yet it must be admitted that, with the exception of this distinction between bank and non-bank credit, the bank had not fully conceptualized the relationship between credit and money. This lack of explicit theorization can be explained by the fact that the relation between the money supply and bank credit (that is, the counterpart) was stable until the late 1960s (Figure 3) and that periods of restrictive credit do in fact lead to a reduction in the growth of the money supply, as I will show in Chapter 4.

Each week at the General Council, meetings began with a ritualized presentation of changes in the Banque de France's balance sheet. Only then did discussions of macroeconomic variables occur, often starting with prices. But the way they were presented and interpreted was neither as generalized, nor as clear and codified as a balance sheet. The Banque de France did not break completely with the prewar tradition: it remained the banks' bank,

---

[63] Chapter 5 presents the means whereby the Banque de France could finance the treasury and considers this distinction. However, I have found some documents and notes in the Banque's archives in the mid-1970s that fully shared the counterpart view that the increase in Treasury bills experienced during this period was the main contribution to the increase in the money supply. It is in line with other ideas studied in the next chapter which burgeoned in the mid-1970s and attributed inflation to other causes than the central bank's actions. See ABF, 1417200405 /1. Note from December 1975 by J. P. Patat, "Les bons du Trésor et le marché monétaire."

devoting itself primarily to discussions of discounting and bank conditions. The broad concept of credit was able to connect this traditional role to a focus on macroeconomic growth that the Banque later acquired.

The Goals of Monetary Policy

As had been the case before the war (Blancheton 2001; Mouré 2002; Duchaussoy & Monnet 2018), the idea that budget deficits would feed inflation was pervasive at the Banque de France. Two mechanisms were considered. First, fiscal deficits are inflationary because they push too much demand when the economy has reached full employment. In January 1957, the governor of the Banque de France sent a letter to the prime minister stating: "From the point of view of safeguarding the currency, there is an incompatibility between full employment and budget deficit. In times of full employment, the budget deficit is bound to lead to inflation."[64]

Second, fiscal deficits are especially inflationary when they rely on money creation. In this way, the bank showed its desire to restrict Treasury advances, even if its ability to do so was severely limited by the risk of political crisis in case of budget crisis. Chapter 5 will study in detail how the Banque lent to the Treasury and the balance of power between the central bank and the government. In any case, the Banque was always reluctant to increase lending to the Treasury and stood ready to implement restrictive measures to offset the inflationary effects of loans to the Treasury. In a letter to the prime minister in 1957, the governor stated very clearly: "It is not without regret that the General Council has resolved to authorize me to sign this agreement. It can only deplore that the bank's balance sheet and monetary situation have once again been burdened by the allowing advances, the harmful character of which is undeniable." He then pointed out that controlling a money supply that had grown as the result of such advances necessarily required credit control: "The state's use of new advances risks leading to an abnormal ballooning of the money supply. To mitigate this risk, new measures in the realm of credit will be indispensable."[65]

The Banque de France was just as conscious of the dangers of budget deficits as it was of the inevitable need to adjudicate between inflation and

---

[64] ABF, PVCG, January 10, 1957.
[65] ABF, PVCG, June 26, 1957. But such measures could not be fully taken before February 1958; see Chapter 3. In this same letter, the governor spells out clearly that credit control is not possible at this time as the bank cannot limit the totality of medium-term credits issued by semi-public credit institutions.

the growth of production (i.e., output-inflation tradeoff). The way that the CNC begged the question in late 1948 is, in this respect, revealing:

The National Credit Council's essential mission in 1948 consisted, as before, in ensuring that, in the realm to which it was assigned, companies did not lack the credit they needed to acquire the supplies they needed, to produce, [and] to distribute; but it also consisted in preventing easy credit from promoting undesirable price increases or allowing it to stand in the way of a desirable decreases. This line of conduct, simple in intent and purpose, does imply, however, in the way it is applied, a constant awareness of credit's dual character: it promotes activity, but it also fuels inflation.[66]

This is very far from the image of a central bank promoting inflation in order to reduce unemployment or believing that goals of price stability and growth can be easily reconciled. This excerpt from the CNC report shows that the need to adjudicate between inflation and production was well understood.[67] Once again, the very nature of credit (increasing both economic activity and inflation) was invoked as the theoretical foundation of its policy.

In this way, the central banks sought a balance that would ensure that credit did not finance overproduction that would lead to inflation. The Banque de France was also familiar with the concepts of "full employment" and "potential production." Thus the 1954 report to which I have already referred clearly states that

credit cannot, without running the risk of destroying as much wealth as it allows to be born, surpass a certain threshold … Thus if the ambition of any monetary policy is to allow the economic system to approach maximum achievable production as much as possible, its responsibility must be to prevent, at least as far its own actions are concerned, this limit from being crossed. It is this difficult balance that monetary authorities will, this year yet again, seek to maintain. (p. 12)

The dual goal of the monetary policy regularly laid out by the General Council's deliberations and in official documents was the preservation of the currency's "internal equilibrium" and "external equilibrium." This goal was not, at first glance, that different from the traditional goals the Banque de France had pursued under the gold standard. Thus, credit restrictions were imposed during periods in which inflation, as well as the balance of

---

[66] ABF, Report of the National Credit Council, 1948, p. 37.
[67] Though the United States' monetary policy took a very different form, Romer and Romer (2002) arrive at a similar conclusion concerning the Fed's policies in the 1950s, which they describe as "crude but fundamentally sensible."

payments deficit, were deemed too high. When they proved inadequate, devaluations were necessary, as occurred in 1949, 1957–1958 and 1969. But it should be emphasized that devaluations always occurred after several months of restrictive policy: the government never carried out a devaluation unless the central bank had previously started to contract internal demand. As Michael Loriaux (1991) has correctly observed, devaluations are mechanisms that France used to safeguard its system for organizing credit without challenging Bretton Woods' rules. However, devaluations were decided once inflation had started to stabilize and seen as a necessary adjustment to boost exports (Blancheton & Bordes 2007). The members of the Banque de France's General Council considered that price stability and low inflation were necessary for the country to benefit from the increase in exports expected from a devaluation. Devaluations went hand by hand with measures of restrictive monetary policy through quantitative controls (see Chapter 4). There is no evidence that they were seen as an opportunity to leave inflation unfettered. At the global level, in accordance with the principles established at the 1944 Bretton Woods conference, devaluations made it possible to avoid that the fixed exchange rate constraint would impose too severe deflationary policies on countries, that would have plunged them into a deflationary spiral similar to that of the 1930s. But these medium-term equilibrium considerations were consistent with a short-term rule that countries should use domestic policy to stabilize inflation and maintain internal equilibrium (Williamson 1985). Achieving this short-term internal objective was also a decisive means of asserting the domestic political legitimacy of general credit policy, as this section emphasizes.

Quantitative Controls versus Interest Rates

The use of direct quantity controls rather than the manipulation of interest rates must thus be understood within the broader context of a *dirigiste* concept of credit. Subsequent chapters will consider various theoretical arguments in favor of such choices, as well as the consequences of this choice on the development of credit and international adjustments. For now, we will limit ourselves to highlighting the fact that the choice of quantity control is naturally conducive to a policy of credit selectivity, as it facilitates exemptions and thus interventions on allocation. This choice seemed self-evident, at least until the late 1950s: it was never theorized and elicited little debate among economists and decision-makers. The Banque de France's employees were content that raising interest rates was no longer efficient and that credit's interest rate elasticity and monetary demand was weak. Thus, they agreed that the discount rate had nothing more than a "psychological" effect.[68] Let us consider the revealing words of Governor Baumgartner as he attempted, in 1951, to convince a skeptical General Council of the need of connecting a lowering of discount ceilings with an increase in the discount rate: "If credit restrictions undoubtedly have a greater practical impact, an increase in the discount rate is an even more significant measure from the standpoint of French as well as foreign opinion. It clearly indicates that every effort will be made to defend our currency."[69]

Discussions about rate manipulation in the 1950s were thus steeped in confusion. Because they were largely seen as inefficient in the fight against inflation, the justifications invoked for rate increases were necessarily laborious and the "psychological" argument struggled to be persuasive. In April 1957, an increase in the discount rate was decided that was not tied to quantitative restriction measures, having as its only goal to send a signal to public opinion. The economist Pierre Dieterlen had the following to say about it:

The reasons on which it [this decision] are based are more varied … These reasons stand in considerable opposition to one another and make a coherent policy difficult. Thus a 3% to 4% discount rate increase last April satisfied no one. Those who do not believe in the discount rate's efficiency found this increase to be useless by definition. Those believe it can be found it useless because insufficient. We will not even mention those who believe it is harmful. (Dieterlen 1957, p. 634)

The Banque de France was primarily interested in the differential between the discount rate and Treasury bonds, as explained earlier, as well as in the differential with other countries.[70] On the domestic front, it would seem that the bank's leaders no longer knew themselves how much importance should be given to the discount rate: if they still paid attention to it, due to its role in the interwar period, its purpose was gradually losing its meaning. Even as inflation and the direction of monetary policy underwent significant variations during the 1950s, the Banque de France's (nominal) guiding interest rate was kept around 3–5%. It remained at 3% in 1954, 1955 and

---

[68] The use of the term "psychological" to describe the discount rate is notably used on several occasions by the governor during sessions of the General Council. ABF. PVCG. Meeting of September 30, 1948 (Monick); meeting of October 11, 1951 (Baumgartner); and meeting of April 11, 1957 (Baumgartner).

[69] ABF, PVCG, October 11.

[70] On the international role of the discount rate, see Baumgartner's statements quoted in Feiertag (2006b, pp. 440–441).

1956, at the very moment when the Banque de France was pursuing an openly expansionary policy (see Chapter 4). Since the inflation rate was below 2% during those years, the discount rate paradoxically reached its maximum in real terms during this period of easy money.

What was the guiding principle of these anti-inflationary measures? My hypothesis is that it must be understood within the broader framework of the institutionalization of credit that I have described by referring to explicit and predefined credit monetary theories. Contemporaries first conceived the organization of credit and monetary control conjointly, connecting them in law before establishing strict rules for controlling inflation and more specific goals for monetary policy. When added to an intellectual framework that was inherited from the interwar years, as well as traditional practices at the bank that drew little inspiration from Anglo-American references, the new conception of credit gave birth to an original way of thinking that was elaborated through practical activity and interaction with the banking system.[71]

The primary difficulties that the central bank confronted in the struggle against inflation and the restoration of balance of payments equilibrium were resistance from the government, as well as from banks and small- and mid-sized business, which suffered the most from restricted credit.[72] After the 1945 law on the "nationalisation of credit," 1948 marked a genuine new beginning for the Banque de France. It established policy instruments and strategies that put an end to postwar hyperinflation and subsequently maintained stable prices – at least until 1957 – while stimulating investment

---

[71] We are not referring here to the theory of *économie d'endettement* (overdraft economy) that developed within the Banque de France in the second half of the 1970s (Lévy-Garboua 1978; Maarek & Lévy-Garboua 1985; Goux 1990) and that some have adopted as an analytical framework (Loriaux 1991; Feiertag 2006b) for understanding this period. The latter was based on the standard models of monetary theory, to which it adds bank debts to the central bank caused by household constraints. Besides the fact that this theory constitutes an after-the-fact rationalization with its own share of assumptions, and which should for this reason become an object of historical analysis, it leaves aside, in the name of modeling, a number of essential characteristics of the French system that prevailed at the very least between the 1950s and 1960s. Thus, adjustment within these models occurred through interest rates, and they gave no role to credit controls and liquidity ratios, whether in connection with money or due to the capacity for selectivity of credit.

[72] This conclusion was often reached at the bank. The complaints of small businesses reached Paris by way of branch banks. In addition to the letters from bankers and business people quoted in the previous section, one can mention this warning from the governor in 1957: "One of the difficulties resulting from a compression of bank credit relates to the fact that, generally speaking, it is small and medium-sized companies that risk to suffer the most from these restrictions." ABF, PVCG, August 12, 1957.

and economic growth in the difficult international and domestic context of the 1950s.

The problem of the efficiency of quantitative instruments for controlling credit was also posed, given the rapid reconstruction of the French banking system, which modified the balance sheet structure of the banks that monetary authorities sought to control. In the late 1950s, the challenge faced by the Banque de France and the government was to adapt credit policy to an economy that had largely turned the page on the immediate problems of postwar reconstruction.

3

Development Then Gradual
Deinstitutionalization: The 1960s and 1970s

The years 1958 and 1959 were a turning point in French political and economic life. The creation of the Fifth Republic was accompanied by an internationalization of the economy, symbolized by the Treaty of Rome in 1957 and the franc's return to full convertibility in 1959, as well as the first steps toward a withdrawal of the state from the economy compared to the previous decade (Quennouëlle-Corre 2000; Chélini 2001; Warlouzet 2010). What some have described as the "liberal and management-based" turn was embodied by the Pinay-Rueff Plan, a series of reforms first implemented in 1959 that primarily sought to reduce the state's debt, reintroduce competition in some sectors and promote international trade (Chélini 2001; Denord 2010). While the birth of the Fifth Republic and the Pinay-Rueff Plan arguably brought about important changes in the French economy, historians often neglect the fact that the stabilization of inflation and the balance of payments had begun in mid-1957 and, above all, in February 1958, with strict and restrictive credit control measures implemented by the Banque de France. It remains a somewhat mythologized vision of the Pinay-Rueff Plan in French history, which ignores the changes in economic policy at the beginning of 1958 and thus also tends to neglect the role of the central bank during this period and underestimate the continuity of the policies implemented.

How did the new fiscal policy of the Fifth Republic affect credit policy? First, it led to a decline in direct assistance to the economy from the Banque de France and the Treasury (see Chapter 5). For the Banque de France, this amounted to a reduction in Treasury advances and a reduction in medium-term credit (Figures 1 and 2). Beginning in the early 1960s, bank participation in the financing of the economy increased in relation to that of the

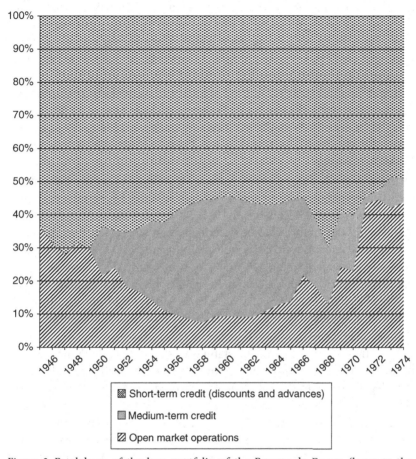

Figure 2 Breakdown of the loan portfolio of the Banque de France (loans to the economy: open market operations, short-term credit, medium-term credit), 1946–1974

Note: These figures display official loans to the Treasury only. See Chapter 5 on how unofficial loans to the Treasury were included in the asset portfolio.

Source: Banque de France's weekly balance sheet (ANNHIS) and author's calculations. I annualized the data taking the annual average value.

Banque de France and public and semi-public institutions. The development of bank credit was once again promoted by the laws of 1966, which gave banks greater freedom of activity and allowed deposits to be better remunerated. The transformations – "debudgetization" (*débudgétisation*)[1]

---

[1] This term was used at the time to refer to decreased direct financing of the economy by the Treasury.

as well as the expansion of the banking sector – necessarily affected monetary policy's tools. Yet, if there was in fact an increase in the volume of financing without direct state intervention, the major principles of interventionist credit policy were not fundamentally questioned. Thus, the legal framework was almost identical to that of the previous period, and the policy of "credit selectivity" was maintained and recognized. Thus, over the course of the 1960s, the Banque de France participated less in bank refinancing, but it notably strengthened its ability to support the development of particular sectors by accepting longer and more varied medium-term credit for rediscounting.

The late 1960s did, however, witness an attempt to render the central bank's interventions more neutral and less selective by introducing minimum reserves in 1967, then, in 1971, by the development of the open market. Yet, this trend could be described as an ambiguous liberalization, in that these reforms were never fully realized and, most importantly, paradoxically engendered new instruments of selectivity that developed over the 1970s. Hybrid means, such as preferential rates or the secondary market of "credit rights" (*marché du désencadrement*), developed, complicating the system and gradually giving credit selectivity a negative connotation at the Banque de France.

With the 1973 revision of the statutes of the Banque de France, which dated back to 1936, the principles of the 1945 law nationalizing credit made their legal entry into the bank's goals and mode of functioning. But they also mark the moment when the government regained control of monetary policy. If, in the 1960s and 1970s, a more liberal conception of economics began to assert itself in a continuous and linear way in matters such as the state budget or competition (Quennouëlle-Corre 2000; Warlouzet 2010), this was not the case for credit policy. However, the internal coherence of credit institutionalization, as well as complementarities with other policies, were seriously disrupted in the early 1970s. In many respects, the Banque de France's policy in the 1970s was very different from that of the previous two decades.

I THE CENTRAL BANK CHANGES … BUT NOT ITS LEGAL FRAMEWORK

Unlike the social norms and the anti-inflation policies, to which I will turn later, the bank's legal framework changed relatively little after 1945. The 1945 law provided the legal framework of credit policy for nearly four decades, and was not affected by the Fifth Republic's new constitution, nor – initially, in any case – by the economic and political crises that were the collapse of the Bretton Woods system, the rising oil prices and stagflation of the 1970s, or the left's electoral victory in May 1981.[2] If the 1945 law remained unchanged, several reforms nevertheless altered the way it was applied. During the mid-1960s, a reform of medium-term credit and new banking laws brought notable amendments to the system, while in 1973, the 1936 statutes of the Banque de France were modified.

The 1966–1967 Reforms: Liberalizing the Banking and Financial System without Abandoning Selectivity

From 1966 to 1967, several laws modified the way banks were regulated. They are generally grouped together under the label Debré-Haberer Laws, after Michel Debré, the finance minister, and his adviser, Jean-Yves Haberer, who together initiated them. They did not amend the 1945 law, but came under the authority of article 14 of this law, which allowed the finance minister, at the CNC's recommendation, to establish rules for banking institutions. The implementation decrees were issued in May 28, 1946 and revised the bank laws of 1941. Without rejecting the principles of the 1945 law, the Debré laws brought new inflections in the way they were implemented.[3] Of these reforms, several participated in the liberalization of the French economy and were based on greater confidence in market forces as a means for mobilizing savings and credit allocation. The decree of January 25, 1966, "on the practice of the banking profession," which authorized deposit banks to engage in investment activities – albeit to a limited degree – thus revised a crucial principle established in the 1941 law.[4] The decree of December 28, 1966 on usury partially liberalized interest rates on deposits (with the introduction of the comprehensive effective rate) and authorized the remuneration of checking accounts. This decree was published the same day that exchange controls were abolished (Teyssier 1973), revealing French leaders' confidence in monetary policy, which they believed would suffice to prevent uncontrolled capital flight: the possibility of short-term arbitrage by depositors was no longer seen as a threat.

---

[2] The bank nationalizations of 1981 did not, in fact, alter the law of December 2, 1945.
[3] The discussions in the finance ministry that led to these reforms have been studied by Quennouëlle-Corre (2005a).
[4] Initially, the effect of this measure on the banking landscape was minimal. But some banks, like Société Générale for leasing contracts, took advantage of it all the same to establish specialized credit affiliates in charge of particular types of financing.

Following the reintroduction of exchange controls in November 1968, the remuneration of checking accounts was, of course, abolished once again.[5]

The banking reforms that Debré wanted were completed by reforms that sought to develop financial markets and were legally independent of the 1945 law. Thus, the orders of September 28, 1967 created the Stock Market Operations Commission (*Commission des opérations de bourse*, or COB) in order to moralize and develop the activity of the stock market (Quennouëlle-Corre 2015; Péréon 2018). It also designed new financial instruments and funds to create a mortgage market and develop financial activities: economically interested combinations (*regroupements d'intérêt économique*, or GIE), real estate companies for commerce and industry (*sociétés immobilières pour le commerce et l'industrie*, or SICOMI), and SICAVs (*société d'investissement à capital variable*, or variable capital investment companies).[6] These measures did not, however, prevent the Paris stock market index from falling until 1979 (Hautcoeur & Le Bris 2010 and Chapter 6).

These reform measures thus clearly sought to stimulate changes in the French banking and financial system so that it could mobilize savings more easily through market mechanisms (such as the remuneration of deposits and the issuing of stock and bonds). The 1966–1967 laws also attest to a conception of the state's role that is more centered on "bank supervision" than "credit management" (to borrow Lacoue-Labarthe's distinction [2007]) but, unlike the reforms that took place nearly twenty years later, in 1984, these did not challenge the second point from a legal perspective.

Though direct state financing of the economy continued to decline, the role of the state – and particularly the central bank – in the allocation and organization of credit was confirmed and even extended by a number of reforms in the mid-1960s. First, several decrees allowed the Banque de France to offer advances against securities to companies that did not previously benefit from them:[7] the Banque de France thus continued to develop the means that would ensure selective financing of the economy.

---

[5] By a general decision of the CNC of May 8, 1969.

[6] The Monory reforms of the late 1970s, like the law on directing savings of July 13, 1978, continued the path opened by the Debré-Haberer reforms.

[7] - Decree of June 13, 1962, authorizing the Banque de France to make advances against obligations, bonds and production shares issued by Électricité de France, Gaz de France et Charbonnages de France (the state electricity, gas and coal company) and guaranteed by the state.

- Decree of August 3, 1963, authorizing the Banque de France to makes advances against unified loans issued by departments (i.e., units of local government), communes (towns and cities), associations of communes, chambers of commerce, port authorities, and organizations that receive guarantees from these collectivities.

The 1966 reform of medium-term credit also confirms this trend. It sought to extend the Banque de France's rediscounting of medium-term credits for company investment and real estate development to credit maturities that had not previously benefited from it: the limit went from five to seven years. One goal of this reform was clearly to support housing construction (Effosse 2003, ch. VIII). To this end, the Banque de France decided that it would henceforth reserve rediscounting for "maturities that are closest to credits," that is, for mobilizing bills whose maturity did not exceed three years at the time the bill was presented. The goal was thus to reduce the inflationary danger of medium-term credit while increasing the central banks' selective power. A note from the Banque's research branch (the *Direction des études*) from 1965 took stock of the proposed legislation:

The planned reform of the rediscounting of medium-term credit is intended neither to systematically encourage the extension of the duration of credits nor to make their financing more difficult. Its essential goal is to establish the distribution of medium-term credit, which until now benefited from an exceptional regulatory framework, which was at once too generous and too restrictive, on a healthier and more sustainable basis. By henceforth allowing investment and building credits the ease of normal rediscounting, though they are still greater than those offered by foreign central banks, the Banque de France will create conditions that are favorable to the expansion of these credits.[8]

While the 1966–1967 reforms are often seen as the advent of Charles de Gaulle's liberal policies in the realm of finance (Quennouëlle-Corre 2000, pp. 497–526, 2005a),[9] one must nevertheless have a comprehensive view of them and see how this period does not represent a straightforward disengagement on the part of the state from credit policy. In particular, the desire to give greater importance to deposit-based financing and the financial market did not challenge the legitimacy or ability of the Banque de France to undertake a policy of sectoral selectivity.

- Decree of July 23, 1963, authorizing the Banque de France to make advances against equity issued by regional development companies.
- Decree of October 29, 1965 authorizing the Banque de France to makes advances against equity issued by the Caisse Nationale des Autoroutes (the National Highway Fund).
- Decree of December 22, 1966, authorizing the Banque de France to make advances against equity issued by the Caisse Centrale de Crédit Hôtelier, Commercial et Industriel (the Central Hotel, Commercial, and Industrial Credit Fund).

[8] ABF, 1397200602/12. Confidential note of September 6, 1965, "Analysis of the Plan to Reform the Rediscounting of Medium-Term Credit" (*Analyse du projet de réforme du réescompte des crédits à moyen terme*).

[9] On their role in the development of consumption credit, see Lazarus (2010).

The Ambiguity of the New Statutes of 1973

The main change directly affecting the functioning of the Banque de France was the revision of the 1936 statutes by the law of January 3, 1973.[10] The 1945 law on the nationalization of the Banque de France and the organization of credit had, in fact, no impact on the central bank's legal status. This notably explains why the Banque de France still had to action "in the name of the National Credit Council" when it imposed new measures relating to monetary policy and regulation.

In the realm of credit policy, the 1973 reform thus marked the entry of some features of the credit nationalization law of December 1945 in the statutes of the issuing institute. In this vein, "credit and money" were officially included among the bank's goals in the first article, thus validating both the distinction and the twofold priority that had prevailed since 1945.

Law no. 73–7 relating the la Banque de France (January 3, 1973):

Article 1:

The Banque de France is the institution which, as part of the nation's economic and financial policy, receives from the state the general mission of managing money and credit. To this end, it tends to the proper functioning of the banking system. The Banque de France's capital belongs to the state.

The new statutes also clarified the CNC's role in formulating monetary policy, in conjunction with the bank's General Council and the government:

Article 4:

The bank contributes to the preparation and participates in the implementation of the monetary policy decided upon by the government and, within the limits of its competencies, the National Credit Council.

But the main goal of the statute revision was to clarify the nature of the relationship between the government and the central bank, which the 1945 law had decided it was best not formalize other than through the nationalization of its capital. The origins of this revision have been notably described by Jean Bouvier (1987) and Michel Margairaz (2008): negotiations between Governor Olivier Wormser and Finance Minister Valéry Giscard d'Estaing were bitter, for it quickly became apparent that the latter intended to take

---

[10] "Loi n°73–7 du 3 janvier 1973 sur la Banque de France."

advantage of the statute revision to place the bank under increasing government control. According to Vincent Duchaussoy (2013, p. 354), the explicit
model of the new reform was the 1946 Bank of England act. This reference
was not insignificant, since the Bank of England was the only one in Europe
whose political dependence on the government was anchored in law (see
Chapter 7). Finally, as Bouvier (1987, p. 29) put it, the "ultimate result
was marked by the fact that the law was deliberately written in a way that
couched a compromise in the broad and vague language of the new statutes.
That which was left unsaid was as important as the explicit language of
certain articles." Even so, article 4 is striking: "monetary policy is *decided*
[*arrêtée*] by the government" (emphasis added). This specification opened
the door to several interpretations, as the term "decided" could mean that
the government registered and validated the Banque de France's decisions
or, on the contrary, that it explicitly commands them. Most importantly,
it is unclear whether the government is meant to set the general goals or
the specific direction of monetary policy. Even so, it cannot be denied that
thanks to this article, the government was given an important legal tool
that could apply pressure on the bank in the event of a dispute, when previously it was confined to its power of nominating the governor and being
represented on the General Council.

But the most important change in relation to the 1936 statutes and the
policy established since 1945 concerned the composition of the Banque
de France's General Council. The 1973 law did in fact replace "members
by right," who represented particular economic milieus (labor, agriculture
and so on) with experts appointed for their economic competence. As soon
as the reform was implemented, Edmond Malinvaud and Raymond Barre
became among the first to join the Banque de France's council as economists.
According to the bank's secretary general, Hubert Morant,[11] this reflected
the government's fear that the members by right would act only on their
particular interest, rather than the general interest. Even if the CNC's composition remained, for its part, unchanged and still represented labor as well
as management, it was indeed a significant change in perspective compared
to 1936 and 1945. In the immediate postwar period, it seemed obvious
that representatives of public and semi-public institutions represented the
French economy's general interest; by 1973, at the Banque de France as well

---

[11] See the article he published in the *Bulletin trimestriel de la Banque de France* in May 1973,
p. 25, cited in Bouvier (1987, p. 30).

as in the government, this was no longer the case. Economic expertise now trumped "republican corporatism."

Finally, the new statutes of 1973 redefined the way the Banque de France financed the Public Treasury. It essentially involved counting as official Treasury advances what had previously appeared as unofficial loans through a rediscounting of guaranteed bonds and loans to the Caisse des Dépôts et Consignations (CDC). Chapter 5 offers an estimate of the unofficial support and thus of the Banque de France's financing of the Treasury. This clarification or regularization sought to make more visible monetary creation that occurred for the purpose of state financing. Most importantly, it merely applied to Treasury support the policy Wormser had pursued since 1971 (see below): rediscounting should no longer be the preferred form of the bank's intervention in the economy, whether it concerned private bills (bank discounting) or public bills (guaranteed bonds or CDC building loans).

The new statutes apparently did little to change credit policy, which was still governed by the 1945 law, but they had two lasting consequences for monetary policy and the way the Banque de France operated. First, monetary policy was indeed taken over by the government, even if Treasury advances were now limited. As we shall see, this partially ratified the practices of finance minister – and soon-to-be president – Valéry Giscard d'Estaing, who constantly claimed responsibility for decisions relating to monetary policy beginning in the late 1960s, notably during the introduction of credit controls in 1969–1970 and 1972. Second, the bank abandoned the principle of joint labor-management (*paritaire*) representation, which had embodied the republican corporatism that arose during the interwar years and the Popular Front: the members of the Council were now appointed on the basis of their "economic competency." This movement, which sought notably to give greater weight to the legitimacy of economic knowledge in policymaking, coincided with the rise within the Banque de France of a Service of Econometric Studies and Research (*Service d'études économétriques et de recherche*, SEER).[12] Collective (*paritaire*) institutions of "coordinated

---

[12] For an analysis of the creation of the econometric service, see Feiertag (2006a). The years 1974–1975 also witnessed the arrival at the bank of young economists who had studied in the United States, such as Jacques-Henri David and Vivien Lévy-Garboua. At the same time, the Planning office also turned to large-scale econometric models (Angeletti 2011). Incidentally, it is in this model that the Phillips curve first appeared in France as a formalized economic relationship used for policy analysis (ibid. p. 56).

capitalism" (Eichengreen 2006) were on the way to be challenged by the rise of economic expertise.

The End of a System

In the course of the 1970s, changes in the law affecting credit policy were infrequent and the institutional shifts resulted primarily from modifications of practices of control and selectivity, as we will see in the next section. Thus, it was not until 1984 that the system's legal foundations would be seriously challenged. I will briefly mention the end of this system in order to take stock of the characteristics that had previously prevailed.

The 1984 law[13] did in fact repeal the "management of credit" (*direction du credit*) section of the 1945 law. The CNC, which became the *Conseil National du Crédit et du Titre* lost its regulatory responsibilities to the Banking Regulation Committee (*Comité de la réglementation bancaire*) and the Credit Institutions Committee (*Comité des établissements de credit*). The liberalization of credit and financial markets that occurred at the same time also represented a shift from the principle of "bank control and credit management [*direction du credit*]" to that of "bank supervision" (Lacoue-Labarthe 2007). These institutional reorganizations represented a desire to give market mechanisms a major role in credit allocation. The CNC's role was now purely advisory on questions of monetary policy and credit – and, in 1993, it would see itself deprived of even that role. The "institutionalization of credit" thus underwent a profound upheaval.

Finally, it was only with the law on the new statutes of 1993 that the Banque de France's responsibility of tending to "credit and money," which was included in the statutes of 1973, officially disappeared.[14] As other laws and measures concerning credit policy were gradually emptied of their content, the disappearance of "credit" as a goal in the 1993 documents merely registered this situation and was barely noticed. The only thing that is generally remembered about the 1993 law is that it made the Banque de France independent of the government.

---

[13] Law 84-46 1984-01-24 JORF, January 25, 1984, which went into effect on July 24, 1984.
[14] The full name and references of the 1993 law are "Loi n° 93–980 du 4 août 1993 relative au statut de la Banque de France et à l'activité et au contrôle des établissements de crédit."

II RISING OPPOSITION AND THE GRADUAL DISAPPEARANCE OF SHARED BELIEFS

Refusing to Change and Reaffirming Principles against Critics: 1958–1964

As soon as it was established in 1945, the *dirigiste* system of credit organization was criticized by some due to the risk it posed to the economy if it proved incapable of opening itself to more competitive principles of allocation. Yet, over the course of the 1950s, the idea gradually came to prevail that a felicitous compatibility existed between the principles of credit allocation developed after the Liberation, protecting the system from inflation, and the existence within the economy of adequate margins for competition. This vision was notably expressed by Governor Baumgartner, following the implementation of new control techniques (temporary credit ceilings) in a letter to the finance minister dated February 6, 1958:

> It goes without saying that the entirety of these measures should not be deemed untouchable. Conceived at the level of the economy as a whole in light of a specific circumstances, credit stabilization should lean one way or the other as the factors defining these circumstances develop. Over time, moreover, the cap on bank credit growth results in a crystallization of existing positions that would be contrary to the normal experience of a competitive sector.[15]

In this declaration, it is clear that Baumgartner does not necessarily contrast competition and economic freedom to state intervention. He embodies a middle way, in which the *dirigiste* or coordinated system can maintain principles of economic competition in some sectors as long as it does not allow economic rents to occur.

Some radical critiques emerged, however, aimed at the system's very foundations. The best known and most radical of these voices was that of Jacques Rueff, who clearly explained in his writings from the late 1950s[16] why the credit system established in 1945, and particularly medium-term credit and selectivity, were inflationary and nefarious to economic development. According to Rueff, the development of competition between banks, the creation of a money market and open market interventions were necessary; the current system was in need of radical reform. Rueff was an important and unavoidable figure on the French political and economic

---

[15] ABF, 1427200301/334. CNC's notes.
[16] See notably his preface to Pavès and Simon (1955) and Rueff (1957).

scene from the 1930s to the 1970s. A liberal economist and reformer, the director of the Mouvement Général des Fonds (the predecessor of the Treasury) under the Popular Front in 1936, then deputy-governor of the Banque de France in 1939, he was, in 1947, one of the founders of the Mont Pèlerin Society, alongside Friedrich Hayek, and an influential critic of John Maynard Keynes, on the French as well as the international scene.[17] In the 1950s, his influence declined, and was confined to the various positions he held while building the European Coal and Steel Community and the European Community. But when De Gaulle returned to power in 1958, Rueff sent a note to Finance Minister Antoine Pinay, which convinced the president to propose the well-known Pinay-Rueff Plan, charged with reforming the French economy.[18] In Rueff's note, in addition to measures against protectionism, for competition and for budget stability, one finds very clear attacks against the credit system: end the Treasury's reliance on the Banque de France, forbid the Banque de France from engaging in medium-term credit rediscounting and make interventions on the money market the Banque de France's primary policy instrument. The measures taken in 1945 were, according to Rueff, uniquely suited to reconstruction and had to be repealed as soon as possible.[19] Rueff was, moreover, a fervent partisan of a return to the gold standard.

It is, consequently, remarkable to see that even if critics of the credit system met with increasing support, they alone were excluded from the Pinay-Rueff proposals of late 1958 and achieved no practical impact. One of the main reasons for excluding credit from the priorities included in Rueff's plan in 1958 was Baumgartner's determined opposition to Rueff and his ideas[20] (Chélini 2001, p. 119; Feiertag 2006b). And when the Banque de France governor then became finance minister from January 1960 to

---

[17] He is known for his sparring matches with Keynes and James Tobin in international journals such as the *Economic Journal* and *Quarterly Journal of Economics*. See Rueff (1929, 1947) and Tobin (1948).

[18] As Chélini notes (2001, p. 106), the world of specialists and politicians was at the time split between two perspectives: one current, represented notably by Albin Chalandon of the UNR and Guy Mollet of SFIO, which was opposed to any devaluations or budget cuts, and a second current, which was more liberal and in the minority, of which Rueff was the dominant figure.

[19] Note of June 10, published in Rueff (1972, p. 153). He would return to this criticism in his "Discours sur le crédit," which was delivered in 1961 (Rueff, 1962).

[20] In his memoirs, Rueff (1977, p. 254) said that he quickly noticed the National Credit Council had full responsibility of credit matters and that his report should not interfere with them.

January 1962, he carried out the liberal reforms in the realm of trade and budget policy, yet without touching credit policy.

While the 1958 Pinay-Rueff Plan shows that there was a strong political will to cut direct financing of the economy by the Treasury and to liberalize commercial exchange,[21] it did not undermine the legitimacy of central bank interventions in credit allocation. On the contrary, in imposing new budgetary discipline on the government, it sought to avoid a replay of the kind of budget crisis that had occurred in 1957, and which led to a request for advances to the Treasury and significant tension between the Banque de France and the ministry. The Banque de France's credit policy emerged from this crisis strengthened and subject to fewer budgetary pressures.

To what extent did Rueff's criticisms spread to society at large? Based on the minutes of the CNC's meetings, they do not seem to have gained much of an audience in the 1960s, but its members were presumably less likely to criticize the system's foundations. It is interesting, for this reason, to consider another assembly, the Conseil Économique et Social (Economic and Social Council, or CES),[22] to which a report was submitted in 1964 by Georges Lutfalla, the president of Nationale, an insurance company. The report, entitled "The Current Situation of Short-Term and Medium-Term Credit," is an analysis of the French banking and financial system. Like many of the publications that have already been cited, it first praises the role of the credit system established in 1945, at the time when the country was being rebuilt, before adopting Rueff's conclusions and advocating – before the 1969 Marjolin, Sadrin and Wormser report, which I will later consider – the creation of a genuine money market. The "opinion" ("*Avis*") referred to in the report's conclusion was put to the entire CES's approval in a non-prescriptive vote. Less liberal members proposed amendments that sought to recall the principles of 1945: credit allocation must respect the goals of the Plan, credit control was essential to this objective and the National Credit

---

[21] In early 1959, France drastically cut back its exchange controls. Thus, in May 1959, 90% of the exchanges between France and the OECD were no longer subject to controls such as licenses, authorizations and quotas.

[22] Created in 1946 to replace the Conseil National Économique (National Economic Council) created in 1924 and abolished by the Vichy regime (Chatriot 2003), the Conseil Économique et Social was preserved by the Constitution of the Fifth Republic. Conceived as a third house alongside the National Assembly and the Senate, its role was purely advisory. The government can ask for its opinion on proposed legislation. Its advice is obligatory on proposed legislation relating to planning and programming related to economic and social matters. It can also provide advice on its own initiative.

Council should play a key role in guiding and allocating credit. The amendments were as follows:

No. 1: Credit discipline is necessary, in order to respect the priorities defined by the Plan and to make available to the latter the means that will ensure it does not remain a dead letter.

No. 2: It is the responsibility of the National Credit Council to determine, in conjunction with the Commissariat Général du Plan, the relevant economic and social criteria guiding credit distribution and the means through which this guidance can be guaranteed.

158 members of the CES were present that day, and both amendments were approved by a wide majority, but without unanimity: 101 for the first, 111 for the second.[23] Overall, the amendments were approved, by large majorities, by members of labor organizations (CGT, CFTC, FO and CGC), agriculture, nationalized companies (including banks), organizations assisting former French colonies, overseas territories, Franc zone countries and artisans. The representatives opposing these amendments were essentially private companies and "individuals chosen due to their competencies" (including Jacques Rueff and Rémy Goussault[24]).

The division over this vote is all the more significant considering that the previous opinion the CES had delivered on credit, in 1953, had produced no disagreement, with most proposals being adopted unanimously, including one specifying that banks had to issue credit "not only in light of the usual criteria of solvency and liquidity, but also that of economic and social usefulness" (p. 45).[25]

The insistence with which the 1964 CES report demanded that the tight bonds between the credit allocation policy defined by the CNC and the Plan's policies be recalled portends a rhetoric that would be heard until the 1970s. This argument, advanced by credit policy's defenders, was based, in fact, on a relationship that was more symbolic than real. The 1945 law, which defined the full scope of the CNC's mission, gave no precise legal status to the bond between the CNC and the Plan, as we have seen, and the connection between

---

[23] The difference between the two votes can be explained primarily by the fact that some of the representatives of the CGT (the Communist trade union) abstained on the first amendment. One possible interpretation could be the opposition of the CGT to the idea of "credit discipline."

[24] On the career of Rémy Goussault, an economic liberal who was close to the Vichy regime and an importance figure in agriculture trade-unionism, see, notably, Cohen (2004, p. 147).

[25] Conseil Economique. Etudes et travaux. Etudes sur le rôle économique du crédit, sa situation actuelle et les réformes que celle-ci appelle. Presented by M. Malterre. Opinion of May 27, 1953.

these two organizations was, in practice, rather episodic and weak: the Plan determined major long-term forecasts, while the CNC adapted its policy more immediately to the sectoral conditions of credit and bank balance sheets. The Plan's commissioner, Pierre Massé, did, however, appear for the first time at the CNC in 1963 in order to establish collaboration between the two organizations. But as Claire Andrieu (1984, p. 396) remarks a propos of this visit, the priorities announced by the Plan were once again too broad to really guide the Banque de France's and the CNC's choices relating to access to rediscounting and recommendations to banks.

The Marjolin–Sadrin–Wormser Report

Consensus began to wither, though remained strong for the moment. Dissent seemed to hail only from a few well-defined milieus, orthodox economists or private companies. It only truly arrived on the scene with the publication of "Report on the Money Market and Credit Conditions" ("Rapport sur le marché monétaire et les conditions de crédit"), requested by the National Assembly in December 1968 and published in June 1969. It is often referred to using the name of its three authors: the Marjolin–Sadrin–Wormser (MSW) report. This report was an immediate result of the inflationary crisis of 1968, which, while primarily due to political turmoil, revived doubts about the French model of organizing credit. It focused, for the most part, on the question of the resources available to the central bank, but, at a more general level, broached the question of state intervention on the credit market. Even if the ideas of this report also met with strong opposition, the identity of its authors – Robert Marjolin, Jean Sadrin and Olivier Wormser – compels us to recognize that its arguments were not isolated. Though they were not radicals and loose cannons in Rueff's mold, all three authors had been involved in establishing the credit policy system and occupied important positions in the French civil service in previous decades.

The trajectories of Marjolin, Sadrin and Wormser, who were all trained as economists, are both astonishing and symptomatic. Their liberal and social economic vision, which made room for Gaullism's interventionist and sovereignist inflections, had shaped the policies of European construction and the common market. Marjolin had been involved in the planning movement in the early 1930s, only to withdraw from it before joining the Popular Front.[26] A friend of many contemporary economists

---

[26] He became an adviser to Léon Blum, with whom he had disagreements over the forty-hour work week.

of multiple theoretical and ideological tendencies, Marjolin participated alongside Rueff and Hayek in the famous Walter Lippmann Conference of 1938, which resulted in the creation of the Mont Pèlerin Society (Denord 2001; Audier 2008). He then became Jean Monnet's assistant and played a decisive role in implementing the first Plan before becoming the Secretary General of the European Organization for Economic Cooperation (OEEC) and, subsequently, European Commissioner. Wormser, for his part, wrote a dissertation in 1938 on the problem of deflation, in which he was critical of the deflationist policies of the 1930s. An avowed Gaullist, he spent much of his career after the war at the Ministry of Foreign Affairs, notably as the head of the Directorate for Economic and Financial Affairs from 1954 to 1966. Though initially very skeptical about European construction, he let himself be convinced that it was necessary, notably by his friend Marjolin. As for Sadrin, he was the director of FINEX, the Directorate of External Finances of the Ministry of Finance, where he established himself as a liberal Europhile (Warlouzet 2010, p. 82). In 1964, he had written an influential report on the reforms of housing finance – for the Finance Minister Valéry Giscard d'Estaing – which recognized the importance of state intervention in this domain while recommending a greater role for the financial markets (Effosse 2003, pp. 515ff.). Like Rueff, these three were trained economists and had acquired mastery of external and notably European affairs over the course of the 1950s. They were, however, more inclined than Rueff to accept Keynesian ideas, on the fiscal as well the monetary front. Marjolin was thus the first economist to defend a thesis on Keynes in 1941, and while he remained critical of the possibility of applying Keynes' theories in a French context, he played a role in promoting Keynes' ideas with the establishment of national accounting in 1947 (Rosanvallon 1987, p. 41).

Between the time of the commissioning of the report and its submission, Olivier Wormser was named governor of the Banque de France, which gave him carte blanche to apply his ideas. A leitmotif of the MSW report was the application of market laws to the realm of credit. This was systematically presented as a necessary goal. The report clearly belonged to a current that believed that the existing system was only suitable to the reconstruction efforts of the 1950s. According to these authors, the need for a competitive system was to be found, in the first place, in the government's policy of internationalizing the economy. It was necessary, to this end, to increase "communication between the French market and the foreign market" (p. 7). The authors insisted on the fact that the increasing internationalization of financial exchanges, the development of the Eurodollars market[27] and the crisis of the Bretton Woods system had made the idea of an independent monetary policy increasingly illusory:

Today, the international monetary system is in a state of crisis – at times acute, at others latent. For nearly fifteen years, the United States' balance of payments deficit has made available to the rest of the world an increasing quantity of dollars, the use of which is, for various reasons, more remunerative outside the United States than in their country of origin. This has resulted in the creation of a kind of vast international money market, in which other currencies have joined the dollars, in which more than three-quarters of all operations are denominated. This extraterritorial market of "Eurocurrencies," which functions outside the control of national monetary authorities and along the margins of fiscal regimes, has as one effect to facilitate the international movement of short-term capital and making an independent monetary policy more difficult for any given country. (p. 6)

The second argument justifying the need for reform presented in the report is that France, according to the authors, suffers from insufficient investment due to an excessively weak supply of capital.[28] The authors were referring here to French banks' difficulty achieving long-term financing through deposits. In the language of the day, this operation was known as "the transformation." The "transformation" became a major subject of conversation at the Banque de France in the mid-1960s, notably at the General Directorate of Credit.[29] According to the partisans of the existing system, the best way to encourage banks to make long-term loans through short-term deposits was to guarantee loans that could be rediscounted by the Crédit National, the Crédit Foncier and the Banque de France. The 1965 reform of medium-term credit prolonged this tendency, even as the 1966 banking laws sought to encourage banks to launch the "transformation" by remunerating long-term deposits more freely (see Chapter 3, Section I). The MSW report, for its part, favored a liberal solution to the transformation problem by advocating the liberalization of bank rates. It criticized

---

[27] On the development of the Eurodollars market, see, notably, Schenk (1998) and Battilossi (2009).

[28] While the state was collecting an ever increasing share of the nation's production, the needs of companies and individuals was growing. The group insisted on this well-known phenomenon, because the conjunction of demands of the state and those of the companies and individuals created a situation in which demand for capital tended constantly to exceed supply, which is an essential characteristic of current times. In this way problems of financing were posed with an unprecedented acuity ... Due to the insufficiency of savings and financing procedures to which it was necessary to resort, this indebtedness resulted too often in the creation of money. (p. 8)

[29] ABF, 133120030179.

head-on the specificities of the French system, namely its fragmentation or specialization – an essential feature of credit selection – and rediscounting. While still recognizing the effectiveness of the current system for financing the state and the economy ("If the method of gathering [funds] might not seem very rational, its advantage is that it is really effective," p. 9) the report's goal was to favor non-directed allocation, in which prices would once again play a role. Indeed, the authors denounced "the a priori assigning of funds, before they had been brought to market" (p. 10).

The charges the report leveled against the system were serious. They challenged the idea that a fragmented system favoring allocation on a sectoral basis under the state's authority was capable of providing the most efficient financing of the economy. Later in the report, the authors assert that the existing system does not allow an allocation of funds on the basis of "profitability."

Without denying that there could be major objections to a reform that took a step toward the creation of vaster market, in which a greater share of collected resources would be demanded as much as it were supplied, our group considers it desirable, if the laws of the market are to function, to put an end as soon as possible to the fragmentation to which it is prone. It is convinced that if such a reform were approved, it would not exactly be the same needs that are satisfied, at the same rate, as at present. Herein lies the difference between authoritarian distribution and market-based distribution. As regards the latter, profitability is the key factor. (p. 10)

Despite Wormser's accession to the Banque de France's head, the report's conclusions did not result in deep reform of the financial system and credit policy. The most important change – which itself was limited – lies in the important role given to the money market in 1971 (see Chapter 3, Section III). The reason for the lack of reforms inspired by the report is the resistance of numerous actors to liberalization, as well as the fact that defects of the French allocation system were not obvious in the late 1960s, as the authors recognized. The 1968 crisis did, of course, appear as a balance of payments and inflation control crisis (due notably to wages), but few saw any reason to challenge the credit allocation system.

Among the various reactions to this report, some notes written by Guillaume Guindey deserve particular attention. Indeed, they offer us a perfect opportunity to grasp the tenor of the arguments at play in France in the late 1960s.[30] Furthermore, Guindey's trajectory and position make him

---

[30] These notes were found in the Banque de France's archives, ABF, 1331200301/29. They circulated among the Direction of Monetary Studies but it's not clear who they were originally addressed to. The pages in the following quotes refer to this document.

someone who was just as representative of the French civil service of this period as the report's three authors. A former director of FINEX, where he was replaced by Sadrin, Guindey was director of the Bank of International Settlements (BIS) from 1958 to 1963, then, beginning in 1965, director of the Caisse Centrale de Cooperation Économique (Central Economic Cooperation Fund, or CCCE).[31] A staunch critic of the recommendation of MSW's report, Guindey reproached the authors for not understanding the French system's coherence and not basing their arguments on satisfactory theoretical justifications.

First, he criticized the fact that the authors did not make the necessary distinction between short-term and long-term credit. Their analysis of "transformation" rested on the illusion that the same resources could create the same credit, which automatically led to a negation of the central bank's role in "transformation." Guindey rehabilitated, in this way, a crucial argument of critics of the interwar banking system and which was reasserted in 1945, that public intervention is capable of ensuring the existence of long-term credit: banks do not have sufficient incentives to create medium- and long-term credit on the basis of deposits. Banque de France rediscounting was not only essential because it provided banks with incentives to make long-term loans, it also allowed for just and efficient credit selection:

[I]t is perfectly normal that a central bank ensures that credit distributed through the banking system, notably credit provided through rediscounting, obeys criteria of sound usage; one of the essential responsibilities of the central bank [*Institut d'émission*] was to ensure that monetary creation did not have the effect, one way or another, of financing immobilized assets. This was not a confusion of the responsibilities of the central bank and other banks, but regular surveillance of bank activity. (p. 14)

Guindey's second criticism asserted that the authors were mistaken in saying that anti-inflationary policy could occur through interventions in the money market. According to Guindey, the error of the MSW report is that it is based on Anglo-American references and that it fails to take sufficient account of the specificity of the French system. Along these lines, he emphasized the paradox of a report that claimed to draw on the Radcliffe report of 1959 while asserting the power of monetary policy, even though the latter implied the primacy of budgetary policy. The MSW report

---

[31] The CCCE is a financial institution that has intervened in overseas departments and territories overseas since 1944. After leaving the BIS, Guindey continued to be a major figure on the international scene and published many noted essays. He was in particular the author of a 1968 report by the OECD (Heller et al. 1968) and lectures on the international monetary system (Guindey 1973; Guindey & Coombs 1980).

repeatedly said that elasticity of demand and the money and credit supply to interest rates is greater than what is usually considered, yet without providing proof. It asserts that fiscal policy has dominated in recent years and that a genuine monetary policy must be put into place by getting the money market to work.[32] Guindey, on the contrary, emphasized that credit control meant that France actually had a monetary policy, unlike the United States and England, where fiscal policy used to be the priority and monetary policy had only been rediscovered: "it is only in the Anglo-American countries and just recently that one sees a certain disenchantment with budgetary measures and a return to fashion of monetary theories that are, after all, rather simplistic (such as the Milton Friedman school)" (p. 20). He concludes:

One sees that the report's authors have assimilated the idea that money is a kind of staple, the availability of which can grow under the influence of rising prices. Yet it is well known that it is credit, and credit alone, which creates scriptural and fiduciary money. The central bank can act on the volume of deposits only by acting on the volume of credit. *Loans make deposits.* (p. 9)

He adds that the report also goes contrary to the French tradition of separating the "properly monetary domain" from the "financial domain" that is reflected in the distinction between commercial banks and investment banks. Conducting a monetary policy by selling and buying securities (i.e. open market operations) strikes him as incompatible with the way French banks create money.[33] For Guindey, the issue is as follows:

We must choose between two conceptions of monetary reality. We must find out if, in France, we are committed to the current conception, which is consistent with our habits, or if we will opt for another, very different conception, which is much closer to that of the British. (p. 9)

Finally, Guindey's third and last major critique of the MSW report was a defense of state intervention in credit allocation. He rehearsed in this way the arguments that were seen many times since 1945, as well as the reference

---

[32] This was also the position defended by Sylviane Guillaumont-Jeanneney in her book from 1968, whose interpretive framework and references are very similar to those of the MSW report, and which aspires to be an application of Gurley and Shaw's theory of financial intermediation (1960) to the French example. Their point of view consists in denying that credit policy was also a means of monetary control, which strikes us as objectionable in light of the actors' own statements in addition to the quantitative results.

[33] On the debate about the (limited) introduction of money market operations in France in the interwar, see Mouré (1991, ch. 4) and, more recently, Duchaussoy and Monnet (2018).

to the "general interest," thus providing evidence that there was not unanimous approval among France's top civil servants regarding the idea that the organization of credit was uniquely adapted to reconstruction:

It would be regrettable to challenge the idea, which has become customary in France since the war, that credit policy must constitute, to the largest extent possible, an auxiliary to economic policy and planning. This idea must, of course, not lead to beliefs that disregard the laws that are unique to monetary phenomena. A compromise must be found between these laws and the needs of economic policy and planning. The French credit system constitutes a compromise of this kind, which is, of course, not perfect and which can be improved. It would not be reasonable to give up to a large extent the use, in the name of the general interest, of credit policy, the use of which is all the more desirable as other instruments have but limited efficiency and flexibility. (p. 11)

The note that Guindey circulated at the Banque de France in response to the MSW report shows the level of disagreement among men of his generation whose trajectories and inclinations were, in principle, similar. At the dawn of the 1970s, two visions of the organization of credit that seemed difficult to reconcile were at odds in the French civil service. These debates did not concern the goals of monetary policy, which everyone believed should make fighting inflation and preserving the "general interest" its primary goal, but the means of arriving at this goal. Yet, it clearly appeared that the choice of these means depended above all on each individual's vision of the organization of credit and of the market's ability to allocate funds and finance investment.

It may seem paradoxical that the MSW report, which united the defenders of a liberalization of the French financial system, was written by an economist who helped introduce Keynes to the French, Robert Marjolin, and that it adopted a theoretical perspective inspired by Keynes and referred frequently to the 1959 Radcliffe report. Thus, it differed considerably from the view of some French liberals, notably Rueff, that the proper functioning of a money market necessarily implied a return to the gold standard (Rueff 1971). But this paradox must be placed within the context of France in the 1960s where monetary debates were primarily about credit's role in a *dirigiste* economy.

The following year, in 1970, the report of the Planning office echoed the MSW report by stating that market forces were an efficient way to allocate funds and that prices reflected the information of agents. It criticized openly the French credit system (p. 12): "the current organization of investment financing mechanisms, characterized by excessive segmentation of circuits and extreme disparity of interest rates, does not promote a fully rational allocation of savings."[34]

From Selectivity to Heterogeneity

Following the 1969 MSW report, credit selectivity was perceived more and more negatively, without yielding a new consensus or a coherent set of policies. During the episode of restrictive monetary policy in 1973, the question of "selectivity" returned to the forefront and triggered a controversy within the bank's General Council. The change in the latter's composition, which, in January, brought into the council "experts" chosen due to their economic competencies,[35] further contributed to renewing the terms of the debate. To a question by Gabriel Ventejol, a CGT trade unionist who belonged as an expert on labor issues, who worried that "if the necessary criteria for directing investment are not set by the central bank, the banks themselves should do so" and who asked for an increase in exemptions aimed at guaranteeing the "selectivity" of credit policy, Governor Wormser ultimately replied that "he did not believe much in selectivity in an economy as complex as the French economy" and "that it is extremely difficult to implement selectivity measures, but rest assured that it will benefit those [the companies] at which it is aimed."[36]

As the controversy relating to selectivity (*sélectivité du credit*) persisted, Governor Wormser decided to organize a debate on this topic at the General Council beginning on May 9, 1974. It continued over several sessions and was interrupted by the change in the governorship that occurred on June 14. It was introduced by defenders of the state's and the Banque de France's

[34] "Rapport sur les principales options qui commandent la préparation du VIe Plan" (July 10, 1970). It was widely discussed at the Banque de France. ABF, 1331200301/183. See also Margairaz (2009a) and Angeletti (2011) on the evolution of the Planning office toward a free-market vision of the economy.

[35] It marked the moment when economists made their first entry into the council, notably Raymond Barre and Edmond Malinvaud. The former, a university professor, had been vice-president of the European Commission, responsible for the economy and finance, from 1967 to 1973. The latter, an economist at the INSEE, enjoyed an international reputation. He was in charge of the Ministry of the Economy and Finance's Directorate for Forecasting from 1972 to 1974.

[36] ABF, PVCG, July 19, 1973. A few months earlier, the Treasury director, Claude Pierre-Brossolette, had created a stir when he declared to the Council that he did not share the opinion of some on the need to develop selectivity because "God knows it is practiced in France – probably a little too much – particularly over the past twenty years or so. And the Banque de France seems, on top of it, poorly placed to do so" (PCVG, May 17, 1973).

role in selectivity. Maurice Gousseau, the representative of the Banque de France's employees, agreed with the position of labor representative Ventejol. He worried that banks "only lend to the wealthy" and deplored how difficult it was to determine if banks allocated their credit based on "economic" goals rather than "purely financial motivations, based on the criteria of profitability." He turned to the usual argument, invoking the general interest: "[G]enuine selectivity – that is, economic selectivity – must tend toward directing access to credit toward companies that respect the priorities defined by public authorities within the framework of the Plan and, more broadly, to steer economic activity toward goals that are consistent with the general interest."[37]

Over the course of lengthy conversations that continued from week to week, a collective position, summed up by the governor and that seemed to have met with consensus, ultimately emerged: that selectivity, which was widely practiced in France, was indispensable to the economy and that the Banque de France had an essential role to play in this realm due to insufficient levels of direct financing from the state (in the realm of budgetary policy). Wormser, in contrast to his remarks in his 1969 report, no longer expressed firm opposition to the current system, but did nevertheless assert that one should not place financial profitability at odds with general economic interest and that it was normal for banks to make decisions on the basis of the former. On this point, Claude Pierre-Brossolette and Raymond Barre agreed with him.[38] The position that was most critical of the existing system was that of Jacques Delors.[39] Even if he, too, did not express the desire for a complete break, he nonetheless made a number of decisive criticisms – which would expand over the course of the decade – by insisting on selectivity's potentially negative long-term consequences for the general interest:

Yet it must be said, however regretfully, that when a given sector of the French economy is placed in a favored situation, it remains there constantly. Thus the favors enjoyed by the Crédit Agricole – though they have been lessened – are an example of the rigidities that establish themselves in an economy and which, by misallocating credit, are one reason for poor adaptation and a source of inflation.[40]

---

[37] ABF, PVCG, May 9, 1974.
[38] In 1976, Pierre-Brossolette became general secretary of the Élysée Palace (i.e., the French presidency) and Raymond Barre became prime minister.
[39] Having joined the Commissariat Général du Plan as head of service for social and cultural affairs, he had been an active member of the CFDT trade union since 1964 and, between 1969 and 1972, worked for Prime Minister Jacques Chaban-Delmas. He joined the Socialist Party in 1974 and was finance minister from 1981 to 1984.
[40] ABF, PVCG, May 9, 1974.

The debate ended with Wormser's eviction from the Banque de France. Once he had been elected president, former Finance Minister Valéry Giscard d'Estaing no longer wanted the Gaullist governor of the Banque de France with whom he had clashed on many occasions during the writing of the new statutes in 1973 and who had dared, in May 1974, to publish in the *Figaro* a letter openly criticizing the government's budget policy. Neither in Wormser's farewell speech, nor in the arrival speech of his successor, Bernard Clappier, would the question of credit selectivity be raised. The two men insisted on the need to develop the money market, but without contrasting it to the principles of the credit policy currently being pursued.

In the years following these debates, French credit policy became schizophrenic. Even as criticism of the existing system grew inside the Banque de France, it paradoxically reinforced credit selectivity through an increasing number of exemptions (Galbraith 1982; Guillaumont-Jeanneney 1991; and below). Beginning in the mid-1970s, critics no longer simply declared that it would be desirable to abandon selectivity, they began to denounce the fact that the specialization and fragmentation of the French banking system – upon which selectivity was in part based – had blocked the possibility of reform. After Wormser's departure, critics no longer expressed themselves openly at meetings of the General Council, but primarily at the General Credit Directorate (*Direction Générale du Crédit*, DGC) and the Directorate of Statistical and Monetary Analysis (*Direction des analyses statistiques et monétaires*, or DASM). Thus, a new rhetoric surfaced, which consisted of denouncing the French credit system's "heterogeneity." The term "heterogeneity" referred to nothing other than the specialization or segregation of the banking system. It appears as a central argument in the debates concerning whether the moment had come to abandon credit ceilings (*"encadrement du crédit"*).[41] In 1978, a Banque de France economist, Jacques-Henri David, held that the policy founded on interest rates and interventions on the money market was poorly adapted to the French banking system due to its "specialization" and lack of "homogeneity." The economist Sylviane Guillaumont-Jeanneney and Director of DASM Robert Raymond replied to him in turn, defending the position that "heterogeneity" was preserved artificially by the existing system and that a change in the instruments of monetary policy would bring an end to it. For Raymond, the preservation of credit controls amounted to

---

[41] ABF, 1415200801/3, "La politique monétaire française sans encadrement du crédit," September 7, 1978. DGC note by Robert Raymond. And "L'encadrement du crédit: une intervention nécessaire?," by J. H. David, with an answer by S. Guillaumont-Jeanneney (*Annales Economiques* 13).

"endorsing the heterogeneity of the banking system by ensuring outside of the money market a significant share of the refinancing that is indispensable to deficit-prone establishments." Guillaumont-Jeanneney also denounced the fact that "the automatic character of refinancing and credit controls contributed to perpetrating this heterogeneity." Inside the DASM, this vision gradually prevailed, thanks notably to Robert Raymond. By the early 1980s, it seems to have met with unanimous approval. A synthetic note by the DASM published in 1981 on the system of credit with preferential rates is, in this respect, symptomatic: it is unsparing in denouncing the fact that use of these rates has increased since 1974 and that they do too much to undermine competition, while also preserving the system's heterogeneity.

Ultimately the system reduces or distorts competition between networks, because some of them enjoy particular advantages conferred by public authorities in gathering their resources or developing their credit operations ... It is true that that special procedures that tend to differentiate some networks in granting credit or gathering savings are by their very nature difficult to call into question; their multiplication, which is thus becoming the norm, makes financial circuits increasingly rigid. A system of this kind renders difficult any determination of the overall costs of the advantages thus agreed upon. ... In industry, horizontal aids thus exist alongside various sectoral interventions; in addition to traditional actions aimed at modernizing the economy have been added, in recent years, support aimed at helping sectors and regions experiencing difficulties. This heterogeneity can also, of course, be found in the realm of credit.[42]

In studies written by the Banque de France between 1980 and 1981, one even finds explicit reference to the argument that holds that credit policy, due to the obstacles it creates in the banking sector, was now at cross-purposes with the goals of the Plan.[43] It is hard to miss the irony of such a reversal: a decade after the controversy surrounding the Marjolin–Sadrin–Wormser report, coordination with planners now constitutes an argument for defending the liberalization of the French financial system.

---

[42] ABF, 1415200801/3.
[43] The purpose of this note is to examine if another controlling technique would not make it possible, without renouncing control over monetary trends – which is necessary for containing domestic inflationary tensions and preserving the franc's position in the EMS – to improve competition in banking and to make credit policy contribute more to economic development and the achievement of the Plan's goals. (ABF, 1415200801/3. November 20, 1981, "Possibilités et limites de politiques alternatives à l'encadrement du crédit")

The position first articulated by Jacques Delors[44] in 1974 before the General Council had become widespread: rents attributed to banks and specialized credit institutions by the Banque de France's policy created inflation and were contrary to the "general interest." In 1945, criticism had been directed against the bankers' "Mathusianism"; in 1975, it was aimed at rents and the banking sector's rigidities. In both cases, it was precisely the opposition between the banks' activities and what was perceived to be the "general interest" that motivated reforms in the financial sector and the Banque de France.

We see the persistent ambiguity in the "perverse effects" argument, on which the critique leveled by some in the Banque de France in the late 1970s against credit policy was based. Albert Hirschman (1991), while primarily associating the perverse effect argument with reactionary rhetoric, also notes that it could be found in progressive discourse: only a radical change can avert catastrophe and make it possible to defend one's foundational ideals.

Norms and beliefs about credit policy inside the Banque de France underwent a very clear evolution in the 1970s and left no doubt as to the nature of future reforms. The system's fragmentation, heterogeneity and selectivity, which had been seen as positive and crucial features of the French system, came to be seen as flaws and obstacles that were contrary to the general interest. The collective norms upon which the institution was founded were called into question.

One must be careful not to interpret new types of discourse on credit as the mere effect of the arrival of neoliberal thinking at the Banque de France. Critiques of the system were based on an analysis of real dysfunction and on the idea that the institution of credit had evolved in a way that was contrary to the principles of national economic interest on which it was supposedly based.[45] Criticisms directed against credit policy within the Banque de France and the Plan matched the analyses of the INSEE (1981) and Sachs and Wyplosz (1986), who suggested that French economic problems in the 1970s were primarily the result of inadequate supply and a decline in business competitiveness at a time when government policy was focused on stimulating demand. When France faced economic troubles in the 1970s – namely inflation and productivity slowdown – there was

---

[44] This position had been articulated as early as 1972 by the economist Serge-Christophe Kolm in an article in a widely discussed article from *Le Monde* (Plessis 1996).

[45] In an article on banking history, the historian Alain Plessis draws a conclusion that is consistent with observations from the period: "Their protests notwithstanding, many bankers often adapted to a sclerotic system which, by assigning each bank a credit allotment based on past experience, protected in practiced their current status" (1996, p. 91).

no difficulty in interpreting them in the light of ideas that put forward the need for market forces and the perverse effects of state intervention. Such discourses had been already well established at the Banque de France since the 1960s. The high inflation of the 1970s had two consequences that may seem paradoxical. On the one hand, it put a brake on the first attempts of free-market reforms begun in 1971 as we will see below, and on the other, it fed even more criticism of the system, based on laissez-faire ideas that had already been in existence for a long time. It is important to note that these reformist ideas, as expressed, for example, in the Lutfalla and MSW reports, were based on the emphasis placed on the "market" as a superior mode of economic organization. References to market forces and the very definition of "a market" remained relatively abstract, and economic theory was not clearly invoked as a justification for market superiority. But it was in contrast to specific forms of state intervention that the argument was constructed. In *The Age of Fracture*, historian Daniel Rodgers (2011, p. 43) asks himself: "The puzzle of the age is not that economic concepts moved into the center of social debate; the riddle is that so abstract and idealized an idea of efficient market action should have arisen amid so much real-world market imperfection." In the case of credit policy in France, we can see here that the answer to this question lies in the fact that it was not the theoretical references that took precedence in the reformist discourses but rather critical analyses of the precise ways in which the state intervened in certain areas.[46] Changing the modes of state intervention in the economy was a very concrete and technocratic vision; references to the market were not made in an abstract context. Thus, as soon as the 1960s, neoliberalism was not a retreat of the state but a call to organize markets in a more "neutral" way. What remains relatively puzzling, and where the reference to ideology but also the sociology of the actors is necessary, is why this set of solutions by the market was preferred to others. On the other hand, it should not be forgotten that criticism did not cover all aspects and that the rediscovery of the market in the late 1960s did not call into question the independence of the central bank, nor did it call for the privatization of banking institutions. We must therefore be careful not to think that a neoliberal corpus appeared at the same time with a comprehensive reform plan. The decisive and well-known role played in France by high civil servants

---

[46] In a very different context, Julia Ott (2011) shows the role of financial securities marketers in promoting laissez-faire ideology and the growth of financial markets in the United States. She shows how references to beneficial outcomes of the market were rooted in current practices and criticisms of existing financial institutions, rather than being mostly inspired by economic theory.

in the appropriation of free-market reformist ideas was also found in the field of monetary and credit policy. The evolution of ideas at the Banque de France was in line with other administrations such as the Planning office, the Finance Ministry or INSEE. The French "neoliberal turn" was a very national phenomenon, not driven by major foreign influences, especially not by "monetarism." It was rooted in the high administration rather than driven by the financial community. It was also an early move, with major statements and reforms as soon as the late 1960s.[47]

Reformers who refused to challenge the principles of credit policy and to endorse the calls for more free-market reforms were convinced that the sclerosis of the system was instead due to the economic rents of the banking system. It is from this perspective that one must understand plans for radical reform that were proposed in 1981 by some political parties or within the civil service. The Socialist Party saw bank nationalization as the system's only salvation and the only means whereby the system could once serve the "general interest" (Plessis, 1996, p. 91), despite the fact that the party had, since 1945, ceased to regard nationalization as an important feature of credit policy. Conversely, the Planning office, adhering to the Banque de France's own conclusions, set as a goal of France's eighth five-year plan the elimination of credit ceilings (*encadrement du crédit*) and ending the exemptions and privileges of public and semi-public credit institutions.[48]

III FROM ATTEMPTS AT LIBERALIZATION TO LOSS OF CONTROL OVER INFLATION

Was the 1945 law organizing credit compatible with monetary policies aimed at encouraging market and interest rate mechanisms? While the Banque de France seemed to be of the opinion that the answer was "yes," it ran up against political and economic resistance that ultimately plunged credit and monetary policy into the deepest uncertainty. In this final section, we will study how approaches to fighting inflation evolved in conjunction with the social norms we have just described.

---

[47] In contrast, studies on the United Kingdom have emphasized the role of the Bank of England as an institution that relays the ideas developed mainly in the financial circles of the City of London (Davies 2012; Needham 2014). On the French neoliberal turn of economists and civil servants, see Théret (1994), Denord (2001, 2010), Abdelal (2007) and Fourcade (2009).

[48] Loriaux (1988, pp. 182–183) presents these proposals. The eighth plan was adopted before François Mitterrand's election. Yet, because it was deemed too liberal, it was replaced by a temporary plan as of the following year.

Within a decade, from the mid-1960s until the mid-1970s, France went from a situation in which it seemed to have found effective tools for fighting inflation that were adapted to its unique banking system to a state of doubt that made it question the ability of monetary policy to actually fight price increases.

The Successes of Quantitative Credit Controls

In the first half of the 1960s, French monetary policy seems to have found, in the direct limitation of bank exposures ("credit ceilings," i.e., *encadrement du crédit*), an efficient tool that perfectly addressed the twofold goal of fighting inflation and credit selection. The experience of these controls in 1958 and between 1963 and 1965 led them to be viewed as exemplary successes, which made possible price stability and a strengthening of balance of payments (cf. Chapter 4).[49]

When credit ceilings came to an end in 1965 in order to make way for a more expansionist policy, the governor, on June 25, 1965, sent a letter to the president of the professional association of banks to assure him that he would bring back this tool if bank credit ever "grew too vigorously."[50] Yet this was not the time for calling matters into question and the refusal to use interest rates was henceforth fully acknowledged. An internal note to the Directory of Statistical and Monetary Analyses from 1966 discussing the wisdom of credit ceilings lists three main justifications for direct quantitative control on bank loans. First, direct credit restrictions makes it possible to not increase rates and thus to avoid attracting foreign capital; second, monetary control through liquidity ratios (*coefficient de trésorerie*) is not, for its part, fast and effective enough, as it does not act "at the very moment when money is created by banks in exchange for providing credit to the economy, but only when the money market has already tightened up." Finally and most importantly,

a reticence towards high rates has gradually emerged in modern industrial countries, to the point that it has become a tradition. As a result, when strong inflationary pressures occur, interest rates set at what is considered an acceptable level remain

---

[49] Noting the absolute success, in relation to growth and price stability of the period between 1959 and 1967, Patat and Lutfalla (1986, ch. 12) described it, in their monetary history of France, as "the great epoch of the Fifth Republic." There was an international consensus at that time, especially in the United States, that French tools of monetary policy were especially effective (Monnet 2013).

[50] ABF, 1331200301/330.

insufficient for fighting the imbalances in the adjustment of savings to investment and in price formation.[51]

The last sentence, while referring to the frequently invoked argument of the insufficiency or inefficiency of a rate policy, nonetheless makes clear one of this argument's crucial (if implicit) assumptions, namely that it applies only to "acceptable" interest rates. In other words, if interest rates are inefficient, it is because the bank keeps them too low. Thus, the refusal to manipulate rates seems deeply anchored in the bank's habits, even if this predisposition is never acknowledged or theorized to a significant degree. Controlling credit was never questioned, even if the note's author regrets certain difficulties experienced by the bank in implementing credit selectivity and considers credit ceilings as an exceptional measure that should not stand in the way of thinking about ways of improving the control of bank liquidity by other means.

The reform of liquidity ratios finally occurred in 1967 with the creation of obligatory reserves. While the negotiations leading to this reform were creating a buzz at the Banque de France, a decree from 1966 that went almost unnoticed and which had few immediate consequences expanded the bank's ability to intervene on the money market. Medium-term bonds issued by credit institutions having a special legal status (Crédit Foncier, CDC and Crédit National) could henceforth be traded on this market.[52] This reform would have later important consequences for the reform of Banque de France loans to the Treasury in 1973 (Chapter 5).

Toward a More "Neutral" Policy: Minimum Reserves

The implementation of obligatory reserves (i.e., cash-reserve requirements) gave rise to considerable controversy, eliciting reticence notably on the part of bankers and Banque de France personnel, who feared that rediscounting would lose its role and that the habits of French monetary policy were being spurned. This reform, which was openly inspired by Germany and the United States, did in fact modify the way in which bank liquidity was controlled by refusing any reference to a sum of discountable loans. Banks were required to have reserves with the central bank that were proportional to the total amount of their deposits. Obligatory reserves replaced the

---

[51] ABF, 1331200301/330. Note from April 1966. Direction des analyses et statistiques monétaires. "Les problèmes de l'action directe sur la progression des encours de crédit."

[52] Decree (December 2, 1966), n° 66–891, pertaining to various Banque de France interventions on the money market.

"Treasury coefficient," (*coefficient de trésorerie*) which had been established in 1961 to replace the "floor" (*plancher*) of government securities, which required banks to maintain a fixed proportion of their holdings in Treasury bills and medium-term bills, excluding ceilings and deposits.[53] The 1967 reform thus prevented the central bank from affecting the level of banks' Treasury coefficients through its rediscounting policy and separated the management of banking liquidity from the holding of Treasury bills. This was a shift from a securities-reserve requirement to a cash-reserve requirement (Monnet & Vari 2017).

This reform, which might seem purely technical and exclusively concerned with monetary control, represents, however, a transformation in the central bank's role in credit allocation. It is, moreover, not insignificant that Michel Debré personally attended the CNC – which was completely unprecedented for a finance minister – on November 9, 1966, to announce and debate this new measure. Debré's pronouncements on this point were unequivocal:

The reserves requirement tends to reintroduce freedom of choice and management of bank assets as a function of natural considerations such as returns and risk assessment. I hope in this way to favor a process that will gradually put rates back in order on the basis of the laws of the market and in a context of competition, the very idea of which has been lost sight of. The same quest to ensure the system's neutrality leads to the principle of uniform constraints, which is indispensable to the reform's success. It is difficult for me to see why the principle of subjection should not apply to all institutions that accept deposits from the public and that, as distributors of credit, participate in the creation of means of payment.[54]

The minister's words made it clear that there was a will to call into question a system based on selecting credit on the basis of criteria that are not strictly determined by the market. The desire for a "neutral" system would seem a departure from the spirit of 1945.

From the beginning of the Fifth Republic until 1968, the Banque de France's anti-inflation policy seems to have found stability, even if there was still some fumbling. Jacques Brunet, who replaced Wilfrid Baumgartner as governor in 1960, was fully in the mold of his predecessor. Pushed toward more liberal practices by Finance Minister Debré, the Banque de France

---

[53] It completed the liquidity ratio imposed in 1948, which established a relation of 60% between deposits and short-term credits (in other words, discounted bills, for the most part), but which was always a tool for prudential control rather than monetary policy (the percentage having not varied over time).

[54] For Debré's remarks, see ABF, 1427200301/29. Séances du CNC. For the modalities of reform see 1427200301/336. Séances du CNC.

remained attached to traditional tools. This was also a period in which the justification of the control of credit as a means for guaranteeing monetary policy's autonomy solidified. Currency returned to convertibility in 1959, capital controls were eliminated in 1966 and the current account was in surplus.

The political and social turmoil of 1968, followed by the end of the Bretton Woods system, shook up these certainties at many levels.

The Money Market Debate and the End of Rediscount Ceilings

As we have seen previously, the publication of the MSW report and the nomination of Olivier Wormser to the head of the bank changed the situation and resulted as of 1971 in an attempt to make interventions in the money market the primary tool of French monetary policy.

The laws of 1938 and 1966 allowed the Banque de France to make partial interventions on the money market (also known in France as the "open market"),[55] but the latter had always given priority to rediscounting by making sure its rate was more attractive for the banks than refinancing on the money market. All that was lacking was the will to make this type of intervention the central bank's primary tool. Wormser's decision implied three changes in procedure. First, the bank raised its discount rate above that of the money market in January 1971. Second, it extended, at the same time, the list of bills eligible for the open market, including commercial paper and rediscounting medium-term credits.[56] Finally, in January 1972, it eliminated rediscount ceilings, which had become useless.[57] To implement this reform, Wormser waited until inflation had been relatively stabilized and the restrictive policy of credit controls decided by his predecessor came to an end in October 1970 (see Chapter 4). As the governor saw things, the time had come to put an end to rediscount ceilings and credit ceilings. These tools were now a thing of the past.[58]

---

[55] This was done respectively through the selling and purchasing of treasury bills and medium-term bills.

[56] Decision of January 21, 1971. See ABF, PVCG, January 21, 1971.

[57] According to the governor, "since the money market is not rationed, every bank will find financing, unless its signature is 'debatable.' Consequently, there is no longer a reason for the Bank to rediscount." ABF, PVCG, Meeting of January 6, 1972.

[58] The charge against the French financial system presented in the MSW report did in fact also address quantitative controls:

According to a first conception, which was widespread in 1945, and which has thus been frequently applied since the end of hostilities, one should construct monetary policy primarily through the use of

There existed before 1971 a money market in France and the central bank sometimes participated in it actively (Figure 2), but it was also entirely subordinated to the rediscounting policy as well as to the constraints of treasury financing.[59] The bank's interventions functioned in only one direction: their sole goal was to provide liquidity, not to absorb it. Put differently, the bank always intervened to lower rates and never to raise them. Indeed, banks initially refinanced themselves mainly through the central bank (*"en Banque,"* as contemporaries put it) and only went to the money market (*"hors Banque"*) when they exceeded their ceilings. Thus, the central bank intervened primarily to prevent the rates of treasury bonds and private bills on the money market from going too high in times when credit was quantitatively restricted. The Wormser reform of 1971 thus sought to make refinancing through the market the primary means for acting on bank liquidity, whereas it had hitherto been simply a means of adjustment, through which the effects of credit restrictions could be calibrated.

Wormser's audacity lay in his belief that a change in the central bank's tools and forms of intervention could precede and trigger the liberalization of the French banking system that he welcomed in his 1969 report. But could he really, through such a simple measure, attack the organization of credit as defined by the 1945 law, as well as the norms, practices and collective values that had developed over time?

Aware of the stakes and of the resistance that his project was likely to provoke, Wormser proceeded step-by-step and prudently. The discussion of the General Council on June 21 and the vote on the eligibility of new bills for the open market demonstrates that he faced what could at best be described as the Council's skepticism, at worst its outright opposition.[60] The governor also admitted that he had not received the support from the French president or the finance minister, with whom he shared his intention to make the

---

quantitative regulations. Regulations make it possible, it is said, by directing credit, to favor such and such activity that has been declared a priority. In this way, it has the advantage of better responding to the demands of an economy in which government interventions are numerous.

It also offers the possibility, to a certain extent, of placing a screen between particular sectors of the national economy and foreign countries. This policy leads not to the unity of the market for money, but to its fragmentation, not to a unity of rates, depending on the nature and duration of credits, but on their plurality. (Marjolin et al. 1969, p. 14)

[59] Information summarized below comes from various articles and notes that are included in ABF, 1330201101/4.

[60] ABF, PVCG, January 21, 1971. The personnel's representative, Maurice Gousseau, voted against. The former budget director, who was now head of Crédit Foncier, Roger Goetze, abstained. As a whole, members were skeptical. No one strongly supported the governor.

money market rate lower than the discount rate. Thus, he suggested that the General Council, as he had promised the minister, consider this measure as "experimental." Wormser thus dodged questions as to whether he thought this proposal would ultimately result in the elimination of discount ceilings. Finally, he attempted to convince the council with an unprecedented argument, explaining that this measure could, in his view, be justified due to the lowering of the discount rates of the Fed and the Bank of England. The Banque de France could thus use the money market rate to follow shifts in international rates, while still maintaining a high discount rate that determined credit conditions in France. As macroeconomic conditions in 1971 were good, Wormser's experimental phase went over relatively well and encouraged him to propose the elimination of discount ceilings on January 15, 1972. This measure, approved by the General Council, triggered a very hostile reaction on the part of the Banque de France's personnel, as well as that of companies and small banks. The grounds for their opposition was a fear of diminished access to credit for companies, as can be seen from the numerous recriminations that came to the Banque de France by way of its branches, which denounced a "premature and inopportune [shift] to the American system."[61] Small and medium-sized companies, notably those receiving financing from regional banks and which faced more difficult access to the money market, suffered from this reassessment of discounting, as the 1969 report had predicted.[62] As for the Banque de France's personnel, represented by the strong personality of Maurice Gousseau, they saw this measure as the end of discounting's traditional role and worried about

---

[61] A revealing example is a telex from the Sète Chamber of Commerce, which was passed on by the Nîmes branch, which spoke of a protest organized by small bankers, small and medium-sized businesses, and wine traders. ABF, 1360200701/242 (transmis à la Banque par succursale de Nîmes). It reads:

[We want to] draw your attention on the serious consequences of this decision. [H]enceforth banks must supply the totality of their commercial paper from their own assets. [T]he inevitable consequence will be that banks will limit discounting to their own clientele. [T]he commercial paper of small and medium-sized companies [will be] seriously hit by this measure. [B]anks risk giving priority to big company paper. [One] estimate[s] that the Banque de France will eliminate bills. [This is a] premature and inopportune American system.

[62] It is difficult to distinguish whether critics were primarily calling into question discounting's longstanding role at the Banque de France or the institution of credit established in 1945 (as seen in the spirited exchange between Wormser and Gousseau, the employees' representative, at the session of the General Council of January 6 (PVCG, January 6, 1972). This can presumably be explained by the fact that other instruments used by the institution, such as selectivity and credit controls, were still in place. Furthermore, the money market and the elimination of ceilings did not, in practice, replace discounting at the Banque de France.

its consequences for the future of the central bank, as well as the French economy.

Over the course of the year, the new way in which the money market was being used gave rise to a concern of a different kind. It quickly became apparent that, at the Banque de France, definitions of this market varied. This lack of coordination reflected different conceptions of the financial system and undermined the institution's functioning. On October 12, 1972, a very technical debate occurred in the General Council as to whether it was opportune for the bank to buy or sell bonds on the money market. Governor Wormser found himself in minority in his own council, several members of which – among them Deputy Governor Jean Saltes – insisting on the necessary distinction between the money market and the financial market, even as Wormser admitted to wanting to connect them. This was followed by a debate over this distinction, which some did not hesitate to describe as "theological." The upshot was the idea, defended notably by Pierre-Brossolette, that the French conception of money market was fundamentally different from that of the English idea of "open market," despite the fact that these words were often used synonymously.[63] This distinction once again reflected the Banque de France's traditional conception – which Wormser sought to refute – that central bank interventions in money creation must necessarily be connected to credit creation and cannot occur through the exchange of financial securities. The defenders of the traditional vision thus demand that the Banque only accept on the money market private securities that it could potentially rediscount (commercial paper, medium-term credit) and not private bonds.

A final measure taken in 1971, which in this instance does not concern the money market but minimum reserves, once again shows how the Banque de France was not prepared to abandon its conception of monetary creation based on credit. On April 1, 1971, banks were required to establish minimum reserves based no longer simply on their deposits but also on the credit they had made available to the economy. This new type of reserve (in proportion to exposures) applied not only to banks, but also to credit institutions (CDC, Crédit National and so on). This type of minimum reserve had no equivalent in Europe at this time, and its goal was, originally, to constitute an alternative to credit ceilings. The principle of this reform was announced at the same time as credit ceilings were lifted, in October 1970, with an explicit objective to avoid "further recourse to authoritarian quantitative limits on credit growth."[64]

[63]   ABF, PVCG, October 12, 1972.
[64]   ABF, 1331200301/162. "Le système des réserves obligatoires," DGC document, 1972.

The 1971 debates on the money market did not entirely overlap with those on credit selectivity. If the extension of this market was in fact a means of further reducing selectivity measures, it also called into question the French discounting tradition that dates to well before World War II (Baubeau 2004; Duchaussoy 2013) and to which the French banking system was accustomed and the Banque de France's employees – notably in the branches – attached. It also seems that open market intervention rested on a conception of monetary creation that was foreign to the Banque de France's habits and doctrine, which were based on credit. Even so, this doctrine, which posited a strong connection between credit, money and price levels, was profoundly challenged in the second half of the 1970s.

The Hybrid Return of Credit Ceilings (*encadrement du credit*)

Thus the development of money market interventions partially contradicted the principles of the credit policy that still prevailed at the beginning of the 1970s, be it the Banque de France's conception of its social purpose or its views about monetary creation. What could thus be described as institutional incoherence was the reason for a return to credit ceilings (though rediscount ceilings were not reestablished) in December 1972. The Banque de France had difficulty accepting this return to direct quantitative limits, which in this instance was done in coordination with a significant and rapid increase of the discount rate; for over a year, Governor Wormser refused to speak of "credit ceilings." True, the limit was placed higher, and thus the constraint was less great than in the past.[65] Most importantly, this measure was imposed by the Finance Ministry, rather than being the bank's initiative. Unlike with previous experiences, no debate within the CNC or the General Council preceded this decision. The return to credit controls, which recognized the inadequacies of the money market due to the low numbers of bills originating from banks was decided following a meeting of the European Community's finance ministers on October 30, 1972. The ministers had agreed to fight inflation through coordinated measures and by setting a quantitative goal (which was not officially announced): the increase in the money supply had to be equal in value to the growth in Gross National Product.[66] During the period of restrictive monetary policy

---

[65] Annual growth was set at 19% then at 17% in 1972 and 1973, as opposed to 10% in 1963 and 12% in 1969.

[66] Jean Truquet, "La 4e expérience française d'encadrement du crédit," ABF, 1415200801/9. See, too, Castel and Masse (1983, pp. 36–37). This decision is also mentioned in James (2012, p. 126).

of 1969–1970, Finance Minister Valéry Giscard d'Estaing had already expressed his desire to make credit controls a full-fledged government policy and to take complete responsibility for it.[67] That Wormser's primary goal was to develop the money market undoubtedly facilitated the transfer of responsibility for credit controls to the government. In the letter he wrote to the Professional Association of Banks to announce the end of credit ceilings in October 1970, the governor had become, on this matter, no more than the government's spokesperson: "As the Economy and Finance Minister informed the National Credit Council last Friday, the improvement of the country's economic and monetary situation makes it possible to end, without further delay, measures aimed at limiting credit that are currently in effect."[68]

The new phase of credits ceilings that began in December 1972 can be distinguished from previous experiences in five different ways. To begin with, ceilings would remain permanent until 1987, whereas they had previously been a short-term measure. Second, they were gradually accompanied by a secondary market of "credit rights," named "decontrolling market" ("*marché de désencadrement*"), which allowed banks that had surpassed their authorized exposure limits to purchase the right to exceed them from banks that were still under the limit. Third, the Banque de France established a mechanism of "supplementary reserves," which required banks that exceeded the credit limit to increase their reserves with the central banks. This reserves mechanism replaced the system of rediscounting penalties that had existed previously. Fourth, the return to credit controls ultimately resulted over the course of the 1970s in a rise in exemptions and was also accompanied by an increase in credits contracted at preferential rates with public and semi-public credit institutions. Finally, the new credit controls policy was accompanied by a policy of money supply targets.

---

[67] More extensive research – notably in the Finance Ministry archives – is needed to support this argument and to understand the origin of this change. Yet, the government's takeover of controlling credit is particularly clear when one reads the press clippings that I consulted (ABF, 133020110/11). In a way that bears no resemblance to earlier experiences, the decision over whether to continue or end credit controls seemed to belong entirely to the prime minister and the finance minister. This is evident in the titles of the newspaper stories: "The government is fine-tuning its calendar for measures to relax credit" (*Nouveau Journal*, December 13, 1969) and "The finance minister will hold on to credit controls after July" (1970, unattributed). Bordo and Eichengreen (2008) have analyzed a similar shift in the United States, where responsibility for monetary policy was partially transferred from the Fed to the Treasury beginning in 1965.

[68] ABF, 133020110/11, "Lettre du Grouverneur," October 27, 1970.

What Were the Primary Stakes of These Deep Institutional Changes?

The limitation of bank exposures did in fact become permanent, yet was less constraining than during earlier periods – 1958–1959, 1963–1965, 1968–1970 (see Chapter 4). A secondary market of "loan transfers" was thus created, on which banks could trade their "spreads," that is, the difference between their actual and their authorized exposures. This market, which was quickly dubbed the "decontrolling market" (*"marché de désencadrement"*) was a response on the part of authorities to interbank operations that were seeking to avoid exposure ceilings and, by the same token, additional reserves. To institutionalize these practices, the bank provided them with a legal framework with a circular of October 31, 1973. A second circular, dated October 13, 1978, further relaxed the rules for trading on this market. Even if this market's volume was relatively modest in relation to total bank exposures,[69] it revealed a profound change in the supervision of credit institutions, as a note from the General Credit Directory of June 16, 1978 emphasized:[70] credit ceilings, which had constrained each bank in a similar but temporary way, became general and permanent constraints to the whole system. And the weight of the constraint for each bank was now determined by market forces. It was a more or less disguised way of granting the market the ability to take into consideration banks' "heterogeneity." Only large banks were active on the decontrolling market, small banks being far more restricted, yet lacking sufficient funds to purchase spreads.

Yet in conjunction with this market, which sought to give more freedom to credit allocation between banks, Sylviane Guillaumont-Jeanneney (1991) has shown that late 1972 marked a return to what she calls "monetary *dirigisme*" and a rejection of the 1971 reform. Whereas the Banque de France favored the development of financial market and the decontrolling market, paradoxically it increased, over the course of the 1970s, the number of exemptions and thus bolstered selectivity (Galbraith 1982). The share of credits exempted from credit controls

---

[69] The transfers made reached 10 billion francs before the 1978 reform, then rose rapidly to around 20 billion. In 1982, the total amount of credit exposures was calculated to be 1,640 billion francs (including 840 for registered banks trading on the market) and transfers on the market reached, on January 4, 23 billion.

[70] ABF, 1360200701/160. NB: This box, as well as the preceding one (1360200701/159), contains most of the information and texts available on the *marché du désencadrement*.

reached 18.5% by 1975 – a figure that had never been attained previously – whereas at the end of 1972 it had only been 8%.[71] The policy of developing the money market was also contradicted by the increase in the share of loans at preferential rates that public and semi-public organizations had granted the economy. Economists of the Banque de France that sought to calculate these loans in the early 1980s found that their share fell rapidly in the early 1970s, from 48% in 1968 to 40.8% in 1974, but rose to 44.6% in 1978.[72] Variations on the money market could not affect the cost of these loans.

Among the other constraints that prevented the money market from functioning, one must emphasize the preferential rate the Banque de France had, since 1972, applied to the rediscounting of medium-term credit for exports outside the European Community and which were lower than open market rates. This preferential access to central bank refinancing was used to the maximum degree by banks in the late 1970s and the growth of the trade deficit blocked any chance of ending it (Guillaumont-Jeanneney 1982, 1991; Le Bourva 1979). Thus, whereas the proportion of fixed rate rediscounting of bank refinancing programs had gone from 93% in 1963 and 70% in 1968 to 15.9% in 1973, it rose back up to 40.5% in 1975, reaching 74.6% in 1980.

The entire array of exemptions, the existence of a "decontrolling" market that the bank found it difficult to supervise, as well as the weak efficiency of control through the money market rendered control of monetary policy increasingly complex and difficult. It is in this context that, beginning in 1973, the bank developed a "credit ceiling bite-mark indicator" (Sterdyniak & Vasseur 1985) derived from a monthly poll of households, companies and banks, which allowed the bank to know to what extent its policy reined in the economy. While use of this indicator must, of course, be understood in the context of the rise of statistical and econometric studies at the Banque de France in the early 1970s, the necessity of consulting public opinion also reveals the difficulties the bank faced in controlling the effects of its policy.

---

[71] See the document by Truquet quoted above in note 66, p. 5. See, too, Guillaumont-Jeanneney (1991, p. 529).

[72] ABF, 1415200801/3. "Possibilités et limites de politiques alternatives à l'encadrement du crédit." November 20, 1981.

Money Supply Targets and the Monetary Theory of Inflation

I will not discuss the implementation of monetary targeting in France in the 1970s in any detail here.[73] But while the targeting of M2's growth did not become official until 1977, it is important to understand that it had been practiced within the Banque de France since 1973. The meeting of Europe's finance ministers in 1972 and the example of the Bundesbank encouraged the bank to move toward the rule that ought to equalize growth of the money supply and that of nominal GDP.

It would, however, be misleading to see this change as the Banque de France's conversion to monetarism: first, because credit growth remained the privileged intermediary goal and second, because targeting did not entail a policy of monetary austerity and a drastic fight against inflation. Quite on the contrary: monetary targeting paradoxically came into effect at the Banque de France at the same time that the idea that inflation was not a monetary phenomenon was on the rise. Thus, in 1975, at a time when targeting was not yet officially practiced, studies by the bank's DASM were in general very skeptical of this new goal. The first econometric analyses conducted by the Banque de France concluded that the money supply was difficult to control. They explained this difficulty by pointing to banks' excessive indebtedness to the central bank: "the size of banks' refinancing needs, given the weakness and irregularity of external assistance as well as the Treasury's limited recourse to monetary creation, led the Banque de France to give primary consideration to its responsibilities to preserve the equilibrium of the banking system, and prevented it from limiting its support."[74] This argument sounds strange in light of the bank's conduct over the two previous decades: henceforth, there would seem to an opposition between credit policy and control of the money supply.

Following a different approach, some of the bank's economists pointed to targeting's clumsiness, due to the excessively high levels of the chosen targets: it was noted, for example, that the money supply increased by only 6% per year during the restrictive period between 1969 and 1970, whereas

---

[73] On the connection between econometric studies and monetary targeting at the Banque de France, see Feiertag (2006a). See Sterdyniak and Vasseur (1985) for a review and definition of M2 targets starting 1977.

[74] ABF, 1417200405 /1. Note from January 8, 1976: "La progression des liquidités et le contrôle de l'émission de monnaie Banque centrale pendant le VIIe Plan."

no target less than 12% was considered during the 1970s.[75] Whereas French inflation reached 11% in 1976 and the Bundesbank had, for its part, adopted, a goal of increasing the money supply by 7% (Beyer et al. 2009), the Banque de France chose 13% as its target for M2 growth. The predictions and simulations undertaken by the bank's various services in 1976 clearly show that implicit inflation targets were never under 11% annually.[76] Needless to say that it was much higher than the average inflation rate since 1948.

The economic slowdown underway since 1973 and the rise in unemployment that began in 1975 were significant factors in justifying the central bank's and government's refusal to establish a policy as restrictive as had been in place in recent decades. In the Banque de France's studies, I found no mention of the Phillips curve as a guide for monetary policy choices.[77] Most important, the new idea emerges that inflation is not a monetary phenomenon, as can be seen in a 1975 note by the DASM:

Monetary restrictions from 1968 and 1973 had a very weak impact on prices compared to earlier restrictive periods. Prices seem to be led by a trend that is completely independent from the rhythm of monetary creation. Under these conditions, the price that must be paid, since 1967, to fight inflation seems excessive in terms of monetary creation and real production in relation to earlier periods. Thus it is not unreasonable to conclude that monetary policy bears little responsibility for the current economic crisis.[78]

According to the Banque's research notes, the factors responsible for inflation were salary indexing and the importation of inflation from the United States. This thesis was premised primarily on the end of the Bretton Woods system and the salary increases agreed upon in 1968.[79] It led to the success of two books by influential economists, François Perroux (1971) and Jean Denizet (1977), and it later reappeared in the report of the eighth "plan" in 1981.

---

[75] ABF, 1417200405 /1. Note from January 7, 1976 by J. P. Patat, "La régulation de la masse monétaire en 1973, 1974, 1975." The unofficial targets of monetary growth in 1973, 1974 and 1975 are, respectively, 15%, 14% and 13%.

[76] ABF, 1417200405 /1. Note by Jacques Pecha from March 1976, "Comparaisons entre les prévisions concernant l'évolution de la dépense nationale brute en 1976 selon les trois variantes de la direction de la prévision."

[77] In France, there was no significant negative relationship between inflation and the unemployment rate during the *Trente Glorieuses*. In the early 1970s, the unemployment rate was not yet a political problem and, according to the INSEE, it did not exceed 3% in 1974. Inflation and unemployment increased in tandem during the 1970s, and it was only the austerity policies launched in 1983 that brought to light the negative relationship between inflation and the unemployment rate.

[78] ABF, 1417200405 /1. Note "L'évolution de l'écart entre PIB et M2 de 1950 à 1975."

[79] The Grenelle Accords raised the minimum wage by 35% and all salaries by 10%.

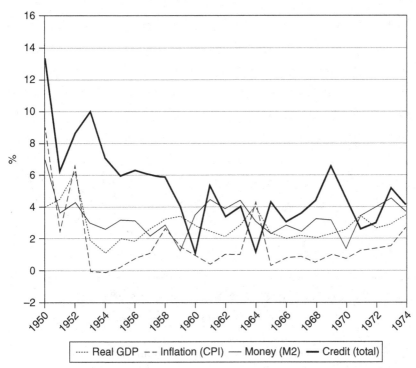

Figure 3 Growth rates of credit, money, GDP and inflation, 1950–1974
Source: CNC and INSEE. Quarterly growth rate (moving average over three quarters).

Figure 3 confirms the uncoupling, between 1968 and 1970, of the money supply growth and nominal GDP growth (i.e., price inflation + real GDP growth), which was noted by Banque de France's services. The two figures soon returned, however, to a similar pattern. The comparative progression of prices and salaries (Figure 4) does in fact demonstrate the size of the salary increases of 1968, but does not allow the subsequent conclusion that a radical change occurred in the progression of the latter and that of consumer prices compared to previous decades. More thorough research would be necessary to assess the validity of the Banque de France's arguments about the changing nature of inflation in the early 1970s.[80]

The utility of monetary targeting was thus the subject of constant debate within the Banque de France during the unofficial experimentation that occurred from 1973 to 1976. The adoption of an official target beginning

---

[80] It is particularly essential to consider the fact that inflation was very much a global phenomenon (Ciccarelli and Mojon 2010).

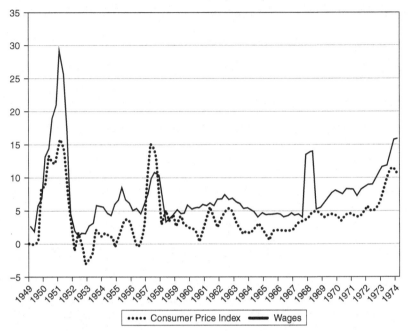

Figure 4 Inflation of wages and the consumer price index, 1949–1974
Source: INSEE (1981), quarterly values, year on year growth rate.

in 1977 was not the result of a conviction, but of a recommendation found in the seventh "plan" of 1976 that savers be provided a nominal anchor in order to promote recourse to the financial market. This new doctrine from the Planning office, which was notably advocated by Treasury director Michel Camdessus, resulted in a "law to direct savings to corporate financing" of July 1978, which eliminated taxes on income invested in stock. The main idea was that it is necessary to promote "long-term savings" in order to ensure a non-inflationary financing of investment.[81] Thus the Banque de France's official announcement of a monetary target in 1977 was essentially motivated by the idea that it would act on inflation not directly but by allowing the development of a financial market, reducing in this way the amount of banking credit. This was in line with a general movement at the end of the 1970s to increase the channeling of households' savings toward the stock market (Quennouëlle-Corre 2015, ch. 8). Targets were maintained

---

[81] ABF, 1417200405 /1. Note of October 24, report of the meeting on "le marché financier et le financement des investissements à l'aube du VIIe Plan."

at a high level in order to prevent them from being greatly exceeded.[82] The discussions of a study group on inflation that was formed at the Banque de France in 1976, consisting notably of the economists Robert Marjolin and Edmond Malinvaud, show there was agreement on the need for a policy focusing on income and financial market liberalization as a way of reducing inflation. The arguments advanced to support the latter distinguish between, on the one hand, nominal interest rates and real interest rates and, on the other, past and anticipated inflation. A money supply target allowed the bank to anchor anticipated inflation and thus made it possible for its agents to anticipate real interest rates, the effect of which was to increase bond purchases even when inflation was high (bond rates at the time were 12% and the inflation rate anticipated by the Banque de France was approximately 10%). Even so, money supply targets, even when high, were widely exceeded (Sterdyniak & Vasseur 1985), which undoubtedly was part of the reason the financial market failed to take off before the "law on savings liberalization," which was adopted in 1978.

The targeting of the money supply's growth thus occurred at the very moment when the monetary theory of inflation had fewer and fewer followers inside the Banque de France. For more than twenty years, the quantitative control of credit (rediscounting ceilings and credit ceilings) had been justified on the basis of the theory that the growth of credit increased the money supply, and thus inflation.[83] In the early 1970s, this relationship seemed broken and inflation was largely attributed to other causes. Quantitative control was thus used for a different purpose and in a far less rigorous way than in previous periods of restrictive monetary policy. It went hand-in-hand with targeting the money supply as a broad goal, which made it possible to develop non-monetary approaches to financing investment, not just as a policy aimed at short-term stabilization. As with Banque de France loans to the Treasury (see Chapter 5), the perceived solution to the inflationary problem was to turn to the financial market. The theoretical coherence that characterized the place of monetary policy in the institutionalization of credit seemed in jeopardy, not least because the national framework in which this reasoning had developed seemed less and

---

[82] In 1976, the government attempted a brief experiment of price controls which, for the first time since 1948, applied to all goods and services. It also placed a cap on salary increases.

[83] Feiertag (2017, p. 220) quotes Pierre Berger, director of research of the Banque, at an international conference in Rome in 1974, saying that "within their traditional concept [credit ceilings], the French authorities are seeking to control the development of money supply."

less appropriate.[84] The fears expressed by Governor Baumgartner in 1958 seemed more real than ever: credit ceilings had to be selective but temporary, in order not to favor economic rents. When the General Commissariat of the Plan declared itself in favor of eliminating credit controls in 1981, it did so in the name of better economic science rather than less restrictive monetary policy. This demonstrates once again how much the meaning of the latter had changed compared to the previous decade.[85]

The conclusions of this study match those of recent studies that have studied how central banks in the United States and England allowed inflation to develop over the course of the 1970s.[86] They are notably similar to those of Batini and Nelson (2005) and Capie (2010), who have shown how the Bank of England adhered to the idea that inflation was no longer primarily caused by an increase in the money supply but by wage policies. Yet, as also importantly highlighted by Needham (2014) in the English case, it does not mean that central bankers neglected the money supply. There have always been some kinds of implicit credit and money targetry at the Banque de France, and extensive studies on this matter were conducted years before official decisions to announce M2 targets in 1977. The Banque de France and the French government arrived at a somewhat similar analysis. They concluded that bringing down inflation solely by controlling credit and money would be too costly for the economy and that what had to be emphasized was a policy of fixed exchange rates, wage regulation, financial liberalization and price controls.[87]

But we have shown how the Banque de France's doctrine during the 1970s must be understood in the context of an institutional evolution that resulted in a reconsideration of the principles upon which monetary

---

[84] Thus beginning in 1977, Banque de France economists attempted to develop a new theoretical framework based on the concept of "overdraft economy," which they freely borrowed from John Hicks (Goux 1990), notably in order to adapt recent theoretical advances in the English-speaking world (in particular the theory of exchange rates, financial intermediation and the determination of interest rates) to the French financial system, which continued to be characterized by a high level of bank indebtedness to the central bank.

[85] At this stage, it may seem strange that exposure limits were still set in general terms. Not until late1984 were they determined on an individual basis, in function of each bank's reserves, which of course brought an immediate end to the decontrolling market. Quantitative limits were finally eliminated in 1987.

[86] A summary of this abundant literature can be found in Romer and Romer (2002) and Bordo and Orphanides (2013).

[87] Price controls were reestablished from 1976 to 1977 and, for the first time since 1949, applied to all goods. During the 1950s and 1960s, they had been used primarily in the case of minimum wages, agriculture and energy (Franck 1979).

policy was based in previous decades. As we see it, the loss of the institutional coherence of the "coordinated capitalism" that Barry Eichengreen (2006) highlighted in the case of the labor market can also be seen in monetary policy. In the early 1970s, the Banque de France's relationship to the banking system, credit allocation, the government and even monetary theory were thrown into disarray, yet no new guiding principles emerged to replace them. The Great Inflation was also the fruit of these institutional changes. Proposals to liberalize financial markets and end credit policy were presented as a solution to high inflation rates.

CONCLUSION TO PART I

These three chapters have shown how the principles that organized credit in France from 1945 until the 1970s were established and evolved. I paid special attention to what I defined as the three components of the institutionalization of credit: the legal framework which defines the relevant actors and distributes their powers, the beliefs about state intervention in credit allocation ("credit selectivity") and monetary policy as a way to control credit in order to fight inflation. These various elements of the institution interacted in ways that were more or less coherent and complementary, often while following different temporalities.

The development of credit policy in France during the postwar decades is not the story of a gradual and unobstructed liberalization. The "debudgetization" and partial liberalization of the economy advocated by the Pinay-Rueff Plan in 1958 initially had no direct application in the realm of credit, save for a decrease in Banque de France advances to the government and in medium-term loans rediscounted by the Banque de France. The bank's support for the economy and its legitimacy in intervening in credit allocation were not called into question at the beginning of the Fifth Republic. In the course of the 1960s, two visions came into conflict: one that claimed that the existing system was justified solely by the need for reconstruction, the other seeing it as a way of ensuring productive investment and the national interest. For many, the decline in medium-term rediscounting and the relative growth of bank loans that occurred during the 1960s were indeed signs that reconstruction was complete; yet they did not challenge the principle of "credit selectivity." From 1966 to 1972, new proposals appeared and promoted the idea that prices and markets had to be given back their distributive role. In a context of economic crisis, the 1970s witnessed the confrontation between these two visions, yet neither truly triumphed over the other and the rules inscribed in the 1945 law were never rewritten. The consequence was a hybrid system, a failed liberalization and a displacement of the terms of the debate: credit was no longer the focal point of inflation control, and discussions came to focus on the preservation of financial advantages, which was favored by French banks' fragmentation or specialization.

In the late 1970s, French monetary policy thus seemed poorly armed to confront the challenge of inflation: the open market was not fully operational, credit controls offered little more than a vast framework avoidance of which had become the norm, and no rules of conduct or coherent doctrine had ever replaced that which had constituted the heart of inflation control over previous decades. One cannot understand the Great Inflation of the 1970s and the subsequent financial liberalization of the 1980s without considering the institutional changes that occurred in the 1970s, which broke with the principles of the two previous decades. Compared to the previous years, contradictions became apparent in the credit policy of the 1970s: some debates and new monetary policy instruments tended to call credit selectivity into question, while others tended to reinforce it. Moreover, theories that explained inflation by citing external causes – other than currency and credit growth – abounded, partially challenging the central bank's role in controlling credit. In terms of central banking, the 1970s were very different from the Bretton Woods period. As Adam Tooze (2014) rightly wrote in a recent text about the need to reconsider the history of the Great Inflation, these were much more adventurous years in terms of policy. By contrast – and against common wisdom – Bretton Woods featured a remarkably strict discipline in terms of fiscal and monetary policy, as the previous chapters have largely exemplified. What we have interpreted as a process of disinstitutionalization in the 1970s – i.e., when principles established in the late 1940s were questioned – can also appear as a time of experimentation and hybrid policy instruments. Either way, it was an age of fracture (Rodgers 2011), rather than the obvious continuation and accomplishment of the postwar model. In this story, terms such as Keynesianism and monetarism add much more confusion to our understanding of the evolution of monetary operations, statements about the stance of monetary policy and the role of central banks in credit allocation. In the French context, they are inadequate to understand the intellectual context and culture of decision-makers.

Thus it is equally misleading to consider the period from 1945 to 1980 in its entirety and to confine oneself to characterizing it as an age of "*dirigisme*," as do many works of political science (Zysman 1983; Schmidt 1996), without recognizing the evolutions and tensions that traversed it.

If the legal framework persists and remains unchanged, the government's and central bank's means of intervention, as well as the way of conceiving the system, vary significantly over time. When one takes into consideration these developments, it becomes more suspect to interpret the rupture of the 1980s solely through foreign experiments, whether it be European integration and the end of Bretton Woods (Loriaux 1991), financial globalization (Perez 1998; Fourcade & Babb 2002), or the shock of Volcker's deflation in the United States. The liberalization of the French financial system in the early 1980s cannot, for its part, be interpreted solely as the inevitable consequence of foreign shocks; it was above all a response to the internal contradictions that became apparent in the course of the 1970s. It simultaneously called into question the various meanings of the term credit control and altered the organization of the banking system and financial markets, as well as the Banque de France's intervention tools.[88]

Even if it is clear that international economic developments – particularly the opening up of financial markets and the economy, the growth of the Eurodollars market, the end of Bretton Woods, the oil crises, as well as the practices and theoretical frameworks of other central banks – had a strong impact on the institution, the idea that credit selectivity had become a way of preserving economic rents that were opposed to criteria of economic profitability and the general interest cannot be traced to exogenous factors. While some analysts (Galbraith 1982; Zysman 1983; Katzenstein 1985) see France in the early 1980s as an example of a "strong" state capable of carrying out major reforms, this conclusion shows, on the contrary, the weakness of divided state (Hall 1986) and a central bank inclined to doubt its ability to control inflation and to direct credit on the basis of unanimously acknowledged criteria.[89] The result was a "disembedding" of credit (Polanyi 1944; Ruggie 1982), in the sense that the idea that it was possible to define economic and social criteria governing the allocation of credit independently of the market mechanism vanished.[90]

---

[88] The effect of liberalization was the development of financial markets sustained by public debt (O'Sullivan 2007) and a reallocation of credit that resulted in reduced concentration and the end to the financing of the least efficient firms (Bertrand et al. 2007). On these reforms, see, too, Guillaumont-Jeanneney (1986) and Mélitz (1990).

[89] For an overall picture of the reform of the French civil service during this period, see Bezes (2009).

[90] There are still some debates on whether, in Polanyi's thoughts, disembeddedness leads to an alternative set of institutions (and a new economic process of reembeddedness) or whether the advent of market society entails an economy actually disembedded from social relations (Behrent 2016). These questions apply here fully.

The story of the Banque de France from 1945 to the 1980s shows that the development of the money market and credit policy can be explained primarily through the relationship between the central bank and other banks. Hence, the previous chapters have studied in detail the operating procedures of the central bank and how bank credit and liquidity was controlled. Government relations changed little, though advances to the Treasury did decline under the Fifth Republic and power dynamics became less favorable to the Banque de France by the early 1970s. It is striking to see that the rhetorical arguments elaborated in the 1970s and which led to the 1984 reforms were remarkably similar to those elaborated in the 1930s that led to the 1945 law. Though these arguments recommended contradictory policies, reforms in both instances were justified by the idea that the Banque de France had abandoned the general interest and privileged economic rents within the banking sector while ignoring investment and growth. This is how the turn to the market and the end of credit policy were motivated. By contrast, arguments about the central bank's independence were absent from the reform plans and criticisms of the Banque de France's policy.

PART II

MANAGING CREDIT

A journey through the last century may, by destroying what Bertrand Russell once called the "dogmatism of the untraveled," help in formulating a broader and more enlightened view of the pertinent problems and in replacing the absolute notions of what is "right" and what is "wrong" by a more flexible and relativistic approach.
Alexander Gerschenkron, *Economic Backwardness in Historical Perspective*, 1962, p. 27

4

Monetary Policy without Interest Rates

Domestic Macroeconomic Effects
and International Issues of Credit Controls

Despite their importance in the history of central banking, the quantitative tools of credit control presented in the previous chapters remain largely absent from the standard literature on the effects of monetary policy. Since traditional econometric methods usually consider interest rates to be the primary instrument of monetary policy, it is difficult to compare the effectiveness of quantitative controls with the standard results obtained by Sims (1992) and Christiano et al. (1999) concerning post-1970s "conventional" monetary policy. As with similar policies in Europe under the Bretton Woods system, we have neither a comprehensive account of the policy decisions of the Banque de France regarding the fight against inflation, nor a quantitative evaluation of their effects.[1]

The first contribution of this chapter is to demonstrate that an effective way to assess the stance of monetary policy when interest rates are not the primary instrument is to follow what monetary economists have called a "narrative approach" (Friedman & Schwartz 1963; Romer & Romer 1989), that is, to examine archival evidence directly concerning policy makers' intentions and decisions. Put differently, the so-called "narrative

---

[1] Sections I–III of this chapter are reproduced from Monnet (2014) with some modifications and updates. I thank the American Economic Association for allowing me to reproduce this published article. Since this publication, Aikman et al. (2016) have provided a thorough quantitative analysis of the effects of quantitative controls in England from 1959. Compared to France, they find a more modest disconnection between interest rates and quantitative controls and a lesser impact of credit controls on macroeconomic variables outside bank loans. These results are indicative of the central bank differences between France and England during this period, despite the overall similarity of the instruments. Klingelhöfer and Sun (2017) provide a similar analysis of Chinese credit controls in a much more recent period (2000–2015) and also note that these instruments are used for achieving traditional monetary policy objectives.

approach" – at least in the way it is used here – is defined as opposed to a purely statistical approach. It aims at characterizing the policy stance (restrictive or expansionary) by looking at the decision process of policy-making rather than by using a single statistical series (such as the interest rates or the money base). It is inherently a historical approach in that it seeks to take into account the full context and evolution of decision-making to assess the objectives of the policy institution. Moreover, it is a way to assess the direction of causation between economic variables and policy actions. I argue below that the very nature of credit policy make the "narrative approach" especially necessary in order to avoid misunderstandings about the policy of the central bank and its effects. It is extremely challenging to assess the stance of monetary policy without interest rates. No reliable quantitative indicator exists concerning French monetary policy from 1948 to 1973, since the central bank had to change its instruments constantly to adapt both to financial innovation and to the circumvention of previous sets of instruments by the banks. Contrary to interest rates, quantitative controls take different forms over time in order to remain effective. Using extensive archival evidence from the Banque de France on the use of a wide set of quantitative credit and liquidity controls, I measure the monetary policy stance with a dummy variable denoting restrictive episodes. In total, six episodes of restrictive monetary policy are identified.

The second contribution of this chapter is to combine the narrative approach with a VAR (vector autoregressive) estimation to demonstrate that quantitative controls on credit and money had a strong influence on nominal and real variables, but not on interest rates. The VAR estimation techniques are frequently used by economists to estimate the effects of monetary policy in other contexts but they had not been used previously to investigate monetary policy without interest rates. I find that monetary policy shocks (i.e., restrictive credit controls) had a significant and sustained impact on production and the price level when I use a "narrative" measure of monetary policy in a VAR, and I find a disconnect between quantities (of money and credit) and prices (interest rates). Conversely, a shock to the discount rate or to the money market rate in a VAR model does not produce significant or consistent responses in production and prices. Indeed, looking at interest rates gives a wrong picture of the effects of central banks' decisions on inflation and production.

These results on the Banque de France's policy cast new light on the importance of monetary policy in the European Golden Age of growth after World War II and under the Bretton Woods system, periods of fixed exchange rates and ubiquitous financial restraints.[2] To date, the literature primarily considers fiscal policy and productivity shocks as factors explaining business fluctuations in Western Europe during the period preceding the Great Inflation (see Battilossi et al. 2010 for a survey). I find monetary and credit policy also mattered. Over this period, monetary policy shocks in France explain approximately 40% of the variance in industrial production and price levels. When policy turned restrictive, industrial production and prices decreased by 5% within twenty months.[3]

The disconnection between interest rates and credit quantities highlighted here has additional important implications for our understanding of the international monetary system during this period. The standard theoretical framework to understand monetary policy and capital controls under Bretton Woods is the Mundell-Fleming model, giving rise to the Mundell trilemma or "unholy trinity of international finance" (Goodman & Pauly 1993; Obstfeld & Taylor 2004; Ghosh & Qureshi 2016). This framework – widely used both in economic history or political sciences – posits that capital controls are necessary to guarantee monetary policy autonomy in a fixed exchange rate regime. The important assumption in this model is that the interest rate is a good indicator of the monetary policy stance or is itself the main instrument of the central bank. As this chapter shows, however, quantitative instruments (credit controls, reserve requirements, etc.) could allow central banks to disconnect their interest rate from the overall domestic monetary policy stance in order to avoid the constraints of international finance. Central banks could let their interest rates in line with international rates while running an autonomous monetary policy on the domestic side through the use of quantitative instruments. Credit controls were a way to escape the constraints of international finance. Then, capital controls were still necessary but not for the reason highlighted in the Mundell framework: capital controls played a role in making credit controls effective. They prevented firms and banks from borrowing from abroad when domestic rediscount or credit ceilings were in place.

---

[2] It is common in the literature to characterize the period from the end of World War II to the Great Inflation as the Golden Age of European growth (Temin 2002). No extant study provides econometric estimations of the effects of French monetary policy over the period due to a lack of appropriate measures. Sims (1992) estimates a VAR on French data from 1966 to 1990, suggesting a very strong price puzzle. Also, using a VAR approach, Bruneau and De Bandt (1999) choose 1972 as a start date, and Mojon (1998) and Clarida et al. (1998) chose 1986. In all of these studies, difficulties that arise using the interest rate as a measure of monetary policy – rather than lack of data – probably motivated the sample choice.

[3] Contrary to most VAR studies, there is no price puzzle, that is prices respond immediately to the policy shocks when they are properly measured.

For simplicity, I use the term monetary policy to refer to the whole set of central bank operations in this chapter. However, two kinds of instrument are distinguished during the analysis since the Banque de France used both direct actions on credit (credit and rediscount ceilings) and controls of the money supply through liquidity or reserve ratios. And, as explained in detail in the first part of the book, monetary and credit policy were intertwined in many respects.

I INSTRUMENTS AND OPERATING PROCEDURES OF THE BANQUE DE FRANCE

As previously described, the Banque de France began pursuing an active refinancing policy in order to support credit growth after World War II. Banks could rediscount bills up to five years (called "rediscountable medium-term credit"), whereas before World War II, the Banque's practice had always been to discount only three-month bills. This discount window policy required strong safeguards to avoid inflationary booms. The central bank started to fight postwar inflation in September 1948 (Casella & Eichengreen 1993), inventing various quantitative instruments to cut price levels rapidly without raising interest rates (Kriz 1951). In subsequent years, the Bank made extensive use of quantitative instruments, and invented many new ones to avoid the two-digit inflation rate which had been seen from 1945 to 1948.

The consensus view of the period is that the official discount rate of the Banque de France "had lost its meaning."[4] As the Bank's management repeatedly pointed out, the discount rate was used primarily for "its psychological effect"[5] because the price elasticity of credit demand was too low and there was no willingness to give a greater role to interest rates and market forces in the allocation of credit (Chapters 2 and 3). Policymakers also called the discount rate a "qualitative" instrument, as opposed to direct credit controls, which they referred to as "quantitative" instruments.[6] Throughout the period, the Banque de France's discount rate remained low, sometimes negative in real terms, and it was adjusted largely in line with

---

[4] "La politique du crédit en France," *Revue du personnel de la Banque de France*, No. 5, November 1954.

[5] This sentiment is notably expressed in ABF, PVCG, September 30, 1948 by Governor E. Monick and in ABF, PVCG, October 11, 1951, p. 511, April 11, 1957, p. 278, by Governor Baumgartner. All quotations are my translations of the original French from the archives of the Banque de France (ABF). Original quotations are available in the online appendix.

[6] Notably expressed by Governor Baumgartner, PVCG, October 11, 1951.

the US interest rate. In Monnet (2016), I showed that the only variable significantly correlated with the discount rate of the Banque de France was the discount rate of the US Federal Reserve (see also Figures 15 and 16). Although they took different forms across countries, quantitative controls on money and credit were not limited to France (see Chapter 7). An easy way to show how unimportant interest rates were during this period is to calculate an anachronistic "Taylor rule" (set as in Taylor 1993, 1998). This rule was designed by John Taylor in the early 1990s to describe the policy of the US Fed and other central banks whose main instruments was the interest rate. Since then it has been used by many, including Taylor (1998), to look at the history of central banking (Orphanides 2003). In a Taylor rule, the interest depends on the inflation rate and the output gap (i.e., deviation of current output from the trend). The nominal interest rate reacts to the inflation rate with a coefficient greater than 1. This is, in theory, the only way for an active monetary policy to stabilize inflation. Figure 5 makes clear that the Banque de France in the 1950s and 1960s did not follow a Taylor rule. The interest rate implied by the Taylor rule is generally much higher than the one set by the Banque de France.[7] Inflation did not increase infinitely, however: in several occasions, price stabilization was not achieved by increasing interest rates to levels that would have been necessary to bring inflation and money growth down by an equivalent amount. This suggests that not only was the discount rate not the Banque de France's main instrument, but it did not reflect the general stance of monetary policy.

There is much anachronism in applying a Taylor rule to postwar France. Part I of the book has already provided information on the many other instruments that were used by the central bank so that interest rates could remain stable. The following sections go deeper into the details and chronology of central bank instruments and monetary policy implementation in order to offer a comprehensive view of how the Banque could affect credit and money creation without manipulating interest rates.

The Banque de France primarily used three main kinds of quantitative instrument: rediscount ceilings (borrowing limits at the central bank window), liquidity or reserve ratios (also called securities and cash reserve requirements respectively) and direct control of bank lending to the economy (credit ceilings).[8] Table 1 shows the primary instruments used

---

[7]   It is lower in 1953, 1954 and 1955 when the Banque ran an expansionary policy while keeping its discount rate almost stable.

[8]   I use the terms rediscount and discount interchangeably when discussing the central bank's refinancing operations as the Banque de France only discounted bank loans (i.e., rediscount) after World War II.

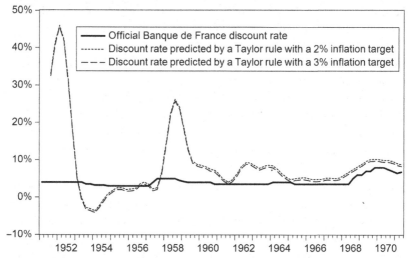

Figure 5 Simulated "Taylor rule" and the actual Banque de France discount rate
Note: the specification of the Taylor rule follows Taylor (1998). The output gap and the
inflation rate are smoothed over three quarters.

over the period and specifies when they were used. The way they functioned
is described in the next section. Table 2 shows all the changes in the values
of these instruments over the period 1948–1973.

Main Instruments Used by the Central Bank

Rediscount Ceilings and Refinancing Operations

Starting in September 1948, the monetary authorities set maximum rediscount limits for individual institutions. The Banque de France determined
these ceilings on a discretionary basis, according to its information on each
bank's needs. Thus, the value of each rediscount ceiling was set for prudential or distributive purposes, but a simultaneous change in all ceilings
could be used to decrease or increase the aggregate quantity of credit in
the economy. For instance, the central bank could decrease all the ceilings
by 10% in order to restrict the supply of bank credit to the economy. The
Banque de France's discount rate remained below the interbank rate until
January 1971 so it was always more beneficial for banks to borrow up to
their rediscount ceiling before seeking financing on the interbank market.
In January 1971, however, the Banque de France began prioritizing the

Table 1 *Instruments of monetary policy*

Type of instruments	Introduction	Abolition	Note
Discount ceilings and penalty rates			
Individual bank discount ceilings	Sep. 1948	Jan. 1972	Several exemptions.
Enfer rate (also called pension A) and *super-enfer* rate (also called pension B)	Oct. 1951	Dec. 1967	
Fixed rate pension	Dec. 1967	Jan. 1972	
Ratios (securities and cash reserve requirements)			
Floor on government paper	Sep. 1948	Sep. 1967	
Liquid asset ratio	Dec. 1960	Jan. 1967	
(*coéfficient de trésorerie*)			
Reserve requirements on liabilities	Jan. 1967	1998	
Reserve requirements on credit	Apr. 1971	Jan. 1987	
Minimum portfolio of medium-term credit	Jan. 1967	Jan. 1985	
Supplementary reserves	Feb. 1970	Jan. 1987	Only when credit ceilings in place.
Credit ceilings			
Central bank authorization for large loans	Feb. 1947	Feb. 1957	
Maximum limit on bank credit growth (credit ceilings)	Feb. 1958	Jan. 1987	Only temporarily before 1972. Several exemptions.

Notes: This table lists the names of all the quantitative instruments used by the Banque de France and specifies when they were first implemented (introduction) and when they were last used (abolition). See the text for details on the use and definition of the instruments.

money (interbank) market over the discount window for its primary refinancing operations. It subsequently set its discount rate above the interbank market rate. Consequently, rediscount ceilings were abolished in January 1972 (Chapter 3).

In October 1951, the Banque introduced two penalty rates for discounts granted in excess of the ceilings: one for the first 10% of credit above the ceiling, and another for credit over and above the first 10% margin. These were known respectively as the "evil rate" (*taux d'enfer*) and the "super-evil rate" (*taux de super-enfer*), or *pension A* and *pension B*. As use of this excess

Table 2 *Changes in the values of the policy instruments in use, 1948–1973*

Bank by bank discount ceiling

Fixed in September 1948; 20% decrease in July and August 1957; 15% decrease in November 1957; 20% increase in June 1968; 20% decrease in November 1968; 10% decrease (20% for discounts above 30 million French francs) in October 1970.

Enfer and super-enfer (i.e., penalty rates)

"Enfer" was 2% above the Bank discount rate until April 1958, 3% above until March 1959, 2.5% until July 1959 and then 1% above. "Super-enfer" was 3% above until July 1957, 5% above until April 1958, 7% until July 1958, 5% until March 1959, 2% above until June 1964, 3.5% until April 1965 and then 2.5%.

Fixed rate pension

Set 2.5% above the Banque de France's discount rate.

Government paper floor (*plancher de bons du Trésor*)

95% of the 1948 level and 20% of new deposits in September 1948); 25% of total deposits in July 1956; 20% in December 1960; 17.5% in June 1961; 15% in March 1962; 13% in January 1964; 10% in May 1964; 7.5% in October 1964; 5% in December 1965.

Liquid asset ratio (*coefficient de trésorerie*)

30% in December 1960; 32% in January 1962; 35% in February 1963; 36% in May 1963; 34% in June 1964; 36% in July 1964; 34% in October 1964; 36% in August 1965; 34% in November 1965; 32% in December 1965; 35% in January 1966; 32% in March 1966; 31% in June 1966; 32% in October 1966.

Reserve requirements on liabilities

2.5% in January 1967; 4.5% in April 1967; 6.5% in July 1967; 8.5% in October 1967; 10.5% in November 1968; 6.5% in June 1969; 6% in January 1970; 8% in June 1970; 10% in July 1970; 9.5% in April 1971; 11.5% in May 1971; 14% in December 1972; (on residents) 11% in March 1972; 15% in July 1972.

Reserve requirements on credit

0.25% in April 1971; 0.5% in May 1971; 1.5% in July 1971; 3% in August 1971; 2% in December 1971; 4% in June 1972; 33% in November 1972; 0% in June 1974.

Minimum portfolio of medium-term credit

20% in January 1967; 19% in May 1967; 18% in June 1967; 17% in July 1967; 16% in November 1967; 14% in June 1968; 13% in July 1968; 14% in November 1968; 15% in October 1969; 16% in April 1970; 14% in July 1971; 12.5% in May 1972; 10% in December 1972; 7% in January 1973.

Supplementary reserves

Proportion of credit exceeding the legal limit and of the institution's total outstanding credit. February to June 1970. Reintroduced in December 1972.

Table 2 (*cont.*)

Central bank authorization for large loans

Loans over 30 million francs in October 1947; 50 million in February 1948; 100 million in April 1950; 500 million in October 1951.

Maximum growth in bank credit (credit ceilings)

Introduced in February 1958, no credit growth (except export credit) allowed. Abolished in February 1959. Reintroduced in February 1963: annual growth in total credit limited to 12%, then 10% in September 1963. Abolished in June 1965. Reintroduced in November 1968: growth in total credit limited to 4% (except rediscountable medium-term credit and housing credit) between September and December 1968, and 1% between September 1968 and January 1969. Then 10% annual growth in 1969, and 6% in the first half of 1970. Abolished in June 1970. Reintroduced in November 1972: 16% maximum growth between September 1972 and September 1973; 12% maximum growth between January 1973 and January 1974.

---

refinancing decreased, the distinction between *enfer* and *super-enfer* was dropped in 1967 and replaced by a single rate called the *fixed rate pension*.

The rediscount ceilings did not apply to medium-term bills (i.e., with maturities of one to five years) which became rediscountable at the Banque de France after World War II. These bills were given preferential treatment in order to finance medium- and long-term investments and economic reconstruction in the 1950s. By the end of the 1950s, once the reconstruction period was largely over, banks were better able to finance themselves and were thus less dependent on the central bank's discount window. The proportion of short-term credit in bank balance sheets had decreased significantly, and it became necessary to control medium-term credit in order to curb credit growth and inflation. Consequently, rediscount ceilings were replaced with credit ceilings as the primary instrument of monetary policy after 1958, although rediscount ceilings were kept and continued to play a role until 1972.

Liquidity and Reserve Ratios

When the Banque de France implemented its rediscount ceilings in 1948, it soon realized that they would be ineffective in restricting short-term credit and liquidity if banks could sell long-term bills to increase their short-term lending (Hirschman & Roosa 1949). Since banks held a large portfolio of Treasury bills at the end of World War II, a decrease in rediscount ceilings would have missed its objective if banks had sold these bills on the money market to acquire liquidity or not renewed them at maturity.[9] Therefore, banks were required to retain a minimum portfolio of Treasury bills, called a "floor" (*plancher*). An increase in the minimum legal portfolio of government paper acted as an automatic restraint on the volume of short-term lending and was an obvious way to help finance the public deficit. This Treasury bill floor was defined on an individual basis for each institution as a ratio of new deposits until 1956, and then as a ratio of total deposits.

The same logic applied to the liquid asset ratio (*coéfficient de trésorerie*) created in 1960, which obliged banks to maintain a minimum ratio between certain components of their liquid or available assets (i.e., government securities and medium-term paper that could be rediscounted at the Banque de France) and certain components of their long-term liabilities.[10] At the beginning of 1960, the amount of medium-term credit that was rediscountable at the Banque de France, as a share of GDP, was four times higher than in 1948. This posed a significant risk for the effectiveness of credit controls since the Banque de France was increasingly being asked to rediscount these medium-term bills. In periods when their liquidity contracted, banks tended to rediscount medium-term paper automatically at the central bank and increase their short-term lending. Increasing the liquid asset ratio led to a reduction in the amount of bank liquidity and helped to avoid the asset substitution that was liable to undermine the effectiveness of rediscount and credit ceilings.

In January 1967, both the liquid asset ratio and the Treasury bill floor were replaced by a standard system of reserve requirements along with a minimum portfolio requirement for medium-term credit. Reserve requirements were initially set as a proportion of banks' demand liabilities (i.e., sight and time deposits), but this definition was extended on February

---

[9] Many central banks used liquidity ratios for this purpose until the 1970s (Monnet & Vari 2017). This mechanism (called securities-reserve requirement in the United States although not implemented in this country) is well explained for example by an economist of the New York Fed in 1957:

> In Belgium, France, Italy and the Netherlands, the ratio were successful in accomplishing their immediate purpose of restraining bank credit through a locking-in of the banks' government securities holdings. Even though the commercial banks in these countries had some leeway in their operations at the time that the ratios were established, the point soon arrived when they no longer were able to sell government securities in order to expand loans to private borrowers. The banks were thus forced to have recourse to central bank credit, the rates for which were increased to discourage such borrowing, and the expansion of bank loans slowed down markedly. (Fousek 1957, p. 63)

[10] This decision was taken together with a decrease in the *plancher de bons du Trésor* from 25% to 20% and was intended to contain the sales of Treasury bills by banks.

23, 1971 to include a proportion of new loans (i.e., a proportion of credit growth for each bank). Until May 1970, banks exceeding their credit ceiling were sanctioned via a reduction in their rediscount ceiling; that is, a limit on their access to the central bank's discount window. After this date, a new system of sanctions was introduced whereby banks exceeding their ceiling were obliged to deposit a share of this excess credit with the central bank. Contrary to the reserve requirement on credit growth, which was permanent, these "supplementary reserves" (or "special deposits") were applied to the amount of credit exceeding the ceiling, and were only imposed when credit ceilings existed.

Credit Ceilings (encadrement du crédit)

Credit ceilings (i.e., direct limits on the growth of outstanding loans) were implemented in France in February 1958. Contrary to the rediscount ceilings and the reserve ratios, they were intended as a temporary restrictive policy, and were repealed when the Banque de France wanted to change the policy stance and reintroduced every time it was necessary to fight inflation. Only after 1974 did the central bank begin to use them as a permanent, though less stringent, technique (Chapter 3). In addition to avoiding an increase in interest rates, the primary justification for credit ceilings was their very rapid effect on lending. The exact method and definitions of direct controls fluctuated between 1958 and 1973 (see Tables 1 and 2). Selective relaxations were occasionally applied in order to favor certain types of lending, such as housing loans or export credit. The definition of direct controls also depended on how they complemented various reserve and liquidity ratios.

Before credit ceilings were implemented in 1958, the Banque de France's practice was to oblige banks to ask for formal authorization before granting large loans above a certain limit. During periods of restrictive monetary policy, the Banque could thus prevent banks from lending large amounts.

Summary

The evolution of the Banque de France's instruments and operating procedures from 1948 to 1973 can be summarized quite easily. Rediscount ceilings and liquidity or reserve ratios were used on a continuous basis, with the Banque changing their values when it wanted to expand or restrict money and credit creation. By contrast, credit ceilings – in use from 1958 to 1973 – were imposed only when the Banque decided to make the monetary policy stance more restrictive, and were lifted the rest of the time. The primary instruments used to curb inflation were rediscount ceilings in the 1950s and credit ceilings in the 1960s (rediscount ceilings were in place in the latter decade, but were less binding). Liquidity and reserve ratios, sanctions and penalty rates were used throughout the period but their definitions changed several times to avoid adverse asset substitution by banks and to maintain the effectiveness of credit and rediscount ceilings.

The Problem of Measuring the Monetary Policy Stance

There are two reasons why a single instrument or a compound index of instruments cannot be used as a measure of monetary policy when ceilings and ratios – rather than open market operations, the money base or interest rates – are the primary instruments of central bank policy.[11]

First, no single quantitative instrument was used – or kept the same definition – over the period. A combination of different instruments always had to be applied, and the particular choice of combination varied over time. As discussed previously, direct bank credit controls had to be supplemented with various liquidity ratios (rediscount and credit ceilings) in order to be effective. For example, if a bank reached its rediscount ceiling, it could sell bonds or substitute demand deposits for time deposits or mid-term credit for short-term credit to increase its liquidity and its ability to lend. Liquidity ratios thus served to block these substitution effects. This argument was frequently advanced at the time within the Banque de France.[12]

Second, and more importantly, even when one instrument was used over a long period, the values of that instrument over time are not commensurable.

---

[11] One additional reason is more common and well known in the literature. Credit or money supplies cannot be used to measure monetary policy because of endogeneity problems and because the central bank does not control credit and money aggregates perfectly (Bernanke & Mihov 1998). Regarding Banque de France policy from 1948 to 1973, the latter argument is more compelling because the central bank always combined controls on the credit supply (i.e., rediscount and credit ceilings) and controls on the money supply (liquidity and reserve ratios). In a previous version of this work (Monnet 2012b), I present a simple model that separates controls on money from controls on credit and shows their ambiguous effect on interest rates.

[12] This explanation can be found in many documents, notably in a note by H. Koch, January 29, 1963, (ABF, 1331200301/10) or in a speech by M. Debré from the Finance Ministry, at the CNC on November 9, 1966 (ABF, 1331200301/11). For example, a preparatory note for the September 1948 CNC meeting states that "the direct limitation of credit creates an excess of funds that banks can finance with deposits. This excess must be invested in government bonds in order to avoid an increase of liquidity." Tobin (1970), Davis (1971), Cottarelli et al. (1986) and Monnet and Vari (2017) discuss these adverse substitution effects from a theoretical viewpoint and assess their consequences for credit control.

What matters is not the nominal value of the ratio or the ceiling, but whether it is constraining. For example, an increase in the Treasury bill floor or in the liquid asset ratio is not a restrictive measure if, as in 1956 and 1962, it only serves to keep pace with the changing composition of banks' balance sheets, without actually imposing a tighter constraint. Hence, it is essential to know the intentions of policymakers, who were observing bank balance sheets and the constraining effects of their instruments, when the decision to change a ceiling or a ratio is taken. This difficulty is compounded by the fact that exemptions were applied to certain instruments at different points in time, and that the combinations of instruments used changed over time. For example, it is difficult to evaluate whether credit ceilings were tighter in 1969 than in 1963; even though 1969 ceilings were lower, they also included important exemptions on medium-term housing credit. For similar reasons, rediscount ceilings in the 1960s are not comparable with those in the 1950s because they were replaced by credit ceilings as the primary instrument of restrictive monetary policy in 1958, and banks were less indebted toward the central bank in the 1960s. Again, it is key to know the intentions of policymakers to be able to compare the stance of policy over time. Instruments of credit control were modified frequently in order to keep them effective and their use depended on how they were combined with others. A 1975 study about monetary policy in OECD countries in the 1960s and early 1970s showed very well how these frequent changes present a challenge for those who attempt to identify the general stance of the central bank's monetary policy. "The use of policy instruments is evolving constantly in the light of the experience gained, and there is always the danger of misinterpreting a temporary relaxation of policy as a more basic modification in the use of the instruments" (OECD 1975, p. 25).

For these reasons, monetary policy that uses quantitative instruments over a long period cannot be measured in the usual way with a single series. It is also impossible to build an index of several continuous series. The choice set of the policymakers is thus not observable; but intentions and objectives can be observed from archival information. For this reason, I follow Romer and Romer (1989) and use archival evidence on policy decisions to build a measure of central bank actions, based on whether or not French central bankers intended to pursue a restrictive policy. Romer and Romer used the term "narrative approach" to characterize their method, in reference to earlier work by Friedman and Schwartz (1963) on US monetary policy, as opposed to an approach where the measure of monetary policy stance and the identification of causation rely exclusively on the use of statistics and econometric models.

II DEFINITION OF RESTRICTIVE EPISODES OF
MONETARY POLICY

This section reports an examination of archival evidence to identify dates when Banque de France board members implemented a restrictive policy through quantitative credit and liquidity controls. I define a dummy variable as 1 when policy is restrictive, and as zero at all other times. I discuss the information set that was available to policymakers, since this is an important factor for the identification of the VAR model in the next section. The dummy variable will be endogenous in the VAR since the Banque reacted to primary economic variables, and it will be ordered first in the VAR since policymakers knew only lagged values of non-policy variables.[13]

In the Banque de France's archives, discussions of monetary policy instruments, including the discount rate, appear under the same heading: Credit Policy (*Politique du Crédit*). At each meeting, the Banque's General Council discussed and stated whether credit policy should be restrictive. The sources I use are largely the minutes from weekly meetings of the General Council (denoted PVCG), minutes from sessions of the National Credit Council (denoted CNC), which met irregularly, and numerous staff documents, notes and letters from the central bank archives. Original quotations in French that were used to construct the dummy variable in this chapter are available in an online appendix.[14]

Forms and techniques of quantitative controls varied greatly over time but their main principles were established in the first anti-inflationary (restrictive) episode of 1948–1950. Many European central banks adopted similar tools at the same time or would follow thereafter during the inflation boom created by the Korean War in 1951. This distinctive French policy also raised interest across the Atlantic, first at the Federal Reserve

---

[13] The approach in this chapter is similar to the Boschen and Mills (1995) type of analysis whose main objective was to deal with the disparate set of instruments used by the US Federal Reserve. According to this approach, in a period when an interest rate was the main instrument of monetary policy, one would measure the changes in the policy stance as the changes in this interest rate. The Romer and Romer approach, in contrast, is mostly concerned with the issue of the possible correlation between policy decisions and other influences on future economic activity. The next section takes a step from the Boschen and Mills approach toward the Romer and Romer-type analysis in providing a longer discussion of identification. I would like to thank David Romer for helping me to clarify this point.

[14] https://assets.aeaweb.org/assets/production/articles-attachments/aej/mac/app/0604/2012-0255_app.pdf

where Albert O. Hirschman and Robert V. Roosa, two economists who would later become prominent figures, wrote a report entitled "Postwar credit controls in France" (Hirschman & Roosa 1949). Two years later, in the *American Economic Review*, a full-fledged article also noticed the novelty of such policies aiming at decreasing inflation and restoring balance of payments equilibrium: "By the middle of 1950, in the comparatively hopeful days before the Korean crisis, France had attained reasonable internal stability and had approached an acceptable international balance. In the rehabilitation and stabilisation of the French franc, credit controls have been an essential instrument, but France's experience with them has remained almost unnoticed on this side of the Atlantic" (Kriz 1951, p. 85).

Six Restrictive Episodes

September 30, 1948 to June 8, 1950
The first episode of quantitative credit control occurred in a context of political instability. To push the government to accept credit restrictions, the Banque de France increased its discount rate by 1 percentage point on September 2, without much effect, and finally decreased it on September 30 by 0.5 percentage point once the government and the National Credit Council had approved restrictive credit controls. The objective of this quantitative credit control was straightforward: to combat inflation by reducing the rate of credit growth. One of the reasons for reducing inflation was that the inflation tax (*seignioriage*) was so high that the government had lost its credibility and could not increase its deficit further.[15]

This new policy had two objectives: first to limit credit expansion in order to reduce the development of monetary facilities; second, to guarantee to the Treasury the resources that it has the right to expect from the banking system.[16] The Banque obtained a commitment from the government that it would continue its financing in a non-inflationary way (i.e., through bond issuance, but with no new advances from the central bank). In addition to discount ceilings, the following measures – considered excessive by many bankers – were introduced: a lower limit on the amount of government securities owned by banks (*floor*), equal to 95% of the amount held by each bank in September 1948, and an obligation for each bank to devote one-fifth of new loans to government bonds.

---

[15] ABF, 1427200301/8, Letter of the Governor, Emmanuel Monick, to M. Filippi, September 17, 1948.
[16] ABF, 1427200301/8, Preparatory notes for the CNC meeting, September 29, 1948.

The end of this episode was more gradual. Throughout 1949, the Banque de France insisted on the importance of these measures.[17] Then, at the beginning of 1950, French monetary authorities began to encounter considerable resistance to their restrictive policy from firms and banks. A relaxation of the policy, consisting primarily of the lifting of rediscount ceilings at the Banque de France, was repeatedly advocated in the Parisian financial press and by business groups. In April 1950, the National Assembly requested that the government and the Banque relax their controls, despite warnings from the Secretary of State for Economic Affairs that it would create inflationary pressures. In May, the Banque de France agreed to shift its policy stance, but kept a constant watch on inflation, especially after the outbreak of the Korean War at the end of June (Kriz 1951). There is some consensus dating the shift of credit policy to between April and June 1950 (Barrère 1951; Kriz 1951; Guillaumont-Jeanneney 1968) due to the adoption of three measures: an increase in the ceilings on loans requiring authorization from the Banque de France (from 50 to 100 million francs) on April 27, an increase in the discount ceiling on May 11 and a reduction of the discount rate on June 8. Given the uncertainty over the end-date of this episode, I try these three different end months (April, May, June 1950) as a robustness check in the econometric analysis with monthly data. This does not apply when using quarterly data.

October 11, 1951 to September 17, 1953

The reasons for implementing credit restrictions in October 1951 were clear, and they were repeated widely at the General Council: inflation kept rising and France was running a permanent current account deficit. Once again, the central bank pointed the finger at the rate of credit growth, which it blamed for fueling the current account deficit.[18] To reduce demand for credit, the Banque began a new and more rigorous application of discount ceilings. Largely due to financial outflows, it also increased the discount rate from 2.5% to 3% and then to 4% on November 8, 1951.

These measures did not go down well with bankers and the business community. For example, there was an interesting exchange between the governor of the Banque de France and the president of the Chamber of Commerce of Paris (letters dating from October 15 and 25, November 30 and December 8), in which the latter complained that the restrictive

[17]   ABF, PVCG, September 1, 1949.
[18]   ABF, PVCG, October 11, 1951.

monetary policy was threatening the development of production and business. The governor replied that combating inflation was a prerequisite for future growth.[19] This exchange highlights the motives behind credit restrictions, and demonstrates that, up to a point, inflation was a clear priority. Production, corporate profits and unemployment were of little concern in monetary policy choices, at least in the short term or at the time of the decision.

The end of the restrictive period came on September 17, 1953, after three weeks of negotiations between the government and central bank. In early September, rumors were already beginning to circulate in the press and among bankers. The central bank lowered the discount rate from 4% to 3.5%, and the National Credit Council adopted important measures to ease credit conditions: rise in the discount ceilings and a 50% reduction in bank tariffs.[20]

(June 26, 1957) February 5, 1958 to February 5, 1959

Faced with inflationary pressures in June 1957, the newly appointed economy and finance minister, Felix Gaillard, changed the direction of economic policy and proposed a series of new measures. To fight inflation, he gave up price controls, which had a counterproductive effect, and to solve the trade deficit, he chose a disguised "devaluation," beginning in August, whereby purchases of foreign currencies were taxed at 20% (Koch 1983, p. 309). Gaillard also requested new advances from the central bank (300 billion French francs) to finance government policies. In reaction to this decision, the Banque de France wanted to "implement limitations on credit in order to offset the flow of money that is going to rush into the money market as a consequence of the new advances to the government. ...

---

[19] I do not deny that a rigorous monetary policy is likely to cause some troubles and real difficulties to the firms, but there is no sign today (looking at the index of industrial production and the level of unemployment) that this policy has pushed the country into a crisis. ... To tell you the truth, the difficulties that firm managers are facing today are essentially due to the recent worsening of an old inflationist situation and not to the monetary policy that has been implemented to fight it. (ABF, 1427200301/15, letter, November 30, 1951)

[20] The governor of the Banque de France – supported by the government – considered these measures necessary, but he also pointed out the contradictions in the government's claims: "We must consider how difficult the government's task is. Indeed, on the one hand it wants French prices to become more competitive and the threat of a rise in wages to disappear, and on the other hand it wants the economic trend to be stronger than in the past. For this reason, one can speak of contradictory views." ABF, PVCG, September 17, 1953.

The limitations can be implemented by two means: liquidity reserve ratio [Treasury floor] or credit ceilings."[21]

Government pressure prevented monetary policy from turning very restrictive. On June 26, the Banque imposed restrictions on consumer credit, extending the Treasury floor (25% of bank assets must be comprised of Treasury bills). In July, discount ceilings were lowered by 10%, and the *super-enfer* penalty rate was increased to 10%. In August, to sustain the disguised "devaluation," discount ceilings were again cut by 10%, and the discount rate was increased from 4% to 5% (from 6% to 7% for the *enfer* rate). On November 28, discount ceilings were lowered by 10% again, and the *enfer* rate increased to 8%, but the governor predicted that these measures "would not create too much difficulty on the money market."[22]

Despite a positive effect on the balance of payments, these restrictive measures were insufficient to curb inflation.[23] For these reasons, the Banque de France – strongly supported by the International Monetary Fund – adopted a stricter policy intended to stabilize internal demand and price levels.[24] Credit ceilings were implemented for the first time on February 5, 1958, drawing opposition from two members of the Banque's General Council (M. Laurent and M. Lambert), who feared an increase in unemployment and a decrease in industrial production.[25] The new decision of the CNC forced banks to restrict their lending to the economy to the same level as in the last quarter of 1957 (+3%, provided banks provided justifications). Banks that exceeded this percentage could be kept away from discounting facilities. The motives were clearly stated in letters from the governor to the economy and finance minister, and to the President of the Professional Bankers' Association:

Regarding private credit, a relentless action had been carried out for a long time in order to fight inflationist pressures. The measures taken in 1957 have led to a slow-down of the growth of bank credit. But these credits have nevertheless continued to grow. Thus, in order to maintain the ongoing effort, it seems necessary to adopt new measures to stabilise the amount of credit directly.[26]

---

[21] ABF, PVCG, June 26, 1957. Note that the term "reserves" here denotes "liquidity ratios" and not "reserve requirements."

[22] ABF, PVCG, November 28, 1957.

[23] The insufficient impact on credit and inflation was discussed at the CNC meeting of February 7, 1958. ABF, 1427200301/334.

[24] The IMF pressures were a strong constraint on the Banque de France's General Council, as was evident in the debates of the February 5, 1958 meeting. ABF, PVCG, February 5, 1958.

[25] ABF, PVCG, February 6, 1958.

[26] ABF, 1427200301/334, letters, February 12, 1958.

This official quantitative credit control ended on February 5, 1959. The reasons for ending the restrictive episode were first a balance of payment surplus, second a need to increase medium-term credit to finance public and private investment and third a commitment by the new political regime in January to run a balanced budget.[27]

There are two possible start dates for this restrictive episode. July 1957 is a meaningful choice since that was when the Banque de France began to lower its discount ceilings. However, the reduction was mild according to the Banque and, above all, it was combined with an increase in advances to the government. The Banque committed to offset the inflationary effect of these advances but it turned insufficient to stabilize inflation in the second semester of 1957. According to most criteria, the true restrictive policy started in February 1958 when the Banque de France admitted and, with the help of the IMF, managed to convince the government that the instruments in place were either too loose or ineffective, and finally implemented stronger measures in line with its objectives. The impact of a different start date for this episode is discussed in Section III.

February 28, 1963 to June 24, 1965

On February 28, 1963, the Banque de France reintroduced a ceiling on the expansion of bank credit. As explained at the Banque's General Council, the reason for the restriction was that "there was an abnormal rise of flows in the money market threatening the internal and external equilibrium of the currency."[28] Thus, whereas bank credit increased by 17.4% in 1962, monetary authorities stated that the total rate of credit growth in 1963 could not exceed 12%. In September 1963, this limit was changed to 10% (from September 1963 to September 1964). The Government paper floor was also increased from 32% to 35% and then to 36% in May. The 10% limit on credit was renewed in September 1964 for another year. Then in June 1965, the Banque ended its official credit control prematurely, a move that the governor said was a strong signal, because "this regulation would have been maintained if the monetary situation had remained the same as it was until recently." It follows that

the suspension of credit ceilings is essentially justified by the fact that banks have recently managed to maintain their credit quite easily within the limits that have been imposed. ... It seems that the moment is well-suited to end these measures. Even though they may not disturb banking activities in general anymore, they

---

[27] ABF, PVCG, February 5, 1959.
[28] ABF, PVCG, February 28, 1963.

cause some malfunctionings because they apply to all kinds of companies and thus create rents and discourage the dynamism of more active firms. There is no reason for maintaining measures that would, in one way or another, lead to a sclerosis of the economy.[29]

Since this restrictive episode was due primarily to inflationary pressures rather than a balance of payments problem (see discussion in Section IV), the discount rate was not increased as much as in 1957; it was raised from 3.5% to 4% in November 1963 and then cut back to 3.5% in April 1965.

November 12, 1968 to October 27, 1970

Due to another large balance of payments deficit, the Banque de France increased its discount rate from 3.5% to 5% on July 3, 1968. The reason was purely to attract capital inflows: "Because of the state of our foreign reserves, in such a situation, it is no longer possible to maintain interest rates clearly inferior to those prevailing on international money markets – especially the US market and the euro-dollar market – … The interest rate must be increased in order to stop the haemorrhage."[30]

This decision regarding the interest rate was taken without any further regard to credit or inflation. Conversely, the rise in the official discount rate (from 5% to 6%) on November 12 reflected a different motivation. First, the justification given for the measure was much broader, highlighting a general demand problem that needed to be addressed through monetary policy: "the evolution of the foreign exchange market, as well as the domestic monetary situation reveal that the abundance of liquidity is not an accident but has been accepted to contribute to a new acceleration of the economy in a context of sustained expansion."[31]

Second, and more importantly, the measures taken were not only "qualitative" (discount rate) but also quantitative; the reserve requirement rose from 4.5% to 5.5% and new official limits were imposed on credit (a maximum of a 4% rise in lending from September 30 to December 31).[32] Contrary to previous restrictive episodes, important exemptions were applied, not just to export credit (the discount rate for export credit was kept at 2%), but also to mid-term housing and consumer credit. According to the governor of the Banque de France, the nature and strength of these restrictions did not differ significantly from 1958 and 1963 because banks

---

[29] ABF, PVCG, June 24, 1965.
[30] ABF, PVCG, March 7, 1968.
[31] ABF, PVCG, November 12, 1968.
[32] The liquid assets ratio had been replaced by the reserve requirement in 1967. Credit growth in the last quarter of that year was 9%.

had always been told to impose restrictions on loans that were not used to finance priority investment, housing construction and exports.[33]

The imitations were extended in 1969 and 1970, although the same exemptions applied, and the rate of credit growth was restricted to 3% for each of those years. In August 1970, a heated debate took place between the finance minister and the Banque de France: although the rate of credit growth had been stabilized, the Banque wanted to wait a few months to be certain of the improvement. By contrast, the finance minister argued that French monetary policy was too strict in comparison with other countries, and that the main indices showed a slowdown in economic activity that would justify a slight relaxation of credit controls.[34] The Banque agreed to decrease its discount rate from 8% to 7.5% to bring it more in line with international standards (Germany and the United Kingdom had a 7% bank rate) but insisted on officially maintaining a restrictive policy as well as keeping its credit controls in place. In October 1970, the ceilings on credit expansion were abolished and the discount rate lowered to 7%. Figure 6 shows some press clippings revealing how credit ceilings were perceived by the press and firms as effective and binding, a brake to investment and expansion.

November 2, 1972 to September 1973
The final restrictive episode is a special case because the end of 1973 was marked by a dramatic change in the way French monetary policy was implemented. One of the reasons for this was the major reform of the money market in 1971, which allowed money market rates to fall below the Banque de France's discount rate (see Chapter 3 section III, and Figure 10). Discount ceilings were abolished in 1972, and the Banque's discount rate, which influenced the money market rate, became a penalty rate. The Banque increased its discount rate slightly on November 2 from 5.75% to 6% to fight inflation, as stated by the General Council: "this measure will first mean, in a symbolic way, that we have entered a period in which money will be more expensive and more difficult to obtain. Second, it will set at a reasonable level the penalty rate applying to banks that do not own enough assets to be traded on the money market."[35]

For similar reasons, the discount rate increased to 7.5% on November 30. Changes in the discount rate were thought to have a similar effect as the former discount ceilings. Most importantly, reserve requirements

---

[33]   ABF, PVCG, November 12, 1968.
[34]   ABF, PVCG, August 27, 1970.
[35]   ABF, PVCG, November 2, 1972.

Figure 6 Press clippings on restrictive and distributive effects of credit ceilings, 1969–1970
Source: Made from pictures of press clippings available in the archives of the Banque de France.

for credit were raised from 4% to 33% of banks' outstanding loans. No other quantitative measures were taken until December 12, 1972 when reserve requirements were raised and ceilings on credit growth were reestablished: the amount of outstanding bank loans on April 3, 1973 could not be more than 19% higher than the amount at April 5, 1972. Since total credit had already grown by more than 12% from April to December 1972, this measure was restrictive. On December 28, the Banque's discount rate was increased to 8%.

For a number of reasons, credit ceilings were not abolished until 1984. However, their role changed radically at the end of 1973.[36] Originally introduced as a temporary, highly restrictive tool, they became a permanent, albeit far less restrictive, upper limit. The credit ceiling was increased in 1974 rather than being abolished while, in June, reserve requirements for credit decreased from 33% to 0%. As argued in Chapter 3, the Banque de France's monetary policy after 1973 was very different from the preceding decades. There was no restrictive episode such as in the 1950s and 1960s. Cash-reserve requirements and interest rates were the main tool of policy. For these reasons, I end my econometric study in October 1973, before the first oil shock. By doing so, I avoid any bias in my analysis caused by a huge supply shock. I also consider that the shock changed the nature of monetary policy. From 1974 onwards, another method of identifying restrictive episodes of monetary policy would be required. Note that the primary conclusions of this chapter are unaffected by the elimination of the period November 1972 to September 1973 from the estimation sample.

Restrictive Monetary Policy and the Economy: A Graphical View

Table 3 summarizes the dates when a restrictive policy was implemented, as identified from narrative evidence (i.e., when the dummy variable is equal to 1).

It is useful to examine simple graphs to see whether there is a correlation between restrictive episodes and economic variables. Figures 7, 8 and 9 show that the cyclical components of the money stock (M2), the industrial production index and the price level experienced a drop during restrictive episodes.[37] The dummy variable is associated with negative monetary downturns of a similar magnitude (between 2% and 4% deviation from trend; Figure 7). Most of the downturns in money, production and prices over the sample are contemporaneous to monetary policy actions. Note that fluctuations in prices are much larger in the first part of the sample.

---

[36] General limitations on credit (i.e., the same for all banks) ended in 1984. Individual limits were abolished in 1987.

[37] The cyclical component of the series was derived using a Hodrick-Prescott (HP) filter over the period 1947–1973. The black vertical line within the 1957–1959 episode in the figures represents the date February 1958 when monetary policy became highly restrictive. In Figure 8, the industrial production cycle shows a sharp decline in May–June 1968 (a few months before the start of restrictive credit controls) because of protests and massive strikes by students and workers.

Table 3 *"Dummy variable" of restrictive monetary policy*

Monthly data		Alternative	Quarterly data		Alternative
10/1948	06/1950	04/1950–06/1950	4:1948	2:1950	–
10/1951	09/1953		4:1951	4:1953	–
02/1958	02/1959	07/1957–02/1959	2:1958	1:1959	3:1957–1:1959
03/1963	07/1965		1:1963	3:1965	
11/1968	11/1970		4:1968	4:1970	–
11/1972	10/1973		4:1972	4:1973	

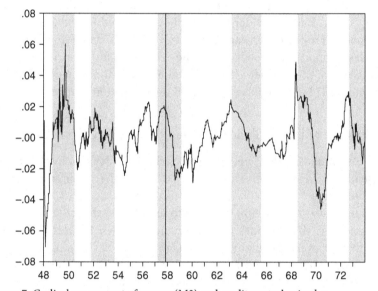

Figure 7 Cyclical component of money (M2) and credit control episodes

The pattern of nominal interest rates (Figure 10) during restrictive monetary policy episodes is also informative. Overall, there is no clear link between monetary policy stance and the value of these rates.[38] Figure 10 shows that the rise in the Bank's discount rate was very modest or non-existent during restrictive episodes. The money market (interbank) rate sometimes experienced a larger increase, but only in the second half of the

---

[38] Real short-term rates were very low throughout the sample, and negative during inflation peaks (1948, 1951 and 1957–1958).

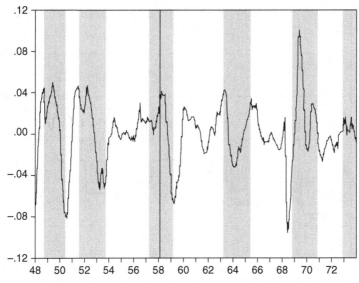

Figure 8 Cyclical component of industrial production and credit control episodes

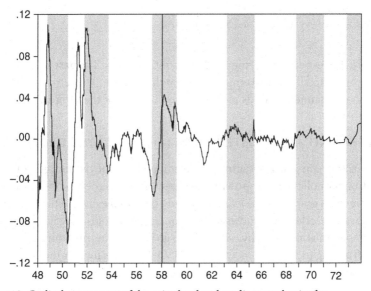

Figure 9 Cyclical component of the price level and credit control episodes

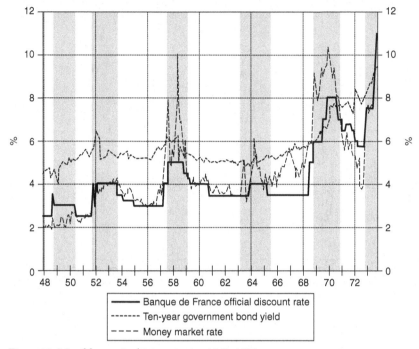

Figure 10 Monthly nominal interest rates, 1948–1973
Sources: CNC; Lévy-Garboua and Monnet (2016).

sample, and especially during the 1968 political crisis. The base lending rate is disconnected broadly from monetary policy stance. The ten-year interest rate on governments bonds is very stable throughout the sample.

III ECONOMETRIC ESTIMATIONS OF RESTRICTIVE POLICIES

This section aims at estimating the average effects of the periods of anti-inflationary policy on the growth rate of the main macroeconomic variables. The previous graphical analysis has already provided evidence that inflation, money and production decreased when quantitative tools were implemented to combat inflation. So, why is it useful to go beyond this preliminary discussion? Turning to an econometric model (VAR) pushes further the analysis in four ways. First, a VAR model can account for possible confounding factors that could bias the interpretation of correlations observed on simple figures. For example, economic or policy shocks that affect output, but are unrelated to Banque de France decisions, are taken into account in the model as they impact past values of the index of industrial production. In the VAR model, each variable depends (linearly) on contemporaneous and lagged values of the other variables. Second, the VAR model will provide us with a variance decomposition analysis, that is that we are able to assess – with a certain margin of error – which share of the variance of main economic variables is explained by the Banque de France's decisions. Third, econometric estimations will provide a more detailed comparison of the distinct effects of quantitative tools and interest rates over the period. In particular, the VAR is more suited than a graphical analysis to detect a significant but small effect of interest rate on economic variables if this effect exists. Fourth, since VAR methods have been the most common tool for estimating the effects of monetary policy in other contexts since the 1980s, we can compare our results with those of other studies conducted in other countries and at different times. This is a simple way of discussing the extent of the impact of the Banque de France's decisions from a broader perspective.

Identification and Specification

The analysis of Section II does not only provide a way to assess when the Banque de France's policy was anti-inflationary. I also use narrative evidence from Section II to inform an identification strategy in the VAR, that is to specify the model to be estimated.[39] Estimating a VAR model requires making an assumption about the timing of relationships between variables. More specifically, one needs to assume that at least one variable does not affect the others within a month. Analysis of policy decisions justifies the following specification of the model: monetary policy is affected by past but not contemporaneous values of economic variables, whereas a monetary policy shock (i.e., unexpected central bank's decision) influences economic variables contemporaneously.[40] It is justified because in the PVCG, the information available to policymakers – especially the economic

---

[39] The dummy variable is thus "ordered first" in the VAR. Since monetary policy decisions appear to be endogenous to most economic variables (i.e., credit, money, inflation and production), I specify that the dummy variable is endogenous in the VAR. This is the same approach used by Shapiro (1994), Boschen and Mills (1995) and Leeper (1997) in their narrative measures of postwar US monetary policy ("Romer dates" or "Boschen and Mills index").

[40] Note that Schreft (1990) also documents an immediate impact on output following the implementation of credit controls by the US Federal reserve in March 1980. My identification considers the effect of agents' expectations more fully than the opposite ordering. Agents are likely to reduce loans, consumption, investments, etc. as soon as a restrictive policy is announced. Note also that the expectation effect can operate in the opposite direction: banks that know they are going to be constrained grant more loans just before the implementation of the control. There is no reason to ignore such a potential effect in identification, whatever the direction.

statistics – refers to values of economic variables in the months preceding policy decisions. Statistics concerning industrial production and consumer prices were available with three-month and two-month delays, respectively.[41] Regarding the effect of policy shocks, letters sent by bankers to the central bank show that banks, households and firms adjusted their behavior immediately after the announcement of the quantitative restrictions. The way I code the dummy variable is consistent with this recursive identification. When a decision is made in the second half of a month, the dummy variable takes the value 1 in the subsequent month and zero in the current month.[42] It is key for our methodology and our results to take into account the duration of credit controls in the VAR model. The dummy variable takes a value equal to 1 for all months when a restrictive monetary policy was in place. Using only the change from an accommodative policy to a restrictive policy (i.e., the dummy equals 1 when the stance of monetary policy shifts) does not fully take into account the behavior of firms and households. Their behavior is not only influenced by a change in monetary policy that happened several months previously, but also by ongoing restrictions on credit and by the fact that if the change in monetary policy is credible, they expect the restriction to last for months or even years. Not considering the duration reduces the accuracy of the estimation since variations in production, money and prices that should be attributed to policy are left unexplained in the model. Hence it is important to bear in mind that the results displayed in the next section will show the responses of macroeconomic variables to a change in monetary policy stance taking into account the duration of restrictive episodes.

Finally, policymakers could have used information regarding contemporaneous and future economic movements beyond the variables that can be included in the VAR model (e.g., industrial production, money, interest rates, prices, trade and credit). This is a common caveat of the VAR methodology. Since the French central bank neither used nor published official forecasts during this period, there is no possibility of constructing a measure of policy shock that is free of anticipatory movements as in Romer

---

[41] The only exceptions were the variables of the central bank's balance sheet (e.g., reserves, gold, etc.) that were available weekly, and the foreign central banks' rates, changes in which were known immediately.

[42] It is worth noting, however, that ordering the monetary stance last in the VAR does not affect the results. Formally, the identification assumption means that the dummy variable D_t is influenced by a vector of past values for all the variables in the system (i.e., including D_{t-n}):

$$D_t = f(Y_{t-n}) + \varepsilon_t$$

and Romer (2004). Regarding industrial production, I found no major anticipated events affecting output that motivated the change of the policy stance. The major drop in output caused by strikes in May 1968 was certainly not expected, and restrictive monetary policy started in November 1968. There is evidence of the use of alternative information concerning future movements in inflation. For example, the government deficit, for which monthly or quarterly data are not available for this period, was an issue in 1957 because the deficit led to an increase in central bank advances to the government, which boosted inflationary pressures. This was a particular issue for the period July 1957 to February 1958. In my benchmark measure (see Section II and Table 3), the dummy does not take the value 1 during this period. A somewhat similar issue occurred in early 1951 when information about the Korean War and US policy raised inflation expectations, and in 1968 when new labor negotiations in May raised the minimum wage and the expected general cost of labor. But these two shocks had already started to influence French consumer prices when the Banque de France implemented its restrictive measures. If anything, this shortcoming in the econometric specification understates the effects of monetary policy shocks on inflation. However, the inability to provide a systematic method of accounting for policymakers' anticipations that are correlated with the variables included in the VAR model remains an important limitation of the analysis and of the following estimates.

Estimations and Results

I estimate a VAR model to simulate the impact of a monetary policy shock on the primary economic variables.[43] The estimation uses monthly

---

where $n \geq 1$ and ε_t is the monetary policy shock.
Ignoring the constant term, the estimated VAR is:

$$Y_t = A_1 Y_{t-1} + A_2 Y_{t-2} + \cdots + A_n Y_{t-n} + C\eta_t$$

where C is a lower triangular matrix with diagonal terms equal to unity, and η_t is a vector of zero-mean, serially uncorrelated shocks with a diagonal variance-covariance matrix. The ordering assumption means the monetary policy shock ε_t is the first element of η_t.

[43] As discussed earlier, an inversion of the moving average representation is required. As pointed out by Leeper (1997), a standard VAR, estimated with OLS, does not respect the dichotomous nature of the dummy variable. If non-linearities are important to determining the dummy, the linear approximation may cause misleading inferences. I checked the robustness of the results using Leeper's method (1997), that is, by estimating the dummy variable equation in the VAR, with a logit estimator (Monnet 2012b), and found

variables.[44] Monthly price levels, interest rates and industrial production are taken from the yearly National Credit Council reports (*Rapports annuels du Conseil National du Crédit*). The price level is the consumer price index from 1950 to 1973. For 1947–1949, I use the wholesale price index since the CPI is not available.

Money (monthly M2, which was also published by the CNC) is taken from Patat and Lutfalla (1986), and the monthly unemployment rate is from Villa (1997). There was no official unemployment rate computed by INSEE before 1968, so that Villa is simply dividing the number of unemployed people on an estimation of the working population.

I will present the alternative specifications with four or six variables which are consistent with the two-variable specification.[45] The main results of the estimations are presented as impulse response functions (IRF) displayed on several figures. Each IRF represents the path of a variable after a change in the monetary policy stance, that is when monetary policy turns restrictive (anti-inflationary). As explained previously, such a change is simply modeled as a shift of a dummy variable from 0 to 1. The dummy variable is denoted Control in the graphs of the IRF. The solid line is the response of a

---

similar results as with OLS (as Leeper did). Gertler and Gilchrist (1994), Carlino and DeFina (1998) and Ramey (2011), among others, also use an endogenous dummy variable in a VAR, with OLS estimations.

[44] The Cholesky recursive identification is better justified with high-frequency data. All variables are logs, except for the unemployment rate and various interest rates which are in percentage points. The benchmark specification includes thirty-six lags. Romer and Romer (1989, 2004) argue that it is necessary to use thirty-six lags to fully consider the effects of US monetary policy. In our sample, the Akaike information criterion (AIC) also confirms that thirty-six months is the optimum lag length for all specifications. The Bayesian information criterion (BIC) favors twelve lags over twenty-four and thirty-six lags. The BIC tends to select too few lags in short samples, and the AIC asymptotically selects lag lengths that are too long (Ng & Perron 2005; Coibion 2012). The shape and magnitude of the impulse response functions presented in the paper are similar when using twelve or twenty-four lags, but estimation with twelve lags is less precise and displays broader standard error bands after ten months.

[45] Following Romer and Romer (2004) and Ramey and Shapiro (1998), my baseline specification included only two variables. The rationale is that all other shocks affecting output are not systemic and do not correlate with monetary shocks, and will thus be considered in the output lags. One important argument supporting this assumption is that there were fewer important oil or commodity price shocks during the period. Thus, criticisms of the narrative approach because of the simultaneity of monetary shocks with oil shocks, such as Hoover and Perez (1994), are less relevant here. Simultaneity of shocks increases estimation imprecision. The potential effects of the wars in Indochina (1946–1954) and Algeria (1954–1962) are more important but, in combination, these wars lasted over sixteen years, more than half of the period, and thus were not temporary shocks. Results are similar when using two, four or six variables.

specific economic variable to the monetary policy change. The shaded area around the solid line (one standard-error band) stands for the uncertainty surrounding the estimation.[46] VAR responses read as follows: after twenty months, industrial production (Figure 11) is 6% lower than it would have been without a monetary policy shock, the price level is 4.5% lower and money (M2) 5% lower. The estimated impact is very significant.[47]

The response of M2 confirms that a shock to the dummy variable is a monetary shock. If one is skeptical about the interpretation of the shock to the dummy variable, this result with the money supply perhaps offers a more intuitive interpretation; after a policy shock that decreases the money supply by 5%, industrial production and the price level also decrease by approximately 5%. The effects on industrial production and on the price level are similar and even more significant in the ten months after the shock. Estimation is more precise when money is included in the VAR and, contrary to many VAR studies (Sims 1992) there is no price puzzle: the price level responds immediately after the anti-inflationary policy has started.[48]

The impulse response functions display three other important features:

- Industrial production starts to fall almost immediately, as early as the second month after the shock. The effect on unemployment (Figure 12) is much more delayed, around ten months. Labor market institutions in France over the period (indexed wages, powerful unions) and the general low level of unemployment may offer good explanations for the lagged response of unemployment. The response of the unemployment rate to a monetary shock is very small, especially compared to the responses of other variables, which confirms that the unemployment-inflation trade-off (i.e., Phillips curve) was not an important preoccupation at the Banque de France during this period. Anti-inflationary policies clearly reduced the growth rate of industrial production but their effect on unemployment was very limited since the French economy was at full employment. When unemployment started to grow markedly around

---

[46] The standard errors are computed using 1,000 bootstrap replications. I display one-standard-error bands. The response of the dummy variable to a monetary shock is normalized such that the dummy takes the value 1 when monetary policy becomes restrictive.

[47] In all specifications, the t-statistic for the estimated effect exceeds 2.5 from the tenth through to the twenty-second months.

[48] This finding contrasts with the results of VAR studies of US monetary policy using the Romer dates or Federal fund rates, which find a very strong price puzzle (Leeper 1997; Christiano et al. 1999).

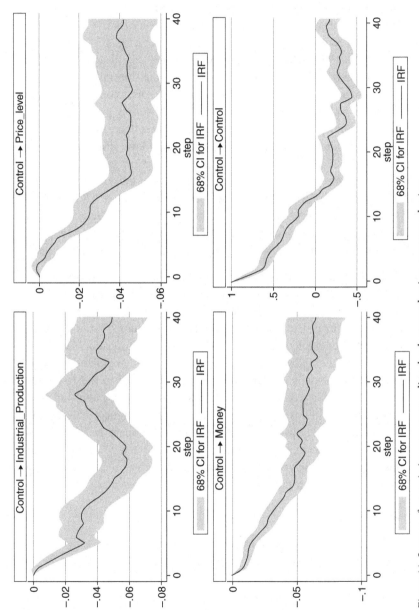

Figure 11 Impact of a restrictive monetary policy shock on production, money and prices
Note: VAR estimated with four variables (dummy, M2, CPI, production).

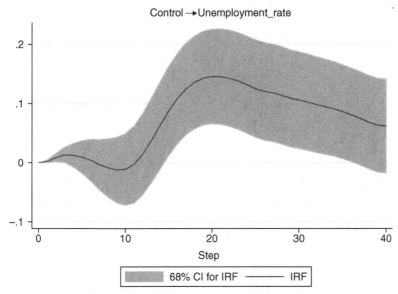

Figure 12 Impact of a monetary shock on the unemployment rate
Note: VAR estimated with two variables.

1973, the Banque de France's economists and policymakers were left with an unknown situation.

- Both for industrial production and unemployment, the marginal impact is maximal after twenty to twenty-five months. Surprisingly, this pattern is similar to the one observed for the United States by Romer and Romer (1989, 2004), despite significant differences in the monetary policy instruments used in the United States and France, and the fact that the disinflation of the early 1980s was not included in the sample.

- These effects are strong. According to the variance decomposition displayed in Figure 13 (a variance decomposition measures the share of the volatility of an economic variable explained by a shock), a monetary policy shock explains approximately 10% of the variance in production and in the price level, and 20% of the variance in M2 after one year. After three years, monetary policy explains around 40% of the variance in industrial production and in the price level and 50% of the variance in M2. The remainder is explained by endogenous shocks to the economy.[49]

---

[49] Only about two-thirds of the variance in the dummy variable is explained by the monetary policy shock after two years, confirming the need to consider the dummy as endogenous in the VAR.

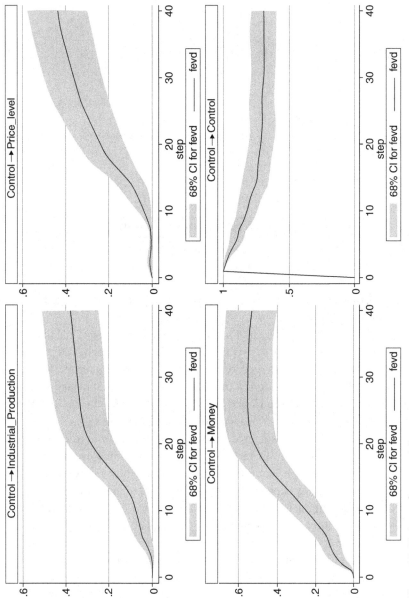

Figure 13 Variance decomposition
Note: VAR with four variables (dummy, M2, CPI, production).

Did monetary policy shocks influence interest rates? Figure 14 shows that there is almost no effect on the money market (interbank) rate. The same result was obtained with the Banque de France discount rate.[50] There is an immediate effect on the money market rate but it is small and temporary while credit restrictions lasted several months. It is either because the Banque offset the effects of credit restrictions on the money market rate (which remained above the discount rate until 1971) through a purchase of Treasury bills, as discussed above, or because the shock did not transmit to the money market because it was not liquid and segmented from other channels of refinancing. Thus, the response of interest rates to a monetary policy shock shows a very strong liquidity puzzle (Gordon & Leeper 1992). Monetary policy does not influence the discount and money market rates, but it does influence production, money, price levels and unemployment in a standard way.

The measure constructed in this chapter can be used to investigate the effects of French postwar monetary policy on many other variables, provided data are available. The long working-paper version of this chapter (Monnet 2012b) displayed results for credit, consumption, investment, central bank reserves and the current account using quarterly data, and all are in line with the results described above. The impact of a policy shock on credit is slightly stronger than the impact on money (about −7% after five quarters), but an estimation using quarterly data shows broader error bands. Not surprisingly, the effect is immediate with short-term credit (with maturity less than a year) while it is significant after two quarters only with medium-term credit. After two years, the cumulative effects are similar. Introducing a wholesale price index into the VAR does not alter the response of the consumer price index (CPI). The response of the wholesale price index to a monetary shock is of a similar magnitude to the response of the CPI. Dividing the sample into two (pre- and post-1958) gives the robust result that the impact of monetary policy is stronger in the first period. This is not surprising given the higher volatility of economic variables experienced in the 1950s. The pattern of the impulse response functions is, however, similar across samples.

Further Discussions about 1957

In Section II, I discussed the fact that the start and end dates of some restrictive episodes may be uncertain (Table 3). Changing the end date of the

---

[50] The absence of a significant effect on the primary interest rate is very robust across many specifications.

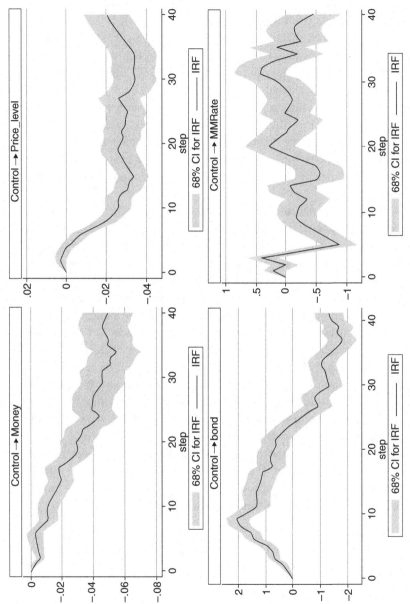

Figure 14 Impact of a monetary policy shock on bond and money market rates
Note: VAR with five variables (dummy, M2, CPI, Treasury rate and money market rate).

first and last episodes slightly has no impact on the results and observations obtained. However, modifying the start date of the third episode (July 1957 rather than February 1958) does change the estimation results. This is because the Banque de France immediately recognized that monetary policy in the second half of 1957 was not restrictive enough to bring down inflation. As a result, new measures were implemented in early 1958, under pressure from the IMF. The econometric specification cannot state whether the measures taken in June 1957 were ineffective or whether they were offset by other factors pushing inflation upward (e.g., fiscal deficits, central bank advances to the government, etc.), which were anticipated at the time of the decision. The estimation results are not reported here, but I discuss them briefly. The price level responds with a lag of about nine months.[51] Production and money respond immediately, but the magnitude of their responses is lower ten months after the shock, in comparison with the benchmark case shown in Figure 11. With the "July 1957" measure, the impact on production was around 2% after ten months, but between 3% and 4% with the "February 1958" measure. After twenty months, the magnitude of the impact on the price level, production and money was very similar regardless of the measure. The difference between the decision and measures taken in July 1957 and February 1958 is reflected consistently and meaningfully in the estimation outcomes. Results are sensitive to the definition of the dummy variable, but I still find that monetary policy has a strong influence on real and nominal variables, and that the pattern of IRFs is similar. The next section demonstrates that this is not the case when using an interest rate as a measure of the monetary policy stance.

Comparisons with Other Measures of Monetary Policy

To assess the relevance and contribution of the "narrative" approach, I compare these results with usual measures of monetary policy. Without specific institutional and historical knowledge of French monetary policy over the period, estimating a VAR with the Banque de France discount rate or with the US Federal discount rate seems reasonable. The rationale for using the Federal discount rate is that we need to find an exogenous measure of monetary policy, and the US rate is an obvious candidate under the Bretton Woods system.[52]

---

[51] This lag is even observed when wholesale and commodity prices are included in the VAR.

[52] For this reason, Mojon (1998) uses the German rate in his study of French monetary policy during the 1980s, under the fixed exchange rate regime of the European Union.

First, the results of a four-variable VAR (Figure 15) show that there are identification problems with a shock to the Banque de France discount rate.[53] Industrial production and the price level respond positively to a rise in the discount rate, and similar results were obtained with the money market rate. This positive effect is inconsistent with standard economic theory. What is captured in the interest rate is not the stance of monetary policy. This can only be understood if we recognize that the Banque de France discount rate is not an equilibrium rate on the domestic credit market (Hodgman 1973).

The "narrative" measure of monetary policy yields better estimations, and is the only one to produce findings that are consistent with economic theory and previous empirical studies on the effects of monetary policy. Using a series of interest rates to measure the stance of monetary policy leads to a misunderstanding of Banque de France policy from 1948 to 1973.

Estimating the VAR with the Federal discount rate (Figure 16) – denoted "Fed" – provides puzzling results. Industrial production and the price level increase after ten months while the Banque de France discount rate ("Bank") also rises. The absence of a negative influence on French production and prices from an increase in the US Federal rate provides additional support for the idea that French monetary policy was strongly autonomous under the fixed exchange rates regime.[54] It is also consistent with the fact that the policy dummy variable I derived in this chapter takes values that are unrelated to the dummy variable computed by Romer and Romer (1989, 1994) for the United States.[55]

Findings of Figure 16 – when compared to Figures 11 and 15 – are very important for one who wishes to understand the Bretton Woods system. Standard economic reasoning (based on interest rates) would predict that either French monetary policy was autonomous if French rates were disconnected from US rates, or – on the opposite – that French monetary policy was not autonomous if the French cycle was influenced by the US rate. The previous results show that the French monetary policy and economic cycle were disconnected from the US interest rate but that autonomy was not caused by a disconnect between French and US interest

---

[53] Using the money market rate as a measure of policy provides similar results. All interest rates were ordered last in the VAR, but again, the primary conclusions are insensitive to the ordering.

[54] Results for the Bretton Woods period, 1948 to August 1971, are similar.

[55] The dates are October 1947, September 1955, December 1968 and April 1974. The only restrictive episode that took place in both countries at the same time is the policy implemented at the end of the year 1968, but it was implemented in France first.

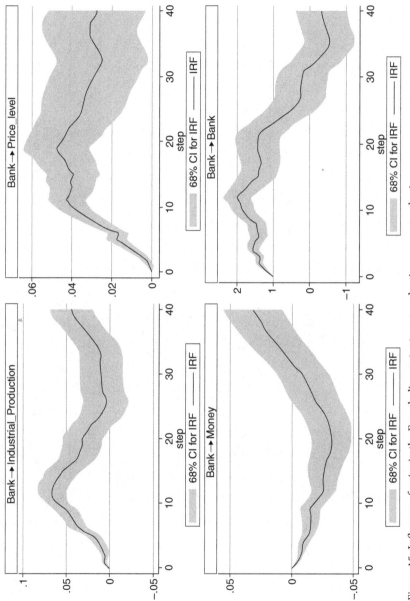

Figure 15 Influence of a rise in the French discount rate on production, money and prices
Note: VAR with four variables (M2, CPI, production, Banque de France discount rate).

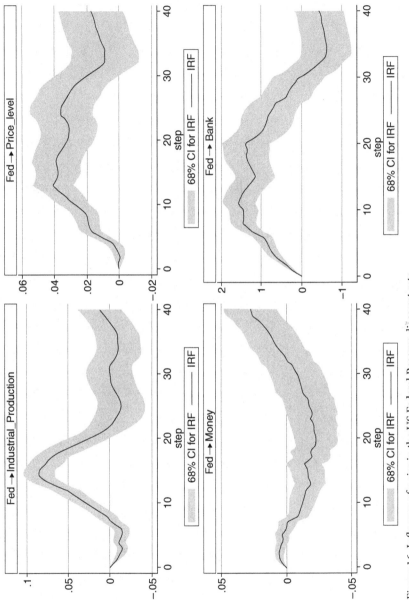

Figure 16 Influence of a rise in the US Federal Reserve discount rate

Note: VAR with five variables (M2, CPI, production, US Federal discount rate, Banque de France discount rate).

rates. The Banque de France discount rate roughly followed the US discount rate because of the exchange rate regime (Figures 16 and 18) but it was in fact largely disconnected from the domestic policy stance because the Banque used quantitative controls. The international and historical issues of this original result are discussed further below.

IV THE INTERNATIONAL DIMENSION

Balance of Payments and Inflation

The Banque de France's policy decisions were taken in a context of fixed exchange rate.[56] As highlighted in the analysis of Section II, the balance of payments was often an explicit objective, together with inflation.[57] When examining the determinants of the dummy variable constructed above (Table 3), I find that the state of the current account and the inflation rate are the two more robust factors influencing the decision of the Banque de France to restrict credit.

The Banque looked at trade deficits, the free-market dollar exchange rate in Paris and, most of all, the stock of foreign reserves, in order to assess the need to restore the "external equilibrium." Conflicts between the "internal equilibrium" (inflation, production and employment) and the "external equilibrium" (balance of payments, exchange rate) were infrequent. When devaluations turned to be necessary in 1949, 1957–1958 and 1969, their action was to limit the severity of domestic restrictive monetary policy, to moderate the external pressure. These were not situations of deflation and rising unemployment coupled with capital outflows, with a straight conflict of objectives between the credibility of the exchange rate and the monetary policy stance. In all but one restrictive episode identified above, the situation was similar: rising inflation, booming production, a growing trade deficit and decreasing foreign reserves (Figure 17). As a result, there was no dilemma for the Banque de France. The only option considered was to impose restrictions on credit in order to decrease inflation, moderate aggregate demand and reduce trade deficit. As said in Part I

---

[56] The argument in this section is developed further in Monnet (2018) with references to other countries.

[57] As explained in Chapter 2, Section III, the policy of the Banque de France was very much in line with the IMF model stating that domestic money creation was the main variable on which the central bank could act to restore balance of payment equilibrium (Polak & Argy 1971; Polak 1997). In Monnet and Puy (2016), we argue that such policies – implemented in European countries and Japan – were in part responsible for the synchronization of business cycles.

Table 4 *Estimation of a (forward looking) reaction function of the central bank*

Explanatory variables	(1)	(2)	(3)	(4)
Inflation	0.23*** (0.00)	0.21***(0.00)	0.23***(0.01)	0.25***(0.00)
Current account		−0.52***(0.00)	−0.54***(0.00)	−0.52***(0.00)
Credit growth		0.02 (0.16)	0.02 (0.12)	0.02 (0.28)
Production cycle		0.04 (0.19)	−0.02 (0.39)	0.02 (0.23)
Unemployment rate				0.01 (0.45)

Notes: P-values are in parenthesis. ***, **, * indicate significance at the 1%, 5% and 10% level respectively. Each right-hand-side variable is instrumented by four lags of its own past value and four lags of the values of other variables. The current account is measured as net exports of goods. Data are monthly. This specification is called a forward-looking reaction function because the current values of the economic variables are instrumented by past values, so that we imagine that policymakers are using historical data to predict the current value of data that they do not know at the time of their decisions.

and studied extensively in the next chapter, if there was a dilemma for the Banque de France, it was rather between monetary policy and fiscal policy: governments of the Fourth Republic were asking for monetary financing of the budget deficit – increasing pressure on money creation – at times when the Banque de France wanted to implement a restrictive monetary policy. The only clear episode of conflict between internal and external equilibria – although it remained modest – occurred in 1963 when France was facing rising inflation while the balance of payments was in surplus. There was not a large trade surplus but a quite rapid increase in capital flows (Figure 18).

Another, but very short-lived, episode of acknowledged conflict between the exchange rate target and monetary policy's objectives occurred in June 1968 (see Section II) when capital outflows and rising US interest rates forced the Banque de France to increase its discount rate, before any move toward a restrictive monetary policy stance.

Credit Controls As a Way to Escape the Trilemma

On both occasions (1963 and June 1968), the Banque de France disconnected the domestic monetary policy objectives (achieved through quantitative controls) from the interest rate. The interest rate was assigned to the external side and other tools were used to manage the rate of credit expansion – and hence inflation – without relying on interest rates. In doing so the Banque

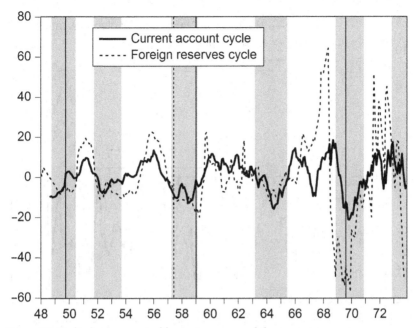

Figure 17 Cyclical component of foreign reserves and the current account
Source: International Financial Statistics (IMF annual volumes). Quarterly data detrended through an HP filter.

was escaping the constraint of international finance, which has been called the "trilemma" or the "impossible trinity" of international finance, after the pioneering work of Robert Mundell (Cohen 1993; Goodman & Pauly 1993; Obstfeld & Taylor 2004). The trilemma posits that it is impossible for a country to have at the same time the following three: fixed exchange rates, capital mobility and monetary policy autonomy. Only two are possible. The easiest way to understand the trilemma is to think about two opposite cases of conflict between the internal and external policy objectives (Mundell 1968, pp. 250–271; Argy 1971; Goodman & Pauly 1993, pp. 54–55).[58] The first case is the one of a central bank that wishes to *decrease* its leading interest rate to *push inflation up* but there is a balance of payments *deficit*. Decreasing interest rates would foster capital outflows, worsen the deficit and threaten the credibility of the peg. On the opposite side, the central bank wishes to *increase* its leading interest rate to *combat inflation* but there

---

[58] Note that in recent macro models (Farhi & Werning 2014), the rationale for capital controls is more complex as capital controls can be welfare improving whatever the exchange rate regime.

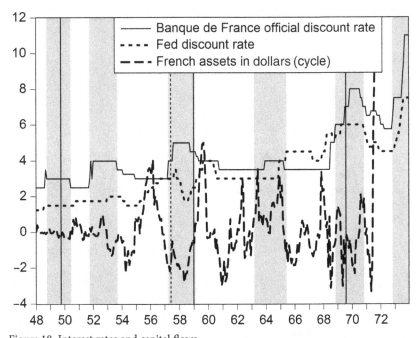

Figure 18 Interest rates and capital flows
Source: International Financial Statistics (IMF annual volumes). Quarterly data detrended through an HP filter. French assets in dollars recorded in the United States by US banks.

is a balance of payments *surplus*: an increase in interest rates would cause *capital inflows* and worsen the surplus. The only option to escape such situations is to impose capital controls. Hence, capital controls help a country to achieve monetary policy autonomy and to maintain the fixed exchange rate at the same time. However, the model of Mundell and the trilemma argument do not consider an alternative option: disconnecting between the interest rates and quantitative controls. This alternative option, not discussed in the subsequent economic and political science literature, was however considered by contemporary economists and policymakers during Bretton Woods (Argy 1971; Monnet 2018). For example, in his survey of central banks' quantitative controls, Hodgman (1973, p. 138) stated clearly that one of the purposes of such tools was: "to check the flow of credit to the private sector without raising domestic interest rates and thus attracting foreign funds through the balance of payment." Conversely, it was possible for the Banque de France to maintain a high discount rate (200 basis points above the average inflation rate) in the mid-1950s and to increase its discount rate in June and July 1968 while implementing an openly expansionary credit policy. From June to early November 1968, the policy of the Banque de France was indeed extremely expansionary in order to sustain economic activity after the strikes of May 1968. The Banque increased its loans to the Treasury through discounting of CDC construction medium-term credit (cf. Chapter 5) and quickly increased rediscounting of medium-term bills of semi-public institutions as well.[59]

Hence, the disconnection between interest rates and quantitative credit controls gave the central bank a way to escape the trilemma when there was a conflict between external and internal objectives. This does not mean, however, that capital controls were unnecessary and superfluous. Capital controls were necessary to make credit controls fully effective when there was a potential conflict between the balance of payments and the domestic monetary policy stance. In 1963, when credit ceilings were imposed and liquidity requirements increased in order to fight inflation, capital controls (both on foreign deposits and foreign borrowing) were also tightened (Teyssier 1973). As stated by the governor of the Banque de France in August 1963, the willingness to restrict borrowing from abroad was justified by the fact that these loans had increased after credit restrictions were imposed on the domestic front at the beginning of the year.[60] Without restrictions on foreign borrowing, firms and households could borrow abroad and would not have been constrained by credit ceilings. Without controls on foreign deposits, banks liabilities could have increased and the liquidity requirements (that forced banks to hold some reserves as a proportion of liabilities) would have been less restrictive. Capital controls had been abolished in France in 1966 and reestablished in May 1968, during the period of civil unrest, in order to limit capital outflows created by political uncertainty. They were again abolished on September 4, 1968 (Mathis 1981). After the May events, capital controls were not anymore necessary since – contrary to 1963 – they did not have to complement credit controls. The conflict between the external objective (attracting capital flows through a rise in interest rates) and the internal objective (expansionary credit policy through active and unrestrained rediscounting and open market

---

[59] Especially loans of Caisse Nationale des Marchés de l'Etat, called "prêts Gingembre" (eighteen-month maturity) starting July. All these expansionary measures are described, for example, in ABF, PVCF, November 12, 1968.

[60] ABF, PVCG, August 8, 1963. The maturity of these loans was decreased from five to two years, their maximum amount from 2 to 1 million and their maximum interest rate from 5% to 4%. Moreover, additional measures were taken to avoid that residents circumvent the law and contract more than one loan from non-residents.

interventions) had been short-lived and limited to the period June–October 1968. Starting November, there was now a common objective to fight inflation and the balance of payments deficit through credit restrictions. Then, capital controls were reestablished on November 28, after the first restrictive measures led to an outflow of liquidity since lending was constrained on the domestic side.

V CONCLUSION

This chapter examined the French experience with temporary quantitative controls from 1948 to 1973 and their macroeconomic effects. Combining a "narrative" approach with VAR estimations, I found that the Banque de France's actions had a strong impact on the economy. By contrast, using interest rates (discount rate or money market rate) as a measure of French monetary policy does not provide consistent results and robust identification. The Banque de France discount rate was used for purposes other than the management of domestic money and credit supply. As acknowledged by contemporary economists and central bankers, it could follow the US interest rate and be disconnected from the domestic monetary policy stance.

This quantitative study elucidates the fact that monetary policy, conflated with credit policy, was neither absent nor passive during the early postwar period in France, before the Great Inflation. It shows that quantitative controls on money or credit can be effective in the short term to decrease output, prices, money and credit. From a methodological point of view, this chapter shows the usefulness of combining an econometric model with a detailed historical analysis of decision-making to assess the economic effects of central bank policy. Quantitative and statistical analyses were needed to prove that credit controls and other quantitative tools had a strong impact on the economy and that the Banque de France's policy was indeed a major driver of the French postwar economic cycle. A detailed analysis of the Banque's archives and a full description of the implementation of monetary policy were necessary to avoid the pitfalls of using unhistorical models to estimate the impact of past monetary policies. This unique combination of historical and quantitative analysis provides results that challenge the usual view of central bank policy during this period. It also demonstrates the importance of taking into account the disconnection between interest rates and quantitative controls to understand central banks' policies during the Bretton Woods era, their autonomy and the function of capital controls. Conventional arguments on the "trilemma of international finance," based on the Mundell-Fleming model, do not take this essential feature of Bretton Woods central banking into account. One key role of capital controls was to make credit controls effective.

5

Blurred Lines

The Two Faces of Banque de France Loans
to the Treasury, 1948–1973

How did the Banque de France finance public debt? What do these monetary techniques tell us about the relationship between the government and the central bank and, more generally, about the nature of the *dirigiste* financial system and postwar credit policy? As with credit policy in general, this chapter shows that a truly stable and singular model of financing of the Treasury by the Banque de France emerged in the late 1940s – albeit partly inherited from the institutional changes of the wars and the 1930s – and was profoundly transformed in 1973, although Banque loans to the government did not stop before 1993. Since the mid-nineteenth century, the standard instruments of government financing by the French central bank were direct long-term loans (advances to the Treasury) whose maximum amount had to be approved by the Parliament. After World War II, this system remained in place and, starting 1948, was supplemented by a hidden method of financing. The hidden part of monetary financing of public debt relied on rediscounting of various assets that were not Treasury bills but were nonetheless direct loans to the Treasury. According to estimations based on different primary sources, I find that from the mid-1950s onwards, almost half of the Banque de France's loans to the Treasury did not appear as such on the Banque's balance sheet. Before 1973, researchers using only official statistics of public debt and the Banque de France's balance sheet are therefore exposed to leaving aside a large part of what monetary financing of public debt really was. In particular, taking into account the hidden financing shows that the share of the Banque's loans to the Treasury in the public debt and assets of the Banque remained stable in the 1950s, whereas official numbers show a continuous decrease. This system was reformed in 1973 in order to make the financing of public debt more transparent, simple and accountable. The nominal maximum amount of Banque de France loans to the government (20.5 billion francs) was then never modified, despite inflation, from 1973 until 1993 when the Banque de France became independent and monetary financing of public debt was abolished.

The 1948–1973 system of monetary financing of public debt reveals some important features of the embedded liberalism of the postwar era, when social legitimacy of economic policies relied much more on the economic outcomes than on their transparency, and when a large share of public debt was non-marketable.[1] These arrangements provided flexibility to state finance and relied on a lack of transparency but it was not a free lunch for the state, although the central bank was not legally independent. Inflation (as well as balance of payments deficits caused by inflation) actually worked as a strong constraint on the ability of the government to rely extensively on monetary financing, as a detailed study of the 1952–1953 and 1957 loans shows. Debates about the opportunity to increase advances to the Treasury were not so different from those of the interwar, when the Banque de France was still a private institution and when governments asking for Banque de France loans had to commit to fiscal rectitude and endorse restrictive monetary policy. As with other elements of credit policy studied in Part I, the financing of public debt was subject to institutional control, either legal or informal. The 1973 reform did not put an end to the financing of public debt by the Banque de France, but it should be interpreted as a sign of a shift toward a system in which transparency and market forces, rather than fear of inflation, acted as limits on the state's ability to take on debt. The gradual shift toward a system of marketable public debt began at the same time, around 1973–1974. It has somehow freed the expansion of public debt from the inflationary constraint and from the reaction of the central bank wishing to counterbalance loans to the Treasury by restrictive monetary policy. It has consequently modified the means of institutional control on the expansion of public debt. After 1973, there was no longer any situation where the Banque implemented anti-inflationary measures to offset the inflationary effects of loans to the Treasury.

---

[1] Marketable (or negotiable) public debt is issued on a market and is transferable to a third party (can be bought and sold on a secondary market). Non-marketable debt is not transferable. Loans with a fixed rate of return from financial institutions to the state are typically non-marketable debt. According to the various documents I have seen, the distinction between negotiable and non-negotiable public debt did not appear in French administration and official statistics before the 1970s (see also Lemoine 2016). The usual distinction that appeared in the reports of the CNC in the 1950s and 1960s was between monetary financing of the public debt (that is loans by banks and the Banque de France) and non-monetary financing (securities). See Abbas et al. (2014) for an attempt to present historical statistics of marketable versus non-marketable debt for a large number of countries.

I THE BASICS OF THE SYSTEM: BANQUE DE FRANCE'S FINANCING OF THE FRENCH GOVERNMENT BEFORE 1948

Advances to the Treasury with Parliamentary Approval

Monetary financing of public debt can be done either through central bank purchases of government securities on the primary market or through direct loans to the government. The long-standing official doctrine of the Banque de France was to use the second option. Since a 1857 law, official loans to the government could take two forms: either permanent or temporary loans. Both types of loans were collateralized by government securities. Temporary loans were justified by exceptional circumstances (war, economic crisis), had a fixed interest rate and had to be reimbursed.[2] Permanent loans were a credit line – with a ceiling – on which the Treasury could draw perpetually, with no interest rate. Temporary loans, as well as any change in the maximum amounts of both types of loans, had to take the form of a legal agreement between the Banque and the Treasury and then be approved by the Parliament. Both types of loans appeared in the official balance sheet of the central bank that was published weekly and received a lot of attention from the press and the financial and political communities. During the two World Wars, the Banque de France fueled inflation by expanding the money base through a sharp increase in advances to the Treasury. These official direct loans accounted for 70% of the balance sheet of the central bank between 1914 and 1918, went down to 10% in the early 1930s, after Poincaré stabilization and the liquidation of war debts, and finally reached 80% in 1945 (Duchaussoy & Monnet 2015, 2018; see Figure 1 in Chapter 2).[3]

The Banque de France accepted government securities (as well as securities of many other public or semi-public institutions, as seen in Part I) as collateral for advances and discount window lending to banks. However, the Banque was not supposed to purchase government securities issued on the primary market nor discount government bills for the account of the Treasury: official advances to the Treasury (approved by the Parliament) had to be used instead. This long-standing informal rule was formalized in

---

[2] The maturity of the loan depended on the agreement with the Treasury that had to be approved by the Parliament.

[3] During World War II, this includes the financing of German troops. Before 1914 – excluding the 1870 Franco-Prussian war – loans to the Treasury accounted for less than 5% of the balance sheet (Duchaussoy & Monnet 2015).

the 1936 new legal status of the central bank (which remained unaffected by the 1945 nationalization and was still in place until 1973). When the possibility of carrying out open market operations was first authorized at the Banque de France in 1938, the law stipulated that direct purchases (i.e., primary market) of Treasury bills from the Treasury were prohibited. In other words, the government could not ask the Banque to buy its debt directly, outside of the official and quite rigid framework of the advances to the Treasury which was monitored by the Parliament.

The Troubles of the Interwar

Despite the rigid system of Treasury loans implemented in 1857, there always have been, however, exceptions and attempts to play with the rules, most prominently after 1914 (Baubeau 2004, pp. 441–442). The most notable ones are particularly important in understanding the historical precedents that central bankers had in mind after World War II and the origins of the laws and institutions they faced. A comparison between the liquidation of war debts after World War I and World War II is also enlightening. For this reason, it is worth paying attention to interwar history in this introductory section. During World War I, the Banque de France discounted directly three-month bills issued by the French government in order to lend to Russia, an ally of the French state. The bills were presented directly by the French government at the Banque de France – rather than by banks or private customers – and money was then deposited on the account of the Russian central bank and used to finance exports from France to Russia. The beneficiary of the loan was Russia but it was in fact direct discounting of French Treasury bills, without being considered as official advances to the French Treasury. Although the scheme stopped with the Russian revolution, bills were renewed every three months until 1928 (Duchaussoy & Monnet 2018). They were not hidden but appeared in a separate category of the balance sheets of the Banque de France as "discounted Treasury bills" and named within the Banque and in parliamentary debates as "discounted Treasury bills on behalf of the Russian government." The normal discount rate of the Banque applied to these bills. After the war, interests received from these operations were deposited on a special account and used to repay the official advances to the French Treasury. This unofficial circuit thus served after the war to reimburse the official loans granted by the central bank to the French state. It ended with the monetary law of June 1928: while official advances were reimbursed through the devaluation of the franc, Treasury bills "held on behalf of

Russia" were converted into bills of a sinking fund created in 1926 (*Caisse autonome d'amortissement*).[4] Discounting of bills of the *Caisse autonome d'amortissement* remained in place until 1952 but it was then a negligible amount of loans to the state. After 1928, it took only a few years for an unofficial form of Treasury financing to reappear. In the first semester 1935, the French government faced a budget crisis and, in May, asked the Banque de France to discount directly the bills presented by the Treasury (Mouré 1991, pp. 177–179). In practice, the Banque committed to rediscount the bills and they were purchased by the three main banks (Crédit Lyonnais, Société Générale and Comptoir d'escompte) and the *Caisse des dépôts et consignations* (CDC), then immediately discounted by the Banque (ibid. p. 177). This led to a large wave of rediscounting of Treasury bills (up to 3 billion francs), at the request of the government. The amount of Treasury bills issued could not exceed a ceiling legally fixed by the Parliament. Given the pre-commitment of the Banque, this operation was equivalent to direct discounting of Treasury bills. These urgent measures were explicitly taken to circumvent the rule requiring that financing of the government took the form of official advances to the Treasury approved by the Parliament. In return, the government committed to restoring the government's budget balance (ibid.; Duchaussoy & Monnet 2018). When the Popular Front came to power in May 1936, it followed the repeated calls of the central bank to normalize the situation. Direct discounting of government paper ceased and official (temporary) advances to the Treasury were increased on June 18th to replace the amount of Treasury bills discounted by the Banque (Duchaussoy & Monnet 2018).[5] The normalization of exceptional Treasury loans in 1936 recognized that the means of government financing had gone out of the tracks and that such exceptional discounting of

---

[4] Blancheton (2001, p. 208) and Baubeau (2004, p. 323) also mentioned episodes in 1924–1925 when rediscounting of Treasury bills eased the financing of the state.

[5] This was ratified by a law on June 23rd. In addition to the direct financing of the state budget, the Banque de France also carries out a number of tasks to help the financing to the Treasury, such as its contribution to bond issuance. The law of November 17, 1897, concluded at the time of the previous renewal of the privilege, already obliged the Bank to participate in Treasury bill issues. In addition, the Banque used to accompany Treasury bill issues with an increase in its discount and advance portfolio to provide liquidity to investors (Ramon 1929; Bazot et al. 2016). The Banque was actively involved in these issues, in particular by opening numerous counters, developing publicity for the bonds and introducing measures to help subscribers, such as the assumption of stamp duties. The Banque's contribution therefore exceeds the distribution and advertising functions, by committing itself to facilitating advances for subscribers of government bonds (Radouant 1921, pp. 123–128).

Treasury bills on demand of the Treasury should not happen again. Almost one month later, the 1936 law carved in stone the fact that the Banque de France could not directly discount government bills.[6] Other tricks had to be found, and they were more complex and more secretive. During World War II, there was no doubt that, as in the previous war, the Banque's primary task was to lend to the government (Baubeau & Le Bris 2017a; see also Figure 1 in Chapter 2). After the war, as the burden of public debt was drastically and quickly reduced by inflation between 1945 and 1948, it was uncertain how the government's financing would be normalized and carried out in the midst of the imperatives and means of credit policy and the political instability of the Fourth Republic. The nationalization of the Banque de France in 1945 had not modified the official rules of advances to the Treasury.

II THE HIDDEN PART OF TREASURY FINANCING, 1948–1973

Description of the System

In addition to the permanent and temporary loans that were officially recorded on the balance sheet of the Banque de France, an unofficial system of state financing was set up after the war and lasted until 1973. Contrary to earlier exceptions to the rules, that had been rather brief and mainly in response to budget crises or as part of war finance, the unofficial postwar arrangement was a regular and important element of monetary financing for almost twenty-five years. Invisible in official statistics, it has not since then given rise to historical analyses that allow assessing its quantitative importance. The following pages therefore present for the first time a comprehensive view of this system and the amounts involved. As will be discussed below, understanding the hidden part of the Banque's financing of the Treasury is not only important for correcting official statistics, but also for understanding the politics of public debt during this period and why it relied on the interconnections (and balance of power) between public institutions rather than on the vigilance of market investors. The two main types of unofficial loans to the Treasury were the following: discounting of *obligations cautionnées* and discounting of CDC construction loans.

---

[6] *Loi tendant à modifier et à compléter les Lois et statuts qui régissent la Banque de France* (24 juillet 1936), article 13.

Discounting of obligations cautionnées *(Guaranteed Bonds) by the Central Bank*

The *obligations cautionnées* are a liability toward the Treasury. They are contracted by firms which cannot pay taxes immediately and thus promise to pay later. It takes the form of an IOU (promise to pay a debt taking the form of a signed paper stating the specific amount owed), namely a promissory note with a three- or four-month maturity. The Banque de France accepted to discount such *obligations cautionnées*, presented at the discount window by the Treasury, which meant that the central bank lent directly to the Treasury, taking the *obligations cautionnées* as a collateral. These direct loans to the Treasury appeared as standard discounting of commercial paper in the balance sheet of the Banque de France rather than as loans to the Treasury (*concours au Trésor*). Neither the public nor the Parliament could know their amount and, outside the Treasury and the central bank, few knew that such a system even existed. *Obligations cautionnées* had been in existence since 1875, but their widespread and systematic use by the Treasury and the Banque de France for the purposes of the state financing emerged in 1948 (see below). Koch (1983, p. 133) provided their annual amounts for the years 1948–1958. In her history of the French Treasury, Laure Quenouëlle-Corre (2000) also mentioned briefly their existence and stressed that this means of financing was unknown to the general public. In her words (I translate): "A Treasury financing channel, however, remains outside the scope of external criticism and for good reason: it is necessary to be at home in the Treasury to know and understand the system of *obligations cautionnées!*" (p. 426).

Discounting of prêts à la construction de la Caisse des Dépôts et Consignations *(CDC Construction Loans)*

The Caisse des Dépôts et Consignations (CDC) is a public credit institution specialized in collecting savings to finance social housing and issuing bonds to finance long-term investments. Loans to firms and banks granted by the CDC to finance construction (of either housing or infrastructures) could be rediscounted at the central bank discount window. There was an informal contract between the Treasury and the CDC: the funds obtained by the CDC from the central bank by discounting construction loans were automatically deposited at the Treasury by the CDC. Thus, when the CDC asked the Banque de France to rediscount these assets (*prêts à la construction*), the Banque de France was making a *de facto* loan to the Treasury. Put differently, when it needed funds, the Treasury could ask the CDC to discount its construction loans at the Banque de France and to deposit the amount received into the account that the CDC made available to the Treasury. The request for financing thus came from the Treasury but was mediated by the CDC and thus limited by the existing amount of construction loans actually granted by the CDC. The maturity of rediscountable construction loans was usually between two and five years (medium-term credit). Until 1964, the discounts of the *prêts à la construction de la Caisse des Dépôts et Consignations* were not distinguished from the discounts of other medium-term credit in the balance sheet of the central bank.[7]

The Official Balance Sheet of the Banque de France
In 1964, as part of a general restructuring of the presentation of the Banque's balance sheet (published weekly), it was decided to distinguish between the guaranteed bonds and the portfolio of commercial paper, as well as between the CDC construction loans and the rediscount of medium-term credit. This accounting change, proposed by the Banque and accepted by the Treasury, was carried out for the sake of clarity and in view of the fact that the use of guaranteed bonds had become a widespread and regular feature of monetary financing, rather than a tool merely used in times of crisis as it had been the case in 1947–1948.[8] In 1963–1964, the financing of the Banque de France to the Treasury as a percentage of GDP was low compared to the previous decade, but the proportion of guaranteed bonds and loans to the CDC was now a significant and regular part of it (Figure 19).

From 1964 to 1973, both types of unofficial financing appeared in a separate column of the balance sheet of the Banque de France but not as loans or advances to the Treasury. Nor were they approved by Parliament. In internal notes at the central bank and the Treasury, and in minutes of the General Council of the Banque de France, however, they were discussed and counted as monetary financing of public debt. Banque de France loans to the state were thus still somewhat encrypted, but their amount was visible in the balance sheet under misleading names. The situation was made more complex in January 1971 when the Banque de France decided to intervene more systematically in the money market (see Chapters 3 and 4) and thus increased its discount rate above the prevailing rate in that market. The CDC decided to go on the market to borrow short-term rather than rediscounting medium-term loans (including construction loans) at the Banque de France.

---

[7] Effosse (2003, p. 386) explains that these loans were indeed used for direct financing of the Treasury and that, during the 1957–1958 budget crisis, the IMF asked if such operations could be stopped.

[8] ABF, PVCG, February 20, 1964.

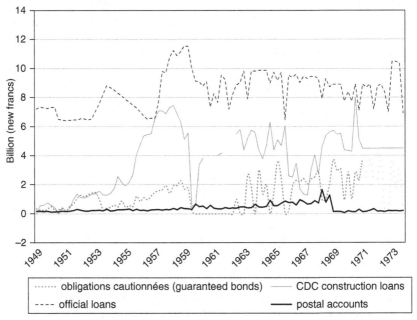

Figure 19 Official and unofficial loans from the Banque de France to the Treasury, 1949–1973
Notes: Billions of new francs. Official loans are the officially published temporary and permanent loans to the Treasury. CDC loans and obligations cautionnées are the hidden part of financing of public debt.
Source: Calculations by author using Banque de France's archives (see the text).

The Banque then lent directly to the CDC on the money market (in the form of a "*prise en pension*," that is, a repurchase agreement).[9] Banque de France's acceptance of medium-term bills issued by public institutions as collateral on the money market was permitted by the 1966 Act (see Chapter 3). The CDC funds available to the Treasury therefore entered the open market portfolio of the Banque, without it being possible to distinguish them from other open market operations, including other loans to the CDC. The discounting of construction loans by the Banque did not, however, stop completely as the CDC arbitraged between money market and rediscounting conditions. The column of CDC construction loans in the balance sheet of the Banque therefore did undergo abrupt and significant variations depending on the spread between the discount and money market rates. In view of the complexity of

[9] ABF, PVCG, February 18 and March 11, 1971.

these operations, the Banque de France took the habit of considering that CDC funds available for the Treasury were equal to 4.5 billion francs, i.e., the tacit maximum amount fixed between these two organizations. But it was becoming difficult for the Banque to know what amount was actually being demanded and used by the Treasury, rather than being short-term liquidity necessary to the CDC. These difficulties, which were a direct result of the 1966 reforms on open market operations and, above all, of the 1971 new policy of the Banque on the money market, were therefore one of the main reasons for simplifying the financial relations between the Treasury, CDC and the Banque de France in 1973. The following sections present and discuss the volume of unofficial financing from 1948 to 1973 and explain how and why the system ended.

Amounts Involved

This previous description of the evolution of monetary means of financing made it clear that it is difficult to provide an accurate and continuous estimate of the amounts involved before 1964 as well as between 1971 and 1973. To get around this problem I have tried to find the distinctions operated internally within the Banque and hidden from the public, based on various notes and, most of all, on presentations and discussions of these figures during meetings of the General Council of the Banque.[10] I have been able to obtain at least one occurrence of amounts of outstanding guaranteed bonds and construction loans to CDC by quarter for the entire period. This makes it possible to build a quarterly series of the Treasury's indebtedness to the Banque de France, including the unofficial part of the financing. In addition, I rely on an internal report of the *Direction Générale du Crédit* (DGC) of the Banque de France written in 1969. This is the only document I found that presents retrospective, comprehensive and disaggregated series of financing to the government – including the unofficial component – over a long period (1950–1967).[11] Annual series from this document are consistent with the quarterly data built from the reading of weekly transcripts

---

[10] In each transcript of the weekly meeting of the General Council, there is a section devoted to Treasury's position (*situation du Trésor*) that is clearly distinguished from the section named "loans to the economy" (*concours à l'économie*).

[11] ABF, 1331200301/219, *Direction Générale du Crédit. Direction des analyses et des statistiques monétaires*. Untitled table, "Concours directs de la Banque de France au Trésor," January 20, 1969. Many other documents mention the *obligations cautionnées* and CDC *construction loans*, but do not provide long-run data that I could compare to the figures mentioned in the transcripts of the General Council.

of the General council (PVCG). In particular, the 1969 document confirms that the discounting of *obligations cautionnées* equaled zero between 1959 and 1962 whereas the discounting of CDC loans was still high during the same period.[12]

Computations are still imprecise for two reasons. First of all, numbers are only stocks at a given point in time and therefore cannot take into account short-term flows that are balanced between two quarters. These flows are potentially significant for guaranteed bonds, which were primarily used by the Treasury to obtain short-term liquidity from the Banque. It would tend to underestimate the amount of guaranteed bonds used by the Treasury. Second, from 1971 to 1973 we have no precise figures since loans to CDC were indistinguishable from other open market operations. The exact amount of Treasury financing through CDC loans lies between the published amount of discounted construction loans and the maximum amount of 4.5 billion francs. In choosing to consider this maximum, my method therefore tends to overestimate the Treasury's use of CDC financing.[13]

Finally, a full assessment of the Treasury's debt toward the central bank also implies taking into account the item "postal current accounts," in line with the internal practice of the Banque.[14] This is the Postal Administration account with the central bank, which is mainly important in regional branches. This item is visible in the weekly statement of the Banque de France over the entire period, although not included in the advances to the Treasury. It is a claim of the Banque against the state, but these accounts are balanced every week and the Treasury had no possibility of using them as a variable means of financing because it could not decide on the amount of these accounts. Accordingly, its share in the Banque's balance sheet is modest and stable over time (2% on average, see Figure 19). While this item should be taken into account in order to provide a full assessment of the loans to the Treasury (as was done by the Banque de France at that time), no general political conclusions can be drawn from it as it is small and does not vary substantially over time.

Guaranteed bonds and construction loans can account for about half of Banque loans to the Treasury during some years of the *Trente Glorieuses*, that is between 1956 and 1959 and then again between 1963

---

[12] According to the document, discounting of *obligations cautionnées* is also equal to zero in 1963, 1964, 1965. In my data, discounting equals zero in the last quarter of each of these years but is positive otherwise.

[13] This was also the assumption made by the Banque in 1973. ABF, PVCG, September 13, 1973.

[14] The Postal Administration account is considered in the 1969 note of the DGC quoted above.

and 1973 (Figure 19). They equaled 35% of total loans from 1949 to 1973 on average, and 43% from 1956 to 1973.[15] Before 1973, researchers using only the series available in the weekly balance sheets of the Banque de France are therefore exposed to leaving aside a large part of what monetary financing of public debt really was. It is also worth noting that, in the publications of the Finance Ministry and in the *Annuaire Statistique de la France* (Statistical Yearbook) of INSEE (National Institute of Statistics and Economic Studies) the debt of the French state toward the Banque de France only included the official advances to the Treasury (*concours au Trésor*). No published sources documented the hidden part of the monetary financing of public debt.

After the war, permanent official advances to the Treasury had been increased in April 1947 in the context of postwar inflation (they nonetheless decreased as a proportion of the Banque's assets and GDP). Then, official Treasury loans remained stable until 1953 and they decreased quickly in proportion to the total balance sheet of the Banque de France, as shown in Figure 20. The picture is very different if we include unofficial loans to the Treasury: the share of total loans in the Banque's assets remained stable in the 1950s. 1959 was an important turning point in French fiscal policies (Quenouëlle-Corre 2000, chs. 6 and 8). The birth of the Fifth Republic was associated with a restoration of fiscal stability which led to a sharp decrease in public debt to GDP ratio.[16] The new government had committed to reduce monetary financing of the public debt in order to keep the price level stable, reimbursing quickly the 1957 official temporary loans and decreasing the use of unofficial facilities. The consequence of fiscal stabilization for the Banque de France was that the nominal amount of official (temporary) and unofficial loans decreased in 1959.[17] They stabilized

---

[15] When I compare the data obtained from the PVCG over 1950–1967 to the series of the 1969 note of the DGC, I find 31% for the former and 32% for the latter.

[16] Figures of public debt are from INSEE (1989). Definitions and statistics of public debt vary for this period, depending on the sources and dates of publication. Reinhart and Rogoff (2009) for example used UN series that show a higher French public debt on average. Statistics are not consistent across the subsequent volumes of the *Annuaires statistiques de la France.* INSEE public debt figures do not include *obligations cautionnées* and presumably not the CDC construction loans, but include official loans to the Treasury from the Banque de France. French debt financing has been underestimated in the economic literature because they used estimates from the United States or INSEE that excluded any hidden financing that is unveiled in this chapter. Taking into account the hidden financing shows stability of public debt to GDP in the 1950s.

[17] The decrease of official advances (and new presentation in the balance sheet of the Banque) was decided in a *convention de Trésorerie* on October 29, 1959.

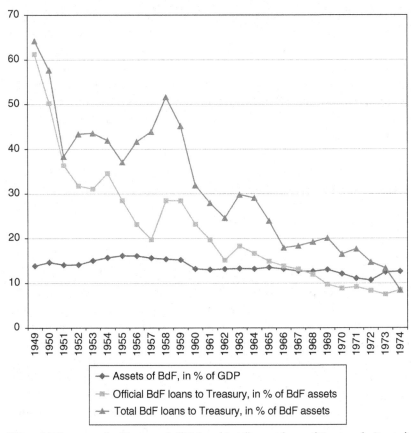

Figure 20 Loans to the Treasury (official and total) as a share of Banque de France's assets
Source: GDP from INSEE (1989), and calculations by author using Banque de France's archives (see the text).

as soon as 1962 so that their share in total assets continued to decrease (Figure 20). *Obligations cautionnées* were less used between 1959 and 1962, at the beginning of the Fifth Republic, because of large budget surpluses. Loans to the Treasury in proportion of total public debt also fell sharply in 1959. Thereafter, as public debt decreased slightly because of budget surpluses until 1967, the ratio of monetary financing over public debt even increased slightly in the mid-1960s (Figure 21). The unofficial side of Treasury loans (especially discounts of CDC loans) increased during the second semester of 1968 and first semester of 1969, before the devaluation

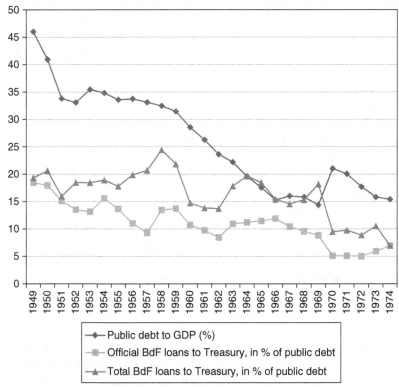

Figure 21 Loans to the Treasury (official and total) as a share of French public debt
Source: Public debt and GDP from INSEE (1989), and calculations by author using Banque de France's archives (see the text).

of the franc, when the country experienced fiscal deficits (Blancheton & Bordes 2007).

End of the System: The 1973 Law and the Path Toward Transparency

Unofficial monetary financing of public debt ended, and came into the bright light, in September 1973 when the government and the central bank decided to make the Banque de France's financing of the Treasury more transparent.[18] The two unofficial types of loans were stopped and

[18] ABF, PVCG, September 13, 1973. The convention was accepted on September 13, published on September 17 and ratified by a law on December 21.

were replaced by an increase in the amount of the official Treasury loans. In many ways, the 1973 normalization seems similar in kind to the ones of 1928 and 1936. All these cases show how long and difficult it was to regularize loans to the Treasury after each of the World Wars, and how, each time, legal change was finally needed to modify or confirm practices that had developed informally over time. However, the unofficial system of postwar financing reformed in 1973 was not limited to short-term financial channels designed for the liquidation of war debts or as ad hoc responses to fiscal crises. Contrary to the chaotic interwar period, unofficial loans to the Treasury during the French Golden Age were a regular and constant feature of the system, including during the years of budget surplus in the 1960s.

With the 1973 reform, the new ceiling of the official loan (20.5 billion francs) equaled the ceiling of the previous official loans (10.5 billion francs) in addition to an estimated value of unofficial loans (10 billion francs). This was a little bit higher than the amount of unofficial loans in 1973. However, it was lower as a proportion of the Banque's assets because of the increase in other types of credit in 1974 (Figure 20). The 1973 law was not an unfavorable deal for the government in financial terms, but it ended the flexibility that had characterized the 1948–1973 period. The nominal value of this ceiling was not changed until 1993 and the real contribution of the monetary financing of public debt decreased quickly as inflation and debt were rising. At the end of 1973, the new amount of official loans from the Banque de France financed around 15% of French public debt, in 1985, 6%, and in 1993, 3%.[19]

---

[19] These are gross numbers. In fact, the net contribution of the Banque de France to the financing of the Treasury was negative starting in the late 1970s according to INSEE (1989, p. 619). This was due to two reasons. First, since 1973 (ABF, PVCG, August 30 and September 13, 1973, and article 5 of the September 17 convention) the benefits from the Exchange stabilization fund were deposited on the account of the Treasury at the Banque de France and were deducted from the maximum amount of Treasury loans. Hence, in practice, when there was a depreciation of the franc relative to floating currencies, the value of the Exchange stabilization fund and Treasury account at the Banque increased and the maximum amount of available Treasury loans decreased. It is why the Treasury tried – without success, because the Banque opposed it – to increase again the ceiling of Treasury loans in 1981. This issue was minor under the fixed exchange rate world of Bretton Woods but became important with floating exchange rates, hence the 1973 decision. The second reasons is simply that, in real terms, the maximum amount of Treasury loans decreased rapidly with inflation so that – whatever the profits of the Exchange stabilization fund in the 1980s – the deposits of the Treasury exceeded Treasury loans starting from the mid-1980s.

III THE POLITICAL ECONOMY OF OFFICIAL
AND UNOFFICIAL LOANS TO THE TREASURY

Political and Economic Limits on Monetary
Financing of the Public Debt (1952–1958)

Besides their economic magnitude, official and unofficial loans to the Treasury were important because of their availability during times of budget deficits such as in 1952–1953, 1957 and 1968, as the direct discounting of government securities had been during the budget and balance of payments crisis of 1935–1936. Rediscounting *obligations cautionnées* and *prêts à la construction* provided flexibility in hard times. As shown in Figure 19, their amount increased quickly between 1954 and 1957, under the Fourth Republic, because they prevented the government from asking for a new official loan from the Banque de France. They made the transition from the war economy to the peace economy smoother. But such flexibility was nevertheless limited. It is not possible to rediscount an asset that did not exist. And the Treasury could not issue *obligations cautionnées* and *prêts à la construction*. Thus, when a serious budget crisis hit, the number of assets in circulation which could be rediscounted was too small. This was particularly the case in the early 1950s, when these operations were still relatively low due to unfinished economic reconstruction. Then, it was necessary for the Treasury to ask for another exceptional temporary official loan, legally approved by a Parliamentary vote. It was done several times in 1953 and 1957. Before that, there had been an important event in February 1952. The *Président du conseil* (prime minister) and Finance Minister Edgard Faure had asked for financial support from the Banque, in the midst of a fiscal and political crisis. His government had just resigned. The Banque accepted to grant a very short-term loan (three weeks) and the governor of the Banque, Wilfrid Baumgartner, sent and made public a letter to Faure which eventually led the latter to be overthrown definitely by the Parliament. The letter contained complaints about the lack of fiscal rectitude, despite restrictive monetary policy, especially in times of balance of payments deficits.[20] More intriguing and unconventional was the form of the loan. Baumgartner did not want to use exceptional temporary advances to the Treasury which

---

[20] See Feiertag (2006b, ch. 3). The debates that led to this letter as well as the letter can be found in ABF, PVCG, February 29, 1952.

generally had a maturity of six months.[21] Instead, he advocated that the Banque would buy Treasury bills on the market. In an implicit reference to the 1935 direct rediscounting of government paper, he refused the option previously used to ask banks to act as intermediaries between the Treasury and the Banque. He stressed that purchases of bills should be made in a transparent manner and with the approval of Parliament, as in the case of temporary advances.[22] Furthermore, a new item was created in the balance sheet of the Banque to make them visible and distinct from usual loans to the Treasury: Treasury bills bought in the money market (*bons du Trésor achetés*). As such they are counted as official loans (*avances directes*) in Figure 19. It was therefore by no means a hidden way of financing the Treasury.[23] The Banque was firm, pushed for a new fiscal policy (and implicitly government renewal) and committed to restrictive monetary policy, while at the same time helping the Treasury to avoid exacerbating the political crisis with a fiscal crisis. The loan was quickly reimbursed after three weeks. However, the same problem reappeared one year later. The Banque again decided to grant a short-term (three-month) loan through the purchase of Treasury bills in the market (25 billion old francs) as well as an increase of the temporary advances (25 billion old francs).[24] The agreement with the Treasury required that dividends received (as the Banque's sole shareholder) at the end of the year, as well as profits from the Exchange Stabilization Fund, should be used to repay the temporary loan. Moreover, the Banque committed to pursue its restrictive monetary policy in order to offset the expansionary effect of the purchase of Treasury bills.[25] On March 24, 1953, a new agreement was signed by the Treasury and the Banque about a purchase of 100 billion old francs of Treasury bills (that had to be reimbursed within three months). It was explicitly mentioned that one of the reasons why – contrary to 1952 – the first loan had not been sufficient was that *obligations cautionnées* were rarer in 1953 than in 1952 (because of the drop in activity caused by deflationary monetary policy), so that the Treasury could not use them for short-term financing.[26] The agreement was

---

[21] ABF, PVCG, February 29, 1952. The amount (25 billion old francs) was chosen to equal – and not exceed – the previous temporary loan granted in 1947 and reimbursed in 1949.

[22] Furthermore, contrary to the interwar period, banks were subject to the *coefficient de Trésorerie*, so that they had to keep most of their Treasury bills as liquidity buffer.

[23] It required an exemption from the decree of June 17, 1938, which defined the operations of the Banque on the open market.

[24] Again the amount was chosen to avoid that the ceiling of temporary advances exceed their previous 1947 maximum. ABF, PVCG, January 22, 1953. The Treasury also received a loan from the Banque d'Algérie (10 billion).

[25] ABF, PVCG, January 22, 1953.

[26] ABF, PVCG, March 23, 1953. Exposé de M. Schweitzer.

renewed on June 15th with a limit of 80 billion francs.[27] On June 22nd, in the midst of a new budget and political crisis (again, the Parliament had not managed to elect a new head of government), the Banque opened a special and temporary account for the Treasury on which the latter could draw within a limit of 50 billion until July 10th. Again, these operations were approved by the Parliament and appeared clearly in the balance sheet of the Banque. The letter sent by the governor to the provisional head of government stated: "the General Council believes that within the deadline set for this new agreement, a Government will be able to set up and implement the economic and financial recovery programme on which monetary consolidation depends."[28] At that time, inflation was no longer rising and the balance of payments was in good shape, so the Banque did not push for a more restrictive monetary policy, but the members of the General Council made it clear that monetary restrictions should be imposed if these new advances to the Treasury were to stimulate inflation.

The political instability of the Fourth Republic continued to push the Banque to increase its lending to the Treasury, despite the sharp rise in unofficial lending from 1955 onwards.[29] Another exceptional way of financing short-term public debt in times of crisis was to allow the Treasury to draw on the credit line of a state-owned company. I have found only one example of such a practice: in October 1957, in the middle of both a political and budget crisis, the government (which had just resigned) asked the Banque de France to use the credit facility of the major electricity firm EDF (Electricity of France).[30] The Banque de France had previously accepted to lend EDF 45 billion old francs, but EDF had only drawn 10 billion of this facility. The Treasury asked to borrow the remaining and committed to reimburse quickly before the end of the year 1957. It was not an official loan and thus did not require a Parliamentary approval. Nevertheless, the Banque de France told Parliament about this operation, and made sure that it was understood by representatives as a very exceptional temporary measure. The rationale for not requiring an official loan and a vote from Parliament was that the political crisis prevented a parliamentary debate on the subject: the Finance Ministry of the government (Felix Gaillard) who

---

[27] ABF, PVCG, March 23, 1953.
[28] ABF, PVCG, June 22, 1953.
[29] During the Fourth Republic, the government (cabinet) could be dismissed if an absolute majority of the National Assembly's members voted against. The Republic had twenty-eight different governments during its short existence (November 1945–January 1959).
[30] ABF, PVCG, October 31, 1957.

has just resigned was running for President of the Council. The debates at the General Council of the Banque de France show that all the members disapproved of such an operation but nevertheless decided to vote for it in order to avoid a stronger political crisis. Regarding central bank independence, it is important to note that, again, the General Council of the central bank was not forced to accept such an exceptional loan (the government had no legal power to force it anyway) but they decided to grant the loan to avoid political instability.

Before this October 1957 episode, there had been an official temporary loan granted by the Banque de France to the Treasury in June 1957. It was legally approved by the Parliament. In order to obtain the vote of the Parliament, the government had to commit to budget cuts, capital controls and temporary taxes (that actually proved insufficient in 1957). Furthermore, the Banque de France started to implement a restrictive monetary policy to counteract the effect of the new loan on inflation (see Chapter 4). According to the governor of the Banque de France, a new loan to the Treasury would mechanically create inflation and the central bank had to restrict credit creation by banks in order to offset the effect of the loan to the Treasury on the money supply and the price level.[31] The same rules applied to a new exceptional loan in November. In December, a report of the Finance Committee of the National Assembly, directed by M. Leenhardt, openly accused the Banque de France of worsening the public deficit by conducting a restrictive monetary policy. The Banque replied that the Parliament had contradictory views because it wanted to both reduce inflation and increase monetary financing of public debt: "inflation cannot be relied on indefinitely when trying to curb inflation."[32] In January 1958, monetary policy turned even more restrictive and in January 1959, when the stance of monetary policy turned back to normal, the new government had committed to a balanced budget and expenditures cuts.

A government could not use too much money creation to finance public deficits without pushing up inflation and then triggering a contractionary monetary policy. As in 1935 – when the Banque increased its discount rate and the government had to embark on a deflationary fiscal policy in order for the unofficial direct purchase of Treasury bills to be acceptable to the Banque – the 1952–1953 and 1957 episodes show that the increase

---

[31] ABF, PVCG, June 20, 1957.
[32] ABF, PVCG, December 19, 1957.

in unofficial or official Treasury loans did not take place without the government and the Banque taking offsetting measures.[33] Some would say that loans from the Banque de France created a moral hazard problem, so that the mere possibility of their existence encouraged governments to go as far as the budgetary crisis. This was not the case anymore however in the 1960s. Yet, *in fine*, legal, economic and political limits on the Banque de France's loans to the Treasury served as a constraint on the expansion of government debt in peacetime. During the Fourth Republic marked by strong political uncertainty, the Banque's loans to the Treasury (compensated by a restrictive policy) had played a role in guaranteeing the stability of the state. Far from signifying a subordination of the central bank to the Treasury, they show the importance of the Banque, and its political power, within the machinery of government during this period.

While the state budget was constantly in deficit during the Fourth Republic, it was almost constantly in surplus starting 1958, until it became in deficit forever from 1975 onwards. The only important exception was 1968, and to a lesser extent 1967 and 1971. In the 1968 episode, the unofficial side of Treasury financing proved to be sufficient to provide short-term liquidity to the Treasury. The government especially relied heavily on discounting of CDC construction loans in the months following the civil unrest and strikes of May 1968, in order to relax the budget constraint.[34]

The lack of central bank independence should not be associated with unfettered monetary financing of public debt. Going beyond stereotypes about the relationship between the central bank and government, we learn a great deal about the functioning of the state and the nature of the financial system when we examine the monetary financing techniques and institutional limits (legal, political, financial) imposed on the expansion of Treasury loans and public debt.

Why Did Some Loans to the Treasury Remain Unofficial?

The reason why about half of the monetary financing of public debt remained unofficial for more than two decades differs from the reason why

---

[33] The situation was however different from 1935 for two reasons. First, during Bretton Woods, the possibility of devaluation was not out of sight. Second, overall the Banque de France's credit policy was clearly supportive of growth, although the central bank wanted to avoid too high inflation rates. Thus, contrary to the interwar period, the balance of power between the Bank and the Treasury was not blocked in a deflationary spiral, but, as we have seen, it was not blocked in an inflationary spiral either.

[34] See discussions on this episode in ABF, PVCG, November 12, 1968.

the central bank accepted or refused to grant new loans to the Treasury. The latter was a problem about choosing the right amount of monetary financing (especially in exceptional circumstances) while the former was a problem of setting common regular practices in a consistent financing framework.

In December 1949, the General Council discussed the fact that rediscounting of the *obligations cautionnées* had increased more than usual (it had existed since 1875 but had always been negligible), and had become a regular way to finance the Treasury deficit since the previous year.[35] It was nevertheless decided that they should not be distinguished in the balance sheet because "their name and their existence is ignored by the public" and "the Treasury fears that that these operations, which are very common, would be interpreted as a direct loan to the Treasury if they appear in a separate line in the balance sheet of the central bank."[36] This 1949 statement contrasts with the practice and the narrative that developed later on, both at the Treasury (Quenouëlle-Corre 2000, p. 426) and at the Banque, as we have seen previously. In August 1973, in front of the General Council, the governor of the Banque de France, Olivier Wormser, explained as follows why the unofficial system should end: "the modernization of the relationships between the Treasury and the central bank [*Institut d'émission*] implies primarily to give up the operations of rediscounting of *obligations cautionnées* and medium-term credit to construction."[37] A week later, the governor stated that the motivation of this reform was to "modernize, simplify, and make neutral" the instruments of monetary financing of public debt. Unofficial loans were indeed abolished and the maximum amount of the official loan to the Treasury was increased by 10 billion francs, which equaled the estimated previous volumes of unofficial financing.[38] As with the *obligations cautionnées* and *prêts à la construction*, the Treasury had to pay an interest rate on the 10 billion francs advances, "so that the Treasury is encouraged not to make use of financing provided by the Banque de France

---

[35] In the preceding years, especially between 1947 and 1949, the Banque lent to banks against Treasury bills and Crédit National bills in a great amount. According to the PVCG, the main objective of these operations was to provide liquidity to the market and they were not seen as unofficial loans to the Treasury. See also Crédit National (1951).

[36] ABF, PVCG, December 29, 1949.

[37] ABF, PVCG, August 30, 1973.

[38] According to a statement of the governor, the discounts of *obligations cautionnées* were 5.5 billion while the discounts of *prêts à la construction* "that benefit from an unofficial arrangement between the CDC and the Treasury" were estimated at 4.5 billion. ABF, PVCG, September 13, 1973.

as a matter of priority and is encouraged to repay it when it has temporary cash surpluses."[39] Debates about this reform at the General Council of the Banque de France show that there was a consensus. Nobody voted against it, not even the members who had been opposed to the 1971 reform of the open market (Chapter 3). However, some wondered why it was necessary to "officialize" and "formalize" such de facto practices that had given flexibility to the Treasury in the past. M. Pérouse, head of the Crédit National, feared negative consequences for the state budget (in 1973, France had a budget surplus) because it would be more difficult to increase monetary financing of the public debt while inflation kept increasing in the early 1970s. M. Pierre-Brossolette, head of the Treasury, replied that the state could still ask "one of its satellites" – that is public banks or public credit institutions – to provide short-term liquidity if it was necessary. Members also agreed that the amount of advances to the Treasury could be increased in the future.

The September 1973 reform should be understood in the context of the "rationalization of public policies" that started in the late 1960s in France (Bezes 2009). Reforms took place following the objectives of simplification and rationalization of state procedures, aiming for more accountability and transparency. It was also in line with the law of January 1973, which redefined the links between the state and the Banque de France and entrenched in law certain practices that had been established since the war (see Chapter 3). Finally, it was a direct consequence of the 1971 new policy of the Banque about open market operations that had increased confusion on the amount of loans to the CDC available to the Treasury. Twenty years before the independence of the central bank and the interdiction of loans to the Treasury, the 1973 reform was a major change in the French postwar system of monetary financing of the public debt as it "rationalized" and made "transparent" all the financial relationships between the Treasury and the Banque de France. I interpret this change as a shift from a system where economic outcomes mattered more than transparency for the legitimacy of public policy, to a system where rules and accountability became the norm in the management of public debt. Accordingly, it was also one of the first important steps of a move away from a system of financing of the public debt that relied on very close financial relationships between the Treasury, the central bank and other public banks and credit institutions such as the CDC, as well as state-owned

---

[39] Ibid. The 1973 law also introduced a new possibility for the Treasury to deposit at the central bank (on a remunerated account) the cash obtained from the sales of Treasury bonds by anticipation (i.e., before the official issuance).

firms such as EDF (Kuisel 1981; Margairaz 1991; Quennouëlle-Corre 2000; Lemoine 2016).

The Turn Toward Marketable Public Debt

According to discussions between the members of the General Council, the 1973 reform was therefore simply aimed at modernizing the financing of the Treasury by the Banque de France. In their view, this was not a major disruption to French public debt management. It is nevertheless remarkable, *a posteriori*, that it was from the following year, in 1974, that the share of marketable debt in French public debt began to grow rapidly, a trend that will never be interrupted thereafter (Figure 22).[40] To be sure, marketable (or negotiable) debt did not develop to replace the loans from the Banque de France. It was a much more general movement that changed the nature of state funding. As discussed by Quennouëlle-Corre (2015), Lemoine (2016) and previously in Chapter 3, the development of public and private marketable debt was a political priority in the late 1970s and early 1980s both in order to reintroduce market forces in the allocation of credit and in order to fight inflation. The government wanted more financial resources but less money creation. In doing so, the government hoped to avoid the criticism that budget deficit was causing inflation because it was financed by the central bank's loans and by deposits of public or semi-public financial institutions at the Treasury. In 1975, the state budget was in deficit again, for the first time since 1968 (INSEE 1989), and inflation was rising, but, contrary to what happened in 1953, 1957 and 1968, it was not followed by a strong contractionary monetary policy aiming at stabilizing the price level. Only fiscal policy was actively used in 1976 (a plan designed by the new Prime Minister Raymond Barre) to counter rising deficits.

IV CONCLUSION: NON-MARKETABLE PUBLIC DEBT AND THE CIRCUIT

The Great Inflation of the 1970s did not coincide with a large monetization of public debt in France. Instead, the central bank's financing to the Treasury decreased in real terms and as a proportion of public debt. Issuance

[40] This graph shows that the history of marketable debt in Western European countries is quite similar. Definitions of marketable public debt are subject to caution and evolved over time. I use the data from Abbas et al. (2014) because of their consistency and comparability. Series published by Jurgensen and Lebegue (1988) show a similar trend but point to a lower share of marketable public over the whole period.

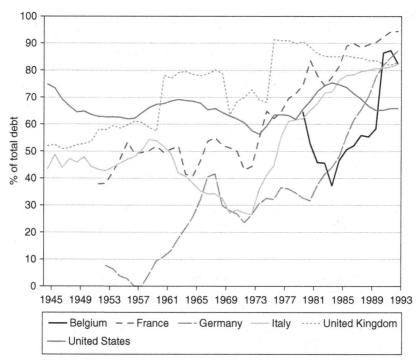

Figure 22 Share of marketable public debt in total public debt
Source: Abbas et al. (2014).

of marketable debt increased in order to provide non-monetary financing to the state. As we have seen in Chapter 3, policy makers at the Banque de France and the Treasury were more and more convinced that inflation was no longer a monetary phenomenon and that a restrictive monetary policy would have been an ineffective remedy. Solutions to fiscal deficits in the 1970s were to turn to the market rather than to the central bank. Contrary to what had happened in the late 1950s, there was no attempt to increase Treasury loans from the Banque de France against a promise of restrictive monetary and credit policies.[41]

Postwar fiscal and political relations between the government and the central bank depended in many ways on past practices. We have seen that the system of Treasury advances approved by Parliament, inherited from the nineteenth century, remained in place and provided an intangible

---

[41] In August 1981, the Banque de France refused to increase advances to the Treasury (Duchaussoy 2011).

reference point for practice and discussion. Similarly, the events of the interwar period and the resulting legal consequences provided a framework as well as a pool of previous practical cases to which references were made. The governor of the Banque de France during the Fourth Republic thus declared that the Banque's nationalization in 1945 had not changed financial relations with the government, and that the decisions to grant loans to the Treasury remained autonomous.[42] However, as with credit policy in general, there is a truly stable and singular model of postwar financing of the Treasury by the Banque that emerged in the late 1940s, albeit partly inherited from the institutional changes of the wars and the 1930s. From World War I to the early 1970s, the financing of the Treasury by the Banque de France was characterized by a high level of loans in proportion to the public debt and frequent recourse to unofficial loans unknown to the public. From 1949 to 1973, this system was marked by a relative stability and regularity of financing methods (much of which remained secret) compared to previous decades and by a gradual reduction in loans compared to the war years. The financial links between the Treasury and the central bank since World War I were part of a general context in which state financing was largely outside the market. This system, which has been widely studied by historians and which in France was called "the Treasury circuit" (Kuisel 1981; Margairaz 1991; Quennouëlle-Corre 2000) was based on the fact that the borders between the state and the main financial institutions (public credit institutions, nationalized banks) were porous. Not only did the government multiply the number of agencies and institutes that issued bonds, but the financing of the public debt relied heavily on these same institutions that lent or deposited money to the Treasury. Writing in 1944 about the interwar economy, the French economist Henry Laufenburger had described this system as the "dedoubling (or duplication) of public credit" (1944, p. 9) and saw similar practices taking place in other countries such as the United States, the United Kingdom and Germany. It is for this reason that the unofficial loans of the Banque de France to the Treasury studied in this chapter – some of which were intermediated by the CDC or nationalized companies – did not appear to

---

[42] Wilfried Baumgartner, governor of the Banque from 1949 to 1960, stated that the nationalization of the Banque de France had not changed the relationship between the Banque and the government as for loans to the Treasury and that the General Council was sovereign in accepting or declining government requests to lend to the Treasury; "the fact that the stocks of the Banque have been transferred to the State has not modified the legal status of the Banque de France." ABF, PVCG, July 17, 1953.

be a heresy but rather a continuation of what was otherwise practiced. The return to the predominance of marketable debt in the 1970s put an end to this system of financing and thus changed the central bank's place in the financing of public debt. The rationalization of the Banque de France's lending to the state in 1973 is therefore a symptom of a more general process at work that is not limited to the role of the central bank. It is the sign of a decade in which rediscovery of the market changed the ways in which credit, whether private or public, was controlled.

6

Financing the Postwar Golden Age

The Banque de France, "Investment Credit" and Capital Allocation

The Golden Age of European Growth (1945–1973) remains an enigma for standard economic and financial theory. How could the era of the highest sustained economic growth ever in Western Europe be associated with "financial repression" and ubiquitous state intervention in credit allocation?[1] The size of financial markets was small, capital controls, credit and interest rates ceilings were the norm and the reconstructing economies faced credit constraints and low savings due to the destruction of collateral during the war. Standard economic approaches that emphasize the virtue of market forces suggest that this environment should have led to a shortage and misallocation of credit. Usual explanations of postwar growth (reconstruction, technological progress, factor reallocation, rise of the consumer society, etc.) do not provide insights on how financial funds were allocated. Whereas the importance of financial development for growth has been extensively studied and documented by many historians and economists, the recent macroeconomic history literature on postwar European economic growth has largely ignored financial factors and credit institutions.[2] The exceptional growth rate of capital accumulation has been recognized as

[1] The term "financial repression" and its use in the growth literature go back to McKinnon (1973). For recent uses, see Battilossi (2003), Allen (2014) and Reinhart and Sbrancia (2015). For a critical survey, see Monnet et al. (2014).

[2] Gerschenkron (1962) remains a standard reference on the relationships between the structure of the financial system and economic growth. A more recent literature has mostly focused on the causal impact of financial development and openness on growth; see for example Levine et al. (2000) and Bordo and Rousseau (2011). On the macroeconomic history literature about economic growth in postwar Western Europe, see Crafts (1995), Crafts and Toniolo (1995), Toniolo (1998), Temin (2002), Eichengreen (2006), Vonyo (2008), Cubel and Sanchis (2009).

a fundamental characteristic of the postwar Golden Age but the financing of such a phenomenon remains unexplained.[3]

The paradox of financial restraints and high growth of capital is especially striking in France, a country whose *dirigiste* financial system featured all the characteristics of "financial repression" (ceilings on credit and interest rates, capital controls, forced holding of government securities), had the lower rate of self-financing among Western European nations (Hautcoeur 1999), and whose stock market capitalization over GDP declined continuously from 1961 to 1975 (Hautcoeur & Le Bris 2010). It led many economists to conclude that the Golden Age of growth occurred despite numerous financial restraints (Voth 2003). Focusing on 1945–1958, Saint-Paul (1993, 1994) points out that, without capital controls, France could have engaged more in foreign borrowing. Reviewing French postwar growth, Sicsic and Wyplosz (1995) suggest that the high growth rates of the 1960s and early 1970s might have even been higher absent widespread public intervention. In a subsequent contribution, Charles Wyplosz (1999) however acknowledges that the correlation between high growth and financial restraints in postwar Europe is a robust fact. But none of these papers is based on a detailed study of the banking system and the allocation of credit.

On the contrary, political scientists and historians working on the French postwar economy have highlighted the strong relationships between industrial policy and credit policy and argued that these policies benefited growth (Cohen 1977; Kuisel 1981; Zysman 1983; Hayward 1986; Loriaux 1991). For example, Michael Loriaux states that "the French state's characteristic ability to promote investment through control over the supply of credit enabled the French to achieve rapid industrial development and industrialization in the 1950s and 1960s" (1991, p. 4). These studies, however, take for granted that credit is good for growth and do not provide a quantitative perspective on the allocation of credit. In particular, two important economic questions have remained unexplored. First, except for some Treasury loans, we do not know if credit (and which credit) indeed financed investment. Credit whose allocation was influenced by the state could have gone to some declining industries, while letting investment be

---

[3] The exceptional rate of capital accumulation during this period is well documented. For example, Barry Eichengreen (1995, p. 38) writes: "Aside from catch-up, the proximate cause of postwar Europe's growth miracle was high investment. Net investment rates in Europe were nearly twice as high as before or since." The French stock of productive capital grew at annual rate of 5.2% from 1957 to 1973. This figure was lower from 1951 to 1957 (2.7%) but still much higher than in the preceding decades: 1.8% from 1893 to 1929 and 0.5% from 1929 to 1951 (Dubois 1985).

mainly financed by retained earnings, short-term bank loans or bonds. Second, we do not know whether such a *dirigiste* system allocated credit only to some "national champions" (the most capital-intensive industries), or, on the contrary, whether the reallocation of capital and credit was an essential feature of the period.[4] Relying on official documents and policy statements, the previously mentioned political science literature on French planning draws a picture of *dirigisme* as being centered on the promotion of growth in only few capital-intensive sectors. The general economic literature on catch-up and industrial policies in various countries adopts a different perspective but reaches similar conclusions (Murphy et al. 1989; De Long & Summers 1991; Calomiris and Himmelberg 1995; Rodrik 1995; Vittas & Cho 1995; Pack 2000; Acemoglu et al. 2006): state intervention works when it manages to "pick the winners" and to create a "big push," but it lacks the flexibility to reallocate credit and capital.[5] Big push strategies and industrial policies were important historically and are appealing from a theoretical point of view but they tend to give a limited and biased picture of what state intervention was really about. From a macroeconomic perspective, it is almost impossible to isolate them from other types of state interventions (such as rediscounting of medium-term credit by the central bank) that spanned various sectors and offered guarantee, incentives and supports to private and decentralized decisions, without substituting for the latter. Hence, in practice, the role of the state in credit allocation was not limited to subsidizing targeted sectors and it offered more scope for adaptability and flexibility. It should be assessed on this basis. There is no doubt that French official discourses emphasized the need for "national champions," but does it mean that financial resources were concentrated in few capital industries only, at the risk of lowering the productivity of capital in those sectors and hampering growth in others? Only a detailed quantitative analysis of credit and capital allocation across sectors can provide

---

[4] Some authors have argued that the reallocation of resources from agriculture to other sectors was a key factor of the postwar Golden Age. But they did not look at the reallocation of resources within the secondary or tertiary sectors. See in particular Temple (2001) and Temin (2002).

[5] A dissenting view is provided by Wade (1992) on postwar East Asian growth who criticized the existing literature as being too centered on the analysis of "picking the winners" strategies (see also Rodrik 1994). On economic theory of catch-up growth, see Acemoglu et al. (2006), for a model with increasing returns to scale that emphasizes that catch-up growth occurs through investment-based strategy in existing sectors whereas growth based on innovation occurred through reallocation and selection. A recent contribution by Lane (2017) studies in great detail the economic effects of South Korean industrial policies implemented in 1973 in a "big push" perspective.

answers to this question and give a more comprehensive picture of postwar growth. Moses Abramovitz (1986, pp. 388–389) suggested that the "trade-off between specialization and adaptability" is a useful lens to look at the process of catch-up growth. It remains to be shown whether postwar capital accumulation and financial development was characterized by specialization, adaptability or both.

This chapter goes beyond the focus on the central bank that characterizes other chapters of the book. The main reason for this is that the only way to appreciate the importance of the Banque de France's rediscounting and credit policy in the postwar economy is to have a broader view of the overall credit allocation. The Banque de France's policy has been integrated into the broad social and economic process of "nationalizing credit." Much of its role was to rediscount credit granted by nationalized banks and public credit institutions. As we will see, the Banque also provided incentives, advice and information to credit institutions. For banks' lending decisions, the possibility of rediscounting could have been as important as the actual rediscounting. The central bank was a key piece of the puzzle, but only one piece, so its role cannot be understood in isolation. A second reason is that we do not have complete aggregated information on the type and nature of loans that the central bank has rediscounted. The identity of the financial institutions that requested the rediscount is easily known, but the CNC has not compiled statistics on the sectoral allocation of the Banque's rediscounted bills. On the contrary, the CNC published credit statistics by sector and the Banque followed these sectoral statistics closely. This chapter uses these statistics to describe quantitatively the allocation of credit in postwar France and explains how the Banque de France could influence this allocation.

Although the aim of the chapter is to put the role of finance and central banks' activist credit policies back into the economic history literature on the European "Golden Age," we are obviously not the first to study some aspects of the French postwar financial system. Recently, Laure Quennouëlle-Corre (2005b, 2015) has provided detailed analyses of French financial institutions and, most of all, of the political relationships and connections that were at the core of the financial system. She sheds light on the role of the state and of civil servants, and rightly emphasizes that the distinction between "market-based" and "bank-based" financial systems is of little use to understand the major role of public credit institutions and financial development over the period. My approach is complementary to hers but we work at a different level of analysis. This chapter aims to understand the means and effects of state intervention in the allocation of credit and, most of all, to characterize the allocation of credit from a quantitative perspective, and discuss to what extent it was related to capital accumulation and economic growth.

I hereby focus on three questions. First, how did state intervention (*dirigisme*) shape the financial system, make it an integrated part of the "postwar coordinated capitalism" (Eichengreen 2006) and create "accommodating institutions generating a social capability for growth" (Abramovitz 1986; Crafts 1995; Toniolo 1998)? Second, what were the means of action of the Banque de France in this environment? Third, how did this institutional configuration affect capital accumulation and capital allocation across sectors? In answering these questions, I follow the approach of Eichengreen, Crafts and Toniolo as I do not take for granted that postwar growth was a natural economic phenomenon that would have happened inevitably. As Nick Crafts (1995, p. 441) wrote: "it seems likely that, far from being automatic, the catching up of the Golden Age depended heavily on making policy decisions that facilitated high investment, technology transfer and promoted more efficient use of factors of production."

Answers to this set of questions point to the decisive role of policies and institutions aiming to develop "investment credit" (*crédit d'investissement*). "Investment credit" was medium- and long-term credit, including those that could be rediscounted by the Banque de France. Defining "investment credit" and presenting its role within the context of the French *dirigiste* economy will be the first step of our analysis (Sections II and III). The second step features a quantitative analysis based on a new database merging credit, revenue and capital statistics for forty sectors of the economy from 1954 to 1974 (Sections IV, V and VI). Because of data availability, the quantitative analysis is focused on 1954–1974, which is the period of the highest growth rates of GDP and capital – taking place after the immediate postwar recovery and the Marshall Plan (Dubois 1985).

This chapter conveys three main messages. First of all, as this introduction has already pointed out, it shows, in an institutional perspective, that the intervention of the state and the Banque de France in the allocation and distribution of credit cannot be limited to support for a few key sectors. The state's intervention, and in particular the role of the Banque de France, was much more complex and wide-ranging, to the point that it is almost impossible to draw a line between private and public credit. Second, the notion of "investment credit," which is present in the CNC's statistics, is essential for understanding how the state and the Banque de France conceived the purpose of credit policy. The distinction between short-term and "investment credit" was at the core of new postwar financial policies and institutions.

The distinction between short-term credit and investment credit is not exactly the same as that between public and private credit, but investment credit is a type of financing mainly supported by the state – and its various ramifications – during this period. It is where we have to look at to assess the role of the state for economic growth during this period. Third, quantitative results show how "investment credit" promoted capital accumulation as well as capital reallocation. By contrast, short-term credit did not. Such a finding not only highlights the small role of commercial banks for postwar financing of capital accumulation. It also contradicts previous studies and the widely held belief that catch-up growth was achieved only through concentration of credit and capital in some main capital-intensive sectors that pulled the rest of the economy. The catch-up process occurred through a reallocation of capital such that "investment credit" – widely supported by the state – and capital increased more in less capital-intensive sectors. In Abramovitz's words, the policy of developing "investment credit" was synonymous with "social capacity for growth," and the postwar system was able to adapt rather than simply be driven by "big push" strategies in capital-intensive industries.

I THE BIRTH OF "INVESTMENT CREDIT" (*CRÉDIT D'INVESTISSEMENT*)

Which institutions were involved in the financing of the economy and, most of all, how did the state shape such institutions and intervene in the allocation of funds? Put differently, what does "state intervention in the financial sector" mean, in the context of the French postwar planned economy? As the first part of this book explained in detail, French politicians had two immediate economic priorities in 1945: increasing investment to rebuild the capital stock and implementing the "nationalization of credit." The first one was essential to reconstruct the economy and it later became a constant claim of the 1950s and 1960s to favor an industry rebirth. The second one was a political objective that built on a large consensus among policymakers from the left to the right, and was especially supported by the center right, the dominant political force of the Fourth Republic. The "nationalization of credit" – as it was called then – was not synonymous with the nationalization of the banking system, although the four major commercial banks and the central bank were nationalized in December 1945. A consensus was built about the quest for growth and the compelling sense of French economic backwardness. According to Richard Kuisel (1981, p. 277): "By 1945, French public authorities had developed a keen sense of economic retardation and accepted the need for expanding and making more use of the nation's economic potential." This climate of change also gave birth to indicative planning. The institutions that organized industrial indicative planning were the Planning Office (*Commissariat Général du Plan*) and the Finance Ministry (including the Treasury). The main institution that supported the "nationalization of credit" was the Banque de France, and especially two new entities within the central bank: the *Conseil national du crédit* (CNC, National Credit Council) and the *Commission de controle des banques* (CCB, Commission of Banking Control) created by the law of December 2, 1945. The latter was in charge of banking supervision while the former was in charge of the allocation of credit, that is to set and monitor the rules of credit allocation and to decide on the main credit policy orientations (see Chapter 2). For this purpose, the CNC created an important service of statistics (*Service central des risques*) that collected monthly statistics on the banking and financial sector. Such a system did not leave a lot of room for the financial market. This service played a key role for defining and constructing statistics on "investment credit." The French stock and bond market reconstructed during the 1950s, mainly because of the issuance of securities by nationalized firms and state-led credit institutions (Marnata 1973; Hautcoeur & Le Bris 2010 and Table 5). In 1960, once the reconstruction of banks' capacities was achieved, the total market capitalization reached an upper bound. Then, its role kept decreasing for fifteen years while the French economy was experiencing high economic growth and credit deepening: in 1973, stock market capitalization to GDP was back to its 1953 level (Marnata 1973; Hautcoeur & Le Bris 2010). The financial market did not provide more than 10% of the total financing of non-financial firms over the period (Table 5).

The postwar *dirigiste* system focused on the development of medium- and long-term credit to firms. Medium- (two to five years) and long-term credits (more than five years) were registered in the CNC statistics as *Crédit d'investissement* ("investment credit"). Before World War II, French banks usually did not lend at a long maturity. The three-month commercial bill (*escompte*) was still the predominant form of banking activity and remained the only type of loans that could be rediscounted at the central bank. The biggest firms raised funds at a longer term on the stock market with the help of banks. The predominance of short-term credit was viewed as the main weakness of the interwar French financial system: during and after the war, much effort was devoted to create or reform financial institutions in order to provide the French economy with secure long-term financing. The public long-term loans from the Treasury were greatly

Table 5 *Loans to the economy versus bonds issued, 1954–1974*

	Loans to households	Loans to non-financial societies	Bonds issued (central government)	Bonds issued (large nationalized firms)	Bonds issued (other non-financial societies)	Bonds issued (credit institutions)
1954	4,270	51,696	7,718	3,840	1,017	3,633
1960	18,730	118,905	11,937	10,357	4,033	8,055
1967	53,790	269,259	15,311	24,073	6,953	26,369
1974	246,450	672,859	15,496	39,166	21,492	78,027

Source: INSEE (1981) and CNC reports. Outstanding loans and bond issued in million new francs.

increased. More power and new attributions were given to the public or semi-public specialized credit institutions (*Credit National, Crédit Foncier, Caisse des dépôts, Banque française du commerce extérieure, Caisse national des marches de l'Etat*) whose role had always been to provide long-term financing (see below). These specialized credit institutions either lent directly to firms or bought Treasury bills and financed Treasury loans; this network was called the "Treasury circuit" (*Circuit du Trésor*). An important reform took place on the monetary side as well, with the Banque de France rediscounting medium-term bills (Chapter 2). This new rediscount policy, potentially very inflationary, deeply changed the activities of French banks since they became allowed to lend at a two to five year maturity and to refinance these loans at the central bank's discount window. Credit controls and rediscount ceilings became usual tools of the central bank in order to limit the growth of credit when the inflation rate was too high.

The activist credit policy led to rapid and steady financial deepening pulled by "investment credit." As shown in Figure 23, the ratio of "investment credit" to GDP increased from 1% in 1949 to 25% in 1973. Both short- and long-term loans increased after the war (as a share of GDP) but financial deepening occurred mainly because of "investment credit." The period from 1954–1955 to 1973, after the immediate postwar recovery, is when the French economy experienced the higher rates of GDP growth and of capital accumulation (Dubois 1985; Sicsic & Wyplosz 1995). Figures 24 and 25 show the share of loans (distinguished by maturity) provided by the various types of financial institutions. Statistics include all loans to firms (loans to households and government are excluded). As in the CNC statistics, we include loans from the central bank in total loans: when a bill was rediscounted at the central bank, the CNC viewed the Banque de France as the ultimate lender to the firm. CDC loans appear in the category "specialized credit institutions" (*organismes spécialisés*) together with *Crédit Foncier, Crédit National, Crédit Agricole* and *Banques populaires*. "Investment credit" includes "medium-term rediscountable" loans that could be accepted at the central bank's discount window.

A distinctive feature of the postwar French banking system is the prominent role of the Treasury, the Banque de France (through rediscounting) and specialized credit institutions, in providing medium- and long-term loans. As emphasized by Quennouëlle-Corre (2005b), such a financial system is described neither as "finance-based" nor "bank-based." Commercial banks were the main providers of short-term loans but not of "investment credit" (Figures 24 and 25). From the early 1960s, the role

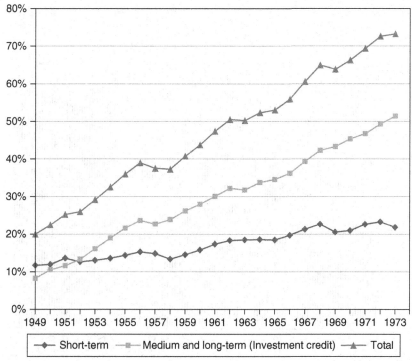

Figure 23 Credit deepening pulled by "investment credit." Credit to GDP (in %), 1949–1973
Sources: CNC annual reports, INSEE (1989).

of the Treasury and the central bank decreased and commercial banks and credit institutions became the main lenders. Such an evolution did not necessarily reduce the ability of the state to intervene in credit allocation through other means (recommendations, exemptions from controls, etc.), as we will explain below.

II THE STATE-LED FINANCIAL SYSTEM AND THE ROLE OF THE CENTRAL BANK

Summing numbers displayed in the previous figures (taking into account that the nationalized commercial banks held around 80% of total banking assets), we can roughly say that the French state had some control over almost 90% of the financial system. Does it mean that there was no room for private and decentralized decisions? State intervention in the allocation of credit was ubiquitous but not altogether centralized.

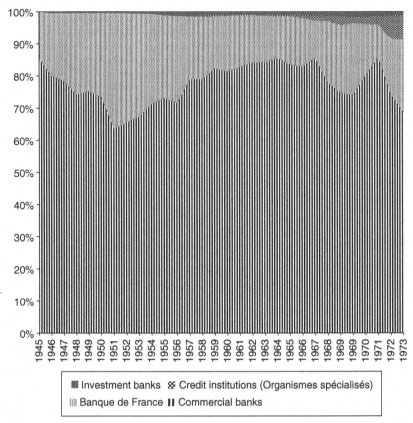

Figure 24 Who provided short-term credit? Breakdown by lender (share in %), 1945–1973
Sources: CNC annual reports; see the text. Loans to corporations.

It would be a mistake to describe the state as a central planner that chose the precise quantity of credit granted to each sector of the economy. First, the state was not a unified body. Coordination did take place between the central bank, nationalized commercial banks, specialized credit institutions and the Treasury, but most of it happened at a very broad level and these administrations agreed on general objectives only. Each administration had different practices and different priorities.[6]

---

[6] Recent historical studies on French administrations have shed light on the singular culture that characterized each of them and often prevented smooth coordination despite the shared goal of French reconstruction and modernization. See Mioche (1987) on the

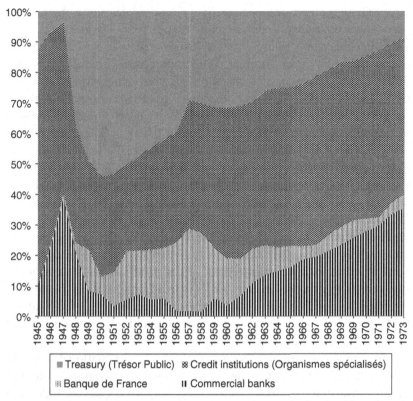

Figure 25 Who provided investment credit? Breakdown by lender (share in %), 1945–1973
Sources: CNC annual reports; see the text. Loans to corporations.

The organization of nationalized banks was also close to that of private banks.[7] Studies of the French Planning office have shown that, except for the First Plan, the guidelines provided by the Planning office were too

first years of the Planning office, Margairaz (1991) on the Finance Ministry and Comité d'investissement, Quennouëlle-Corre (2000) on the Treasury, Feiertag (2006b) and Duchaussoy (2013) on the Banque de France. Andrieu (1984) first pointed out the frequent conflicts between the government and the Banque de France as well as the lack of official coordination between the CNC and the Planning office.

[7] The well-informed economist and journalist Andrew Shonfield (1965, p. 171) wrote:

Postwar nationalization of the major French banks, which it is sometimes suggested was a key factor in the development of economic planning, has no relevance whatsoever to the tight control established by the Government over the French credit system. The fact [is] that the banks after nationalization were run by the same type of manager and, on exactly the same commercial principles as before ... It was not public ownership but the traditional "mixed enterprise," the fertile diffusion of public and private power, which was used to take charge of the capital market.

large to have a direct influence on banks' lending decisions; their direct impact was limited to Treasury loans (Baum 1958; Hackett & Hackett 1963; Bauchet 1964; Shonfield 1965; Andrieu 1984). Second, most of the interventions were indirect. With the exception of loans granted directly by the Treasury, state entities did not choose the identity of the borrower nor the amount of the loan. Providing information, giving incentives to banks through the rediscount window, backing projects or investments realized by private firms or banks, were the main tools of public intervention. This was especially the case for the Banque de France and the CNC.

I describe below the five main types of state intervention. While the role of the Treasury has been studied in previous publications (Margairaz 1991; Quennouëlle-Corre 2000, 2005b), we emphasize other types of influence on credit allocation, beyond direct lending. Among other things, it sheds light on the central role played by the central bank. Since the decisions were not centralized, it is not an easy task to identify exactly the objectives pursued by the administrations, banks and *organismes spécialisés*. The main rhetoric of the Planning office and the CNC was to foster productive investment and to serve social and national interests. But the question remains about the criteria chosen to define such vague terms as "economic utility" or the "national interest." In the late 1940s, the CNC issued recommendations to banks in order to avoid shortage in food and raw products supplies (especially sugar and meat) while the Plan focused on the development of energy and metallurgy. In the following decades, according to CNC reports and Banque de France notes, the main objectives of credit selectivity were to promote exports, to avoid overproduction and limit inventories in some specific sectors such as agriculture, to support regional development, to meet social needs such as housing and, finally, to help "creative destruction" in some sectors where activity was seen as too traditional. The subsections below will provide examples of such objectives and policies followed by the CNC. It is impossible to track every decision that was taken inside the Banque de France and the Treasury, nor by the banks, but it should be recognized that there were a variety of criteria and objectives and that these choices did not necessarily encourage the financing of incumbents and did not only support the largest industries. In addition, the Banque de France's tools were used not only to directly promote certain sectors, but also to accompany the financial reforms undertaken in some of these sectors, including those aimed at developing market financing, as in the housing sector in the late 1960s. As explained in Part I of the present book (especially in Chapter 3), credit policy was also about creating and organizing markets and developing new financial instruments.

Loans from the Treasury

Treasury loans financed long-term projects viewed as priorities by the Finance Ministry. Most were deemed a sequel to the Marshall Plan investments. The Treasury was in charge of the *Caisse autonome de Reconstruction* and the *Fonds de Modernisation et d'Equipement* (FEM) that granted reconstruction loans and would become the *Fonds de Développement Économique et Social* (Economic and Social Development Fund, or FDES) in 1954 (Wilson 1957, ch. VII; Margairaz 1991, pp. 1033ff.; Lynch 1997, p. 89). Loans were at below market rates. Most FDES funds were granted by the Treasury but some were granted by the *Crédit National* or the *Caisse des dépôts and Consignations* (CDC). Their allocation followed government policies but managerial independence was maintained within firms (Quennouëlle-Corre 2000, pp. 113–120). Although FDES loans were crucial for some sectors (mainly siderurgy, gas and electricity supply), new loans remained limited after 1950, compared to the total amount of new "investment credit." For this reason, the share of Treasury loans in total outstanding loans decreased continuously after 1950 (Figure 25). Starting from the mid-1950s, CDC loans replaced the FDES loans in many sectors, especially housing and construction. FDES's role also decreased because French nationalized firms obtained an easier access to the bond market over time and, starting in 1959, the new government of the Fifth Republic decided to decrease loans financed by government deficits (Chapter 3).

Loans from Public and Semi-Public Institutions

Contrary to nationalized commercial banks, specialized credit institutions (*organismes spécialisés*) were formally asked to follow the main orientations of the national credit policy defined by the CNC, the Planning office or the Government. The *Crédit National* and the *Caisse des dépôts et consignations* (CDC) specialized in financing of construction, machinery and equipment. The *Crédit Foncier* aimed to finance housing. Public housing was financed by the CDC rather than by the *Crédit Foncier*. Agricultural credit was mostly financed by the *Caisse nationale du Crédit Agricole* (CA), an organization that enjoyed financial autonomy but received guidelines from the Ministry of Agriculture. It was closely associated with government policies aiming at modernizing French agriculture, but loans' decisions were not taken by the Ministry (Gueslin 1988, p. 110). Whereas the *Crédit Foncier* issued bonds, the CA was a mutual savings bank. In the field of the financing of small- and medium-sized firms, the *Banques populaires* (a group of regional cooperative banks) were what the *Crédit Agricole* was to agriculture.

These institutions could lend at below market rates. According to a retrospective study written at the Banque de France in 1983, 49.5% of French loans were granted at a preferential rate in 1969 and 40.8% in 1975.[8] Bonnet (1968) shows that, in 1959, 34.25% of long-term loans were granted at a rate below the discount rate of the central bank, 37.5% at a rate between the discount rate and the bond market rate, and 28.25% at a rate at least equal to the bond market rate. These figures were 30.5%, 45% and 24.5% in 1964.

Rediscounting by the Central Bank

The intervention of the state through rediscounting must be distinguished from direct loans. This type of intervention aimed to encourage the development of both private and public loans rather than providing direct subsidies. The *Crédit Foncier*, CDC and *Crédit National* rediscounted medium-term banking loans and could ask the Banque de France to rediscount the loans they had already refinanced. Rediscounting was thus a powerful tool used by the central bank and some specialized credit institutions in order to foster the development of banking loans and to affect their allocation. The total value of rediscounted loans by public institutions is not necessarily a good measure of the extent of public intervention in the allocation of credit because bankers' decision to lend was in fact influenced by the ability to rediscount.

The Banque de France used rediscounting to affect credit allocation in four ways. First, from 1948 to 1972, each bank was assigned a rediscount ceiling. There were no fixed rules for setting their amount. The main criteria were the share of deposits in banks' balance sheets and their "economic utility," namely their ties with industries at the local level, and their specialization by sector. Second, the Banque de France accepted to rediscount housing and construction loans up to seven years in 1966, officially supporting the development of

---

[8]   Archives of the Banque de France (ABF), 1331200301/10).

these sectors.[9] Third, the central bank could issue guidelines and send information to banks, and commit to rediscount loans granted to some sectors and for specific economic activities. It could also give advice directly to banks, in the form of general recommendations, at the national level (for the production and storage of butter, sugar, canned product until the mid-1950s, mostly for housing, agriculture and exports afterward) or at the local level, through its 220 branches that surveyed the needs of the sectors. It was implicit (and sometimes explicit) that the Banque de France rediscounting policy would be in accordance with such guidelines. For example, when the French economy increased its openness to trade in 1959, the Banque de France implemented a large survey in order to measure the reactions of some sectors that were supposed to suffer from trade liberalization. It asked the directors of the branches to gather information on firms. Then the CNC encouraged the branches and the banks to use this information to compare the performance of firms in their local area to the national performances.[10] Fourth, for some very specific activities only, the central bank announced publicly the maximum amount of loans it would rediscount. It was however limited to agricultural credit and credit to exports.[11]

Whatever the means used to influence credit allocation (discount ceiling, guidelines, commitment to rediscount, etc.), the central bank always stated that rediscounting was contingent on the justification of real needs and would not take place automatically. Banks were discouraged to lend to unprofitable firms. For example, in 1953–1954, bankruptcies of retail stores increased greatly but the Banque de France stated that these exits were a "necessary cleansing." The Banque de France decided to follow government policies aiming at developing department stores, and let many unprofitable retail stores fail.[12] "Creative destruction" was also a feature of the *dirigiste* system.

Exemptions

This tool was used by the CNC in order to favor some sectors or activities when limits on credit expansion were imposed in order to combat

---

[9] Negotiations took place at the *Direction générale de l'escompte* (DGE). Amount of ceilings for some years as well as discussions over whether they should be increased are found in ABF, 1360200701/239, 1360200701/72, 1397200602/12.

[10] ABF, 1331200301/10. Letters from H. Fournier.

[11] ABF, 1331200301/10.

[12] ABF, *Résumé des rapports économiques des directeurs des succursales*. August 1954– September 1955.

inflation. They were used to support housing credit and mostly credit to exports. Credit to exports was always exempted from quantitative credit ceilings during episodes of restrictive monetary policy (Chapter 4). Such a policy strongly favored sectors producing tradable goods. When credit ceilings were imposed again in 1968, housing credit was exempted. The exemptions on housing credit took place while, beginning in 1965–1966, the French government was attempting to shift housing finance from specialized credit institutions to banks and to develop a genuine mortgage market (Effosse 2003, ch. VIII). Thus, the Banque de France's decisions were consistent with housing finance reforms and temporary monetary policy instruments (credit ceilings) were used in line with the general credit policy guidelines.

Compulsory Guidelines by the National Credit Council

The archives of the Banque de France and *Conseil National du Crédit* (National Credit Council or CNC) show little evidence of compulsory guidelines that forced the banks to lend (or prevented them from lending) to specific firms or sectors. These were not the main instruments of public intervention in the allocation of credit. The few examples available in the archives of the CNC are related to agricultural credit and were intended to avoid overproduction.[13] For example, the Ministry of Agriculture decided to control loans to the chicken farming business because it was concerned with overproduction and big inventories. In July 1961, it asked the Banque de France and the CNC to prevent banks from lending to businesses that raised more than 5,000 chickens. The limit was then extended to 16,000 chickens in 1963.[14] However, this "chicken example" is not representative of the central bank's interventions in the allocation of credit throughout the *dirigiste* period. By contrast, it shows that the CNC had the legal and institutional power to impose quotas of loans to specific sectors or products, but it was not commonly used. It relied instead on other kinds of incentives that left the ultimate responsibility to banks and credit institutions.

---

[13] The Planning office neither used nor recommended such practices but further research may find that similar guidelines were occasionally issued for other industries.

[14] ABF, 1331200301/10. Letters from the Ministry of Agriculture to the Governor of the Banque de France.

III CREDIT STATISTICS AND THE UNDEFINED BORDERS OF STATE INTERVENTION

The previous description has shown how difficult it is, in such a *dirigiste* economy, to disentangle credit allocated through a pure market process from credit allocated by state intervention. This is in line with the conclusions of Aymard (1960, pp. 63–85), an enlightening contemporary book devoted to the respective roles of the state and the private sector in the postwar French economy. It explains why such a distinction was not made in the statistics published by the CNC, nor by economic studies. Trying to identify "subsidized" loans in the archives of the CNC would be a dead end. However, CNC statistics distinguished clearly between short-term loans and "investment credit," reflecting the emphasis given to the latter in political and financial circles. Statistical categories were a mirror of policy objectives. They were published in order to help the banks, the central bank and public credit institutions to assess the overall allocation of credit or their own distribution of loans.

Such statistics by sector, which have not been used yet by economic historians in a comprehensive way, offer a nice opportunity to answer simple questions: did "investment credit" promote investment? Was it granted to a small number of sectors only, or did it enable the reallocation of capital? Previous sections have described policy decisions and financial institutions that aimed to facilitate high investment. We now need to investigate whether this aim was fulfilled. In order to study the overall allocation of credit in postwar France, I use the sectoral data on credit computed by the CNC that include all types of loans received by a sector. Contrary to current sectoral data about firms' financing that rely on debt, this historical source makes it possible to study the allocation of loans rather than the leverage or external financing of firms. Below, we describe the sources, the construction (merging credit and corporate tax statistics) and the limitations of a unique but complex database.

Credit Statistics

CNC statistics are outstanding loans at the end of the quarter.[15] Despite its richness, this source is neither comprehensive nor perfect. First, there

---

[15] These quarterly sectoral statistics are published in the appendix of the *Rapport annuel du Conseil national du crédit et du titre*, consulted at the Banque de France archives. For some sectors, subsectors were also reported.

was a lower limit on credit that had to be declared by banks (50,000 "new" francs until 1962 and 100,000 thereafter). Since this amount was very small, it was not likely to matter for loans that financed investment and growth. Second, these statistics were constructed from declarations by bankers themselves. The CNC imposed controls and sanctions in case of cheating but banks tended to underreport loans of the last quarter of a year and to report the numbers on the first quarter of the following year. The use of yearly data diminishes this problem. Third, the CNC provides the stock of credit granted to each sector for each quarter but does not provide a breakdown of these sectoral loans by lending institution. Fourth, the exact duration of the loans is not specified and it is impossible to calculate exactly the new flows. Fortunately, the data are quarterly and distinguish between three-month commercial bills (*Effets commerciaux*) and other short-term loans (*Autres crédits à court terme*). Moreover, there is a separate category for "investment credit" (*Crédit d'investissement*), that is, all loans whose maturity exceeded two years. I measure the annual total amount of *effets commerciaux* granted by financial institutions to a sector within a year as the sum of quarterly values. The rationale for adding these figures is to obtain the total amount of borrowed funds that could be used each year to finance a sector. This is necessary to compare the choice of financing between rollover short-term debt or borrowing long-term funds. Other short-term loans usually had a maturity between three months and two years. Two alternative methods were used to compute their total annual stock: the highest value or the mean of the four quarters. The difference between the two methods is actually negligible since the amount of these loans is very stable. Results reported use the second one. Finally, the annual outstanding stock of medium- and long-term credit is measured as the end of the year value of the column *Crédit d'investissement*. "Investment credit" and "other short-term loans" are available from 1950, whereas "commercial bills" are available only starting 1956.

Corporate Tax Statistics

Statistics of the CNC do not include any other information by sector. However, the tax administration constructed and published data by sector (from corporate tax statistics) whose categories were mostly similar to CNC's. Matching databases produced by two different administrations obviously comes at a cost since some categories are not the same or are not continuous. In 1968, the CNC and the Finance Ministry decided to standardize the two databases. The 1968 conversion table helps to build

continuous series but it is impossible to recover all the sectors. This is especially true for either the very small or the broadly defined sectors. Thus,
the sample is restricted to forty sectors whose definitions were similar and
continuous in the two databases. They amount to 68% of total revenues in
the economy, 50% of firms, 69% of the wages, 66% of the capital stock and
65% of credit on average over the period 1954–1974. These shares are pretty
stable over the twenty years but slightly decreasing overall. Sectors that are
excluded are either very small or non-industrial sectors (as in toys, the-
ater or music instruments) or big public sectors that did not receive credit
from financial institutions (the defense industry, the army, hospitals and
the public cultural industry). Because of discontinuity in data, it is impossible to build a series of loans to the banking industry. In 1971, the INSEE
(National Institute of Economics and Statistics) and the Finance Ministry
decided to implement a new nomenclature (Desrosières 1972). In 1975 the
tax and the CNC statistics were reformed in order to follow the new INSEE
nomenclature: there is no way to recover the ancient categories except at a
high level of aggregation (seven sectors up to 1959, ten afterwards).

These tax statistics were published in irregular supplements of *Statistiques
et études financières* – a series issued by the Finance Ministry – and usually available with a lag (e.g., statistics of taxes in 1960 are published in
1963). Statistics on 1965 and 1966 were never published (probably because
of the 1968 long strikes and the disruption of publication in this year).
Corporate tax statistics cannot be used for our study before 1954 because
only the number of firms and the revenue were published.[16] The statistics
published in *Statistiques et études financières* are an incomplete mix of
balance sheet and income statement for each sector. Some important categories of usual balance sheets and income statements are missing, probably because they were too difficult to aggregate and harmonize at the
sectoral level. The information available from 1954 to 1974 in the tax
statistics is the following: number of firms, inventories, tangible fixed assets
(*immobilisations*), wages and revenue (*chiffre d'affaires*). Note that we use
the terms "capital," "capital stock," "fixed assets" and "tangible fixed assets"
interchangeably in the following analysis. The measure of capital in the tax
statistics is gross. Revenues are counted before taxes, which is important to

---

[16] There are two regimes in the French corporate tax system: *forfait* and *bénéfices réels*. The
firms in the first category are small and pay a fixed amount negotiated at the sector level,
whereas the firms in the second category pay a proportion of their profits. Many small
firms paid the *forfait* but their share in total revenue is negligible.

allow a comparison between sectors (since different VAT regimes applied across sectors).[17]

Additional Remarks on the Statistics by Sector

A note of caution should be added regarding the quality of the corporate tax statistics. Valuation of tangible fixed assets is subject to the usual caveats of a firm's balance sheet. Firms periodically revaluated their fixed assets, but not every year. For example, *Statistiques et études financières* mentions that there was a substantial reevaluation by firms in 1959.[18] This revaluation was made by all sectors: the tax administration asked firms to value their capital at the 1959 prices in order to account for the postwar inflation. Firms might also have different methods of valuation (of asset prices and depreciation) that may change over time. Hence, year on year changes in the stock of capital may be explained by accounting reasons rather than by new flows of capital. Moreover, although some revaluations took place, some fixed assets are still valued at the price they were purchased.[19] Revenues are also subject to accounting changes and manipulations (e.g., firms may smooth benefits and revenues over years for tax reasons). It is why national accounts combine balance sheets of firms with surveys of production, consumption and capital when they build annual series. Although there is no evidence that accounting methods systematically differed across sectors, issues about annual growth rates are likely to be important and to differ across sectors since data of monopolistic sectors – such as gas or electricity – are more dependent on year on year accounting changes of one single firm. As a consequence, annual changes of sectoral variables must be interpreted with great caution and are likely to be noisy. For this reason, this chapter focuses only on the analysis of *average values* (growth rates and ratios) over years, by sector, rather than on yearly growth rates within a sector. In doing so, reevaluations are smoothed over several years.

Moreover, it has been impossible to reconstruct valued added and gross investment for each sector. Instead, we have total revenues and the capital stock. It is sufficient to link the allocation of credit to important financial ratios (such

---

[17] Starting 1968, much more information is available including debt, depreciation (*amortissement*), benefits and dividends, revenue after taxes and purchases.

[18] See also Delestré (1979).

[19] According to the definition of *immobilisations* available in the *Statistiques et études financières*.

as the capital to revenue ratio) for a large number of sectors.[20] National account data over this period would allow a disaggregation of production and investment at the level of seven branches only, without possibility to link them to credit statistics (Delestré 1979; Dubois 1985). By contrast, my database distinguishes between a large number of branches within the primary and mostly, secondary and tertiary sectors. Thanks to a large number of sectors, it provides a unique perspective to study the allocation of credit and capital between sectors, which could not be done in previous studies of French growth.[21]

IV INVESTMENT CREDIT AND CAPITAL ACCUMULATION

Did "investment credit" really finance capital accumulation? As explained previously, the institutions and state-led financial network that emerged after 1945 intended to finance investment, claiming that market mechanisms and private commercial banks had failed to do so in the interwar period. If "investment credit" deserves its name, we should observe that sectors that received more of it were also the sectors that accumulated more capital. However, there are several reasons why it may not be the case. State policies may have systematically picked sectors using little capital. Thus, other sectors in need of more capital would have turned to the bond or stock market, or would have relied on short-term borrowing from nationalized commercial banks to finance long-term investment, as was the case before World War II. Capital-intensive sectors may also have preferred other forms of financing. It would have been the case if alternative forms of financing were cheaper, or if receiving loans from public credit institutions sent a negative signal to other potential lenders. Financial models with asymmetries of information and imperfect financial markets emphasize the following tradeoff: long-term credit protects firms against repudiation and favors investment but a preference for long-term credit sends a signal that a firm is not able to roll over short-term loans (Diamond 1991; Hart & Moore

---

[20] In the financial and accounting literature, the capital to revenue ratio is usually called the "fixed-asset turnover ratio."

[21] When I compare the average capital to revenue ratios of my database to the capital to production ratios estimated by INSEE (1981) I obtain close figures. The values of the ratios in my database are 0.5 in agriculture, 2.3 in energy, 0.4 in construction, 0.5 in manufacturing, 1.6 in transport, 0.4 in services and 0.8 for total, while in the INSEE database, they are respectively 1, 2.4, 0.4, 0.7, 2.8, 0.7 and 0.9. Note, however, that the definitions of the branches of INSEE (published in 1981) are not exactly similar to mine (some of the sectors in my database are split into two INSEE branches [energy and manufacturing, or transport and manufacturing, for example]).

1994). In such a framework, state interventions that favor medium- and long-term loans can lead the "best" firms to prefer short-term financing in order to signal themselves as less risky. For these reasons, it would be possible that sectors that accumulated more capital were not those that received more "investment credit." Postwar accumulation of capital could have been mostly financed by other sources, e.g., short-term banking loans, bonds or equity. If it were the case, it would cast doubt on the effectiveness of new postwar financial institutions and policies described in previous sections.

Although state support to "investment credit" was massive, alternative forms of financing were neither shut down nor legally impossible: nationalized commercial banks could provide short-term credit and the stock and bond markets were open.[22] According to most recent estimates retained earnings to revenue were stable from 1958 to 1973 (the self-financing rate fluctuated between 65% and 70%), after decreasing in the immediate postwar decade.[23]

In Figure 26(a), I have plotted the mean of the fixed-asset turnover ratio (i.e., capital to revenue ratio) by sector, against the mean of the ratio of "investment credit" to revenue. Average values are calculated over the full sample. Values of coefficients of the linear regression line are displayed below both graphs. The positive slope of the linear fit line implies that sectors that had more capital (as a share of their revenue) received more "investment credit" (as a share of their revenue). Interestingly, I find a negative slope when I draw a similar figure for short-term credit (cf. Figure 27[a]). There are two possible interpretations: first, short-term credit was mainly intended to provide liquidity for commercial transactions and had no relationship with investment and capital allocation or, second, short-term credit was used by firms with few investment opportunities that had no access to long-term financing.

These findings are not driven by outliers. When I exclude the seven most capital-intensive sectors (whose capital to revenue ratio exceeds one), I still find a positive correlation between capital and "investment credit" and a flat line in the case of short-term credit (see Figure 26[b] and Figure 27[b]).[24]

---

[22] However, firms needed authorization to issue bonds, and the Treasury was making sure that the timing and volumes of issue were not damaging government bond issue. According to Marnata (1973, p. 96), the sector that issued the highest share of stocks and bonds over the period was the financial sector (including nationalized banks and public credit institutions).

[23] Estimates differ about its values before 1958 but it was higher and decreased continuously, starting around 100% according to Pierre Villa (see Hautcoeur 1999).

[24] The seven more capital-intensive sectors are electricity, gas, siderurgy, coal mining, iron mining, rail transport and road transport. In Figure 26(b) and Figure 27(b); we also

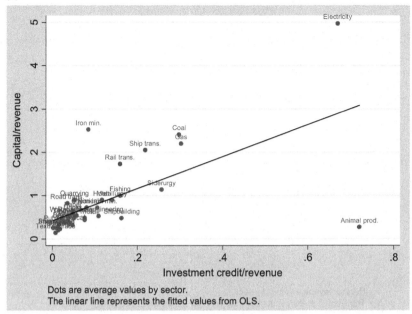

Dots are average values by sector.
The linear line represents the fitted values from OLS.

(b)

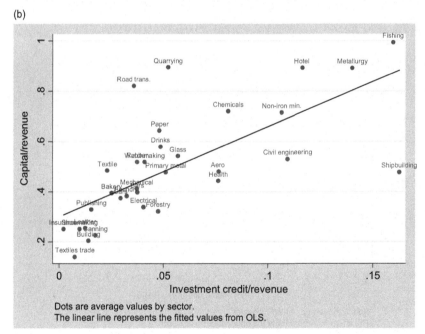

Dots are average values by sector.
The linear line represents the fitted values from OLS.

Figure 26 Correlation between investment credit and capital, by sector, 1954–1974

(a) All sectors

(b) Less capital-intensive sectors

Notes: In (a), the coefficient of the OLS regression is 3.67 (std = 0.14) and R2 = 0.4; in (b), the coefficient of the OLS regression is 0.12 (std = 0.6) and R2 = 0.01.

Sources: CNC annual reports and author's calculation. See the text.

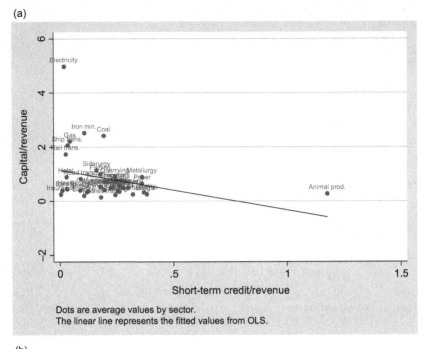

(a)

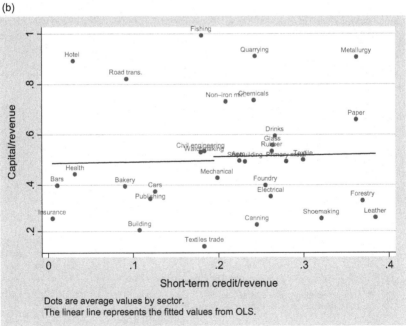

(b)

Figure 27 Correlation between short-term credit and capital, by sector, 1954–1974

(a) All sectors

(b) Less capital-intensive sector

Notes: In (a), the coefficient of the OLS regression is –1.47 (std = 0.14) and R2 = 0.1; in (b), the coefficient of the OLS regression is 0.05 (std = 0.07) and R2 = 0.0.

Sources: CNC annual reports and author's calculation. See the text.

Conclusions are similar when I run estimations including both ratios of short-term and investment credit as explanatory variables.[25]

A different question is whether there is a positive correlation across sectors between the real growth rate of "investment credit" and the real growth rate of the capital stock. Figure 28 shows that the correlation is significantly positive. Capital grew more in sectors where "investment credit" grew more. It is also robust when we control for the real growth rates of revenue (Table 6).[26] By contrast, the correlation is not significant for short-term credit. Besides, the most important conclusion to draw from Figure 28 is that the positive correlation between growth rates of credit and capital is not driven by the most capital-intensive sectors. The most capital-intensive sectors (electricity, gas, siderurgy, coal mining, iron mining, rail transport, road transport) were not those that grew more on average: they do not appear in the northeast region of Figure 28. The revealing fact that the sectors that had more capital (and more investment credit) in proportion of their revenues were not those in which capital and credit grew more rapidly is of first order importance for our understanding of the growth process and capital allocation during this period, and to this we now turn our attention.

V   REALLOCATION OF CAPITAL ACROSS SECTORS

Was the growth of capital during the catch-up process mostly driven by a limited number of capital-intensive sectors or was there a reallocation of capital across sectors over time? This is, first, a very descriptive question whose answer is interesting to understand the nature of economic growth during the postwar Golden Age. As such, Carré et al. (1972) and Delestré (1979) have provided evidence that the stock of capital grew faster in manufacturing industry and services (starting in the mid-1950s) than in the energy and transport sectors that were more capital intensive.[27]

---

exclude the animal production sector (whose credit to revenue ratio is much higher than the average), in order to improve the graphical presentation. It does not affect the general conclusion. The animal production sector had an easy access to medium-term credit through the *Crédit Agricole*, a cooperative financial institution devoted to agriculture.

[25] Results not displayed here for the sake of brevity.

[26] To obtain real values, I deflate nominal values by the deflator of the investment of non-financial societies provided by INSEE. According to the between estimator (balanced panel of forty sectors, Table 6, column 3), if the annual growth rate of investment credit was 1 pp higher in sector A than in sector B, then the annual growth rate of the stock of capital was 0.19 pp higher in sector A.

[27] According to INSEE (1981), the real stock of capital grew annually by 6% from 1954 to 1973 in manufacturing industry and services, and by 4% in energy and transport, whereas

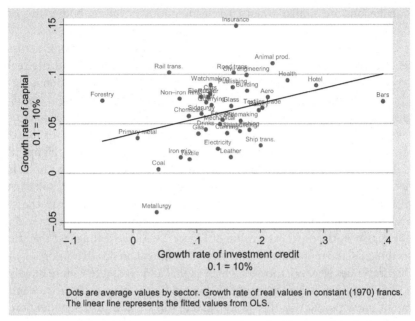

Dots are average values by sector. Growth rate of real values in constant (1970) francs.
The linear line represents the fitted values from OLS.

Figure 28 Annual growth rates of investment credit and of the capital stock, by sector,
1954–1974
Notes: The coefficient of the OLS regression is 0.15 (std = 0.01) and R2 = 0.12.
Sources: CNC annual reports and author's calculation. See the text.

Second, this is also a question whose answer is telling about the ability of
the planned economy and state-led financial institutions to favor reallocation
and increase productivity.[28] As highlighted in the introduction of this chapter,
the common opinion considers that state intervention in the financial sector
and industrial policies during catch-up growth are mostly focused on some
few capital-intensive industries rather than on the reallocation of funds and
selection of most productive firms. While some authors view such a concentration as beneficial, many view government intervention in the financial

the ratio of capital to value added was 5 on average in energy and transport but 2.5 in
industry and 1.6 in services.
[28] It is sufficient to define productivity as the "apparent productivity" (the ratio of capital to
output). The argument is that, if there are decreasing returns and capital increases more
in sectors where the ratio of capital to output is already high, then new investment is less
likely to provide as much revenue as before, and the productivity of capital is likely to
decrease. Such an argument also holds under constant returns to scale if the capital shares
are similar across sectors.

Table 6 *Correlation between the growth of credit and the growth of the capital stock*

	All sample	Less capital-intensive sectors
Dependent variable: average growth rate of capital by sector (in %)		
Investment credit (growth rate in %)	0.17 * (0.09)	0.27 *** (0.09)
Short-term credit (growth rate in %)	−0.06 (0.09)	−0.19 (0.12)
Revenue (growth rate in %)	0.86 *** (0.15)	0.97 *** (0.15)
Constant	−0.01 (0.01)	−0.03 *** (0.01)
Adjusted R-square	0.59	0.69
Number of sectors	40	33

Notes: Standard errors in parentheses. * p-value < 0.1, ** p-value < 0.05, *** p-value < 0.01. Real growth rate calculated using the deflator of investment of non-financial societies (INSEE). Average values calculated over the period 1956–1974 (values for 1965 and 1966 are missing). Total of 600 observations for the all sample, and 495 for the less capital-intensive sectors.

sector as being unable to reallocate funds to more productive and less capital-intensive industries. In this perspective, Sicsic and Wyplosz (1995) looked at the total stock of credit in France in seven branches in 1956 and observed that the more capital-intensive industries received more funding, from which they conclude that state subsidies and government policies favored too much capital-intensive sectors (energy and transport) and prevented a necessary reallocation of capital. According to them, the preferential treatment of these industries may have been maintained for too long and was detrimental for growth, at least in the 1950s. However, studying capital allocation from 1958 to 1973, the same authors found that factor reallocation took place, but they did not make connections with the allocation of credit.

Capital to Revenue Ratios and Convergence

As previously mentioned, a comparison between the sectors in Figures 26 and 28 show no evidence that capital and "investment credit" grew more in the more capital-intensive sectors. To assess this statement, I compute the correlation between the average growth rates of credit (or investment) on one hand, and, on the other hand, the capital to revenue ratio at the beginning of the period. Figure 29 shows evidence of a negative correlation between the capital to revenue ratio in 1954 and the average growth of capital over 1954–1974. It is only slightly weaker when the more capital-intensive sectors are excluded (Figure 29[b]). Figure 30 presents a similar

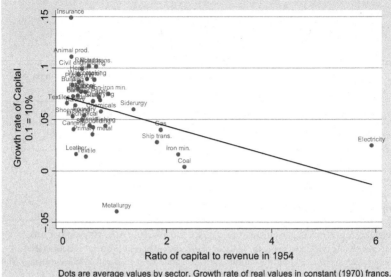

(a)

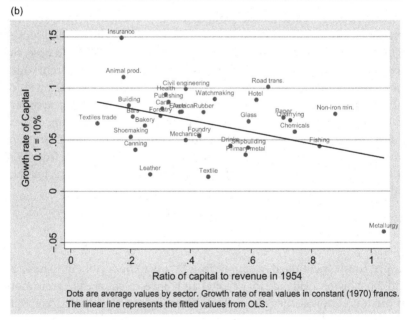

(b)

Figure 29 Correlation between the capital to revenue ratio in 1954 and the average growth of capital over 1954–1974

(a) All sectors

(b) Less capital-intensive sectors

Notes: In (a), the coefficient of the OLS regression is –0.01 (std = 0.005) and R2 = 0.18; in (b), the coefficient of the OLS regression is –0.06 (std = 0.02) and R2 = 0.16.

Sources: CNC annual reports and author's calculation. See the text.

(a)

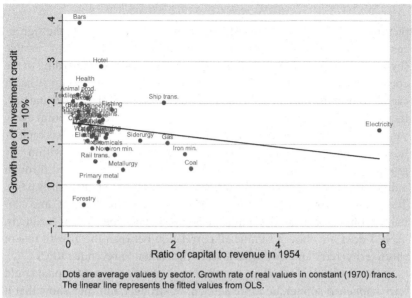

Dots are average values by sector. Growth rate of real values in constant (1970) francs. The linear line represents the fitted values from OLS.

(b)

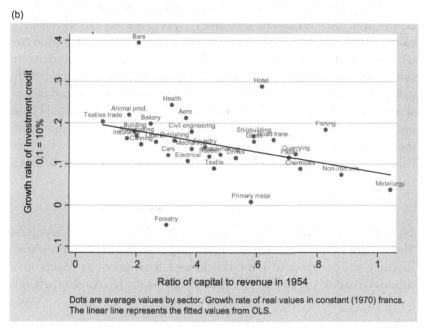

Dots are average values by sector. Growth rate of real values in constant (1970) francs. The linear line represents the fitted values from OLS.

Figure 30 Correlation between the capital to revenue ratio in 1954 and the average growth of investment credit over 1954–1974

(a) All sectors

(b) Less capital-intensive sectors

Notes: In (a), the coefficient of the OLS regression is –0.01 (std = 0.005) and R2 = 0.04; in (b), the coefficient of the OLS regression is –0.13 (std = 0.06) and R2 = 0.14.

Sources: CNC annual reports and author's calculation. See the text.

picture for the growth of "investment credit." Table 7 assesses the significance of these results. I simply regress the mean of the dependent variable (by sector) on the 1954 value of the explanatory variable.[29] According to the coefficients in columns 1 of Table 7, we can conclude that if sector A had a capital to revenue ratio in 1954 equal to 1 and sector B had a ratio equal to 2, then the stock of capital in sector A grew faster by 1 percentage point every year (on average). Coefficients are stronger for the sample with less capital-intensive sectors because the difference between ratios is lower within this group: a difference in the annual growth rate of 1 pp is achieved through a difference in the ratio of 0.17 instead of 1 (since the coefficient is 0.06). These results provide additional evidence that "investment credit" and capital accumulation shared a similar destiny over the period. Accordingly, Table 7 does not show a significant correlation between the growth rate of short-term credit and the initial level of the capital to revenue ratio.

Such correlations are silent on whether the reallocation of capital could have happened sooner, be more efficient or stronger, but they show that it did occur, and that is was supported by a parallel reallocation of "investment credit" from the more capital-intensive sectors to the less capital-intensive sectors. Finally, if such a convergence was likely to increase the productivity of capital, as suggested by simple theory and previous studies, we should observe that there was a higher increase of (apparent) productivity in the most capital-intensive sectors, where the accumulation of capital was slower. Otherwise, the lower growth of capital in those sectors would have only reflected lower output growth. The last columns of Table 7 show that, indeed, the effectiveness of the use of capital increased more (i.e., the capital to revenue ratio decreased more) in the most capital-intensive sectors.

Discussion on Revenue and Value Added

Up to now, capital intensity was measured as a share of sectoral revenues. This is right from accounting and financial points of view but it is unsatisfactory if one wants to draw conclusions from previous results in a national accounts perspective. We need to discuss the relationship between

---

[29] Note that this convergence might be partly explained by the fact that the more capital-intensive sectors had older equipment that was not fully revalued over the period. But if it were the case, the negative correlation would be weaker in the second half of the sample. We find that the correlation is in fact higher in the 1960s, which seems consistent with Sicsic and Wyplosz's observations of a larger reallocation of factors after 1958 (a period when the accumulation of capital was also faster). Results are available upon request; not reported because of space constraints.

Table 7 *Capital and credit convergence (in function of the capital to revenue ratio)*

Dependent variable	Average growth rate of capital over 1954–1974 in %		Average growth rate of investment credit over 1954–1974 in %		Average growth rate of short-term credit over 1956–1974 in %		Average growth of the capital to revenue ratio	
	All sample	Less capital-intensive sectors	All sample	Less capital-intensive sectors	All sample	Less capital-intensive sectors	All sample	Less capital-intensive sectors
Capital to revenue ratio in 1954	−0.01***	−0.06**	−0.01**	−0.13**	−0.01	−0.00	−0.02***	−0.02***
	(0.01)	(0.02)	(0.01)	(0.06)	(0.02)	(0.03)	(0.00)	(0.01)
Constant	0.07***	0.09***	0.15***	0.21***	0.04***	0.05***	0.01**	0.01***
	(0.01)	(0.01)	(0.02)	(0.03)	(0.01)	(0.01)	(0.01)	(0.01)
Adjusted R-square	0.14	0.20	0.04	0.14	0.06	0.00	0.34	0.54
Number of sectors	40	33	40	33	40	33	40	33

Notes: Standard errors in parentheses. * p-value < 0.1, ** p-value < 0.05, *** p-value < 0.01.
Real growth rate calculated using the deflator of investment of non-financial societies (INSEE).
Average values calculated over the period 1954–1974 (values for 1965 and 1966 are missing). Total of 600 observations for the all sample, and 495 for the less capital-intensive sectors.

a financial measure of capital intensity (capital over revenue) and a productivity measure of capital intensity (capital over value added). Sicsic and Wyplosz (1995), using a decomposition of factor productivity and data for ten large branches only, have provided evidence of factor reallocation for the period 1958–1973: capital grew less in the relatively more capital-intensive sectors. But they did not discuss the potential role of finance in this reallocation. Can we extend their result and then draw links between credit allocation, capital reallocation and the increased capital productivity? Unfortunately, corporate tax statistics do not provide enough information to construct reliable measures of value added for forty sectors. We are left to discuss whether the negative correlation we have observed so far would be different when using value added instead of total revenues (production). A first part of the answer is given by the fact that the sectors that are the most capital intensive in the dataset (with a capital to revenue ratio greater than one) are those that are notoriously more capital intensive when intensity is measured as a share of value added. The six sectors with the highest capital to revenue ratio in the database all belong to the transport, mining and energy branches that are the most capital-intensive ones in the aggregated data used in previous studies on French growth (Carré et al. 1972; Delestré 1979; Sicsic and Wyplosz 1995). They did not have the highest average growth rates of investment and "investment credit" over the period. Hence, at least for the most capital-intensive sectors, the convergence observed in my data is consistent with previous works that matched (for fewer industries, at a higher level of aggregation) estimations of capital and of value added.

As an additional robustness check, I compute pseudo "capital to value added ratios" for the forty sectors using the series of production, intermediate consumption and value added available for seven main broad branches in INSEE. To obtain such pseudo ratios I multiply the capital to revenue ratio of one sector by $1/(1 - \alpha)$, where α is the share of production devoted to intermediate consumption in the branch to which the sector belongs to. Such an exercise has important limits because the ratio of value added to production is probably not constant within a branch. It is only tried here in order to assess whether differences in the share of intermediate consumption would break the hypothesis of factor reallocation over this period. As shown in Table 8, we still find negative relationships, i.e., evidence of reallocation of capital over the period.

The less capital-intensive sectors had the highest growth rates of capital stock and of apparent productivity of capital. Values of coefficients are lower than in previous tables because a given change in the capital to revenue ratio

Table 8 *Capital and credit convergence (in function of the pseudo capital to value-added ratio)*

Dependent variable	Average growth rate of capital over 1954–1974 in %		Average growth rate of investment credit over 1954–1974 in %		Average growth rate of short-term credit over 1956–1974 in %		Average growth of the capital to revenue ratio	
	All sample	Less capital-intensive sectors	All sample	Less capital-intensive sectors	All sample	Less capital-intensive sectors	All sample	Less capital-intensive sectors
Capital to value-added ratio in 1954	-0.004***	-0.003**	-0.006*	-0.019*	-0.004*	-0.003·	-0.009***	-0.005*
	(0.001)	(0.001)	(0.003)	(0.010)	(0.002)	(0.005)	(0.003)	(0.003)
Constant	0.069***	0.068***	0.153***	0.169***	0.042***	0.054***	-0.001	-0.001
	(0.01)	(0.01)	(0.014)	(0.032)	(0.013)	(0.011)	(0.012)	(0.004)
Adjusted R-square	0.20	0.16	0.06	0.08	0.07	0.00	0.21	0.10
Number of sectors	40	33	40	33	40	33	40	33

Notes: Standard errors in parentheses. * p-value < 0.1, ** p-value < 0.05, *** p-value < 0.01.
Real growth rate calculated using the deflator of investment of non-financial societies (INSEE).
Average values calculated over the period 1954–1974 (values for 1965 and 1966 are missing). Total of 720 observations for the all sample, and 440 for the less capital-intensive sectors. See the text for the assumptions underlying the estimation of value added.

implies a larger change in the capital to value added ratio (since the latter equals the former multiplied by $1/(1 - \alpha)$). Such estimations cast doubt on the hypothesis that differences in the share of intermediate consumption across sectors would be sufficient to create a negative relationship between capital to revenue ratios and capital to value-added ratios across sectors. The main problem with these estimations is that less capital-intensive sectors have quite similar capital to revenue ratios (usually between 0.4 and 0.8): their ranking is thus more likely to change if the ratios of value added to revenue differ across them. Available information is however too limited to implement a more precise robustness check and to account for differences in the share of intermediate consumption within branches. Regarding the overall convergence between the most and the least capital-intensive sectors, however, my results are in line with previous studies and are not biased by relative share of intermediate consumption across sectors.

VI   CONCLUSION

Many previous studies emphasized the joint role of capital accumulation and institutions in postwar growth (Abramovitz 1986; Crafts 1995; Toniolo 1998; Eichengreen 2006). Credit policy had however remained out of the scope of this literature. This chapter has studied how capital accumulation was financed, the role and definitions of activist credit policies, and how capital and financial flows were jointly allocated across sectors. My institutional analysis highlights that the allocation of credit in such a planned economy was not the result of a centralized process with a rigid system of quotas. The complex institutional configuration, as well as the omnipresence of the state at various levels of the financial system (direct loans, rediscounting, guidelines, incentives, ownership of financial institutions, etc.), makes it impossible to distinguish between credit that was allocated in a pure market process from credit that was allocated in a pure *dirigiste* way. The more important postwar change in the financial system was the emphasis given by state policies, and in particular by the Banque de France, to medium- and long-term credit ("investment credit") in order to finance capital accumulation. As a result, financial markets were sidelined and commercial banks played a minor role for the financing of investment (though growing in the 1960s).

A quantitative analysis based on disaggregated sectoral data of the economy over twenty years has shown that this institutional configuration produced an allocation of "investment credit" that was able to support capital accumulation and productivity gains. The stock of capital grew more on average in the sectors in which the growth rate of "investment credit" was higher.[30] But the sectors that experienced the highest growth rates of the stock of capital and "investment credit" were not the most capital-intensive ones. Thus, the most capital-intensive sectors were also those that experienced higher gains of (apparent) productivity of capital. It would not have been the case if the *dirigiste* system had overflowed these sectors with too much credit without reallocating funds toward less capital-intensive sectors. Besides capital accumulation and financial deepening, the postwar Golden Age is also the story of capital and credit reallocation. Such results could hopefully lead to comparative research across different countries, including both Western and Eastern European economies.[31]

This study is not a causal analysis of the effect of credit on growth over this period, but it gives arguments to include finance and credit policies within the set of "social capabilities for catch-up" during the postwar European Golden Age, as it shows how capital accumulation and reallocation were financed by new peculiar institutions in a way that was compatible with economic growth. Yet, my quantitative analysis is too limited to state whether the postwar *dirigiste* system, or another type of financial system, could have worked more effectively and led to higher (or lower) growth rates. This, and many other questions, remains unanswered. A business history analysis would be much needed to study how and why decisions to invest were taken in such an environment where the price system played a limited role. Finally, future work should be devoted to explore the evolution of credit allocation after 1973 (sources used in this chapter do not provide series after 1974) and why the system was finally reformed in the mid-1980s.[32] Readers should also bear in mind that – because of data limitations – the quantitative estimations presented here say nothing about the early postwar period, before 1954, and the immediate effects of the Marshall Plan.[33] The

---

[30] This is also consistent with Benard (1974) who finds a convergence of marginal of capital across some sectors.

[31] Financial systems differed greatly during this period despite widespread strong state interventions (Shonfield 1965).

[32] Using firm-level sources, Bertrand et al. (2007) show evidence of misallocation in 1985, when the financial system was liberalized. Loriaux emphasizes the role of international factors: "But as the international economic constraints of the 1970s overloaded the state with contradictory demands, interventionism met with fewer and fewer successes" (1991, p. 4).

[33] The stagnation of investment that took place between 1949 and 1953 is a well-known peculiarity of French postwar growth (Mairesse 1971; Bouvier 1979; Bonin 1987; Saint-Paul 1994; Sicsic & Wyplosz 1995). It contrasts with the high rate of growth of GDP in 1950 and 1951 (as a result, the ratio of investment to GDP decreased quickly from 17% to 14% between 1950 and 1953). Bouvier (1979) shows that the stagnation of total investment is essentially due to the decrease of investment by nationalized firms and by the construction

empirical analysis in this chapter has many limitations, but I hope that it will at least help to avoid mischaracterizing the postwar credit policy as a rigid system that focuses solely on the directed financing of certain industrial sectors.

sector (BTP). Carré et al. (1972, p. 289) argue that this phenomenon might be explained by the reallocation of capital to productive investment in 1950 whereas the years 1946–1949 focused on the reconstruction of basic equipment infrastructure. Saint-Paul (1994) and Sicsic and Wyplosz (1995) argue that it was an inefficient outcome explained by controls on the banking and financial sector. Unfortunately, the sectoral database does not allow us to study the allocation of capital before 1954. None of the explanations mentioned above can be dismissed or verified. It should be nonetheless remembered that 1950 and 1951 had the highest growth rate of GDP of the whole decade, which may support Carré et al.'s argument. The growth rate then fell in 1952 and 1953 because of the restrictive monetary policy (Chapter 4). Was the early 1950s drop in investment necessary to reallocate factors or was it suboptimal? Did investment suffer more than consumption and GDP from the 1948–1949 restrictive monetary policy and then did not recover when the second episode of restrictive policy started in October 1951? Was it an adverse effect of the Marshall Plan (banks were reluctant to finance nationalized firms that already received Marshall loans)? These are hypotheses for further research. The results have nonetheless shown that the inefficiency of state intervention in the banking sector cannot be taken for granted.

The Rise and Fall of National Credit Policies

Implications for the History of European Varieties of Capitalism and Monetary Integration

This chapter has two main objectives. The first is to show that credit controls and policies were widespread in Europe after World War II, but that there were significant differences between countries in the way they were implemented.[1] Put differently, other central banks pursued policies similar in kind to the French policies described in the previous chapters (intervention in credit allocation and recourse to quantitative controls), but the very nationalistic nature of credit policies made them extremely different in practice, because they were rooted in various financial and political systems. The second objective of this chapter is to take stock of both national differences and the general importance of credit policies in Western Europe to inform historiographical debates on the construction of the European monetary union (EMU). Once the historical importance of central bank credit policies in postwar Europe is recognized, it becomes natural to wonder whether the reforms and rejection of these policies in the 1970s and 1980s were linked to the process of European monetary integration. The end of credit policies in European countries has been a key phenomenon for achieving the convergence of central bank practices and the reduction of state interventionism in the allocation of credit. The EMU was built on this ground. However, there is no evidence that reforms of credit policies in the Member States have been undertaken for the purpose of achieving monetary integration. As seen in France in Part I (Chapter 3), the criticisms and decline of credit policies appear to have been a process rooted in national debates, practices and policies that began in the late 1960s. Like their birth, the end of credit policies was a deeply national

---

[1] The first part of this chapter is a substantially revised version of some sections of Monnet (2016). Monnet (2016) contains a detailed presentation of the balance sheets of main central banks and estimations of policy reaction functions.

process. In the 1970s, debates among European central banks focused on monetary targeting and exchange rate alignment, whereas, at the same time, debates in national central banks focused on reforms of credit controls and activist selective credit policies.

This chapter is a first attempt to provide an overview of the differences in the design and role of central banks in Western European countries from the end of World War II until the 1970s, after discussions on European monetary integration started to grow following the 1970 Werner report (McNamara 1999; James 2012; Mourlon-Druol 2012). It focuses on France, Italy, Germany, the United Kingdom, Netherlands and Belgium, that is, the biggest democratic economies at that time in Europe as well as the first members of the European Community.[2] It raises more questions than it solves, and several of its conclusions are likely to be called into question as the history of credit policies and of the convergence of European central banks' practices is still being written. But, in spite of the limited primary sources and scarce secondary literature on which this chapter is based, I think it is important to conclude with some first thoughts on the link between the end of credit policy and the construction of monetary Europe, a topic that has not been yet addressed in historical studies.

In the following pages, I observe the national differences in credit policy through four aspects: i) legal and political responsibilities of central banks; ii) banking supervision and the links between central banks and the banking system; iii) monetary policy instrument; and, finally, iv) credit policy and economic planning. A first conclusion is that the differences across central banks partly reflect usual categories of "varieties of capitalism." The common distinction between market capitalism (United Kingdom), managed capitalism (Germany) and state capitalism (France) is at work under Bretton Woods central banking.[3] But the differences cannot be represented on a linear scale. The Bundesbank had the widest responsibility in banking supervision, the Banque de France was the most interventionist in credit allocation and the Bank of England was the most involved in managing and financing of government debt. Considering the Bank of England as a singular case rather than the rule may also reshape the discussions about postwar central banking.[4] The Bank of England was

---

[2] Luxembourg did not have a central bank before 1998.

[3] About this distinction, see notably Shonfield (1965), Hall and Soskice (2001), and especially Schmidt (2003) and Fioretos (2011).

[4] Histories of the changing role of central banks over the twentieth century usually focus on the Bank of England as the main example of postwar central banking in the "Keynesian era," 1945–1973. See Goodhart (2011) and Singleton (2011, ch. 8).

mostly applying and supporting government controls and fiscal policy, while the central banks in France and Italy were more heavily involved in directed credit. The role of the Bundesbank cannot be understood out of the context of the German trade policy and the federal organization of the state. Based on these observations, I discuss briefly some hypotheses about the main factors explaining the differences in credit policy between countries. Among political and cultural factors, the role and organization of the state (especially federalism versus centralization of power) and beliefs about state intervention ("market ideologies," in Shonfield's words) and monetary theory played important roles. The legacy of World War II (including the occupation of Germany) also stands as an obvious explanation of the different paths followed by central banks. Among economic factors, the inherited structure of the financial system greatly influenced the relationship between the central bank, the nation state and the economy.[5] The second part of the chapter (Sections IV and V) then shifts our attention to the attempts to liberalize credit markets and reform credit policies from the late 1960s to the mid-1980s. It shows that debates on these reforms were strikingly absent from the discussions at the meetings of the governors of European central banks and from the publications of the European Community (EC) Monetary Committee. The decline of credit policies and the construction of the EMU appear as two parallel historical processes that converged in the late 1980s only.

I THE INTERNATIONALIZATION OF CREDIT POLICIES

Credit Policies in the History of Central Banking

The post-World War II years and the development of the welfare state led to a reconfiguration of the nation states that exacerbated disparities in economic policies (Esping-Andersen 1990; Milward 2000). Credit and monetary policies had no reason to be excluded from this process. Whereas the economic literature has mainly focused on central bank independence, historical and political-science studies – including the previous chapters of this book – have pointed out that the main post-World War II changes lay in the new role of central banks in the financial systems, and not only in

---

[5] Among other important factors that should be discussed, wages and income policy, military relationships with the United States and exchange rate policy are left to further research.

government financing (Zysman 1983; Loriaux 1991; Conti et al. 2009). In a recent history of central banking in the twentieth century, John Singleton calls the many changes that occurred in 1945 the "First revolution in central banking" (Singleton 2011, ch. 7). Although he devotes more attention to the subservience of monetary policy to fiscal policy, he concludes that central banks and commercial banks were brought into "closer touch than ever before." After World War II, European democracies not only turned to capital controls in order to avoid the constraint of international finance, they also built new institutions in order to integrate more closely monetary policy to industrial policy, banking policy and fiscal policy. For central banks, the "nationalization of monetary policy" was not a passive process aiming to protect the economy from international shocks but a set of active policies in order to reconstruct the country and growth potential. French policies studied in the previous chapters were not an exception. An overview of European monetary policies published in 1956 by the French Finance Ministry thus concluded that the history of central banking had led to an apparent contradiction: the economic and political power of central banks had greatly increased at the same time that the *legal* power of government over central bank also kept increasing.[6] Based on legal capacities, central banks were more powerful institutions than ever. Their political power depended on the singular relationships with the government. There was a common movement across countries toward activist credit policies and increasing relations between the government and the central bank, but their institutional forms depended greatly on national characteristics. Before going into the details of national singularities, it is worth examining how European policies were viewed from the United States, the leading monetary and political power. This perspective from abroad helps to understand how a distinct common model was identified by contemporaries despite large differences between central banks.

US Perspectives on European Credit Policies

In several countries, most importantly Italy and France, the new role of central banks was integrated in a set of policies officially called the "nationalization of credit" (*nationalisation du crédit, nazionalizzazione del credito*). This term was not synonymous with the legal nationalization of financial

---

[6] Ministère de l'Économie et des Finances, "Le contrôle du crédit en France et à l'étranger," *Statistiques et Études Financières*, Supplément, n° 90, 1956, p. 636.

institutions but meant that many institutional complementarities were established in order to allocate credit alongside social and national priorities. However, credit policies were not a Franco-Italian specialty. Nor were they limited to the early postwar period. A staff report prepared in 1971 for the Committee on Banking and Currency of the US House of Representatives chaired by Wright Patman offers an interesting foreign (and mostly favorable) description of central banking out of the United States, with a particular emphasis on West European countries (France, West Germany, United Kingdom, Italy, Netherlands, Sweden).[7] Its title was particularly explicit about the function of central banks and their credit policy: "Activities by Various Central Banks to Promote Economic and Social Welfare Programs" (Thurow 1971).[8] The report summarizes the aims of the central banks under scrutiny as follows:

Central banks in most countries designate certain sectors of the economy that are to receive favorable treatment from the central bank. This means either making loans in these favoured sectors at below market rates of interest or making credit more available in these sectors than it would be if so-called market forces were allowed to operate. In some cases this is done to aid preferentially particular

---

[7] Other countries included in the study were Mexico, Yugoslavia, Israel, India and Japan.

[8] This report was commissioned and presented by Wright Patman, the chairman of the House committee on Banking and Currency. Patman was a prominent figure of the US Congress associated with southern democrats. He repeatedly attacked the US banking system, and the Federal Reserve system during his long career as a representative (Meltzer 2003, pp. 588–589; Conti-Brown 2017, pp. 201–209). Patman had chaired important hearings in 1951–1952 about instruments of the Fed (Tobin 1953; Meltzer 2003, p. 715) and had proposed more control of the Congress on the Fed in the mid-1960s (Meltzer, 2010, pp. 650–659). In his introduction to the 1971 report, Patman explicitly wished that the report would push the United States to adopt policies pursued by foreign central banks "which are active participants in the allocation of credit" and that "necessary corrective actions will be taken to make our central bank system perform in a way which can truly be said to be in the public interest." The report was written by a team of MIT economists led by Lester Carl Thurow. The other authors were Peter Temin, Alan Blinder, Joseph Quinn and Ernesto Tironi. These authors were associated with the "Keynesian school" in US academia: Thurow served in Lyndon Johnson's Council of Economic Advisors and wrote about the war against discrimination and poverty, Temin would later be known as a fierce opponent to Milton Friedman's monetarist interpretation of the US Great Depression and Blinder, who became vice-chairman of the Board of Governors of the Federal Reserve System in 1994–1996, had just received his doctorate supervised by Robert Solow. Besides Patman's introduction, the tone of the report is mostly favorable to credit policies implemented in other countries. A few years later, other US authors, especially Hodgman (1973, 1974) also provided a presentation of European credit policies with a much more critical tone. Although the political views of Thurow (1971) and Hodgman (1973, 1974) markedly differed, both provide good and quite similar descriptions of credit policy outside of the United States.

sectors and in some cases this is done to offset the uneven impacts of private money markets. (p. 1)

Although the report acknowledged important differences across objectives and functions of central banks, the involvement of central banks in credit allocation was seen as a similar feature. Many other characteristics of central banking highlighted in this report show strong similarities with French credit policy that I described in the previous chapters. As for instruments of central banks, the report states:

A wide range of instruments have evolved for achieving these specific objectives. They include special rediscounting privileges, direct loans and investments, special reserve requirements and credit ceilings, channeling of private investment funds, direct credit controls, approval over individual loans, exemptions from normal restrictive regulation and control over non-bank financial intermediaries. (p. 3)

As in France, interest rates and open market operations were not the main instruments of the central bank, neither to allocate credit (credit policy) nor to affect short-run fluctuations of money, production and prices (monetary policy): "Open-market operations typically are not used. ... Discount rates play a minor role in short-run policies, often only as a signal of central bank intentions. The main tool of short-run policy consists of quantitative restrictions on credit" (p. 4).

The report emphasized the difference between foreign practices on the one hand and the widespread use of open market operations in the United States on the other hand. Finally, another striking similarity with French central banking is that the lack of legal independence of the central bank did not mean that she was a powerless institution. As described in Part I of this book and Chapter 5, the central bank was part of a general state apparatus where the balance of power varied depending on the stability of governments and various institutional linkages. Interconnections between the government, the Treasury and the central bank did not mean that the latter was under the control of the former. Only the Bank of England was seen as mostly obeying the orders of the government. This was seen, again, as a strong difference with the United States:

The Banque de France plays a role that is very similar to that played by the Treasury Department in the United States, as part of the overall economic machinery of government. ... Despite its government ownership, the Bank of the Netherlands is almost entirely independent of the government. ... In practice the prestige of the recent governors of the Bank of Italy and the instability of Italy's governments has meant that the Bank has had a role far more important than was intended in the laws establishing it. (p. 5)

As I have underlined many times in the previous chapters about the French case, what central bank independence meant in the postwar context cannot be isolated from the fact that the lines between various state organizations as well as between private and public sectors were in fact blurred. The 1971 US Congress report formulated this explicitly about Japan, where credit policy closely resembled that of France and Italy.[9]

I quoted widely from this 1971 report because, like Fousek (1957) and Hodgman (1973, 1974), it shows how American postwar economists identified a particular model of European central banking (that also resembled closely central banks' policies outside of the United States on other continents, especially Japan, South Korea, Israel and Latin American countries), based on central bank intervention in credit allocation and the use of quantitative credit controls rather than on open market operations and interest rates. In 1981, an additional report for the US Congress on credit policies in European states was published (to my best knowledge, it was the last one), with, again an explicit title: "Monetary Policy, Selective Credit Policy and Industrial Policy in France, Britain, West Germany and Sweden" (Galbraith et al. 1981).[10] Of course, the interest of US economists in foreign credit policies did not start in 1971. Staff economists of the Federal Reserve had started to identify and study European credit controls as soon as the late 1940s (Hirschman & Roosa 1949). A few years later, in his book on foreign central banks, the New York Fed economist Peter Fousek (1957) noted that: "many foreign countries have since the war employed a wide range of monetary devices to affect specific economic activities or financing operations directly ... The purpose and scope of selective credit controls abroad has generally been much wider than in the United States" (p. 61). Fousek showed a strong skepticism toward the

---

[9] The Bank of Japan is legally subordinated to the Ministry of Finance but its position cannot be understood without recognizing that independence is at best a fuzzy concept in Japan where even the line between public and private are not firmly drawn. In some sense all agencies and firms are part of a national economic plan to promote economic growth. The Bank of Japan is much more powerful than the Federal Reserve Board. (Thurow 1971, p. 6)

[10] Important insights from this report are found again in Zysman (1983) who was one of the authors of the 1981 report, under the direction of the Keynesian economist James Galbraith. More than the previous ones, this report emphasized the differences between credit policies in European countries as well as their decline in most countries. In England, now led by Margaret Thatcher, credit policy was viewed as being nonexistent. In Germany, it was viewed as decentralized and implemented by regional banks. In Sweden, it was mostly focused on housing. Only in France it was still perceived as a key policy intertwined with industrial policy.

ability of foreign central banks to influence the allocation of credit without causing harm to the market economy, but he acknowledged that quantitative restraints on credit at the general level have proved an effective means to fight inflation in some countries (p. 76).

Although the US never fully engaged in credit policy and selective credit controls, some were implemented to fight inflation.[11] The US interest in foreign credit controls went beyond mere curiosity. The 1971 Congress report referred to above should be interpreted as part of a long-term discussion of the relative merits of credit controls and of foreign experience with them. Selective credit controls were used in the United States in 1948–1951 (Schreft 1990). Important debates took place in the US Congress in 1951–1952 in the Subcommittee on General Credit Control and Debt Management and finally led to a repeal of selective credit controls (Tobin 1953; Schreft 1990; Meltzer 2003, pp. 715ff.). In the 1950s, debates continued on the opportunity to introduce liquidity ratios (securities-reserve requirements) widely used in France and Europe both as a way to fight inflation and secure government financing (see Chapters 2 and 4 and Monnet & Vari 2017).[12] Debates frequently reemerged at the US Congress in the 1960s about the opportunity to impose selective credit controls, especially to regulate consumer or real estate credit (Schreft 1990; Romer & Romer 1993; Owens & Schreft 1995; Corder 1998, ch. 5; Meltzer 2010, chs. 2 and 3). Arguments against credit controls emphasized their lack of effectiveness in a system with many financial substitutes to banking loans – contrary to financial systems in continental Europe and Japan – as well as their authoritarian nature. The focus of US proposals in the 1960s was more on avoiding inflationary credit booms than on implementing a wide-scale interventionist credit policy as the one eventually proposed in the 1971 Congress report (Thurow 1971). After a visit to the Banque de France in March 1966, officials of the Federal Reserve of New York showed a genuine interest in the European instruments of credit ceilings and were impressed by their success in mitigating inflation.[13] In 1969, a Credit Control Act was passed and enabled the President of the

---

[11] A list of these tools used by the Fed is provided by Elliott et al. (2013).

[12] The "availability doctrine," first developed at the Fed by Robert Roosa emphasized the importance of credit quantities rather than interest rates for the conduct of monetary policy (Tobin 1953). It served as a rationale for attempts to regulate liquidity through ratios and targets of bank reserves in the 1950s (Miller 1956; Monnet & Vari 2017). In the availability doctrine credit rationing arises because banks shift their portfolio from business loans to Treasury bills. There is no need to have direct credit controls to obtain credit rationing without movements in interest rates.

[13] ABF, 1397200602/12. Various letters from NY Fed officials.

United States to ask the Federal Reserve Board to use regulation on credit to fight inflation.[14] Credit controls were finally implemented in the US to fight inflation in 1980 by the Carter administration and led to a sharp initial disinflationary episode and economic recession (Schreft 1990; Goodfriend & King 2005). It would be a mistake to ignore the role of such instruments and of the 1969 Credit Control Act in the history of the Fed. The Fed was nonetheless deemed an exception, especially in comparison with Western Europe and Japan, the other leading economic powers of this period where the role of the central bank in credit allocation was recognized as essential and much more extensive. The 1971 US Congress report is also striking evidence that, contrary to what a usual retrospective view of central bank history suggests, debates on central banks in the late 1960s and early 1970s were not centered on the Phillips curve. Although the report was written by MIT economists close to Solow and Samuelson, this term did not appear in the description of monetary policy in other countries. The authors did, however, take inflation into account because they repeatedly reiterated that the main objectives of foreign central banks – in addition to intervention in credit allocation – were to control inflation, and that inflation control was closely linked to balance-of-payments equilibrium. As I explained about France in Chapter 3, the debates on credit policy and central bank instruments were very isolated from the academic debate between Keynesians and monetarists. On the other hand, it is clear from the report that the main political issues were the extent and instruments of central banks' intervention in credit allocation.

Credit policy was therefore not the prerogative of France but a key common feature of postwar central banking, although – as we will see below – the Banque de France was arguably one of the most interventionist central banks together with the Banca d'Italia. Strangely enough, little attention and no comparative studies have been devoted by historians to national differences in central banking across Europe and to their economic and political consequences. Nor has the "varieties of capitalism" literature in political sciences devoted much attention to diversity in central banking before the 1980s. Yet, as the US studies mentioned above already pointed out, there were many national peculiarities behind the widespread

---

[14] *Credit Control Act, December 23, 1969, Public Law 91–151, 83, Stat. 376.* "Whenever the President determines that such action is necessary or appropriate for the purpose of preventing or controlling inflation generated by the extension of credit in an excessive volume, the President may authorize the Board to regulate and control any or all extension of credit" (section 205 a).

use of credit controls.[15] The book that is seen as the seminal contribution to the "varieties of capitalism" perspective, Shonfield (1965), emphasized the role of central banks, especially in France and Italy, but did not provide a systematic comparison of their policies. Writing about the central bank of Italy, Shonfield put forth an argument that is now familiar to the reader of this book: "the heart of the Italian system of control over lending and investment is the central bank" (p. 180).

II SIMILARITIES AND DIFFERENCES BETWEEN COUNTRIES

Legal and Political Responsibilities

It is well known that the degree of independence of the central bank from the government was considerably reduced during and after World War II (Siklos 2002; Singleton 2011). But differences in legal and political independence across countries were very important. There was a considerable gap between *de facto* and *de jure* control by the government.[16] Political practices and bargaining power between central banks and government varied not only between countries with similar legal frameworks but also within a country over time. This caveat was already noted by contemporary observers: the report of the Monetary Committee of the European Community published in 1972 underlined that, more than the legal framework, "the degree and methods of collaboration between government and central bank depend to a large extent on the personalities involved" (EEC 1972, p. 13).[17]

West Germany is without a doubt the country where legal independence became the most important. But during the first decade of the Bretton Woods system, German central banking remained very dependent on the Allies' policy, especially on that of the United States (Holtfrerich & Iwami

---

[15] See also Holbik (1973), in addition to Hodgman (1973, 1974). Goodman (1992) focused on central bank independence (in three countries) rather than on credit policies. Useful technical documents, published by international institutions, on central banks' legal framework and instruments during this period are EEC (1962, 1972), BIS (1963), OECD (1975). I will rely on them below.

[16] This argument was already made, among others, by Siklos (2002, ch. 2), Fforde (1992) and Capie (2010) about the Bank of England, Bouvier (1987) and Feiertag (2006b) about the Banque de France.

[17] Similar remarks were made in the comparative study published by the French Finance Ministry in 1956. Ministère de l'Économie et des Finances, "Le contrôle du crédit en France et à l'étranger," *Statistiques et Études Financières*, Supplément, n° 90, 1956, p. 637.

1999). As shown by Monica Dickhaus (1998) and Carl-Ludwig Holtfrerich (2008), the independence of the central bank was the result of the fear of the Allies of giving power to a centralized German government and of a strategy tò avoid a new hyperinflation. The structure of the German system was created by the Allies in order to copy the US Federal Reserve system. Before the birth of the Bundesbank in 1957, it comprised the central banks of the Länder (*Landeszentralbanken*) and the Bank deutscher Länder created by a decree on March 1, 1948. The central banks of the Länder acted as central banks within their areas of jurisdiction and they were legally independent even though their members were appointed by the parliaments of the Länder. The law of August 10, 1951 specified that the Bank deutscher Länder might not contradict the general policy of the government but that "it is not subject to instructions from any political body or public office." Members of the Federal government had the right to attend the meetings of the Central Bank Council and could propose motions to it but they could not vote. The 1957 Act maintained this independence and only made the system more centralized: the *Landeszentral banken* were now branches of the Bundesbank. The capital was still owned by the German state.

Other European central banks enjoyed less independence, even though, in practice, none of them was completely subject to the instructions of the government. The central banks of the United Kingdom, France and the Netherlands were completely nationalized while the Banque nationale de Belgique was half-nationalized and the Banca d'Italia kept its 1936 status (i.e., shareholders should be public institutions).[18] In these countries, the members of the board were appointed by the government (BIS 1963). Besides capital property and the appointment of the board, the extent of the government interventions was usually not clearly defined and it let a lot of room for various interpretations and practices. Belgium prohibited instructions from the government to the central bank, but the finance minister exercised his control through a Government commissioner that had a veto in respect of any measure "contrary to the interests of the State." Only in the United Kingdom did the 1946 law stipulate that the government could give to the Bank of England all the instructions that "it thinks necessary in the public interest."[19] In other countries, the nature of the relationships between the government and the central bank

[18] The Nederlandsche bank is still a society with limited liability but the law sets that the state is the only shareholder.
[19] Bank of England Act 1946, art. 4.

was not stipulated in the law. Belgium, Italy and France changed the capital structure of their central bank but founded their new monetary policy on laws (banking laws and central banks' status) passed in the 1930s or during the war. The Netherlands, which had not passed any banking law in the 1930s, constructed a new financial architecture between 1948 and 1952 where the central bank became the center of the puzzle. In the 1952 act, the Nederlandsche Bank was officially given the task to supervise the credit system (Mooij & Prast 2002).

The main postwar institutional innovations in continental Europe lie in the creation of committees in charge of credit policy. They were related to the central banks in a variety of ways. But, again, it seems that the practice was more important than the law. In France, the National Credit Council (*Conseil National du Crédit*), created in December 1945, belonged to the Banque de France and was always chaired by the governor, but the president was the finance minister. Nevertheless, the latter attended the meetings only twice over twenty years (Andrieu 1984, and Part I). In Italy, credit policy was exercised by the Interministerial Committee for Credit and Savings (*Comitato Interministeriale per il Credito e il Risparmio*) created by law in 1947. The governor of the Banca d'Italia participated in the meetings and the Banca had the operational authority and inspired most of the measures.[20] EEC (1972, p. 17) thus concludes that

the government's powers to lay down general guidelines for monetary policy do not prevent the Bank of Italy from filling a role of great importance. Wide discretionary powers have been conferred on it for the application to the banking system of ministerial directives and it enjoys almost complete autonomy as regards the way in which it controls the banks.

The centralization of several committees (discount committee, commission of banking supervision, foreign exchange operations, etc.) within the central bank was important in Germany, the United Kingdom and France. In Italy and in Belgium, the most important committees were not part of the central bank. Belgium is the most striking case because the banking commission (*Commission bancaire*), the open market commission (*Fonds des rentes*) and the rediscount committee (*Institut de réescompte et de garantie*) did not belong to the central bank. But the Banque Nationale de Belgique was represented in all these institutions (Cassiers & Ledent 2005, pp. 64–68).

---

[20] Cf. Ministère de l'Économie et des Finances, "Le contrôle du crédit en France et à l'étranger," *Statistiques et Études Financières*, Supplément, n° 90, 1956, p. 638.

The next sections will investigate whether these legal and organizational frameworks were related to important differences in the conduct of monetary policy.

Banking Supervision and Relationships with the Banking System

Postwar central banks were widely involved in banking and financial regulation. But prudential supervision was not the main purpose for regulating the banking system. The central bank set legal interest rate ceilings, credit ceiling and liquidity ratios, so that banking regulation was not separated from monetary policy actions. This is in striking contrast with the nineteenth century when banking regulation was nonexistent in most countries, as well as with post-1980s central banking where banking regulation was clearly disconnected from the management of monetary policy.[21]

The most important consequences of the postwar reforms were first the integration of monetary policy and banking regulation (which was not necessarily done in the 1930s banking acts) and, second, the development of public credit institutions as substitutes to banks. As we will see in the next section, central banks' responsibility in regulation and banking supervision is not mechanically related to the extent of their intervention in credit allocation (and then economic planning). The strongest and widest supervisors were not necessarily the central banks that were more involved in planning and in credit allocation. In France, there was a separation between commercial banks (nationalized and private) that were regulated by the *Commission de contrôle des banques* and the semi-public credit institutions that were regulated by the Treasury. In Italy, the Committee for credit and savings was responsible for the supervision of commercial banks and public credit institutions. In Germany, a specific debate on banking regulation took place because of the Federal system (Franke 1999). Initially, pursuing the role of the 1939 banking act, there was a proposal in 1948 to coordinate the banking supervisory authority of the Länder with the directives issued by the Bank deutscher Länder. Finally, after long negotiations, the Banking Act of 1961 assigned responsibility for supervising credit institutions and the subsequent new category of financial services institutions to the Federal Banking Supervisory Office (*Bundesaufsichtsamt für das Kreditwesen* or BAKred),

---

[21] Before World War II, there was substitutability between banking regulation and monetary policy: countries that concentrated their note issues in central banks earlier were less in need of a banking code (Grossman 2010, pp. 123–138). See Toniolo and White (2015) and Mourlon-Druol and Schenk (2016) for a history of postwar banking regulation and supervision.

which was set up as an independent superior Federal authority reporting to the Federal Minister of Economics. The Bundesbank then became responsible for implementing supervision in practice. This movement toward a more effective and centralized banking regulation was described by Charles Kindleberger (1984, p. 320) in these terms: "The centripetal character of banking is illustrated in this gradual organization of German banking into an hierarchical structure despite the efforts of occupation authorities, largely at American instigation, to decentralize the system and to root it widely in the states."

The result was a very powerful banking supervision in the hands of the Bundesbank that covered a very high number of institutions. In many ways, this was the broadest regulatory coverage at that time in Europe for a central bank since, in the other countries, (public) credit institutions were supervised by governments (Galbraith et al. 1981, p. 102). The main reason for such a broad coverage was the tradition of universal banking that prevailed in Germany, whereas in Italy, France, Belgium and the Netherlands, there was a somewhat clear distinction between "monetary institutions" that create money from deposits and "financial or credit institutions" that rely on other sources of refinancing (state ownership, bonds issue). In Belgium, the independent *Commission bancaire* was in charge of banking supervision but kept constant relationships with the Banque Nationale (Cassiers & Ledent 2005, p. 67). In the Netherlands, the powers of banking controls were exercised by the central bank itself. The thrift and semi-public credit institutions were supervised by the government (BIS 1963). The Bank of England again stands as a notable exception. The Bank was not officially in charge of banking supervision before the Banking Act of 1979 – as there was not even a legal definition of a bank – and had no legal authority to force banks to comply with credit controls. The system only rested on Section 4.3 of the 1946 Bank of England Act that allowed the central bank – with approval from the Treasury – to "make recommendations" and "issue directions" to bankers.[22] The traditional proximity between the Bank of England and the cartel of main English banks nevertheless allowed the implementation of informal supervision and the enforcement of reserve and credit requirements. For example, negotiations took place between the Bank and the main banks in order to set a common liquidity ratio (30% of the total deposits) in order to ensure financial stability. The ability to control the banks (including through a legal basis and a broad statistical coverage of banking credit and assets) was not as complete as on the continent. This issue was little discussed within the Bank of England before

[22] I thank Duncan Needham for bringing this to my attention.

the 1970s (Capie 2010, ch. 12; Needham 2014; Mourlon-Druol & Schenk 2016), and it greatly limited the possibility of providing qualitative and formal guidelines such as those issued by the Banque de France (see Chapter 6). The Bank of England disliked credit controls, which were however favored by HM Treasury to keep a low Bank rate (Aikman et al. 2016). It explains in part the amused reactions of the board members of the Banque de France to the publication of the Radcliffe report in 1959 (see Chapter 3).

Instruments of Monetary Policy and Credit Controls

Short-term stabilization of the price level and balance of payments deficits was achieved through different means across Europe. Four main types of instruments were used (see Chapter 4): the discount rate, open market operations, liquidity or reserves ratios (i.e., securities-reserve requirements or cash-reserve requirements) and credit controls (discount ceilings or direct limits on credit expansion). Most of the countries used all of them but the weight given to each of them was very different.

The Bank of England gave priority to the discount rate and to open market operations even though it used controls on bank lending as well as various types of reserve requirements (Aikman et al. 2016). The West German central bank gave priority to the discount rate and to reserves requirements, but also used rediscount ceilings on several occasions. France, Italy, Belgium and the Netherlands (as well as Scandinavian countries) used all of them with a special emphasis on the third and fourth types, especially credit ceilings (BIS 1963; EEC 1962, 1972). In all these countries, the discount rate was a limited indicator of the stance of monetary policy. It was mostly set in line with the US discount rate while the domestic fight against inflation relied on quantitative controls, as explained by Hodgman (1973) and Monnet (2016, 2018; see also Chapter 4 of this book). In line with the French practices described in the previous chapters, other countries also gave priority to quantitative credit controls rather than to interest rates or open market operations. Other central banks, as well as international institutions, were aware that it was possible "to assign the interest rate to the external side and to find ways of managing the rate of credit expansion without relying wholly on interest rates," as noted by Milton Gilbert, the head of the Monetary and Economic department of the Bank of International Settlements (BIS).[23] In his survey of credit controls

---

[23] BIS Archives, H.S.380, "Domestic and external equilibrium, European objectives and policies," paper presented at the annual meeting of the American Economic Association,

in Western Europe, Hodgman (1973, pp. 137–138) identified four reasons for this reluctance to change interest rates (i.e., their maintenance below market clearing level) and the preference for quantitative controls:[24]

financing government debt at lower interest rates than market preferences would permit; decreasing inflation without raising domestic interest rates and thus without attracting foreign funds through the balance of payments; influencing the allocation of credit to priority uses (selective controls) and, finally, blocking channels of financial intermediation and thus assisting a restrictive general monetary policy by impeding a rise in velocity.

Central banks favored credit controls because they were a way to combat inflation and restore the balance of payments equilibrium (traditional goals of monetary policy) while influencing the allocation of credit (between sectors and between private and public financing) and playing a role similar to capital controls. Estimations of the determinants of the central bank's discount rate show that it responded significantly to the output gap and the inflation rate only in West Germany (Monnet 2016). According to these econometric results, only the German bank rate was significantly affected by changes in production and prices. Using a different specification, Helge Berger (2003) also found that the Bundesbank policy responded to output and inflation over this period. This result seems to be quite specific to Germany. They are not straightforward to interpret, however. They can be interpreted differently depending on our knowledge of the other instruments used by the central bank and their view about monetary policy. In the English case, for example, the non-significance of these coefficients possibly reflects the claims of the Radcliffe report that monetary policy was not effective. Contrary to central banks in Italy or France, the Bank of England used its discount rate quite frequently but mostly believed in fiscal policy and wage policies to stabilize inflation. In France, Belgium or the Netherlands, these econometric results may reflect the fact that alternative instruments were used and that, indeed, signals on foreign markets through interest rates were disconnected from the management of credit expansion (see Chapter 4). In Italy, the absence of significant relationships is simply explained by the stability of the discount rate over fifteen years. It was neither a domestic tool, nor a signal sent to foreign markets. Furthermore, even the German results show

December 29, 1964. See also Katz (1969, pp. 4–6). See Monnet (2018) for further references and similar quotes from Italian, French and Austrian central bankers.

[24] In the same year, Johnson (1974) provided theoretical rationale for such credit controls.

that the response of the rate to inflation was below one, which means that the interest rate alone was not enough to stabilize inflation. Indeed, the Bundesbank mostly relied on cash-reserve requirements during this period. I do not have sufficient space here to provide a complete picture of the use of these instruments that have been already reviewed in a comprehensive way in EEC (1962, 1972). I focus instead on discussing the link between these instruments and the extent of central banks' interventions in credit allocation.

Credit Policy and Economic Planning

As highlighted by Hodgman (1973, 1974), West Germany was the country where selective credit controls were less used and the Federal government and the central banks were more reluctant to intervene in credit allocation. The United Kingdom and the Netherlands occupied an intermediate position, although Hodgman considers the UK planning experience (1948–1951) to be part of the third (more interventionist) group of countries. In the Netherlands, the whole set of credit controls were used but there were attempts to avoid too many distributive effects. The coordination with industrial policy was not so stringent and qualitative guidelines were not systematic. This was in part due to the lower importance of (semi) public credit institutions. In Belgium, Italy and France, credit policy became a prominent feature of the financial system and state intervention had an influence in almost every sector. In the words of Hodgman (1974, p. 138), "the principle of controlling credit flows and interest rates to serve national economic interests is fully accepted and has been extensively applied in practice in these three countries." In these three countries, credit policy notably relied on the new ability of the central banks to refinance banks or public credit institutions at a long maturity (usually up to five years). The most activist credit policies in European countries were very similar to the one implemented by the Bank of Japan (Patrick 1962; Cargill et al. 1997; Werner 2002b).

It is noteworthy that these differences in the extent of credit policy do not strictly reflect the differences in the status of the central banks and the organization of banking supervision highlighted in the previous section. West Germany had the more independent central bank, universal banking and thus centralized banking supervision, and was the less interventionist in credit policy. Nevertheless, before the creation of the Bundesbank, the Bank deutscher Länder was involved in the financing of the reconstruction through an active credit policy. The policy was mainly based on the *Kreditanstalt für Wiederaufbau* (*KFW*, Credit institution for reconstruction), created in 1948 and charged with facilitating credit for postwar reconstruction. Even though it was originally forbidden, the central bank soon started to grant long-term loans to the Kreditanstalt and thus supported the reconstruction of the priority sectors and export-oriented industries (Grünbacher 2004, pp. 84–87). In the autumn of 1948, a few months after its creation, the Central Bank Council of the Bank deutscher Länder implemented selective rediscount ceilings to fight inflation while favoring credit to exports: it was decided to rediscount bank bills for acceptance credit only if they served to finance foreign-trade transactions or administratively ordered storage (Holtfrerich 1999, p. 326). All over the period, the Bundesbank favored credit to exports through rediscounting and managed capital flows through a selective definition of cash-reserve requirements (different ratios applied to foreign and domestic assets). Hence, although the Bundesbank's role in direct financing and the definition of priority sectors remained limited, it would be mistaken to neglect its selective credit policy toward export-led growth that was a key component of what Holtfrerich (1999, p. 342) called "monetary mercantilism" that aimed "to promote exports and block competition from imports."[25] Some authors (MacLennan et al. 1968) have also argued that the limited role of the Bundesbank in credit allocation across sectors was explained by the fact that large state-owned banks (*Landesbanken*) played such a role at the regional level. Thus, the Bundesbank did not have a direct but an indirect role in supporting regional activist credit policies.

In England, economic planning, supported by Keynesian thoughts and policies, was an important part of British economic policy and state intervention over this period (Tomlinson 1996; Ringe & Rolling 2000; O'Hara 2007).[26] The involvement of the British state in industrial policy, public investment and wages determination was strong. But contrary to France or Italy, the role of the central bank in credit allocation and economic planning remained very limited. Direct controls on consumer loans and construction or machinery investment were implemented

---

[25] According to Shonfield (1965, pp. 285–286), this policy dates back to when Vocke was replaced as President of the Bank by Blessing in 1957. Shonfield argues that Blessing openly kept up credit and money in the system to support exports, and then reacted to booms by tightening credit.

[26] Tomlinson (1981) challenged the Keynesian inspiration of these policies and emphasized instead how they were designed as strategic economic planning influenced by socialism.

during the war and lasted until the mid-1950s but they were not administered by the central bank (Dow 1965, ch. VI). The government issued investment guidelines and controlled banking credit through exports targets and steel allocation in some industrial sectors but it was not the Bank of England's attribution and it was disconnected from monetary policy instruments (Dow 1965, pp. 149–150; Ross 2004). The Bank of England financed the government that then invested in some priority sectors. Contrary to other central banks, the Bank of England did not refinance long-term bills and only accepted the usual three-month bills of exchange. The network of public credit institutions and the role of the central bank in credit selectivity (notably through the discount window) that existed in Belgium, Italy, France or even West Germany, was not a part of British economic planning. The primary role of the Bank of England was to be the banker of the government, managing and intervening on the gilt-edged market, and its balance sheet was mostly composed of government securities.

Selective credit controls were both interventionist measures in the allocative process and tools to control the money supply and inflation. The dual role of credit controls is fundamental to understand central banks' practices in postwar Europe. However, credit ceilings and selective credit controls could be used in countries where the role of the central bank in credit allocation remained limited. This was the case in England, for example, where, as in the United States, credit controls have sometimes been used to combat inflation, but the central bank has had little involvement in direct lending to specific sectors and in setting guidelines to encourage banks or public credit institutions to increase or reduce their lending to certain sectors. Thus, while it is important to recognize the intrinsic allocative effect of credit ceilings, the use of credit ceilings should not be equated with strong intervention of the central bank in the allocation of credit. The ability of the central bank to intervene in the allocation of credit depended heavily on the nature of the relationships with other financial institutions. In France, we have seen that the financial and political relations with public and semi-public credit institutions, as well as rediscounting medium-term credit, were decisive in this respect. In Germany, the postwar role of the central bank is strongly linked to the KFW and to the relations with regional state-owned banks. National credit policies were thus strongly embedded in national financial systems. It explains why they took such different forms.

III EXPLAINING THE DIFFERENCES

Organization of the State, Structure of the Financial System and Ideology

Three main factors are likely to explain differences in credit policies between countries: organization of the state (degree of federalism), the structure of the financial system, and the political views on state interventionism and monetary theory. Of course, these factors influenced each other. A simple look at credit policy in Western Europe would support the idea that federalism works "as a commitment to preserving market incentives" (Qian & Weingast 1997) since Germany was the country that used less credit selectivity and economic planning. However, it should not be forgotten that the structure of the banking system at the Länder level was oligopolistic and ensured close relationships between industries and banks. The German system could be viewed as a delegation of "credit planning" from central to regional level – with a key role of the regional oligopolistic banking sector – rather than a pure market-economy (MacLennan et al. 1968, p. 72). On the contrary, the French centralized state relied mostly on numerous nationwide state-owned institutions. Without taking a position on the different degrees of interventionism between a centralized state and a federalist state, the organization of the state certainly appears to be a key factor explaining the role of the central bank in granting credit.

A second factor – partly linked to the first one – is the structure of the financial system. Contemporary economists all noticed that credit controls worked well only in a system that was mostly bank-based and where there were few substitutes to state-led financial intermediation. This was true for both meanings of credit controls: their function to allocate credit across sectors as well as their function to limit inflation. Frequent arguments stated that an oligopolistic banking system was more adapted to the implementation of quantitative credit controls than a unit banking system like in the United States where compliance with the general rules was more difficult to verify (Fousek 1957). The role of large state-led non-bank financial institutions and the limited role of the stock market, typical of continental European capitalism, were also viewed as key features for the implementation of credit policy. In England, the central bank had relatively limited legal capacity to enforce credit controls, as seen above and exemplified by the discussions of the Radcliffe report (see below), whereas non-bank private financial institutions and the stock market could easily replace bank loans. There were numerous ways to circumvent credit controls and use uncontrolled financial intermediation (Ross 2004).[27] Finally, the absence of a fully functioning money market, and the priority given to the discount window of the central bank for refinancing was also an essential ingredient of the effectiveness of credit control. This argument was for example put in front by proponents of the theory of an overdraft economy, especially in France and Japan (Loriaux 1991). It explains why the reform of open market operations in France in 1971 was viewed as a key departure from the standard credit policy that had prevailed since the late 1940s (see Chapter 3). More generally, both critics and defenders of credit policies emphasized the importance of the segmentation of the financial system for the working of credit policies. It is straightforward that in an economy where a unique price clears financial markets and where there is always a substitute for a type of financial asset, it is almost impossible to intervene in the allocation of credit. Without segmentation of financial markets, it is impossible to control credit in one sector only, to isolate domestic assets from foreign assets or to disconnect quantities from prices. Indeed, in a unregulated and fully integrated financial system, a restriction of credit quantities always increases interest rates. Of course, the segmentation of financial markets was largely endogenous to credit policy. Maintaining the segmentation of the financial system by regulating creditor and depositor interest rates, subsidizing loans, setting barriers to entry, imposing capital controls, was also an essential dimension of credit policies. Yet, the segmentation was also inherited from the peculiar history of the national financial system: oligopoly in the banking sector, differences between regional and national markets, political and financial power of state-owned credit institutions, etc.

Finally, ideological views on the role of the state and beliefs about the functioning of financial markets can also explain differences in credit policies.[28] Many studies had highlighted the strength of national economic cultures, mainly ordoliberalism and *Soziale Marktwirtschaft* in Germany, Keynesianism in England and *dirigisme* in France.[29] But the role of the state and the market process is not the only dividing issue on which central banks had different views. The role of money in the economy and the power of monetary policy were also highly debated topics that were obviously very

---

[27] In line with this argument, Aikman et al. (2016) found that credit controls in England between 1959 and 1971 affected mostly bank lending but had a limited effect on production and especially inflation.

[28] Shonfield (1965) used the term "market ideologies."

[29] On the role of Keynesianism in England, see Booth (2001) for a survey and Tomlinson (1981) for a dissenting view. On ordoliberalism, see Allen (2005) among others.

influential for the conduct of policy and were shaped by national intellectual debates. This is most strikingly illustrated by the Radcliffe report in England (Capie 2010, ch. 3). This report both reflected the conventional view of the Bank of England in the 1950s and introduced some changes on the conduct of monetary policy in the 1960s. It is considered as a manifesto of the Keynesian doctrine on monetary policy. The report claimed that the only possibility for the Bank of England to influence economic activity was through changes in the Bank rate supported by open market operations. Then it concluded that monetary policy could never be very effective because the Bank had no sufficient instruments to influence directly the money supply and that open market operations had a limited effect. It also revealed the skepticism of the Bank of England's officials toward restrictions on lending (credit ceilings), which would nevertheless later be used (Blackaby 1978, pp. 224–226). It implied that fiscal policy was much more suited for fighting inflation.

The conclusions of the Radcliffe report are in sharp contrast with the way monetary policy was considered in other European central banks where quantitative credit controls were more important instruments than open market operations and where policy makers considered the power of the central bank on money and the economy as much more important. In Germany, even though monetary targeting was not adopted in 1957, money growth (bank liquid reserves) remained one of the objectives and implicit target of the Bundesbank and reserves requirements were deemed an effective way to regulate money supply, bank reserves and economic activity (Lohmann 1994; Holtfrerich 1999).

These different views on state intervention and monetary policy were developed and strengthened as a corporate culture of the institutions. These cultural and sociological factors may explain a large part of the differences across central banks' practices at that time. No international common framework emerged because of these differences. This changed tremendously and rapidly in the 1970s, both because of the inflation crisis and because the weight of research and statistics departments within central banks, as well the links between academia and central banks, increased (Feiertag 2006a; Capie 2010, ch. 13).

The Consciousness of Otherness: A Bundesbank Perspective on the Banque de France

In Chapter 3, I studied the reaction of the members of the General Council of the Banque de France to the Radcliff Report. It showed how much divergence there could be across the channel on the relations between the central bank and the banks as well as on the purpose of credit policies. In a previous section of the present chapter, I have also presented French views on foreign central banking that emphasized important differences despite similarities in the use of selective credit controls, as well as US views on European central banks that identified a particular model of central banking abroad. These documents are all enlightening to understand the actors' perceptions of policy differences between central banks. A note written in August 1964 by an economist of the Bundesbank, Thomas Buch, after a visit to the Banque de France, is also particularly telling on the difference between French and German credit policies.[30] It confirms the importance of the three factors previously highlighted. Buch first wrote that the instruments of French monetary policy heavily distorted competition. He expressed a great concern about the non-respect of the neutrality of competition (*Wettbewerbsneutralität*) and the fact that credit controls created rents for the incumbents. When he asked the officials at the Banque de France about this problem, he had been told that credit controls were actually a means to prevent the exclusion of the weaker banks from the market. Then Buch wondered whether Germany should adopt French monetary and credit instruments.[31] He answered negatively and first mentioned a "cultural" argument: French households, firms and banks were more used to a *dirigiste* government. Second, he pointed out that the French banking system was more homogeneous. The Banque de France could discuss with only one professional association of bankers, while in Germany there were many divergent interests between the banks, especially between regional banks. He also noticed that French banks were more indebted toward the central bank. Most importantly, he highlighted the difference between institutions that financed short- and long-term credit. In France (see Chapter 6), banks financed short-term credit and a part (about a half in the mid-1960s) of medium-term

---

[30] Banque de France archives, 1330201101/1. NB: the note was written in German for the Bundesbank and then sent to the Banque de France as a courtesy. I also found that the answers by German and French officials written to a BIS questionnaire (found in the BIS archives: BISA, H.S. 363), dated from 1962, reached similar conclusions.

[31] In 1964, French monetary policy had experienced great successes since the 1958 stabilization. The 1963 disinflationary plan, using direct credit controls, had been very effective (and still ongoing in 1964). The Netherlands, the United Kingdom and Italy were using similar instruments. It was thus a legitimate question for the Bundesbank to know whether the Banque de France instruments should be copied.

credit, but long-term credit was only financed by semi-public credit institutions (Crédit National, Caisse des dépôts, etc.). Hence, the central bank could impose credit controls on banks only in order to fight inflation without damaging long-term investment too much. In Germany, according to him, because of universal banking, it was impossible to discriminate the maturity of credit using credit controls.

IV   THE FALTERING END OF CREDIT POLICY

In the early 1970s, a number of European central banks, like the Banque de France, began implementing reforms to give more room to open market operations, reduce the extent of credit controls and, more generally, give the market a greater role in the allocation of credit. Because of the very nature of credit policy, the desire to reduce its ambition and give more room to markets required reforms of both the central bank's instruments and of the banking and financial system, as explained in France in the 1969 Marjolin–Sadrin–Wormser report (Chapter 3). A similar process of liberalization took place in several European countries (both Community and non-Community) in 1969–1971, in particular in the United Kingdom, Spain and, to a lesser extent, Italy. But in the years 1972 and 1973, however, when inflation increased and became a major problem for European countries and Community institutions – even before the first oil shock – several countries took a step backwards, considering the "liberalization" of credit policy and monetary policy instruments as one of the reasons for their difficulty in controlling inflation. In the United Kingdom, the liberalization programme starting in September 1971 was explicitly called "competition and credit controls" (CCC) and was intended to replace the latter (credit controls) with the former (competition). Credit rationing by cost (interest rates) replaced rationing by control (Needham 2014, p. 3). Taking stock of the failure of CCC two years later in the autumn of 1973, the Bank of England introduced the "corset" in December, which placed a limit on the growth of bank deposits to control the money supply (Hodgman 1971; Gowland 1978; Capie 2010, ch. 10; Needham 2014, pp. 50–72; Goodhart 2015). Control of credit and money by interest rates and market forces had been suspended. Some countries, such as Denmark and Italy, for the first time used credit ceilings (i.e., direct limitation of the growth of banking credit outstanding) whereas they had previously used other types of quantitative instruments only (Oksanen 1974; Blomgren-Hansen 1977; Cotula &

Padoa-Schioppa 1971; Cotula & De Stefani 1979; Gaiotti & Secchi 2012). In West Germany, the project of introducing credit ceilings was seriously proposed and discussed within the Bundesbank, but it was abandoned, particularly under the influence of Finance Minister Helmut Schmidt, who feared embracing the French model of credit control and its management (Von Hagen 1999, pp. 414–415). The process and timing in other European countries were very similar to what happened in France, as described in Chapter 3. We therefore find a similar paradox: credit ceilings were undergoing a revival in the mid-1970s after an aborted wave of liberalization, and in a less restrictive form in the fight against inflation than what had previously been present in the 1950s and 1960s. Furthermore, this process coincided with the rise in monetary targeting by central banks. Selective credit ceilings were quantitative objectives that could be coupled with money targeting while being consistent with the traditional purposes of selective credit policy.

The widespread and regular use of selective credit ceilings provided new arguments for critics, who saw them as a factor of the productivity crisis (in that it maintained inefficient rents for certain sectors) and of the inflationary crisis (in that it allowed part of the loans to increase for reasons of selectivity). From the late 1970s to the mid-1980s, at a different pace depending on the country, credit policy was attacked again, then eventually reformed and lost its importance in favor of refinancing operations on a money market increasingly open to various institutions and financial securities. The full process of financial liberalization was contemporary with the implementation of deflationary policies in the early 1980s, but it is not confused with them; deflationary policies were conducted in Europe with instruments that go far beyond the powers of central banks (budgetary policy, wage indexation). Some countries, such as England, led these two policies together, while others, such as France and Italy, initially stabilized inflation in the early 1980s with quantitative credit control instruments before embarking on a major liberalization program. The United States also began its deflationary policy in 1980 with a credit control program (Schreft 1990), as we have seen earlier. It was the United Kingdom, under the impetus of Margaret Thatcher, which opened the way toward the end of credit policy, with the abandonment of the corset in 1980 and a wave of liberalization. France is a country where these reforms were most drastically implemented in 1984, with the creation of a real money market in less than two years, culminating in the end of credit ceilings (Cerny 1989; Mélitz 1990; Loriaux 1991; O'Sullivan 2007). Financial liberalization was intrinsically linked to changes in monetary policy implementation (Alexander & Enoch 1995; De Melo & Denizer 1997; Borio 1997). Activist credit policies were delegitimized, open market operations and interest rates replaced quantitative credit controls.

It is impossible to give a detailed chronology of the reforms in each country during the 1980s. A very synthetic and rough overview can be obtained from the "liberalization indices" (starting in 1973) published retrospectively by the International Monetary Fund, which reflect the presence of "credit control," "interest rate control," "capital controls" and various elements of banking or financial regulation (Abiad et al. 2008). We can see from this database that a strong movement toward liberalization of credit policy took place between 1979 and 1987, including for the United States and Japan, with a concentration of reforms between 1984 and 1986 for the countries of Western Europe.[32] This movement is characterized by the opening up of the money market (and therefore by an increase in central bank intervention on the latter), the end of direct control and credit selectivity, and the end of regulated interest rates. In the 1987 annual report of the European Banking Federation, this process was explicitly described as follows: "the desire to less regulate the financing of the economy by administrative techniques that have the disadvantage of rigidifying behavior has gradually led to giving interest rates and their variations greater role than before ... In most countries, the use of monetary policy as an instrument of selective and sectoral credit policy has declined or almost disappeared" (pp. 2–3).[33]

This was the state of central banking in the late 1980s, when the process of European monetary integration began. It was radically different from what prevailed in the late 1960s, when the first monetary union plans were developed. It is important to bear in mind that, as in France with the Marjolin–Sadrin–Wormser report, the first attempts to reform credit policy and liberalize the banking systems and the instruments of central bank intervention started in the late 1960s. In the 1970s, both credit policy reforms and the EMU construction project were put on hold, but the discussions and proposals on these two subjects did not cease. Was there a connection between these two processes?

---

[32]   Greece, Spain and Portugal being the latest countries to introduce liberal interest rate and credit control reforms. On the Spanish case, see Perez (1997, 1998).

[33]   I translate excerpts from this report, consulted in French in the library of the central bank of Belgium (*Rapport annuel de la Fédération bancaire européenne, 1987*).

V WHAT IS THE LINK WITH EUROPEAN MONETARY INTEGRATION?

The end of credit policy, linked to financial liberalization, is not specific to Europe (Borio 1997; Loriaux et al. 1997). But within the European framework, it cannot be denied that it has profoundly affected the way in which central bank practices and financial systems partly converged before the EMU was established. The subject of this book is not the reforms of the 1980s and even less the creation of the EMU, but we must ask ourselves whether the first political projects of the EMU in the early 1970s (following the publication of the Werner report in 1970) could have had an effect on the reform of credit policies in France and in other countries of the European monetary community. As I have pointed out on several occasions in this book, credit policy meant that the instruments of central banks differed considerably from one country to another because they were adapted to the particularities of national financial systems. Credit controls also reinforced segmentation within national financial systems and were complemented by capital controls or played a similar role to capital controls. In this respect, it seems in retrospect that the end of credit policies was a precondition for European monetary integration. Although there was no plan to end or reform credit policies in the Werner report, it was clear in the early 1970s that the instruments and operating framework of central banks needed to be harmonized in order to move toward monetary union. In a report published in 1972 about instruments of European central banks, the EC Monetary Committee stated that "the means by which these [instruments of central banks] are used often reveal particular structural and institutional characteristics which will make their gradual harmonization in the Community framework more difficult. This harmonization is nevertheless a necessary precondition for arriving at a monetary policy which can lead to the achievement of economic and monetary union" (EEC 1972, preface).

Given the frequent contacts between the central banks of the European Community in the 1970s and 1980s, particularly in the context of the European exchange rate regime (James 2012; Mourlon-Druol 2012), it might therefore be thought that the end of credit policy and the convergence of central bank instruments linked to it was undoubtedly an important theme of European policy at that time. It seems likely that reforms of credit policy have been coordinated at European level to ensure freedom of capital movement, reduce state intervention in financial systems and allow convergence of central bank instruments. This hypothesis is all the more justified since intervention in credit allocation was one of the most visible and debated characteristics of central banks during this period, particularly in Europe (as highlighted for example in the reports to the US Congress of 1971 and 1981 mentioned above), and reforming credit policy was a most important policy issue within central banks, as shown by the debates in France studied previously (Chapter 3) or equivalent discussions that I have been able to see in the archives of the Italian central bank.[34] However, this hypothesis is not verified, as we will see in the next section. In transcripts of the regular meetings of the governors of the EC central banks or in various reports and key documents published by the EC Monetary Committee, there is no evidence of any plan to reform credit policy in the Member States. This confirms what I observed in the French case, namely that the reform of credit policy was essentially a domestic process rather than imposed from abroad. This striking paradox gives an interesting insight into the history of credit policies, financial liberalization and European monetary integration.

From Werner to Delors: The Disappearance of Credit Policy

The history of EMU is marked by the publication of two landmark reports. In 1970, the Werner report put the idea of such a union on the table and defined a step-by-step program to achieve it. In 1989, the Delors report reinvigorated the idea of a single currency and laid the foundations for the future Maastricht Treaty.[35] Historians have clearly demonstrated the importance of these reports while questioning the idea of a discontinuity in discussions on monetary union and insisting instead on the long process of political concertation that, from 1970 to 1988, resulted in the recommendations of the committee chaired by Jacques Delors (Dyson &

---

[34] In a 1977 memorandum, Governor Baffi criticized the rigidities of credit policy and announced his commitment to reform (Archives of the Banca d'Italia, Documenti n° 4, Novembre 1977, I flussi del credito in un'economia aperta, p. 11). In 1981, several internal reports of the Banca insisted on the need to open up a real money market and denounced the risks that the direct control of credit exposed the economy to by dragging it into a spiral where any anti-inflationary action requires ever more administrative control (see ABI, Documenti, n° 60, Giugno 1981, Le autorità monetarie e gli impieghi alternativi del risparmio, Mario Sarcinelli). In 1984, Governor Campi made a speech to the Italian Senate, testifying to the desire to liberalize the financing system of the Italian economy and credit policy, while stressing the difficulties of this transition (ABI, Documenti, Febbraio 1984, n°119, Politica industriale e strutture finanziarie, Carlo Campi, Governatore).

[35] Pierre Werner, *Report to the Council and the Commission on the Realization by Stages of Economic and Monetary Union in the Community*, Luxembourg, October 8, 1970. Jacques Delors, *Report on Economic and Monetary Union in the European Community, April 17, 1989, Committee for the Study of Economic and Monetary Union*.

Featherstone 1999; James 2012; Mourlon-Druol 2012). We also know how close their contents are. Yet, a major difference between them was neither noticed nor discussed in previous works on the subject: while the Werner report repeatedly mentions "monetary and credit policy," in particular to explain the need to "centralize" it, "coordinate" it and define the "general guidelines" jointly, the Delors report discarded the term "credit policy" and referred only to "monetary policy." Fiscal policy, exchange rate policy, capital controls and financial markets remained at the center of the 1989 report, but credit policy – and its association with monetary policy – had disappeared.

Prior to the Werner report, the Segre report published in 1966 on the "development of a European capital market" had already mentioned that the end of capital controls would have significant consequences for credit policy and monetary policy by making them potentially less autonomous, and that it required greater convergence of credit policy to allow genuine market integration.[36] The report acknowledged that "credit policy, balance-of-payments policy and capital market policy overlap a great deal" (p. 97). As mentioned earlier, the 1972 report of the EC Monetary Committee on central bank instruments (EEC 1972), which was a direct consequence of the Werner report – the previous edition dated back to 1962 (EEC 1962) and directly followed the 1957 Treaty of Rome and the creation of the EC Monetary Committee in 1959 – also viewed the convergence of instruments, including credit controls, as a necessary condition for monetary integration, but it did not specify whether such convergence would require the abolition of credit controls and other selective quantitative tools. In the annual reports on the activities of the Monetary Committee that followed this report (EEC 1972), there was never a plan to harmonize or abolish credit controls, nor criticisms about the perverse effects of selective credit controls such as the ones found, for example, in the reports of the French Planning office (Chapter 3).[37] When describing instruments used by central banks to fight inflation, the Monetary Committee was nevertheless mentioning the various quantitative instruments used by European central banks. Discussions and proposals were focused on money targets, exchange rates policies and the functioning of the European Monetary System (EMS), and capital controls. The following section looks at whether credit policy

[36] Claudio Segre, *The Development of a European Capital Market. Report of a Group of Experts Appointed by the EEC Commission*. November 1966.

[37] I have consulted online the various annual Reports on the Activity of the Monetary Committee, available on the Archives of European Integration (http://aei.pitt.edu).

and credit controls were discussed during the meetings of the Committee of Governors of the European Community.

The Silence of the Committee of Governors on Credit Policies

The Committee of Governors of the central banks of the European Community, set up in 1964, met at the Bank for International Settlements in Basel, which had already hosted consultations on the European Payments Union in the 1950s. Among central bank governors, the issue of exchange rate policy was constantly being discussed. The various positions expressed during these debates have been studied by Emmanuel Mourlon-Druol (2012) and Harold James (2012) in an exhaustive way.[38] Indeed, the recurrent themes in the Committee's transcripts in the 1970s were the issues of exchange rate fluctuation margins, inter-central bank credit to enable each country to defend fixed parity, swaps with the US Federal Reserve, participation in the fixed exchange rate system, and the European unit of account (ECU). The introduction of the "monetary snake" after the end of the Bretton Woods system, the creation of the European Monetary Cooperation Fund in 1973, and then of the EMS in 1979 gave rise to lengthy debates among the governors. With a view to maintaining the fixed exchange rate regime and avoiding excessive balance of payments imbalances between countries, the Committee regularly focused on the objectives and results of monetary policy in the Member States. In October 1972, the members of the Committee gave their strong and total approval to the proposals of the Commission and the European Council of Finance Ministers (ECOFIN) to coordinate the quantitative objectives of each country's policies in the form of a rule equalizing the growth of the money supply and nominal

---

[38] The archives I consulted are the transcripts of the monthly meetings. They are available in full (in French only) online at www.ecb.int/ecb/history/archive/agendas/html/index.en.html. Transcripts of monthly meetings of the Committee are not declassified after December 1986. The governors of the EEC central banks were members of the Delors Committee, which was set up in 1988. On the history of this group, see Scheller (2011) and James (2012). A few hints or discussions may have escaped my analysis, but it would be surprising if an important plan or debate on this topic were not mentioned in these discussions or documents. The analysis of the minutes in this chapter remains relatively brief in terms of presenting the topics discussed or not addressed during the meetings of the Committee of Governors. It may be complemented by a more detailed study of the speeches in this committee and the reports that underpin them. My analysis of the main debates on monetary instruments below is close to the analytical framework developed by Mitchel Abolafia (2004), which shows how debates within the central bank take the form of interpretative techniques based on the tension between technical discourses and accounts of experience delivered by experts.

GDP (James 2012, p. 126). These proposals notably led to the creation of a committee of experts (the so-called "Bastiaanse" committee, named after its chairman) to monitor the "monetary situation" of member countries and report to the Committee of Governors every three months. However, this coordination did not lead to the harmonization or publication of a strict common monetary policy rule or target. The governors regularly stressed that they thought that monetary policy was no longer able – unlike in previous decades – to cope with inflationary pressures on its own. In addition, several governors thought that a money (or credit) target was not a reliable objective.[39] It was often stressed that instruments of central banks depended heavily on the structure of the domestic financial system. There were numerous discussions on money targets between the governors but they never reached a consensus on a common European rule. In 1976 and 1978, the EC Monetary Committee recommended to the European Council and Commission that it was not advisable to define common monetary targets because the financial systems of European countries were too different.

Discussions within the Committee of Governors and reports of the EC Monetary Committee about exchange rates, capital controls and money targets often showed strong differences of opinion between central banks and national experts. But the very fact that a discussion was engaged presupposed a certain agreement: at least the participants agreed on what was at stake. In the field of credit policy and the structures of the national banking and financial systems, there was, on the contrary, a lack of a minimum agreement that would make it possible to put the topic on the agenda. The few attempts in this direction did not succeed. On November 13, 1973, the governors discussed the creation of the expert group on "Harmonization of monetary policy instruments" (eventually created in June 1974 and also headed by Bastiaanse), in line with the recommendations of the Werner report and the EEC (1972) report. Given the diversity of central bank instruments and the widespread use of selective credit controls – which

---

[39] See, for example, the criticism of money targets by the Belgian governor, Cecil de Strycker, on May 11, 1976: "The meaning given to money supply varies considerably in the Community; for some countries, this aggregate is an objective, while for other countries it is only an assumption" (translated from French by the author). On February 16, 1976, he had stated

Given the wide discrepancies in the conceptions of monetary policy and in the structures and financial institutions of member countries, it seems more useful, at least in the short term, that the member countries seek the appropriate use of the various existing instruments, rather than a systematic harmonization of monetary policy objectives and instruments that would be too far removed from reality. (translated from French by the author)

were clearly described in EEC (1972) – the Committee may have given a broad meaning to the term "instruments" and therefore a broad mandate to the committee of experts on this issue. This was not the case: the committee on the "harmonization of monetary policy instruments" merely elaborated and presented a reflection on money targets alone. "Instruments" was taken as synonymous to "targets." At the November 1973 meeting, some governors (especially Wormser, from France, and Ziljstra, from the Netherlands) objected to the following recommendation: "The structure of the banking system in the final stage of economic and monetary union should also be considered."[40] Their objection closed the door to any consideration on quantitative credit controls, the implementation of which was closely linked to the characteristics of the national banking system. Thus, when the report on the harmonization of monetary policy instruments was presented in June 1976, its only purpose was to harmonize the calculation of money supply targets (which did not succeed). It did not mention selective credit controls or even credit ceilings that were applied in all countries except West Germany at that time. It is striking to see how the discussions at European level diverged from the central banks' actual means of intervention at national level. Meanwhile, discussions on a joint European supervision of credit institutions (i.e., including non-bank institutions) took place between March and October 1975 but also led to a dead end.[41] Among the reasons put forward for not pursuing this project, the English and Dutch governors stressed that the national central banks had already taken sufficient measures to avoid problems of "vulnerability" in the banking system. Once again, the link between credit policy and the banking system was not discussed between governors. These discussions clearly show that the management of credit and banking institutions was a national rather than a European issue. So was credit policy.

Because of the governors' reluctance to address credit policy issues, it was not until May 1977 that the Committee first referred to "credit ceilings." The governor of the Bank of Italy, Paolo Baffi, acknowledged the effectiveness of this instrument in controlling inflation, but regretted that it "distorts the

---

[40] The following month, in December 1973, it was also definitively decided not to set up a new committee responsible for consultations "on central banks' monetary and credit policy" with the newly created European Monetary Cooperation Fund to ensure exchange rate stability. This is the only time that the notion of "credit policy" appears in the committee's deliberations in the 1970s, and it was to mean that it must be excluded from discussions on cooperation in exchange rate policies.

[41] On the failed initiatives to plan a European banking union in the 1960s and 1970s, see Mourlon-Druol (2016).

structure of bank assets." Baffi's remark echoed important and recurrent criticisms within national central banks during this period but did not lead to a discussion on the agenda of the Committee. However, the governors decided to include credit ceilings in the remit of the expert group on the harmonization of instruments. The Bastiaanse group therefore included credit aggregates in the statistics it presented to governors, as a counterpart to the money supply. Experts of the group discussed whether it was preferable to target credit growth or money supply growth, but they did not ask why and according to what procedures credit ceilings were used in an interventionist way in the allocation of credit.[42] Again, "instruments" was taken as synonymous to "targets." In February 1979, Bastiaanse defined the harmonization of monetary policy instruments as follows: "Harmonization means the use of a concept by all member countries, such as harmonized M2 or credit, in order to define a common monetary policy stance." Selective credit controls, giving priority to certain sectors, and subsidized loans were not discussed. Some governors, especially those of the Netherlands (Zijlstra) and England (Richardson) then criticized openly the group of experts: "the differences in the choice and application of instruments to achieve the same intermediate objective, as well as the causes of these differences, such as the variety of financial structures etc., should be examined pragmatically from one country to another. Such studies would be more useful than monetary and financial forecasting."[43]

A few months later, in July 1979, following criticisms by the governors, Bastiaanse proposed an analysis of the difference in the instruments used by central banks. The group's report mentioned

four closely related factors, which may explain the differences between the monetary policy instruments used by the various EEC member countries:

1) The strategy of monetary authorities, some of whom trust implicit self-regulation by economic agents while others believe that specific controls are necessary;

2) The financial structure;

3) Institutional differences: in some countries, monetary authorities do not have the legal powers to use certain instruments. The absence of these instruments reflects either fundamental policy principles or the peculiarities of the relationship between government and the central bank;

---

[42] The 21st report of the EU monetary committee in 1980 was a follow-up to these discussions. It discussed money targeting as well as "domestic credit expansion" (DCE), that is, the credit targeting apparatus used by the Bank of England at that time.

[43] Remark by Richardson, meeting of February 1979.

4) More general economic considerations: for example, small open-economy countries that participate in a stable exchange rate system and whose interest rate policy is subject to external constraints, tend to make a different choice than larger countries that enjoy a greater autonomy in interest rate policy.

All these arguments are reminiscent of those mentioned in the previous sections of this chapter (see also Hodgman 1973, 1974). It is the only time in the Committee of Governors that it was mentioned that central bank instruments depended on the modes and degree of state and central bank intervention in the economy (and thus on the belief in the free market), whereas this was an essential characteristic of the credit policy of the time. This is the first and last time, therefore, that all of the central banks' assignments and operating methods were really discussed. However, this discussion was immediately closed and did not give rise to any plan to harmonize the key elements of credit policy that Bastiaanse had stressed: belief in the role of state, financial structure, regulatory powers of central banks.

Contrary to the liberalization of capital flows, which had already been mentioned earlier and was once again the focus of attention with the 1986 white paper and the 1989 Delors report, credit policy and the harmonization of banking structures did not appear in these reports or in the preparatory documents that are now available to historians. Harold James, who had been able to consult the minutes of the Committee of Governors until 1992 for his book *Making the European Monetary Union* (James 2012), did not recount any debate on this subject, while the issues of monetary objectives, the link between fiscal and monetary policy and the end of capital controls were widely discussed. The end of credit policy that I have documented earlier was not a topic discussed at the European level, although at the time it was a major development for central banks. When Michel Camdessus replaced Renaud de la Genière as governor of the Banque de France in November 1984, he praised the free-market reforms put in place by his predecessor: "to convince the Government to restore market mechanisms – and first of all the money market – their place and protect them from too many public interventions that are still justified in the moment but sclerotic." To achieve this objective, he announced "the disappearance of credit ceilings (*encadrement du credit*)" and "resolute action against financial segmentation, subsidized loans and directed credit."[44] Indeed, a few weeks before de la Genière had praised the end of credit ceilings in order "to replace a brutal and uniform quantitative

---

[44] ABF, PVCG, November 15, 1984.

regulation by market mechanisms and arbitrage based on the cost of the different methods of financing [interest rates]."[45]

Such statements about the need to abolish definitely the methods and goals of credit policy – which are reminiscent of Wormser's argument in 1969–1971 (Chapter 3) – are not found in the discussions of the Committee of European governors. It is a priori particularly remarkable that the disappearance of credit policy has not been the subject of any official coordination with a view to achieving the EMU. There are no links or plans between those of Werner and Delors that would explain why the abandonment of credit policy is essential to monetary union and would attempt to impose or even suggest this path for European countries. The reason why credit policy does not appear in the Delors report is that it was already in agony in Europe at the time of writing. Our contention is that it was not at the transnational or European level, but at the national level and according to different processes in different countries, that the exit from credit policy was negotiated.[46] This observation is in line with Kathleen McNamara (1998, 1999)'s constructivist thesis that the European Union is the result of the convergence of "neoliberal" policies implemented in the main European countries without the European Economic Community necessarily being at the origin of these policies. However, it is important to note the difference between the history of credit policy and the history of capital controls studied by McNamara. The abolition of capital controls was eventually discussed at the European level (until the Single European Act of 1986) in the context of the creation of a single market and exchange rate policy. In the domain of credit policy in the 1970s and early 1980s, the European Union was not the driver of national reforms. By contrast, it is key to recognize that the EMU, as it was built in the 1990s, was the product of a convergence of central banks' practices and policies that had shifted away from activist interventions in credit allocation. The end of activist credit policies in

---

[45] ABF, PVCG, October 15, 1984.

[46] Laurent Warlouzet (2017) observes quite a similar process for industrial policy and planning in the 1970s. He documents the failure of some European planning projects (in particular the 1976 Maldague report) at the same time as the decline of planning policies at the national level. Although European central banks were involved in a common exchange rate system in the 1970s, we do not observe in the domain of credit policy what Orfeo Fioretos (2011) has documented about trade or agricultural policies, where, he argues, multilateral strategies of government at the European level shaped the national trajectories of capitalism.

interventionist states (Loriaux 1997) meant that European central banks were now ready "to play the market" (Jabko 2006).

VI CONCLUSION

This chapter aimed to go beyond the French case and to emphasize that the role of credit policy is key to understanding the history of central banking in other countries, especially in Western Europe, since World War II. Overall, I found that there were significant differences in the role of central banks, and that the history of the Bank of England and the Federal Reserve – which until now has received the most attention in the economic and historical literature – is not representative of what central banking was like in the postwar world.[47] The strong national embeddedness of central banking during this period explains why no European central bank stood out as a benchmark or as an example for the others, but all were, to some extent, involved in intervening in credit allocation. Differences in financial systems, beliefs in public intervention in the economy and the organization of the state stand out as prominent explanations of differences in implementation and extent of credit policies. If we look at the history of credit policies in postwar Europe, we realize that it is then impossible to fully understand the historical process of European monetary union without integrating into it the evolution of central banks that have paved the way for the convergence of monetary practices on which EMU, as we know it today, has been built. Credit policy was in decline when the Delors report gave final impetus to EMU. Thus, there was no attempt to draw up a European credit policy led by a European central bank, nor was there any attempt to coordinate or encourage at the European level the reforms of credit policies that had already taken place at the national level.[48]

---

[47] In a recent paper based mostly on the English experience, Charles Goodhart (2011, p. 140) concludes that central banks in the 1950s–1970s had three roles: the provision of advice on policy to the government, the administration of the government's panoply of controls, and the management of markets (debt management, liquidity management and foreign exchange operations). Indeed, central banks of the European Community performed such roles, but only the Bank of England entirely performed debt management. Furthermore, as I have shown, credit policies outside of the United Kingdom went much beyond the mere administration of "the government's panoply of controls."

[48] In the words of historical institutionalism in political sciences (Streeck 2005; Fioretos et al. 2016), we could speak of "unintended consequences" to speak about this historical process, meaning that the reforms of credit policy were not implemented in order to achieve European monetary integration. The monetary union then appears as an unintended consequence of the convergence of national frameworks of central banking.

Conclusion

The goal of this book has been to understand the instruments, goals and consequences of the Banque de France's policy during the greatest period of economic growth in the country's history. In contrast to the widely held view that monetary policy was passive, entirely subject to budget policy and lacking autonomy due to the fixed rate system, the previous chapters have shown the extent to which the Banque de France's role during this period was robust and economically decisive. By pursuing a policy of credit development, the bank contributed to expansion and the rebuilding of productive capital during the *Trente Glorieuses*. By intervening in credit allocation in various ways, it supported the transition to growth through investment and the reallocation of capital. By establishing rigorous instruments for controlling money and credit, and imposing its own views in the face of occasionally reluctant or unstable governments, it was able to keep the inflation rate at a moderate level and to guarantee, in this way, the legitimacy and successful functioning of the *dirigiste* system. By alternating between expansionary policies and credit restriction, it largely shaped the French economy's short-term economic cycle. By disconnecting the price of credit from its quantity, in a context characterized by capital controls, it acquired the means to pursue a relatively autonomous monetary and credit policy. More generally, it helped to formulate a definition – specifically, a statistical definition – of "investment credit" and non-inflationary credit, describing "good" credit in contrast to poor credit. In this way, it played a key role in the institutionalization of what contemporaries called "the nationalization of credit." These actions occurred at a time when government financing was one of the central bank's major preoccupations and in which external constraints tied to the exchange rate system were ubiquitous and devaluations occurred quite frequently. One cannot speak of "monetary policy" during this period without considering its interactions with budgetary and exchange rate policy, yet it can be reduced to neither of these interactions. This book will have achieved its task if it has managed, overcoming entrenched prejudices, to convince the reader that the role of central banks in the postwar economy cannot simply be described in terms of inflationary financing of public deficits. One cannot speak of investment, fighting inflation, capital allocation, economic cycles, and debt and credit during this period without having to consider the role of monetary authorities. Readers are welcome to draw their own conclusions about the advantages or perverse side-effects of such a system, but I hope that the scale and complexity of the Banque de France's policy during the *Trente Glorieuses* will now be better understood, as well as, more generally, the role that central banks played in the postwar period and the Bretton Wood system, before the "Great Inflation" of the 1970s. This policy is best understood as a "credit policy" (*politique du credit*), as it was referred to at the time. Its main goal was to expand and properly allocate credit to help promote economic growth. This was combined with a second objective: controlling credit, when required, in order to avoid high inflation rates, destabilizing international capital flows and banking crises. The connection between monetary policy, the public debt and balance of payments must also be understood as elements of the credit policy framework. Finally, if France was undeniably one of the European countries in which credit policy occurred on a vast scale and in which state intervention was particularly extensive, similar traits can be found elsewhere during this period, particularly in Japan and Western Europe, that is, in countries in which central banks, via the G10, played a predominant role during the 1960s in preserving the international monetary system's stability.[1]

THE HISTORICAL AND POLITICAL CONSEQUENCES OF THE END OF CREDIT POLICY

These observations, I believe, have important consequences for the economic and political history of the second half of the twentieth century. It follows that the profound transformation of central banks in the 1980s and 1990s – especially in "advanced" economies – must be understood primarily in terms of the end of credit policy.[2] The latter is intrinsically tied to

---

[1] On the G10's role in central bank cooperation under the Bretton Woods system, see James (1996), Toniolo and Clement (2005), Monnet (2013).

[2] Building on Milton Friedman (1969), Goodfriend and King (1988) provided the clearest theoretical and political justification for distinguishing monetary policy from credit policy (which they call "banking policy" and "lending policy"). Their argument also offers a good description of the changes in monetary policy underway in the United States as financial

the liberalization of financial markets and the decline of industrial policy. Central bank independence, which attracted great attention in economic and political science literature, was, of course, a major phenomenon in the 1990s, but it was only a symptom of credit policy's end.[3] It seems most likely that independence is less the result of rational learning about the best ways to limit inflation (which, incidentally, had ultimately been controlled during the 1980s without independence), as one often wants to believe, than the culmination of reforms that significantly limited and depoliticized central banks' functions. Once credit policy came to an end, central banks could be seen as neutral institutions, whose decisions did not disturb the operation of financial markets and who engaged in technical economic issues more than general policy debates. The end of credit policy was thus the historical condition of possibility of central bank independence. It was symptomatic of this trend that the 1993 law granting the Banque de France its independence simultaneously eliminated the "money" and "credit" management goals from its mandate, and that this occurred only a few years after credit ceilings came to an end and financial markets were liberalized between 1984 and 1987. Understanding the end of credit policy also makes it possible to grasp why bank regulation and supervision, beginning in the 1980s, pursued goals that were primarily microeconomic and distanced itself from macroeconomic issues related to credit cycle, despite the fact that, since World War II, bank regulation instruments (liquidity ratios, reserves, credit increase limits and maximum interest rates) were used above all to achieve macroeconomic goals and to control credit and capital flows. It was not until the aftermath of the 2008 financial crisis that central banks once again

deregulation was occurring in the 1980s. These changes were greater in other countries, as the US central bank made less use of credit policy to support and finance other policies (notably housing policy and industrial policy; see Thurow 1971), though the Fed did use non-price rationing at the discount window and credit control to fight inflation (Schreft 1990; Corder 1998, ch. 5). In Europe, this process has been less often described and theorized, though the financial liberalization of the 1980s has been the subject of numerous studies. It has been customary, especially in France, to describe it as the end of the overdraft economy (Loriaux 1991), but, as we have seen, this characterization is too limited to allow one to grasp credit policy in all its aspects and mechanisms. Concerning Japan, Richard Werner (2002a, 2002b) has provided a critical account of changes in central bank policy during the 1980s as it relates to financial deregulation. Finally, a number of publications have described the end of quantitative instruments of credit control (such as *encadrement de credit* in France) used by central banks in the 1980s and 1990s, but focus exclusively on the technical aspects of implementing monetary policy (Goodhart 1989; Borio 1997). See Chapter 7 for further references.

[3] A recent book by Peter Conti-Brown (2017) about the history of the Federal Reserve shows how, in practice, the notion of independence is much more complex that what is usually considered.

decided that certain bank regulation tools could be used to guide credit expansion at a macroeconomic level.

The reconsideration and subsequent end of credit policy on the part of central banks was a slow and non-linear process, the rhythm and scale of which varied by country, lasting from the 1970s to the early 1990s. Leaving aside financial liberalization, to which it was inherently tied, this process was connected to three major trends in the financial and monetary history of this period that must be reconsidered from this perspective: the "Great Inflation" of the 1970s, the end of the Bretton Woods system and the construction of Europe's monetary union. High inflation in the 1970s had multiple causes (the oil crisis, increasingly accommodationist budget and monetary policies due to rising unemployment, the end of the Bretton Woods system, lower productivity and so on). But it also coincided, in many countries, notably France, with a transitional period in which central bank instruments that had been used over the previous three decades were called into question. Thus, I have described the 1970s as a period in which institutional coherence began to fragment and in which, more concretely, the central bank lost control over the effects of its instruments and, consequently, over its ties to the banking sector, notably due to the rise of international capital flows and to the growing complexity of the credit controlling system. In many respects, the inflation of the 1970s was a symptom of the first, poorly controlled changes to credit policy and it contributed, in turn, to delegitimizing the *dirigiste* policies pursued since the war's end.

Understanding central bank credit policy also strikes us as indispensable to grasping how the Bretton Woods system operated. The classical macroeconomic model for an open economy (the Mundell–Fleming model, which results in a "triangle of impossibility" or "trilemma") tells us that the only way to guarantee the autonomy of monetary policy in a fixed exchange rate system is to impose capital controls. This theory gradually became the main framework for interpreting the motives, functioning and benefits of capital controls under the Bretton Woods system (Goodman & Pauly 1993; Obstfeld & Taylor 2004; Ghosh & Qureshi 2016 and so on). The historical analysis proposed in this book has, however, shown that this line of reasoning tends to overlook the fact that capital controls were also conceived as a complement to credit policy, rather than as instruments motivated solely by a desire to maintain differentials between domestic and international interest rates. Intervention in credit allocation could have been diverted and rendered ineffective if commercial banks had used these funds to invest abroad. Similarly, credit controls for fighting inflation would have had little effect if companies and banks had been able to obtain unlimited financing from abroad. Capital controls – except in exchange rate crises – can be seen as an integral feature of credit policy. Thus, Bretton Woods' capital controls were not instruments conceived by states after the fact, in order to give themselves more wiggle room, but were, rather, a major component of their domestic intervention policy, with which the postwar international system had to contend. They guaranteed the autonomy of monetary policy through a rationing mechanism rather than through a price mechanism, and they extended domestic credit controls to the international level.[4] It follows that the end of credit policy profoundly altered the nature and purpose of capital controls – even as many countries, especially in Europe, held on to a system of fixed exchange rates – and turned these into one of their primary instruments for resolving short-term crises, rather than a structural feature of central bank policy.

The broader process I have been describing also had a decisive influence on the construction of the European monetary union. It is evident, in retrospect, that the process of monetary integration might have taken a different form and may, perhaps, have been impossible with central banks with powers that varied radically by country and were deeply tied to national budgetary and industrial policies, granting particular institutions and sectors priority (i.e., non-competitive) access to credit. The end of national credit policies – and the reduction of capital controls that accompanied them – was thus a decisive stage in the convergence of the practices and goals of European central banks. This does not, however, mean that one should conclude – falling for a backwards and anachronistic interpretation – that monetary integration would have been impossible without this process,[5] nor that the end of credit policy was imposed on various countries by European authorities. As we have seen in the case of France in the early 1970s, challenges to credit policy occurred primarily at a national level, among top civil servants and bankers, with little significant influence or pressure coming from abroad. Drawing on archives of discussions occurring in the committee of governors of European central banks during

---

[4]   This conception of capital controls has also been suggested by Helleiner (1996). A particularly explicit formulation of this idea has been presented by Erik Hoffmeyer (2000), the former Chairman of the Board of Governors of Danmarks Nationalbank from 1965 to 1994, who explains the considerable complementarity between what he calls "domestic financial repression" (i.e., credit controls) and "external financial repression" (i.e., capital controls).

[5]   Monetary integration in some countries, such as Germany in the nineteenth century, occurred with interest rates and rediscounting practices that varied from region to region. In the interwar period, regional Federal Reserve banks in the United States also had different interest rates and discounting policies.

the 1970s and early 1980s, I was struck by the absence of any conversation of the question of credit policy reforms (compared, for instance, to questions about monetary money targets or exchange rate levels), whereas this issue was crucial and ubiquitous when it came to national matters, even within central banks. These hypotheses – examined in Chapter 7 – must still be confirmed, but everything seems to suggest that the end of credit policy in European countries was uncoordinated and was, on the contrary, the outcome of national processes, as this policy (like budgetary policy) was too deeply related to the state's key functions for decisions relating to it to be negotiated with and imposed by European authorities.

DIRECTIONS FOR FUTURE RESEARCH

There remain a number of unanswered questions, which this study has only touched upon. Our level of analysis has essentially been macroeconomic and institutional, overlapping, at times, with studies of political decision-making, statistics and the history of ideas. The microeconomic level and actors in companies and financial institutions are barely mentioned. Thus, the social history of credit and decisions about loans and investment have been addressed only briefly, through references to earlier works and by situating them within a broader framework of credit policy (Effosse 2003, 2014; Lazarus 2010, 2012). Much remains to be written about articulating macroeconomic and political history and business history. This would notably make it possible to reflect on the credit policy's persistence in some realms, beyond the 1980s, despite the uncoupling of monetary policy and credit policy that occurred over time. Indeed, the French state continued to pursue a credit policy in some domains (Lazarus 2012), housing credit continued to be subsidized, and the interest rates of certain forms of savings regulated, while consumer credit was subject to many norms. In this way, the history of the state's intervention in the allocation and regulation of credit does not end with the disassociation of credit policy and central bank policy.

Economists may reproach this book for not having assessed and examined state intervention in credit allocation from the standpoint of efficiency. Would a different kind of policy have allowed for a better form of credit allocation and faster investment and production growth? The difficulties in answering this question have been mentioned a number of times. Constructing and testing counterfactual hypotheses is impossible if one is to take full account of the specificity of the postwar context. For this reason, I focused on estimating macroeconomic effects and describing macroeconomic trends, and I did not speculate on simulating alternative policy scenarios. Yet, once again, it is reasonable to believe that a more fine-grained microeconomic analysis of detailed data from businesses would provide a better description of resource allocation and investment decisions.

Going beyond the question of economic efficiency, the analyses presented in this work encourage us to ponder the conception of democracy that constituted the framework of interventionist policy in credit allocation and distribution. As written recently by Herrick Chapman (2018), the postwar period witnessed a revival and institutionalization of the tension between the democratic and the "technocratic." We have seen how, after the war, there was a strong desire – accompanied by a real desire to act at the institutional level – to give the Vichy regime's statist-corporatist policies a republican form, in which the nation's different interests were represented in decision-making and a central role was given to collective consultations. Membership of the National Credit Council and the General Council of the Banque de France reflected this approach through 1973. But the way in which these authorities operated – particularly the National Credit Council – was quite different from the idea of a "little parliament" that some had called for. Admittedly, this type of authority allowed for an expression of disagreement and the representation of various interests; in practice, however, it often ratified decisions that the civil service or the Banque's Governor had already made. The rapid and relatively improvised implementation of these structures, as Philippe Mioche (1987) described so well in the case of the *Commissariat Général au Plan*, left some power in the hands of the civil service, which, for its part, guaranteed the continuity and permanence of state intervention. Thus, the role of top civil servants appears as absolutely critical in decision-making and, more than anything, in the development of the instruments and the parameters of state intervention over time. One way that postwar institutions resolved problems relating to the scale of the new structures that needed to be implemented, on the one hand, and the significant political conflicts and different ideas about the "nationalization of credit," on the other, was to attribute increasing power to the civil service and its economic experts. Conflict within the civil service existed; there were considerable cultural and political differences between its various branches and different generations; and one must be careful not to describe the state during this time period as if it represented the forward march of a uniform and autonomous technocratic rationality.

But it is just as important to avoid succumbing to the idea, which is often presented in print, that these economic policies arose from collective consultation and a broad representation of national interests. As discussed previously, several French historical monographs on sectoral or ministerial policies have already reached similar conclusions. Yet, there is still important work to be done to understand, in France and beyond, the foundations of political decision-making processes in a postwar "negotiated," "embedded" (Ruggie 1982) or "coordinated" (Eichengreen 2006) economy, as well as of their democratic legitimacy and the nature of their subsequent development.

The study of monetary policy presented here, and notably the central bank's financing of the public debt, has shown how the intertwined finances of the various components of the state bureaucracy were opaque and kept outside of public and parliamentary discussions. In another domain, that of price indices and inflation, technocratic and political control over statistics resulted, at times, in challenges from labor unions or even some civil servants (Touchelay 2017), reflecting the difficulties that a *dirigiste* model faces in relying fully on negotiation, as well as the perennial mistrust resulting from the opacity of political decision-making process and an obedient civil service. It is in no way contradictory that this lack of transparency existed at the same time as a significant growth in economic (and particularly macroeconomic) statistics, including those used for credit policy, and of official forecasts. At the heart of the *dirigiste* system established after the war, there lay a tension between the celebration of negotiation as a method for formulating public policy and faith in the authority of the economic engineers and the top civil servants who contributed to economic planning (Fourquet 1980). And despite the deep transformations in the civil service and the forms of state intervention that began to occur in the late 1960s, this tension seems to have largely survived the challenges aimed at *dirigisme*. A major study is still needed on the nature of economic information, its use by the government, the civil service and "civil society" organizations during the *Trente Glorieuses*. The institutional-analysis perspective elaborated in Part I would benefit from such research. I have emphasized the importance of the development of sectoral credit statistics in the institutionalization of credit policy and the use of macroeconomic statistics in monitoring the institution, notably to avoid credit surpluses in some sectors or an excessively inflationary expansion of credit. But the use of such statistics by companies and other bureaucracies (such as the industry or agriculture ministries, for example) has been mentioned only in passing. Similarly, the way in which restrictions on spreading certain economic statistics might have been used to protect credit policy in the face of potential external critics could be the focus of more in-depth research.

THE RETURN OF THE REPRESSED: THE TRANSFORMATION OF CENTRAL BANKS SINCE 2008

The reader may well ask what lessons can be drawn from this book for contemporary debates about monetary policy – particularly because, as I mentioned in the Preface, the instruments used by central banks in Europe and the United States since the 2008 crisis resemble those used in the 1950s and 1960s. I shall conclude with a few thoughts on this topic. First, it seems that if parallels exist between central bank policies of the *Trente Glorieuses* and contemporary monetary policy, they can be more clearly found in so-called "emerging" economies (such as China, India, Brazil and Turkey), where credit policies similar to those pursued by France and other European countries until the 1970s are still practiced: the central bank's goal is to control inflation and exchange rate stability, but it also acts to guide credit toward priority sectors, capital controls are a structural component of monetary policy and state intervention in credit allocation and so on.[6] At present, it is not clear that these countries will chose to completely reconsider these policies, as Europe did in the 1980 and 1990s. One must refrain from conceiving of economic development as a succession of obligatory stages converging toward a single model. Yet, it is, even so, undeniable that these countries have already, for the most part, begun the transition toward a liberalization of their financial systems and given interest rates a greater role. Even if the end result of this transition takes an entirely different form than it did in Europe, European history in the 1970s and 1980s nonetheless offers important clues for thinking about the stakes of central bank development in emergent countries. In particular, it calls attention to the difficulties that central banks have historically faced in shifting from a model defined by the control of quantities to a model defined by the control of interest rates and the "open market." It is important not to underestimate the length of this transition period or the difficulties in keeping inflation and international financial flows stable when a central bank must test and get used to new instruments. Finally, at a time when European central banks are reinstituting forms of credit control that they had completely

---

[6] On credit policy and central banking in India, see Ray (2013, 2017); on China, see Sun (2016) and Klingelhöfer and Sun (2017). On Africa and the Middle East, see Cobham and Dibeh (2009).

abandoned (which they now call "macroprudential," as we shall see below), it is in fact highly probable that central banks in emergent countries will maintain the current credit control tools they use to limit inflation and capital flows (notably reserve requirements), while also gradually using them to ensure financial stability (macroprudential) as their economies become more financially open. Many countries have begun to evolve along these lines, simply by affixing the term "macroprudential" to tools they were already using and by considering potentially new uses, at the outer reaches of monetary policy and financial stability and exchange rate policy. One might however wonder if this sudden borrowing of a foreign vocabulary will not trigger confusion and, paradoxically, heighten difficulties related to the direction of credit policy in these countries if it creates an artificial distinction between monetary policy and macroprudential policy, when both remain fundamentally intertwined, notably in the way they fight inflation. The international institutions that advise these countries should be wary of new and imported vocabulary that overlooks the specificities of credit policies still practiced by these countries and tends to erase the historical experience of other central banks.

Let us return now to countries that are considered economically "advanced," notably Europe, the United States and Japan. Two features of the policies they have implemented since the 2008 financial crisis recall the 1950s–1970s.[7] First, central banks began once again to lend broadly to banks rather than to intervene in more limited ways to target an interbank interest rate, and they even revived a system of long-term lending (LTRO for the European Central Bank and the Funding for Lending Scheme for the Bank of England) that is similar to the kind of medium-term rediscounting practiced by the postwar Banque de France, which this book has studied. Second, central banks have given themselves new instruments to control credit in quantitative terms as well as bank liquidity, with the goal of limiting, in certain cases, the expansion of credit and thus the risk of financial crisis (i.e., systemic risk). This new policy, which is dubbed "macroprudential," seeks to guarantee financial stability. In this way, it has been dissociated from monetary policy, even if this task has also been assigned to central

---

[7] Siklos (2017) offers a comprehensive review and description of the main changes in central banks' operations and objectives since the 2008 crisis as well as of the challenges ahead. A much shorter description is available in Kelber and Monnet (2014). Although the term "credit policy" has been banned from official discourses on the evolution of central banking, it remained at the center of some alternative proposals to reform central banks; see for example Konczal and Mason (2017).

banks.[8] Macroprudential instruments bear a striking resemblance to credit policy's instruments during the 1950s and 1960s: they involve control mechanisms that operate on quantities rather than prices; they can be sectoral (if a credit bubble is detected in the housing sector, for example); and they combine liquidity ratios and credit ratios.

Despite these similarities, there are two major differences related to the context in which these instruments were implemented. The first is that macroprudential policy is seen as disconnected from monetary policy and that credit controls in this context are, consequently, viewed as mainly affecting financial risk and the likelihood of a crisis, rather than monetary policy's traditional goals, i.e., inflation and employment. Yet, as we have seen, postwar credit policy did not make this distinction and, on the contrary, used quantitative credit controls to limit inflation and to act on the price and production cycle. The second difference is institutional in nature: after World War II, credit control occurred in conjunction with government policies of sectoral allocation, industrial policy and management of the public debt. This policy was not, consequently, assigned to an independent agency that was disconnected from government policy. Awareness of these two differences invites reflection on the stakes confronting macroprudential policy at present. There are reasons to believe that, unlike in the 1950s and 1960s, inflation, money and credit are now less connected than previously (Schularick & Taylor 2012), since not all credit is bank credit, economies are more open and the non-bank financial system is less indebted to central banks. But studies of this topic, notably the connection between inflation and credit, are still limited, and their conclusions necessarily depend on the banking system's structure. Interactions between monetary policy and macroprudential policy will probably differ depending on a national financial system's characteristics. Many recent macroeconomic models relating to macroprudential policy are premised on the hypothesis of a disconnect with monetary policy (which is seen as based on interest rates), rendering them incapable of considering the interactions and overlapping between them, whereas partial equilibrium models relating to the implementation of monetary policy show, on the contrary, how the use of macroprudential instruments makes it necessary to modify the way monetary policy operates (Bech & Keister 2013; Monnet & Vari 2017). If we can learn anything from history, it is that we should not take for granted the distinction between monetary policy and macroprudential policy, given how conflated they

---

[8] Clement (2010) provides a history of the term "macroprudential" that was first coined in the late 1970s but not used before the recent financial crisis.

were in the past, and that monetary policy should not be reduced to interest rates. This conclusion is particularly true for "emerging market" economies today, but it is not, in principle, limited to them.

A broader question relates to the distributive consequences of macroprudential policy and its interactions with government policy, independent of monetary policy. Are these consequences compatible with central bank independence? Some specialists on the history of monetary policy, such as Charles Goodhart, predict that central bank independence will necessarily decline or must at least be revised if the scope of central bank intervention continues to expand (Goodhart 2011; Goodhart & Lastra 2017). If independence was, as we have seen, a consequence of the end of credit policy, then a return to certain forms of credit control could indeed pose a challenge to their independence, or at least alter its institutional form by requiring more extensive control and democratic debate over central bank decisions. As it relates to such questions, the French example studied in this book is, of course, too limited, and it is necessary to consider the full range of historical experiences. Returning to the analytical framework used in the first part of this book, one might argue that post-2008 central banking has yet to achieve complete institutional coherence, in which legal structures, collective beliefs and ideas about ensuring the institution's stability and durability are interconnected. These difficulties reflect the fact that the conviction that, historically, brought an end to credit policy (based on the idea that it could and must be separated from monetary policy) has been significantly undermined: is it really possible to have a "neutral" monetary policy, which would have no impact on the way financial markets normally operate?

This question, which is now very explicitly being posed anew, has always accompanied the history of central banks, and each historical period has provided a different institutional answer, without ever settling the debate once and for all. From the nineteenth century to the interwar period, at a time when central banks were still private institutions (banks like any others to which states assigned the privilege of currency emission) governments placed regulatory constraints on them to limit their competitive advantages and used them to finance the public debt. Yet, they were still the object of serious criticisms, on the grounds that a financial elite had been given control over currency emission. Central banks had implicitly been assigned the task of ensuring financial stability in their capacity as the "banks' bank," exposed to the risks of their counterparts, yet often without formal regulation. The subsequent period, which is the subject of this book, put an end to private management of central banks and integrated the latter into the numerous realms in which the state intervened, pushing back against the idea of neutral intervention and eliminating the boundaries between monetary policy and other forms of state economic policy. Newly created instruments of bank regulation also helped in the implementation of these other policies. Deemed at once too powerful and too dependent on the state, central banks were then later confined to a role that was more limited and independent of the political calendar and democratic elections. Bank regulation refocused itself on microeconomic monitoring. But it became apparent that this role was too weak to prevent banking crises, limit the systemic effects of such crises and guarantee the state's credit. In the process, the distributive implications of central bank interventions resurfaced, like the return of the repressed. It seems likely that we are witnessing the emergence of a fourth historical moment – one that remains, for now, unstable and uncertain.

Bibliography

Abbas, S. A., Blattner, L., De Broeck, M., El-Ganainy, M. A. & Hu, M. (2014), "Sovereign debt composition in advanced economies: A historical perspective," IMF Working Paper No. 14–162, International Monetary Fund.

Abdelal, R. (2005), "Le consensus de Paris: la France et les règles de la finance mondiale," *Critique internationale* 28(3), 87–115.

(2007), *Capital Rules: The Construction of Global Finance*, Harvard University Press, Cambridge, MA.

Abiad, A., Detragiache, E. & Tressel, T. (2008), "A new database of financial reforms," IMF Working Paper No. WP/08/266, International Monetary Fund.

Abolafia, M. Y. (2004), "Framing moves: Interpretive politics at the Federal Reserve," *Journal of Public Administration Research and Theory* 14(3), 349–370.

(2010), "Narrative construction as sensemaking: How a central bank thinks," *Organization Studies* 31(3), 349–367.

Abramovitz, M. (1986), "Catching up, forging ahead, and falling behind," *The Journal of Economic History* 46(2), 385–406.

Acemoglu, D., Aghion, P. & Zilibotti, F. (2006), "Distance to frontier, selection and economic growth," *Journal of the European Economic Association* 4(1), 37–74.

Acemoglu, D., Johnson, S., Querubio, P. & Robinson, J. A. (2008), "When does policy reform work? The case of central bank independence," *Brookings Papers on Economic Activity* 2008, 351–417.

Adams, W. J. (1989), *Restructuring the French Economy*, Brookings Institution, Washington, DC.

Adler, M. D. (2000), "Expressive theories of law: A skeptical overview," *University of Pennsylvania Law Review* 148(5), 1363–1501.

Aglan, A., Margairaz, M. & Verheyde, P., eds. (2003), *La Caisse des dépôts et consignations, la Seconde Guerre mondiale et le XXe siècle*, Albin Michel, Paris.

(2011), *Crises financières, crises politiques en Europe dans le second XIXe siècle: la Caisse des dépôts et consignations de 1848 à 1918*, Librairie Droz, Genève.

Aglietta, M. (1992), "Genèse des banques centrales et légitimité de la monnaie," *Annales. Économies, Sociétés, Civilisations* 47(3), 675–698.

Aglietta, M. & Orléan, A. (2002), *La Monnaie entre violence et confiance*, Odile Jacob, Paris.

Aikman, D., Bush, O. & Taylor, A. M. (2016), "Monetary versus macroprudential policies: Causal impacts of interest rates and credit controls in the era of the UK Radcliffe report," NBER Working Paper No. w22380, National Bureau of Economic Research.

Alesina, A. & Summers, L. H. (1993), "Central bank independence and macroeconomic performance: Some comparative evidence," *Journal of Money, Credit and Banking* 25(2), 151–162.

Alexander, W. E. & Enoch, C. (1995), "The adoption of indirect instruments of monetary policy," IMF Occasional Paper No. 126, International Monetary Fund, Washington, DC.

Allen, C. (2005), "Ordo-liberalism trumps Keynesianism in the Federal Republic of Germany," in B. Moss, ed., *Monetary Union in Crisis: The European Union as a Neo-Liberal Construction*, Palgrave, London, pp. 199–221.

Allen, W. A. (2014), *Monetary Policy and Financial Repression in Britain, 1951–59*, Palgrave Macmillan, Basingstoke, UK.

Amable, B. (2003), *The Diversity of Modern Capitalism*, Oxford University Press, Oxford, UK.

Amable, B., Guillaud, E. & Palombarini, S. (2012), "Changing French capitalism: Political and systemic crises in France," *Journal of European Public Policy* 19(8), 1168–1187.

Anderson, E. S. & Pildes, R. H. (2000), "Expressive theories of law: A general restatement," *University of Pennsylvania Law Review* 148(5), 1503–1575.

Andrieu, C. (1983), "Genèse de la loi du 13 juin 1941, première loi bancaire française (septembre 1940–septembre 1941)," *Revue Historique* 269(2), 385–397.

(1984), "A la recherche de la politique du crédit, 1946–1973," *Revue Historique* 271(2), 377–417.

(1991), *La banque sous l'Occupation, Paradoxes de l'histoire d'une profession*, Presses de Sciences Po, Paris.

(1996), "Regards sur la genèse de la pensée nationalisatrice: la nationalisation des banques sous la IIIe république," *Le Mouvement social* (175), 149–177.

Angeletti, T. (2011), "Faire la réalité ou s'y faire? La modélisation et les déplacements de la politique économique au tournant des années 1970," *Politix* 3(95), 47–72.

Aoki, M. (1996), "Towards a comparative institutional analysis," *Japanese Economic Review* 47(1), 1–19.

(2007), "Endogenizing institutions and institutional changes," *Journal of Institutional Economics* 3(1), 1–31.

Ardant, H. (1953), *Technique de la banque*, PUF, Paris.

(1954), *Introduction à l'étude des banques et des opérations de banque*, Dunod, Paris.

Argy, V. (1971), "Monetary policy and internal and external balance," *International Monetary Fund Staff Papers* 18(3), 508–527.

Audier, S. (2008), *Aux origines du néo-libéralisme: Le colloque Lippmann*, Editions Le Bord de l'eau, Paris.

Aymard, P. (1960), *La banque et l'Etat: la politique économique et l'évolution des techniques bancaires en France depuis 1945*, A. Colin, Paris.

Barrère, A. (1951), "La politique du crédit en France depuis 1945," *Revue économique* 2(5), 513–542.

Batini, N. & Nelson, E. (2005), "The U.K.'s rocky road to stability," Working Paper No. 20, Federal Reserve Bank of St. Louis.

Battilossi, S. (2003), "Capital mobility and financial repression in Italy, 1960–1990: A public finance perspective," Working Paper No. 2003-02, Universidad Carlos III de Madrid, Instituto Figuerola.

(2009), "The eurodollar revolution in financial technology: Deregulation, innovation and structural change in Western banking in the 1960s–70s," Working Paper No. 2009-10, Universidad Carlos III de Madrid, Instituto Figuerola.

Battilossi, S., Foreman-Peck, J. & Kling, G. (2010), "European business cycles and economic policy, 1945–2007," in S. Broadberry & K. O'Rourke, eds., *The Cambridge Economic History of Modern Europe*, Vol. 2, Cambridge University Press, Cambridge, UK.

Baubeau, P. (2004), " 'Les cathédrales de papier' ou la foi dans le crédit. Naissance et subversion du système de l'escompte en France, XVIIIe–premier XXe siècle," PhD dissertation, Paris X-Nanterre.

(2011), "Gaston Roulleau et l'étude des effets de commerce ou la tension entre statistiques fiduciaires et conceptions métallistes," *Histoire & mesure* 26(1), 221–242.

Baubeau, P., Lavit d'Hautefort, A. & Lescure, M. (1994), *Histoire publique d'une société privée: le Crédit national, 1919–1994*, Albin Michel, Paris.

Baubeau, P. & LeBris, D. (2017a), "La deuxième guerre mondiale," in M. Lutfalla, ed., *Une histoire de la dette publique en France*, Garnier, Paris, pp. 159–178.

(2017b), "La IVe République," in M. Lutfalla, ed., *Une histoire de la dette publique en France*, Garnier, Paris, pp. 179–208.

Bauchet, P. (1964), *Economic Planning: The French Experience*, Heinemann, London.

Baum, W. C. (1958), *The French Economy and the State*, Princeton University Press, Princeton, NJ.

Bazot, G. (2014), "Local liquidity constraints: What place for central bank regional policy? The French experience during the Belle Époque (1880–1913)," *Explorations in Economic History* 52, 44–62.

Bazot, G., Bordo, M. D. & Monnet, E. (2016), "International shocks and the balance sheet of the Bank of France under the classical gold standard," *Explorations in Economic History* 62, 87–107.

Bech, M. L. & Keister, T. (2013), "Liquidity regulation and the implementation of monetary policy," BIS Working Papers No. 432, Bank for International Settlements.

Behrent, M. C. (2016), "Karl Polanyi and the reality of society," *History and Theory*, 55, 433–451.

Belin, J. (1951), "Le crédit au commerce extérieur," *Revue économique* 2(5), 637–646.

Bénabou, R. & Tirole, J. (2011), "Laws and norms," NBER Working Paper Series No. 17579, National Bureau of Economic Research.

Benard, M. (1974), "Rendement économique et productivité du capital fixe de 1959 à 1972," *Economie et statistique* 60(1), 7–15.

Berger, H. (2003), "La Bank deutscher Länder et le 'miracle économique' allemand, la politique monétaire de l'Allemagne dans les années 1950," in O. Feiertag & M. Margairaz, eds., *Politiques et pratiques des banques d'émission en Europe (XVIIième–XXième siècle)*, Paris, Albin Michel, pp. 623–655.

Bernanke, B. S. & Mihov, I. (1998), "Measuring monetary policy," *The Quarterly Journal of Economics* 113(3), 869–902.

Bernhard, W., Broz, J. L. & Clark, W. R., eds. (2003), *The Political Economy of Monetary Institutions*, MIT Press, Cambridge, MA.

Bertrand, M., Schoar, A. & Thesmar, D. (2007), "Banking deregulation and industry structure: Evidence from the French banking reforms of 1985," *The Journal of Finance* 62(2), 597–628.

Besse, P. (1951), "Le Conseil national du crédit," *Revue économique* 2(5), 578–590.

Bessis, F. (2009), "L'institution comme réalisation du collectif," *Tracés* (17), 73–87.

Beyer, A., Gaspar, V., Gerberding, C. & Issing, O. (2009), "Opting out of the great inflation: German monetary policy after the breakdown of Bretton Woods," ECB Working Paper No. 1020, European Central Bank.

Bezes, P. (2009), *Réinventer l'État: les réformes de l'administration française (1962–2008)*, Presses universitaires de France, Paris.

BIS (Bank of International Settlements) (1963), *Eight European Central Banks*, Praeger, New York.

Blackaby, F. (1978), *British Economic Policy, 1960–74*, Cambridge University Press, Cambridge, UK.

Blancheton, B. (2001), *Le Pape et l'Empereur*, Albin Michel, Paris.

Blancheton, B. & Bordes, C. (2007), "Débats monétaires autour de la dévaluation du franc de 1969," *Revue européenne des sciences sociales* (XLV-137), 213–232.

Bloch-Lainé, F. & Bouvier, J. (1986), *La France restaurée, 1944–1954: dialogue sur les choix d'une modernisation*, Fayard, Paris.

Blomgren-Hansen, N. (1977), "Bank credit ceilings as an instrument of money and capital movements control: The experience of Denmark, 1970–74," *The Scandinavian Journal of Economics* 79(4), 442–456.

Boff, R. B. D. (1968), "The decline of economic planning in France," *The Western Political Quarterly* 21(1), 98–109.

Boltanski, L. & Thévenot, L. (2006), *On Justification: Economies of Worth*, Princeton University Press, Princeton, NJ.

Bonin, H. (1987), "L'année 1954: un cas de sortie de crise. Temps court et temps long en histoire économique contemporaine," *Annales. Economies, Sociétés, Civilisations* 42(2), 347–367.

(2003), "Le Crédit lyonnais, la Société générale et les autres: essai d'appréciation des rapports de force (1864–1966)," in B. Desjardins, ed., *Le Crédit lyonnais, 1863–1986*, Droz, Paris, pp. 725–749.

Bonnet, J. (1968), "Etude des taux d'intérèt en France de 1959 à 1964: Le coût du crédit, analyse des taux des prèts des intermédiaires nanciers," *Revue économique* 19(1), 86–129.

Bonoldi, A. & Leonardi, A., eds. (2009), *Recovery and Development in the European Periphery (1945–1960)*, Duncker & Humblot, Bologna.

Booth, A. (2001), "New revisionists and the Keynesian era in British economic policy," *The Economic History Review* 54(2), 346–366.

Bopp, K. R. (1954), "Central banking objectives, guides and measures," *The Journal of Finance* 9(1), 12–22.

Bordo, M. D. (1993), "The Bretton Woods international monetary system: A historical overview," in M. D. Bordo & B. J. Eichengreen, eds., *A Retrospective on the Bretton Woods System: Lessons for International Monetary Reform*, University of Chicago Press, Chicago, pp. 3–108.

Bordo, M. D. & Eichengreen, B. J., eds. (1993), *A Retrospective on the Bretton Woods System: Lessons for International Monetary Reform*, University of Chicago Press, Chicago.

Bordo, M. D. & Eichengreen, B. (2008), "Bretton Woods and the Great Inflation," NBER Working Paper Series No. 14532, National Bureau of Economic Research.

Bordo, M. D. & Haubrich, J. G. (2010), "Credit crises, money and contractions: An historical view," *Journal of Monetary Economics* 57(1), 1–18.

Bordo, M. D. & Orphanides, A., eds. (2013), *The Great Inflation: The Rebirth of Modern Central Banking*, University of Chicago Press, Chicago.

Bordo, M. D. & Rousseau, P. L. (2011), "Historical evidence on the finance-trade-growth nexus," NBER Working Paper Series No. 17024, National Bureau of Economic Research.

Bordo, M. D., Monnet, E. & Naef, A. (2017), "The Gold Pool (1961–1968) and the fall of the Bretton Woods system: Lessons for central bank cooperation," NBER Working Paper No. w24016, National Bureau of Economic Research.

Borio, C. (1997). "The implementation of monetary policy in industrial countries: A survey," BIS, Monetary and Economic Department, Working Paper Vol. 47, Bank for International Settlements.

Boschen, J. F. & Mills, L. O. (1995), "The relation between narrative and money market indicators of monetary policy," *Economic Inquiry* 33(1), 24–44.

Bossuat, G. (1992), *La France, l'aide américaine et la construction européenne 1944–1954*, 2 vols. Paris, CHEFF.

(1998), "La France et le FMI au lendemain de la seconde guerre mondiale: les raisons de la tension," in CHEFF, *La France et les institutions de Bretton Woods, 1944–1994*, CHEFF, Paris, pp. 17–33.

Bouvier, J. (1973), *Un siècle de banque française*, Hachette, Paris.

(1979), "L'investissement et son financement en France, 1945–1952," in *Le rôle des capitaux publics dans le financement de l'industrie en Europe occidentale*, Bruylant, Bruxelles.

(1987), "Les relations entre l'État et la banque de France depuis les années 1950," *Vingtième Siècle. Revue d'histoire* 13(1), 23–34.

Broz, J. L. (1998), "The origins of central banking: Solutions to the free-rider problem," *International Organization* 52(2), 231–268.

(2009), *The International Origins of the Federal Reserve System*, Cornell University Press, Ithaca, NY.

Broz, J. L. & Grossman, R. S. (2004), "Paying for privilege: The political economy of Bank of England charters, 1694–1844," *Explorations in Economic History* 41(1), 48–72.

Bruneau, C. & De Bandt, O. (1999), "La modélisation VAR structurel: application à la politique monétaire en France," *Economie et Prévision* 137(1), 67–94.

Calomiris, C. W. & Himmelberg, C. P. (1995), "Government credit policy and industrial performance: Japanese machine tool producers, 1963–91," The World Bank, Policy Research Working Paper No. 1414.

Capie, F. (2010), *The Bank of England: 1950s to 1979*, Cambridge University Press, New York.

Capie, F., Goodhart, C., Fischer, S. & Schnadt, N. (1994), *The Future of Central Banking: The Tercentenary Symposium of the Bank of England*, Cambridge University Press, Cambridge, UK.

Cargill, T. F., Hutchison, M. M. & Ito, T. (1997), *The Political Economy of Japanese Monetary Policy*, MIT Press, Cambridge, MA.

Carlino, G. & DeFina, R. (1998), "The differential regional effects of monetary policy," *Review of Economics and Statistics* 80(4), 572–587.

Caron, F. (1982), "Le plan Mayer: un retour aux réalités," *Histoire, économie et société* 1(3), 423–437.

Carré, J., Malinvaud, E. & Dubois, P. (1972), *La Croissance française, un essai d'analyse économique causale de l'après-guerre*, Le Seuil, Paris.

Casella, A. & Eichengreen, B. (1993), "Halting inflation in Italy and France after World War II," NBER Working Paper Series No. 3852, National Bureau of Economic Research.

Cassiers, I. & Ledent, P. (2005), *Politique monétaire et croissance économique en Belgique à l'ère de Bretton Woods (1944–1971)*, Banque Nationale de Belgique, Bruxelles.

Castel, M. & Masse, J. (1983), *L'encadrement du crédit*, Presses universitaires de France, Paris.

Cerny, P. (1989), "The 'Little Big Bang' in Paris: Financial market deregulation in a dirigiste system," *European Journal of Political Research* 17(2), 169–192.

Chapman, H. (2018), *France's Long Reconstruction: In Search of the Modern Republic*, Harvard University Press, Cambridge, MA.

Chatriot, A. (2003), *La démocratie sociale à la française. L'expérience du Conseil national économique, 1924–1940*, La Découverte, Paris.

Chaurand, D., Joly, H., Verheyde, P., Kohser-Spohn, C., Hellwinkel, L., Hamelin, D., Fitzgerald, E. P. & Grevet, J. (2008), *L'épuration économique en France à la Libération*, PU Rennes, Rennes.

CHEFF (1998), *La France et les institutions de Bretton Woods, 1944–1994*, CHEFF, Paris.

Chélini, M. (1998), *Inflation, État et opinion en France de 1944 à 1952*, CHEFF, Paris.

(2001), "Le plan de stabilisation Pinay-Rueff, 1958," *Revue d'histoire moderne et contemporaine* 48(4), 102–123.

Chélini, M-P. & Warlouzet, L. (2017), *Calmer les prix: l'inflation en Europe dans les années 1970/Slowing Down Prices*, Presses de Sciences Po, Paris.

Christiano, L. J., Eichenbaum, M. & Evans, C. L. (1999), "Monetary policy shocks: What have we learned and to what end?," in J. B. Taylor & M. Woodford, eds., *Handbook of Macroeconomics*, Vol. 1, Part A, Elsevier, Amsterdam, pp. 65–148.

Ciccarelli, M. & Mojon, B. (2010), "Global inflation," *Review of Economics and Statistics* 92(3), 524–535.

Clarida, R., Gali, J. & Gertler, M. (1998), "Monetary policy rules in practice: Some international evidence," *European Economic Review* 42(6), 1033–1067.

Clavert, F. (2009), *Hjalmar Schacht, financier et diplomate, 1930–1950*, Peter Lang, Bruxelles.

Clement, P. (2010), "The term 'macroprudential': origins and evolution," *BIS Quarterly Review*, March, 59–67.

Cobham, D. & Dibeh, G. (2009), *Monetary Policy and Central Banking in the Middle East and North Africa*, Taylor & Francis, London.

Cobham, D. & Serre, J. (2002), "A characterization of the French financial system," *The Manchester School* 68(1), 44–67.

Cohen, A. (2004), "Vers la révolution communautaire," *Revue d'histoire moderne et contemporaine* 51(2), 141–161.

(2012), *De Vichy à la Communauté européenne*, Presses universitaires de France, Paris.

Cohen, B. J. (1993), "The Triad and the unholy trinity: Lessons for the Pacific region," in R. Higgott, R. Leaver and J. Ravenhill, eds., *Pacific Economic Relations in the 1990s: Cooperation or Conflict?* Lynne Rienner, Boulder, CO, pp. 133–158.

Cohen, S. S. (1977), *Modern Capitalist Planning: The French Model*, University of California Press, Berkeley.

Coibion, O. (2012), "Are the effects of monetary policy shocks big or small?," *American Economic Journal: Macroeconomics* 4(2), 1–32.

Conti, G., Feiertag, O. & Scatamacchia, R., eds. (2009), *Credito e nazione in Francia e in Italia (XIX–XX secolo)*, Pisa University Press, Pisa.

Conti-Brown, P. (2017), *The Power and Independence of the Federal Reserve*, Princeton University Press, Princeton, NJ.

Corder, K. (1998), *Central Bank Autonomy: The Federal Reserve System in American Politics*, Routledge, New York.

Cottarelli, C., Galli, G., Reedtz, P. M. & Pittaluga, G. (1986), "Monetary policy through ceilings on bank lending," *Economic Policy* 1(3), 674–710.

Cotula, F. & De Stefani, P. (1979), *La politica monetaria in Italia. Istituti e strumenti*, il Mulino: Bologna.

Cotula, F. & Padoa-Schioppa, T. (1971), "Direct credit controls as a monetary policy tool," *Banca Nazionale del Lavoro Quarterly Review* 98.

Crédit National (1951), "Le Crédit national, établissement de crédit à moyen et long terme," *Revue économique* 2(5), 657–674.

Crafts, N. (1992), "Productivity growth reconsidered," *Economic Policy* 7(15), 387–426.

(1995), "The Golden Age of economic growth in Western Europe, 1950–1973," *The Economic History Review* 48(3), 429–447.

Crafts, N. F. R. & Toniolo, G., eds. (1995), *Economic Growth in Europe since 1945*, Cambridge University Press, Cambridge, UK.

Crouch, C. (2005), *Capitalist Diversity and Change: Recombinant Governance and Institutional Entrepreneurs*, Oxford University Press, Oxford, UK.

Crouzet, F. (1972), "Réactions françaises devant les conséquences économiques de la paix de Keynes," *Revue d'histoire moderne et contemporaine* 19(1), 6–26.

Cubel, A. & Sanchis, M. T. (2009), "Investment and growth in Europe during the Golden Age," *European Review of Economic History* 13(2), 219–249.

Cukierman, A. (2008), "Central bank independence and monetary policymaking institutions: Past, present and future," *European Journal of Political Economy* 24(4), 722–736.

Davies, A. (2012), "The evolution of British monetarism, 1968–1979," University of Oxford, Discussion Papers in Economic and Social History No. 104.

Davis, R. G. (1971), "An analysis of quantitative credit controls and related devices," *Brookings Papers on Economic Activity* 1971(1), 65–104.

De Kock, M. (1974), *Central Banking*, Crosby Lockwood Staples, London.

De Long, J. B. (1997), "America's only peacetime inflation: The 1970s," NBER Working Paper Series No. 84, National Bureau of Economic Research.

De Long, J. B. & Summers, L. H. (1991), "Equipment investment and economic growth," *The Quarterly Journal of Economics* 106(2), 445–502.

De Melo, M. & Denizer, C. (1997), "Monetary policy during transition: an overview," World Bank Research Policy Paper No. 1706.

Delestré, H. (1979), "L'accumulation du capital fixe," *Economie et statistique* 114(1), 33–47.

Denizet, J. (1977), *La grande inflation: salaire, intérêt et change*, Presses universitaires de France, Paris.

Denord, F. (2001), "Aux origines du néo-libéralisme en France," *Le Mouvement Social* 195(2), 9.

(2010), "Les rénovateurs du libéralisme," in L. Bonelli & W. Pelletier, eds., *L'Etat demantelé*, La Découverte, Paris, pp. 31–41.

(2012), "Les idéologies économiques du patronat français au 20e siècle,"*Vingtième Siècle. Revue d'histoire* 114(2), 171–182.

Desrosières, A. (1972), "Un découpage de l'industrie en trois secteurs," *Economie et statistique* 40(1), 25–39.

Diamond, D. W. (1991), "Debt maturity structure and liquidity risk," *The Quarterly Journal of Economics* 106(3), 709–737.

Dickhaus, M. (1998), "Fostering 'the bank that rules Europe': The Bank of England, the Allied Banking Commission, and the Bank Deutscher Länder, 1948–51," *Contemporary European History* 7, 161–179.

Dieterlen, P. (1954), *Quelques enseignements de l'évolution monétaire française de 1948 à 1952*, A. Colin, Paris.

(1957), "La politique monétaire française, cinq ans de stabilité," *Revue économique* 8(4), 613–648.

Dieterlen, P. & Rist, C. (1948), *The Monetary Problem of France*, King's Crown Press, New York.

Djankov, S., Glaeser, E., La Porta, R., Lopez-de-Silanes, F. & Shleifer, A. (2003), "The new comparative economics," *Journal of Comparative Economics* 31(4), 595–619.

Dow, J. (1965), *The Management of the British Economy 1945–60*, Cambridge University Press, Cambridge, UK.

Dubois, P. (1985), "Ruptures de croissance et progrés technique," *Economie et statistique* 181(1), 3–31.

Duchaussoy, V. (2011), "Les socialistes, la banque de France et le mur d'argent (1981–1984)," *Vingtième Siècle. Revue d'histoire* 110(2), 111–133.

(2013), "Histoire de l'organisation et de la gouvernance de la Banque de France (1936–1993). La constitution d'une institution de marché," PhD dissertation, Université de Rouen.

Duchaussoy, V. & Monnet, E. (2015), "Les circuits du financement de l'Etat par la Banque de France," in F. Descamps & L. Quenouëlle-Corre, eds., *La mobilisation financière pendant la Grande Guerre. Le front financier, un troisième front*, IGPDE, Paris, pp. 121–151.

Duchaussoy, V. & Monnet, E. (2018), "L'impact de la Grande guerre dans les relations de trésorerie entre l'État et la Banque de France (1914–1936)," in M. Margairaz & O. Feiertag, eds., *Banques centrales dans la Grande Guerre/Central Banks in the Great War*, Presses de Sciences Po, Paris.

Dupont, P. (1952), *Le controle des banques et la direction du credit en France*, Dunod, Paris.

Dutailly, J. (1981), "La crise du système productif," *Economie et statistique* 138(1), 3–20.

Dyson, K. (2014), *States, Debt, and Power: "Saints" and "Sinners" in European History and Integration*, Oxford University Press, Oxford, UK.

Dyson, K. & Featherstone, K. (1999), *The Road to Maastricht: Negotiating Economic and Monetary Union*, Oxford University Press, Oxford, UK.

Edelman, L. B. (2004), "Rivers of law and contested terrain: A law and society approach to economic rationality," *Law & Society Review* 38(2), 181–198.

EEC (European Economic Community) (1962), "The instruments of monetary policy in the countries of the European Economic Community," report of the Monetary Committee Luxembourg, Office for Official Publications of the European Communities.

(1972), "Monetary policy in the countries of the European Economic Community: Institutions and instruments," report of the Monetary Committee Luxembourg, Office for Official Publications of the European Communities.

Effosse, S. (2003), *L'invention du logement aidé en France: l'immobilier au temps des Trente Glorieuses*, CHEFF, Paris.

(2014), *Le crédit à la consommation en France, 1947–1965: de la stigmatisation à la réglementation*, CHEFF, Paris.

Eich, S. & Tooze, A. (2016), "The great inflation," in A. Doering-Manteuffel et al. eds., *Vorgeschichte der Gegenwart. Dimensionen des Strukturbruchs nach dem Boom*, Vandenhoeck & Ruprecht, Göttingen.

Eichengreen, B. (1992), *Golden Fetters: The Gold Standard and the Great Depression, 1919–1939*, Oxford University Press, New York.

Eichengreen, B. J. (1995), "Institutions and economic growth: Europe after WW II," in N. Crafts & G. Toniolo, eds., *Economic Growth in Europe Since 1945*, Cambridge University Press, Cambridge, UK, pp. 38–72.

(2006), *The European Economy Since 1945: Coordinated Capitalism and Beyond*, Princeton University Press, Princeton, NJ.

(2007), *Global Imbalances and the Lessons of Bretton Woods*, MIT Press, Cambridge, MA.

Eichengreen, B. & Flandreau, M. (2009), "The rise and fall of the dollar (or when did the dollar replace sterling as the leading reserve currency?," *European Review of Economic History* 13(3), 377–411.

Eichengreen, B. & James, H. (2003), "Monetary and financial reform in two eras of globalization," in M. D. Bordo & A. Taylor, eds., *Globalization in Historical Perspective*, University of Chicago Press, Chicago, pp. 515–548.

Eichengreen, B. & Temin, P. (2000), "The gold standard and the Great Depression," *Contemporary European History* 9(2), 183–207.

Elgie, R. & Thompson, H. (1998), *The Politics of Central Banks*, Routledge, London.

Elliott, D. J., Feldberg, G. & Lehnert, A. (2013), "The history of cyclical macroprudential policy in the United States," Working Paper No. 8, Office of Financial Research, US Department of the Treasury.

Esping-Andersen, G. (1990), *The Three Worlds of Welfare Capitalism*, Princeton University Press, Princeton, NJ.

Esposito, C. (1991), "French international monetary policies in the 1940s," *French Historical Studies* 17(1), 117–140.

Farhi, E. & Werning, I. (2014), "Dilemma not trilemma? Capital controls and exchange rates with volatile capital flows," *IMF Economic Review* 62(4), 569–605.

Feiertag, O. (1993), "Polémique sur la politique du crédit au printemps 1953: l'attaque de l'économie nationale, la défense des autorités monétaires," *Etudes et documents* 5, 585–600.

(1995), "Le nerf de l'après-guerre: le financement de la reconstruction entre l'Etat et le marché (1944–1947)," *Matériaux pour l'histoire de notre temps* 39(1), 46–51.

(2001), "Finances publiques, mur d'argent et genèse de la libéralisation nancière en France de 1981 à 1984," in S. Bernstein, P. Milza & J. L. Bianco, eds., *les années Mitterrand, les années du changement (1981-1984)*, Perrin, Paris.

(2003), "Les banques d'émission et la croissance économique en Europe (1945-1973)," in O. Feiertag and M. Margairaz, eds., *Politiques et pratiques des banques d'émission en Europe (XVIIe-XXe siècle)*, Albin Michel, Paris, pp. 595-622.

(2006a), "Greffe économétrique et genèse de l'école de la banque de France (1969-1985)," in O. Feiertag, ed., *Mesurer la monnaie*, Albin Michel, Paris, pp. 213-245.

(2006b), *Wilfrid Baumgartner: Un grand commis des finances à la croisée des pouvoirs*, CHEFF, Paris.

(2007), "Administrer la monnaie: pour une histoire des banques centrales comme organisations," *Entreprises et histoire* 48(3), 73-91.

(2009), "Le système financier français face à la désindustrialisation (1974-1984): la faute aux banques?," in P. Lamard & N. Stoskopf, eds., *Une décennie de désindustrialisation*, Picard, Paris, pp. 37-49.

(2017), "Les banques centrales face à la 'grande inflation' (1968-1979)," in M-P. Chélini & L. Warlouzet, eds., *Calmer les prix/Slowing Down Prices*, Presses de Sciences, Paris, pp. 213-244.

Feiertag, O. & Plessis, A. (2000), "Conjoncture et structures monétaires internationales en europe à la fin des années trente," *Revue économique* 51(2), 277-290.

Fioretos, O. (2011), *Creative Reconstructions: Multilateralism and European Varieties of Capitalism After 1950*, Cornell University Press, Ithaca, NY.

Fioretos, O., Falleti, T. G. & Sheingate, A., eds. (2016), *The Oxford Handbook of Historical Institutionalism*, Oxford University Press, Oxford, UK and New York.

Fforde, J. (1992), *The Bank of England and Public Policy, 1941-1958*, Cambridge, Cambridge University Press, UK.

Fontaine, L. (2014), *The Moral Economy: Poverty, Credit, and Trust in Early Modern Europe*, Cambridge University Press, New York.

Fossier, A. & Monnet, E. (2009), "Les institutions, mode d'emploi," *Tracés* (17), 7-28.

Fourastié, J. (1979), *Les Trente Glorieuses ou la révolution invisible de 1946 à 1975*, Fayard, Paris.

Fourcade, M. (2009), *Economists and Societies: Discipline and Profession in the United States, Britain, and France, 1890s to 1990s*, Princeton University Press, Princeton, NY.

Fourcade, M. & Babb, S. L. (2002), "The rebirth of the liberal creed: Paths to neo-liberalism in four countries," *American Journal of Sociology* 108(3), 533-579.

Fournier, H. (1951), "La commission de controle des banques," *Revue économique* 2(5), 591-599.

Fourquet, F. (1980), *Les Comptes de la puissance: histoire de la comptabilitée nationale et du Plan*, Recherches, Paris.

Fousek, P. G. (1957), *Foreign Central Banking: The Instruments of Monetary Policy*, Federal Reserve Bank of New York, New York.

Franck, L. (1979), *Les prix*, PUF, Paris.

Franck, L. R. (1953), "Planisme français et démocratie," *Revue économique* 4(2), 195-219.

Frank, R. (1998), "Bretton Woods: un esprit plus qu'un système," in CHEFF, ed., *La France et les institutions de Bretton Woods, 1944-1994*, CHEFF, Paris, pp. 9-14.

Franke, G. (1999), "The Bundesbank and financial markets," in Deutsche Bundesbank, ed., *Fifty Years of the Deutsche Mark*, Oxford University Press, Oxford, UK, pp. 219-266.

Friedman, M. (1968), "The role of monetary policy," *American Economic Review* 58(1), 1–17.

(1969), *The Optimum Quantity of Money*, Transaction Publishers, New York.

Friedman, M. & Schwartz, A. J. (1963), *A Monetary History of the United States, 1867–1960*, Princeton University Press, Princeton, NJ.

Gaiotti, E. & Secchi, A. (2012) "Monetary policy and fiscal dominance in Italy from the early 1970s to the adoption of the euro: A review," *Bank of Italy Occasional Papers* No. 171.

Gaïti, B. (2002), "Les modernisateurs dans l'administration d'après-guerre l'écriture d'une histoire héroïque," *Revue française d'administration publique* 102(2), 295–322.

Galbraith, J. K. (1982), "Monetary policy in France," *Journal of Post Keynesian Economics* 4(3), 388–403.

Galbraith, J., Cohen, S. & Zysman, J. (1981), "Monetary policy, selective credit policy and industrial policy in France, Britain, West Germany and Sweden," a study prepared for the use of the Joint Economic Committee, Congress of the United States, June 26, US GPO, Washington, DC.

Gavin, F. J. (2004), *Gold, Dollars, and Power: The Politics of International Monetary Relations, 1958–1971*, University of North Carolina Press, Chapel Hill, NC.

Gersbach, H. & Hahn, V. (2004), "Voting transparency, conflicting interests, and the appointment of central bankers," *Economics & Politics* 16(3), 321–345.

Gerschenkron, A. (1962), *Economic Backwardness in Historical Perspective*, Harvard University Press, Cambridge, MA.

Gertler, M. & Gilchrist, S. (1994), "Monetary policy, business cycles, and the behavior of small manufacturing firms," *The Quarterly Journal of Economics* 109(2), 309–340.

Ghosh, A. R. & Qureshi, M. (2016), "What's in a name? That which we call capital controls," IMF Working Paper No. 16/25, International Monetary Fund.

Gide, C. (1930), *Cours d'économie politique*, Sirey, Paris.

Gillard, L. (1978), "Nouvelles réflexions sur les découpages du système industriel," *Revue d'économie industrielle* 6(1), 121–130.

Gille, B. (1959), *La banque et le crédit en France de 1815 à 1848*, Presses universitaires de France, Paris.

Goode, R. & Thorn, R. S. (1959), "Variable reserve requirements against commercial bank deposits," *Staff Papers International Monetary Fund*, 7(1), 9–45.

Goodfriend, M. & King, R. G. (1988), "Financial deregulation, monetary policy, and central banking," *Economic Quarterly, Federal Reserve Bank of Richmond* 74(3), 3–22.

Goodfriend, M. & King, R. (2005), "The incredible Volcker disinflation," *Journal of Monetary Economics* 52(5), 981–1015.

Goodhart, C. (1985), *The Evolution of Central Banks*, MIT Press, Cambridge, MA.

(1989), *Money, Information and Uncertainty*, MIT Press, Cambridge, MA.

(1998), "The two concepts of money: Implications for the analysis of optimal currency areas," *European Journal of Political Economy* 14(3), 407–432.

(2011), "The changing role of central banks," *Financial History Review* 18, 135–154.

(2015), "Competition and credit control: Some personal reflections," *Financial History Review* 22(2), 760–779.

Goodhart, C. & Lastra, R. (2017), "Populism and central bank independence," *Open Economies Review*, 1–20.

Goodman, J. (1992), *Monetary Sovereignty: The Politics of Central Banking in Western Europe*, Cornell University Press, Ithaca, NY.

Goodman, J. B. & Pauly, L. W. (1993), "The obsolescence of capital controls? Economic management in an age of global markets," *World Politics* 46(1), 50–82.

Gordon, D. B. & Leeper, E. M. (1992), "In search of the liquidity effect," *Journal of Monetary Economics* 29(3), 341–369.

Goux, J. (1990), "Les fondements de l'économie de découvert a propos de la théorie de la liquidité de Hicks," *Revue économique* 41(4), 669–686.

Gowland, D. (1978), *Monetary Policy and Credit Control: The UK Experience*, Taylor & Francis, London.

Greif, A. (2006), *Institutions and the Path to the Modern Economy: Lessons from Medieval Trade*, Cambridge University Press, Cambridge, UK.

Greif, A. & Laitin, D. (2004), "A theory of endogenous institutional change," *American Political Science Review* 98(4), 633–652.

Grenard, F. (2010), "L'administration du controle économique en France, 1940–1950," *Revue d'histoire moderne et contemporaine* 57-2(2), 132–158.

Grenard, F., Le Bot, F. & Perrin, C. (2017), *Histoire économique de Vichy*, Perrin, Paris.

Grossman, R. (2010), "The emergence of central banks and banking regulation in comparative perspective," in S. Battilossi & J. Reis, eds., *State and Financial Systems in Europe and the USA: Historical Perspectives on Regulation and Supervision in the Nineteenth and Twentieth Centuries*, Aldershot, Ashgate, pp. 123–138.

Grünbacher, A. (2004), *Reconstruction and Cold War in Germany: The Kreditanstalt für Wiederaufbau (1948–1961)*, Ashgate, Burlington, VT.

Gueslin, A. (1988), "Crédit agricole et agriculture en France au XXe siècle," *Économie rurale* 184(1), 107–115.

Guillaumont-Jeanneney, S. (1968), *Politique monétaire et croissance économique en France, 1950–1966*, Armand Collin, Paris.

(1982), *Pour la politique monétaire. Défense d'une mal aimée*, PUF, Paris.

(1986), "L'ouverture du marché monétaire. Vers une politique libérale des taux d'intérêt?," *Revue de l'OFCE* 14(1), 87–106.

(1991), L'alternance entre dirigisme et libéralisme monétaire 1950–1990, in M. Lévy-Leboyer & J. C. Casanova, eds., *Entre l'Etat et le marché*, Gallimard, Paris, pp. 507–543.

Guindey, G. (1973), *Mythes et réalités de la crise monétaire internationale*, J. Delmas, Paris.

Guindey, G. & Coombs, C. A. (1980), *Réflexions sur le système monétaire international*, Fondation Per Jacobson, Basel.

Gurley, J. G. & Shaw, E. S. (1960), *Money in a Theory of Finance*, Brookings Institution, Washington, DC.

Gusfield, J. R. (1984), *The Culture of Public Problems: Drinking-Driving and the Symbolic Order*. University of Chicago Press, Chicago.

Hackett, J. & Hackett, A. (1963), *Economic Planning in France*, Harvard University Press, Cambridge, MA.

Hall, P. A. (1986), *Governing the Economy: The Politics of State Intervention in Britain and France*, Oxford University Press, New York.

Hall, P. A. & Franzese, R. J. (1998), "Mixed signals: Central bank independence, coordinated wage bargaining, and European monetary union," *International Organization* 52(3), 505–535.

Hall, P. A. & Soskice, D. (2001), *Varieties of Capitalism: The Institutional Foundations of Comparative Advantage*, Oxford University Press, Oxford.

Hall, P. A. & Thelen, K. (2009), "Institutional change in varieties of capitalism," *Socio-Economic Review* 7(1), 7–34.

Hart, O. & Moore, J. (1994), "A theory of debt based on the inalienability of human capital," *The Quarterly Journal of Economics* 109(4), 841–879.

Hautcoeur, P-C. (1999), "L'auto financement: questions de méthode et tentative de cadrage macro-économique pour la France (1914–1990)," *Entreprises et histoire* (22), 55–77.

Hautcoeur, P.-C. & Le Bris, D. (2010), "A challenge to triumphant optimists? A blue chips index for the Paris stock exchange, 1854–2007," *Financial History Review* 17(2), 141–183.

Hayward, J. E. S. (1986), *The State and the Market Economy: Industrial Patriotism and Economic Intervention in France*, Wheatsheaf Books, Brighton, UK.

Helleiner, E. (1996), *States and the Reemergence of Global Finance: From Bretton Woods to the 1990s*, Cornell University Press, Ithaca, NY.

(2014), *Forgotten Foundations of Bretton Woods: International Development and the Making of the Postwar Order*, Cornell University Press, Ithaca, NY.

Heller, W. W., Goedhart, C. & Guindey, G. (1968), *Politique budgétaire et équilibre économique: lessons du passé, problèmes et perspectives*, OCDE, Paris.

Hennessy, E. (1992), *A Domestic History of the Bank of England, 1930–1960*, Cambridge University Press, Cambridge, UK.

Hicks, J. (1974), *The Crisis in Keynesian Economics*, Basic Books, New York.

Hirschman, A. O. (1991), *The Rhetoric of Reaction*, Harvard University Press, Cambridge, MA.

Hirschman, A. O. & Roosa, R. V. (1949), "Postwar credit controls in France," *Federal Reserve Bulletin*, April, pp. 348–360.

Hodgman, D. (1971), "British techniques of monetary policy: A critical review," *Journal of Money, Credit and Banking* 3(3), 277–289.

(1972), "Selective credit controls," *Journal of Money, Credit and Banking* 4(2), 342–359.

(1973), "Credit controls in Western Europe: An evaluative review," in *Credit Allocation Techniques and Monetary Policy*, Federal Reserve Bank of Boston, Boston, pp. 137–161.

(1974), *National Monetary Policies and International Monetary Cooperation*, Little, Brown and Co, Boston.

Hoffman, P. T., Postel-Vinay, G. & Rosenthal, J. L. (2000), *Priceless Markets: The Political Economy of Credit in Paris, 1660–1870*, University of Chicago Press, Chicago.

(2018), *Dark Matter Credit: The Development of Peer-to-Peer Lending and Banking in France*, Princeton University Press, Princeton, NJ.

Hoffmann, S. (1963), *A la recherche de la France*, Seuil, Paris.

Hoffmeyer, E. (2000), "Decisionmaking for European economic and monetary union," Report No. 62, Group of Thirty.

Holbik, K., ed. (1973) *Monetary Policy in Twelve Industrial Countries*, Federal Reserve Bank of Boston, Boston.

Holtfrerich, C-L. (1999), "Monetary policy under fixed exchange rates (1948–1970)," in Deutsche Bundesbank, ed., *Fifty Years of the Deutsche Mark. Central Bank and the Currency in Germany Since 1948*, Oxford University Press, Oxford, UK, pp. 321–403.

(2008), "Monetary policy in Germany since 1948: National tradition, international best practice or ideology?," in J.-P. Touffut, *Central Banks as Economic Institutions*, Edward Elgar, Cheltenham, UK, pp. 22–51.

Holtfrerich, C.-L. & Iwami, T. (1999), "Postwar central banking reform: A German-Japanese comparison," in C.-L. Holtfrerich, J. Reis & G. Toniolo, eds., *The Emergence of Modern Central Banking from 1918 to the Present*, Ashgate, Aldershot, UK, pp. 69–110.

Hoover, K. D. & Perez, S. J. (1994), "Money may matter, but how could you know?," *Journal of Monetary Economics* 34(1), 89–99.

Hyman, L. (2011), *Debtor Nation: The History of America in Red Ink*, Princeton University Press, Princeton, NJ.

INSEE (1974), *Fresque historique du système productif*, Les Collections de l'INSEE., Paris.

(1979), *La Crise du système productif*, INSEE, Paris.

(1981), *Le mouvement économique en France, 1949-1979: séries longues macroéconomiques*, INSEE, Paris.

(1989), *Annuaire rétrospectif de la France: séries longues macroéconomiques*, INSEE, Paris.

Iversen, T. (1999), "The political economy of inflation: Bargaining structure or central bank independence?," *Public Choice* 99(3), 237–258.

Jabko, N. (2006), *Playing the Market: A Political Strategy for Uniting Europe, 1985-2005*, Cornell University Press, Ithaca, NY.

James, H. D. (1996), *International Monetary Cooperation Since Bretton Woods*, Oxford University Press, New York.

James, H. (2012), *Making the European Monetary Union*, Harvard University Press, Cambridge, MA.

Jeanneney, J. (1976), *François de Wendel en République: l'argent et le pouvoir, 1914-1940*, Le Seuil, Paris.

Johnson, O. E. G. (1974), "Credit controls as instruments of development policy in the light of economic theory," *Journal of Money, Credit and Banking* 6(1), 85–99.

Judt, T. (2006), *Postwar: A History of Europe Since 1945*, Penguin, New York.

Jurgensen, P. & Lebegue, D. (1988), *Le trésor et la politique financière*, Montchrestien, Paris.

Kaldor, N. (1960), "The Radcliffe report," *The Review of Economics and Statistics* 42(1), 14–19.

Katz, S. I. (1969), "External surpluses, capital flows, and credit policy in the European Economic Community, 1958 to 1967," Princeton Studies in International Finance No. 22, Department of Economics, Princeton University.

Katzenstein, P. J. (1985), *Small States in World Markets: Industrial Policy in Europe*, Cornell University Press, Ithaca, NY.

Kelber, A. & Monnet, E. (2014), "Macroprudential policy and quantitative instruments: A European historical perspective," *Financial Stability Review* 18, 151–160.

Kelsen, H. (1967), *Pure Theory of Law*, University of California Press, Berkeley.

Kindleberger, C. P. (1984), *A Financial History of Western Europe*, Oxford University Press, Oxford, UK.

Klingelhöfer, J. & Sun, R. (2017), "Macroprudential policy, central banks and financial stability: Evidence from China," Working Paper No. 79033, University Library of Munich, Germany.

Koch, H. (1983), *Histoire de la Banque de France et de la monnaie sous la IVe République*, Dunod, Paris.

Konczal, M. & Mason, J. W. (2017), *A New Direction for the Federal Reserve: Expanding the Monetary Policy Toolkit*, Roosevelt Institute, New York.

Kriz, M. A. (1951), "Credit control in France," *American Economic Review* 41(1), 85–106.

Kuisel, R. F. (1981), *Capitalism and the State in Modern France: Renovation and Economic Management in the Twentieth Century*, Cambridge University Press, Cambridge, UK.

(1993), *Seducing the French: The Dilemma of Americanization*, University of California Press, Berkeley.

Lacan, L., Lazarus, J., Perrin-Heredia, A. & Plot, S. (2009), "Vivre et faire vivre à crédit: agents économiques ordinaires et institutions nancières dans les situations d'endettement," *Sociétés contemporaines* 76(4), 5.

Lacoue-Labarthe, D. (2007), "Du controle à la supervision bancaire: le tournant des années 1980," *Communication aux Journées de la Mission historique de la Banque de France*, 15 & 16 novembre 2007.

Lamoreaux, N. R. & Rosenthal, J. (2005), "Legal regime and contractual exigibility: A comparison of business as organizational choices in France and the United States during the era of industrialization," *American Law and Economics Review* 7(1), 28–61.

Lane, N. (2017), "Manufacturing revolution: Industrial policy and networks in South Korea," working paper.

Laufenburger, H. (1944), *Crédit public et finances de guerre, 1914–1944*, Librairie de Médicis, Paris.

Lavoie, M. (1984), "The endogenous flow of credit and the post Keynesian theory of money," *Journal of Economic Issues* 18(3), 771–797.

Lazarus, J. (2010), "Le crédit à la consommation dans la bancarisation," *Entreprises et histoire* 59(2), 28.

(2012), *L'épreuve de l'argent. Banques, banquiers, clients*, Calmann-Lévy, Paris.

Le Bourva, J. (1979), "Les établissements de crédit en France," *Revue économique* 30(1), 88–120.

Le Merrer, P. (2012), "L'affirmation de l'économie comme discipline scientifique: une histoire française particulière," *Tracés* HS(3), 163–174.

Le Van-Lemesle, L. (2004), *Le Juste ou le Riche: l'enseignement de l'Économie politique 1815–1950*, CHEFF, Paris.

Leclercq, Y. (2010), *La banque supérieure: la Banque de France de 1800 à 1914*, Classiques Garnier, Paris.

Leeper, E. (1997), "Narrative and VAR approaches to monetary policy: Common identification problems," *Journal of Monetary Economics* 40(3), 641–657.

Lefranc, G. (1966), "Le courant planiste dans le mouvement ouvrier français de 1933 à 1936," *Le Mouvement social* (54), 69–89.

Leijonhufvud, A. (1968), *On Keynesian Economics and the Economics of Keynes: A Study in Monetary Theory*, Oxford University Press, New York.

Lemercier, C. (2008), "Discipliner le commerce sans corporations," *Le Mouvement Social* 224(3), 61–74.

Lemoine, B. (2016), *L'ordre de la dette: Enquête sur les infortunes de l'État et la prospérité du marché*, La Découverte, Paris.

Lepage, S. (1999), "La direction des finances extérieures face à la modernisation et à la nécessité de restaurer la puissance internationale de la France (1946–1950)," *Histoire, économie et société* 18(2), 255–274.

Lescure, M. (1982), *Les banques, l'État et le marché immobilier en France, à l'époque contemporaine, 1820–1940*, EHESS éditions, Paris.

(2010), "La politique du crédit et le financement des districts industriels en France (1945–1965)," in L. Tissot, ed., *Histoire de territoires: les territoires industriels en question XVIIIe–XXe siècles*, Editions Alphil, Neuchâtel, pp. 193–224.

Lescure, M. & Plessis, A., eds. (1999), *Banques locales et banques régionales en France au XIXe siècle*, Albin Michel, Paris.

Lessig, L. (1998), "The new Chicago school," *The Journal of Legal Studies* 27(S2), 661–691.

Levine, R., Loayza, N. & Beck, T. (2000), "Financial intermediation and growth: Causality and causes," *Journal of Monetary Economics* 46(1), 31–77.

Levy, J. (2012), *Freaks of Fortune: The Emerging World of Capitalism and Risk in America*, Harvard University Press, Cambridge, MA.

Lévy-Garboua, V. (1978), "Le taux de change et la politique monétaire dans une économie d'endettement," *Annales de l'INSEE* (32), 3–32.

Lévy-Garboua, V. & Monnet, E. (2016), "Les taux d'intérêt en France: une perspective historique," *Revue d'économie financière* 121(1), 35–58.

Lévy-Garboua, V., Oudiz, G., Villa, P. & Sterdyniak, H. (1978), "Change, inflation et intérèt: un modèle," *Revue économique* 29(5), 866–926.

Lévy-Leboyer, M. & Casanova, J. (1991), *Entre l'État et le marché: l'économie française des années 1880 à nos jours*, Gallimard, Paris.

Lohmann, S. (1994), "Designing a central bank in a federal system: The Deutsche Bundesbank, 1957–1992," in P. L. Siklos, ed., *Varieties of Monetary Reforms: Lessons and Experiences on the Road to Monetary Union*, Kluwer Academic Press, Boston, pp. 247–278.

Loriaux, M. (1988), "States and markets: French financial interventionism in the seventies," *Comparative Politics* 20(2), 175–193.

Loriaux, M. M. (1991), *France After Hegemony*, Cornell University Press, Ithaca, NY.

Loriaux, M. (1997), "The end of credit activism in interventionist states," in M. Loriaux et al., eds., *Capital Ungoverned: Liberalizing Finance in Interventionist States*, Cornell University Press, Ithaca, NY, pp. 1–16.

Loriaux, M., Woo-Cumings, M., Calder, K., Maxfield, S. & Perez, S., eds. (1997), *Capital Ungoverned: Liberalizing Finance in Interventionist States*, Cornell University Press, Ithaca, NY.

Lynch, F. (1984), "Resolving the paradox of the Monnet plan: National and international planning in French reconstruction," *The Economic History Review* 37(2), 229–243.

(1997), *France and the International Economy: From Vichy to the Treaty of Rome*, Routledge, London.

Maarek, G. & Levy-Garboua, V. (1985), *La Dette, le boom, la crise*, Economica, Paris.

MacLennan, M. C., Forsyth, M. & Denton, G. (1968), *Economic Planning and Policies in Britain, France and Germany*, Frederick A. Praeger, New York.

Madero, M. (2012), "Interpreting the Western legal tradition: Reading the work of Yan Thomas," *Annales. Histoire, Sciences Sociales* 67(1), 103–122.

Mahoney, J. & Thelen, K., eds. (2009), *Explaining Institutional Change: Ambiguity, Agency, and Power*, Cambridge University Press, Cambridge, UK.

Mairesse, J. (1971), "L'estimation du capital fixe productif. Méthode chronologique," *Economie et statistique* 25(1), 33–55.

Mantoux, E. (1946), *La Paix calomniée ou les conséquences économiques de M. Keynes*, Gallimard, Paris.

Marchal, J. (1967), *Monnaie et crédit: Le système monétaire et bancaire français*, Editions Cujas, Paris.

Margairaz, M. (1991), *L'Etat, les finances et l'économie: histoire d'une conversion, 1932–1952*, CHEFF, Paris.

(2008), "L'impossible réforme des structures de la Banque de France (1967–1974)," in M. Margairaz & O. Feiertag, eds., *Gouverner une banque centrale. XVII–XXIemes siècles*, Albin Michel, Paris, pp. 456–456.

(2009a), "Le temps de la politique du crédit en France (années 1930–1980)," in G. Conti et al. eds., *Credito e nazione in Francia e in Italia (XIX–XXe secolo)*, Pisa University Press, Pisa, pp. 119–136.

(2009b), "Les politiques économiques sous et de Vichy," *Histoire@Politique* 9(3), 93.

Margairaz, M. & Rousso, H. (1992), "Vichy, la guerre et les entreprises," *Histoire, économie et société* 11(3), 337–367.

Marjolin, R., Sadrin, J. & Wormser, O. (1969), *Rapport sur le marché monétaire et les conditions du crédit. Demandé, par décision en date du 6 décembre 1968*, Documentation Française, Paris.

Marnata, F. (1973), *La bourse et le financement des investissements*, A. Colin, Paris.

Mathis, J. (1981), "L'évolution des mouvements de capitaux à court terme entre la France et l'extérieur de 1967 à 1978," *Économie & prévision* 47(2), 27–58.

Mayer, T. (1999), *Monetary Policy and the Great Inflation in the United States: The Federal Reserve and the Failure of Macroeconomic Policy, 1965–1979*, Edward Elgar, Cheltenham, UK.

McKinnon, R. I. (1973), *Money and Capital in Economic Development*, Brookings Institution Press, Washington, DC.

(1993), *The Order of Economic Liberalization: Financial Control in the Transition to a Market Economy*, JHU Press, Baltimore, MD.

McNamara, K. R. (1998), *The Currency of Ideas: Monetary Politics in the European Union*, Cornell University Press, Ithaca, NY.

(1999), "Consensus and constraint: Ideas and capital mobility in European monetary integration," *Journal of Common Market Studies* 37, 455–476.

(2002), "Rational fictions: Central bank independence and the social logic of delegation," *West European Politics* 25(1), 47.

Mélitz, J. (1990), "Financial deregulation in France," *European Economic Review* 34(23), 394–402.

Mélitz, J. (1991), "Monetary policy in France," CEPR Discussion Paper No. 509.

Meltzer, A. H. (1959), "The behavior of the French money supply: 1938–54," *Journal of Political Economy* 67(3), 275–296.

(2003), *A History of the Federal Reserve*, Vol. 1, University of Chicago Press, Chicago.

(2010), *A History of the Federal Reserve*, Vol. 2, University of Chicago Press, Chicago.

Miller, E. (1956), "Monetary policy in a changing world," *The Quarterly Journal of Economics* 70(1), 23–43.

Milward, A. S. (2000), *The European Rescue of the Nation-State*, Routledge, London.

Mioche, P. (1987), *Le Plan Monnet, genèse et élaboration, 1941–1947*, Presses de la Sorbonne, Paris.

Mojon, B. (1998), "Monetary policy under a fixed exchange rate regime, the case of France 1987–1996," CEPII Working Paper No. 14.

Monnet, E. (2012a), "Politique monétaire et politique du crédit en France pendant les Trente Glorieuses, 1945–1973," PhD dissertation, EHESS and Paris School of Economics.

(2012b), "Monetary policy without interest rates: Evidence from France's Golden Age (1948–1973) using a narrative approach," Working Paper No. 32, European Historical Economics Society (EHES).

(2013), "Une coopération à la française. La France, le dollar et le système de Bretton Woods, 1960–1965," *Histoire@ Politique* 1, 83–100.

(2014), "Monetary policy without interest rates: Evidence from France's Golden Age (1948 to 1973) using a narrative approach," *American Economic Journal: Macroeconomics* 6(4), 137–169.

(2015), "La politique de la Banque de France au sortir des Trente Glorieuses: un tournant monétariste?," *Revue d'histoire moderne et contemporaine* 62(1), 147–174.

(2016), "The diversity in national monetary and credit policies in Western Europe under the Bretton Woods system," in M. Margairaz & O. Feiertag, eds., *Les banques centrales et l'État-nation/Central Banks and the Nation State*, Presses de Sciences Po, Paris, pp. 451–488.

(2017), "French monetary policy and the Bretton Woods system: Criticisms, proposals and conflicts," in G. Scott-Smith & J. S. Rofe, eds., *Global Perspectives on the Bretton Woods Conference and the Post-War World Order*, Palgrave Macmillan, Cham, Switzerland, pp. 73–87.

(2018), "Credit controls as an escape from the trilemma: The Bretton Woods experience," *European Review of Economic History*.

Monnet, E. & Puy, D. (2016), "Has globalization really increased business cycle synchronization?," IMF Working Papers No. 16/54, International Monetary Fund.

Monnet, E. & Vari, M. (2017), "Liquidity ratios as monetary policy tools: Some historical lessons," mimeo, Banque de France.

Monnet, E., Pagliari, S. & Vallée, S. (2014), "Europe between financial repression and regulatory capture," Bruegel Working Paper No. 2014/08.

Mooij, J. & Prast, H. (2002), "A brief history of the institutional design of banking supervision in the Netherlands," WO Research Memoranda No. 703, Netherlands Central Bank, Research Department.

Moulévrier, P. (2002), *Le mutualisme bancaire: le Crédit Mutuel, de l'Église au marché*, Presses Universitaires de Rennes, Rennes.

Mouré, K. (1991), *Managing the Franc Poincaré: Economic Understanding and Political Constraint in French Monetary Policy, 1928–1936*, Cambridge University Press, Cambridge, UK.

Mouré, K. (2002), *The Gold Standard Illusion: France, the Bank of France, and the International Gold Standard, 1914–1939*, Oxford University Press, Oxford, UK.

Mourlon-Druol, E. (2012), *A Europe Made of Money: The Emergence of the European Monetary System*, Cornell University Press, Ithaca, NY.

(2016), "Banking union in historical perspective: The initiative of the European Commission in the 1960s and 1970s," *Journal of Common Market Studies* 54(4), 913–927.

Mourlon-Druol, E. & Schenk, C. (2016), "Bank regulation and supervision," in Y. Cassis, R. S. Grossman & C. Schenk, eds., *The Oxford Handbook of Banking and Financial History*, Oxford University Press, Oxford, UK, pp. 395–419.

Mundell, R. (1968), *International Economics*, Macmillan, New York.

(2000), "Currency areas, exchange rate systems and international monetary reform," *Journal of Applied Economics* 3, 217–256.

Murphy, K. M., Shleifer A., & Vishny R. W. (1989), "Industrialization and the big push," *Journal of Political Economy* 97(5), 1003–1026.

Musacchio, A. (2008), "Can civil law countries get good institutions? Lessons from the history of creditor rights and bond markets in Brazil," *The Journal of Economic History* 68, 80–108.

(2010), "Law and finance c. 1900," NBER Working Paper Series No. 16216, National Bureau of Economic Research.

Needham, D. (2014), *UK Monetary Policy from Devaluation to Thatcher, 1967–82*, Springer, London.

Ng, S. & Perron, P. (2005), "A note on the selection of time series models," *Oxford Bulletin of Economics and Statistics* 67(1), 115–134.

Nishimura, S. (1995), "The French provincial banks, the Banque de France, and bill finance, 1890–1913," *The Economic History Review* 48(3), 536–554.

Nord, P. G. (2010), *France's New Deal: From the Thirties to the Postwar Era*, Princeton University Press, Princeton, NY.

North, D. C. (1990), *Institutions, Institutional Change, and Economic Performance*, Cambridge University Press, Cambridge, UK.

Obstfeld, M. & Taylor, A. M. (2004), *Global Capital Markets: Integration, Crisis, and Growth*, Cambridge University Press, New York.

OECD (Organisation for Economic Co-operation and Development) (1975), *The Role of Monetary Policy in Demand Management: The Experience of Six Major Countries*, OECD Monetary Studies Series, Paris.

Offer, A. (2014), "Narrow banking, real estate, and financial stability in the UK c. 1870–2010," in N. Dimsdale & A. Hotson, eds., *British Financial Crises Since 1825*, Oxford University Press, Oxford, UK, pp. 158–174.

(2017), "The market turn: From social democracy to market liberalism," *Economic History Review* 70(4), 1051–1071.

O'Hara, G. (2007), *From Dreams to Disillusionment: Economic and Social Planning in 1960s Britain*, Palgrave, Basingstoke, UK.

Oksanen, H. (1974), "The discount window and monetary policy: The case of Finland," *The Swedish Journal of Economics* 76(4), 434–448.

Olson, M. (1982), *The Rise and Decline of Nations: Economic Growth, Stagflation, and Social Rigidities*, Yale University Press, New Haven, CT.

Orphanides, A. (2003), "The quest for prosperity without inflation," *Journal of Monetary Economics* 50(3), 633–663.

O'Sullivan, M. (2007), "Acting out institutional change: Understanding the recent transformation of the French financial system," *Socio-Economic Review* 5(3), 389–436.

Ott, J. C. (2011), *When Wall Street Met Main Street*, Harvard University Press, Cambridge, MA.

Overy, R.-J. (1995), *War and Economy in the Third Reich*, Clarendon Press, Oxford, UK.

Owens, R. E. & Schreft, S. L. (1995), "Identifying credit crunches," *Contemporary Economic Policy* 13(2), 63–76.

Pack, H. (2000), "Industrial policy: Growth elixir or poison?," *The World Bank Research Observer* 15(1), 47–67.

Page, S. (1993), *Monetary Policy in Developing Countries*, Routledge, London.

Patat, J. & Lutfalla, M. (1986), *Histoire monétaire de la France au XXe siècle*, Economica, Paris.

Patel, K. K. (2016), *The New Deal: A Global History*, Princeton University Press, Princeton, NY.

Patrick, H. T. (1962), *Monetary Policy and Central Banking in Contemporary Japan*, Vol. 5. Bombay University Press, Bombay.

Pavès, L. & Simon, P. (1955), *Le crédit à moyen terme*, Presses universitaires de France, Paris.

Paxton, R. (1972), *Vichy France: Old Guard and New Order, 1940–1944*, Barrie & Jenkins, New York.

Péréon, Y.-M. (2018), *Moralizing the Market: How Gaullist France Embraced the US Model of Securities Regulation*, John Hopkins University Press, Baltimore, MD.

Perez, S. A. (1997), "From cheap credit to the EC: The politics of financial reform in Spain," in M. Loriaux, K. Woo-Cumings, S. Calder, S. Maxfield & S. Pérez, eds., *Capital Ungoverned: The Dismantling of Activist Credit Policies in Interventionist States*, Cornell University Press, Ithaca, NY.

     (1998), "Systemic explanations, divergent outcomes: The politics of financial liberal-ization in France and Spain," *International Studies Quarterly* 42, 755–784.

Perroux, F. (1971), *Inflation, dollar et euro-dollar*, Gallimard, Paris.

Pessis, C., Topçu, S. & Bonneuil, C. (2013), *Une autre histoire des Trente Glorieuses. Modernisation, contestations et pollutions dans la France d'après-guerre*, La Découverte, Paris.

Philip, A. & Monceau, A. (1936), *La toute-puissance bancaire et la nationalisation du crédit*. Avant-propos de Jules Moch, Librairie populaire, Paris.

Piketty, T. (2014), *Capital in the Twenty-First Century*, Harvard University Press, Cambridge, MA.

Pineau, C. (1938), "La nationalisation du crédit," *Revue Banque et bourse* (14), 91–110.

Plessis, A. (1985), *Régents et gouverneurs de la Banque de France sous le Second Empire*, Champion, Genève.

     (1991), "Les banques, le crédit et l'économie," in M. Lévy-Leboyer & J. C Casanova, eds., *Entre l'État et le marché: l'économie française des années 1880 à nos jours*, Gallimard, Paris, pp. 332–367.

     (1996), "Les banques françaises dans les grandes crises du 20e siècle," *Vingtième Siècle. Revue d'histoire* 52(1), 85–93.

     (1998), *Histoires de la Banque de France*, Albin Michel, Paris.

     (2001), "La révolution de l'escompte dans la France du XIXe siècle," *Revue d'histoire du XIXe siècle* 23, 143–163.

Polak, J. J. (1997), "The IMF monetary model at forty," IMF Working Paper No. 97/49, International Monetary Fund.

Polak, J. & Argy, V. (1971), "Credit policy and the balance of payments," *Staff Papers International Monetary Fund* 18(1), 1–24.

Polanyi, K. (1944), *The Great Transformation: Economic and Political Origins of Our Time*, Rinehart, New York.

(1957), 'The economy as instituted process," in K. Polanyi, C. Arensberg & H. Pearson, eds., *Trade and Market in the Early Empires: Economies in History and Theory*, The Free Press, New York; Glencoe, IL, pp. 243–270.

(1963), "Ports of trade in early societies," *The Journal of Economic History* 23(1), 30–45.

Posner, R. A. (1974), "Theories of economic regulation," *The Bell Journal of Economics and Management Science* 5(2), 335–358.

Primiceri, G. E. (2006), "Why inflation rose and fell: Policy-makers' beliefs and US postwar stabilization policy," *The Quarterly Journal of Economics* 121(3), 867–901.

Qian, Y. & Weingast, B. (1997), "Federalism as a commitment to preserving market incentives," *Journal of Economic Perspectives* 11(4), 83–92.

Quennouëlle-Corre, L. (2000), *La direction du Trésor: 1947–1967: l'État-banquier et la croissance*, CHEFF, Paris.

Quennouëlle-Corre, L. (2005a), "Les réformes bancaires et financières de 1966–1967," in E. Bussière, ed., *Michel Debré, un réformateur aux Finances*, CHEFF, Paris, pp. 85–117.

Quennouëlle-Corre, L. (2005b), "The state, banks and financing of investments in France from World War II to the 1970s," *Financial History Review* 12(1), 63–86.

Quennouëlle-Corre, L. (2015), *La place financière de Paris au XXe siècle: Des ambitions contrariées*, CHEFF, Paris.

Radouant, J. (1921), *Les Rapports de la Banque de France et de l'État particulièrement pendant la guerre de 1914–1918*, Rousseau, Paris.

Ramey, V. A. (2011), "Identifying government spending shocks: It's all in the timing!," *The Quarterly Journal of Economics* 126(1), 1–50.

Ramey, V. A. & Shapiro, M. D. (1998), "Costly capital reallocation and the effects of government spending," *Carnegie-Rochester Conference Series on Public Policy* 48, 145–194.

Ramon, G. (1929), *Histoire de la Banque de France d'après les sources originales*, Grasset, Paris.

Ray, P. (2013), *Monetary Policy: Oxford India Short Introductions*, Oxford University Press, Delhi.

(2017), "Political economy of central banking in India," in R. Nagaraj & S. Motiram, eds., *Political Economy of Contemporary India*, Cambridge University Press, Cambridge, UK, pp. 25–50.

Reinhart, C. M. & Rogoff, K. (2009), *This Time Is Different: Eight Centuries of Financial Folly*, Princeton University Press, Princeton, NY.

Reinhart, C. M. & Sbrancia, B. (2015), "The liquidation of government debt," *Economic Policy* 30(2), 291–333.

Ringe, A. & Rollings, N. (2000), "Responding to relative decline: The creation of the National Economic Development Council," *The Economic History Review* 53(2), 331–353.

Rodgers, D. T. (2011), *Age of Fracture*, Harvard University Press, Cambridge, MA.

Rodrik, D. (1994), "King Kong meets Godzilla: The World Bank and the East Asian miracle," CEPR Discussion Paper No. 944.

(1995), "Getting interventions right: How South Korea and Taiwan grew rich," *Economic Policy* 10(20), 55–107.

Romer, C. D. & Romer, D. H. (1989), "Does monetary policy matter? A new test in the spirit of Friedman and Schwartz," in *NBER Macroeconomics Annual*, Vol. 4, MIT Press, Cambridge, MA, pp. 121–184.

(1993), "Credit channel or credit actions? An interpretation of the postwar transmission mechanism," NBER Working Paper Series No. 4485, National Bureau of Economic Research.

(1994), "Monetary policy matters," *Journal of Monetary Economics* 34(1), 75–88.

(2002), "The evolution of economic understanding and postwar stabilization policy," NBER Working Paper Series No. 9274, National Bureau of Economic Research.

(2004), "A new measure of monetary shocks: Derivation and implications," *American Economic Review* 94(4), 1055–1084.

Rosanvallon, P. (1987), "Histoire des idées keynésiennes en France," *Revue française d'économie* 2(4), 22–56.

(1998), *Le Peuple introuvable: Histoire de la représentation démocratique en France*, Gallimard, Paris.

(2000), *La démocratie inachevée: Histoire de la souveraineté du peuple en France*, Gallimard, Paris.

Ross, D. (2004), "Domestic monetary policy and the banking system in Britain 1945–1971," in R. Michie & P. Williamson, eds., *The British Government and the City of London in the Twentieth Century*, Cambridge University Press, Cambridge, UK, pp. 298–321.

Roulleau, G. (1914), *Les règlements par effets de commerce en France et à l'étranger*, Dubreuil, Frèrebeau et cie, Paris.

Rousso, H., ed. (1987), *La Planification en crise: 1965–1985*, Editions du CNRS, Paris.

Rueff, J. (1929), "Mr. Keynes' views on the transfer problem," *The Economic Journal* 39(155), 388–408.

(1947), "The fallacies of Lord Keynes' General Theory," *The Quarterly Journal of Economics* 61(3), 343–367.

(1957), "Eléments pour une théorie du taux d'escompte et de la balance des comptes," *Revue économique* 8(4), 529–559.

(1962), *Discours sur le crédit*, CELSE, Paris.

(1971), *Le péché monétaire de l'Occident*, Plon, Paris.

(1972), *Combats pour l'ordre nancier: mémoires et documents pour servir à l'histoire du dernier demi-siècle*, Plon, Paris.

(1977), *De l'aube au crépuscule: autobiographie de l'auteur*, Plon, Paris.

Ruggie, J. G. (1982), "International regimes, transactions, and change: Embedded liberalism in the postwar economic order," *International Organization* 36(2), 379–415.

Sachs, J. & Wyplosz, C. (1986), "The economic consequences of President Mitterrand," *Economic Policy* 1(2), 262–322.

Saint Marc, M. (1983), *Histoire monétaire de la France, 1800–1980*, Presses universitaires de France, Paris.

Saint-Paul, G. (1993), "Economic reconstruction in France: 1945–1958," in R. Dornbusch, W. Nolling & R. Layard, eds., *Postwar Economic Reconstruction and Lessons for the East Today*, MIT Press, Cambridge, MA, pp. 83–114.

(1994), "Monetary policy in economic transition: Lessons from the French postwar experience," *European Economic Review* 38(34), 891–898.

Sauvy, A. (1946), *Chances de l'économie française*, Presses Universitaires de France, Paris.

Scheller, H. K. (2011), "Le Comité des gouverneurs des banques centrales de la CEE et l'unification monétaire européenne," *Histoire, économie & société* 4, 79–99.

Schenk, C. (1998), "The origins of the eurodollar market in London: 1955–1963," *Explorations in Economic History* 35(2), 221–238.

Schenk, C. R. (2010), *The Decline of Sterling: Managing the Retreat of an International Currency, 1945–1992*, Cambridge University Press, Cambridge, UK.

Schmidt, V. A. (1996), *From State to Market? The Transformation of French Business and Government*, Cambridge University Press, Cambridge, UK.

Schmidt, V. A. (2003), "French capitalism transformed, yet still a third variety of capitalism," *Economy and Society* 32(4), 526–554.

Schreft, S. L. (1990), "Credit controls: 1980," *Economic Review, Federal Reserve Bank of Richmond* 17(6), 16–36.

(1992), "Welfare-improving credit controls," *Journal of Monetary Economics* 30(1), 57–72.

Schularick, M. & Taylor, A. M. (2012), "Credit booms gone bust: Monetary policy, leverage cycles, and financial crises, 1870–2008," *American Economic Review* 102(2), 1029–1061.

Shapiro, M. D. (1994), "Federal reserve policy: Cause and effect," in G. Mankiw, ed., *Monetary Policy*, NBER, University of Chicago, Chicago, pp. 307–334.

Shaw, E. S. (1973), *Financial Deepening in Economic Development*, Oxford University Press, Oxford, UK.

Shonfield, A. (1965), *Modern Capitalism: The Changing Balance of Public & Private Power*, Oxford University Press, Oxford, UK.

Sicsic, P. & Wyplosz, C. (1995), "France, 1945–1992," in N. Crafts & G. Toniolo, eds., *Economic Growth in Europe Since 1945*, Cambridge University Press, Cambridge, UK, pp. 210–239.

Siklos, P. L. (2002), *The Changing Face of Central Banking: Evolutionary Trends Since World War II*, Cambridge University Press, Cambridge, UK.

Siklos, P. L. (2017), *Central Banks into the Breach: From Triumph to Crisis and the Road Ahead*, Oxford University Press, Oxford, UK.

Sims, C. A. (1992), "Interpreting the macroeconomic time series facts: The effects of monetary policy," *European Economic Review* 36(5), 975–1000.

Sims, C. A. & Zha, T. (2006), "Were there regime switches in U.S. monetary policy?," *American Economic Review* 96(1), 54–81.

Singleton, J. (2011), *Central Banking in the Twentieth Century*, Cambridge University Press, Cambridge, UK.

Sterdyniak, H. & Vasseur, C. (1985), "Encadrement du crédit et politique monétaire," *Revue de l'OFCE* 11(1), 105–136.

Stoskopf, N. (2002), *Les patrons du Second Empire. Banquiers et financiers parisiens*, Ed. Cénomane, Paris.

Streeck, W. (2005), "Rejoinder: On terminology, functionalism, (historical) institutionalism and liberalization," *Socio-Economic Review* 3(3), 577–587.

Sun, G. (2016), *Reforms in China's Monetary Policy: A Frontbencher's Perspective*, Springer, London.

Sunstein, C. R. (1996), "On the expressive function of law," *University of Pennsylvania Law Review* 144(5), 2021–2053.

Swedberg, R. (2003), "The case for an economic sociology of law," *Theory and Society* 32(1), 1–37.

Taylor, J. B. (1993), "Discretion versus policy rules in practice," *Carnegie-Rochester Conference Series on Public Policy* 39(0), 195–214.

(1998), "An historical analysis of monetary policy rules," NBER Working Paper No. w6768, National Bureau of Economic Research.

Temin, P. (2002), "The Golden Age of European growth reconsidered," *European Review of Economic History* 6(1), 3–22.

Temple, J. (2001), "Structural change and Europe's Golden Age," CEPR Discussion Paper No. 2861.

Teyssier, L. (1973), *Le Controle des changes en France: de 1932 à 1972*, Librairie du commerce international, Paris.

Théret, B. (1994), "La consécration républicaine du néolibéralisme," in B. Jobert, ed., *Le tournant néolibéral en Europe*, L'Harmattan, Paris, pp. 29–86.

Thévenin, P. (2009), "L'institution, la casuistique et l'historien. Hommage à Yan Thomas," Tracés. *Revue de science humaines* (17), 331–386.

Thomas, Y. (1991), "L'institution de la majesté," *Revue de synthèse* (3–4), 331–386.

(1993), "L'institution civile de la cité," *Le Débat* 74(mars–avril), 23–44.

(2002), "Présentation 'Histoire et droit'," *Annales. Histoire, Sciences Sociales* 57(6), 1425–1428.

Thurow, L. C., ed. (1971), "Activities by various central banks to promote economic and social welfare programs," a staff report prepared for the Committee on Banking and Currency, US House of Representatives, 91st Congress, second session.

Tobin, J. (1948), "The fallacies of Lord Keynes' General Theory: Comment," *The Quarterly Journal of Economics* 62(5), 763–770.

(1953), "Monetary policy and the management of the public debt: The Patman Inquiry," *The Review of Economics and Statistics* 118–127.

(1969), "A general equilibrium approach to monetary theory," *Journal of Money, Credit and Banking* 1(1), 15–29.

(1970), "Deposit interest ceilings as a monetary control," *Journal of Money, Credit and Banking* 2(1), 4–14.

Tomlinson, J. (1981), "Why was there never a 'Keynesian Revolution' in economic policy?," *Economy and Society* 10(1), 72–87.

(1996), *Democratic Socialism and Economic Policy: The Attlee Years, 1945–1951*, Cambridge University Press, Cambridge, UK.

Toniolo, G. (1998), "Europe's Golden Age, 1950–1973: Speculations from a long- run perspective," *The Economic History Review* 51(2), 252–267.

Toniolo, G. & Clement, P. (2005), *Central Bank Cooperation at the Bank for International Settlements, 1930–1973*, Cambridge University Press, Cambridge, UK.

Toniolo, G. & White, E. N. (2015), "The evolution of the financial stability mandate: From its origins to the present day," NBER Working Paper No. w20844, National Bureau of Economic Research.

Tooze, A. (2006), *The Wages of Destruction*, Allen Lane Books, New York.

Tooze, A. J. (2014), "Who is afraid of inflation? The long shadow of the 1970s," *Journal of Modern European History* 12(1), 53–60.

Touchelay, B. (2007), "La monnaie dans les discours du CNPF entre 1947 et 1969: un révélateur des relations entre le patronat et les gouvernements," *Revue européenne des sciences sociales* XLV(137), 233–250.

(2017), "Mesurer l'inflation, un processus délicat," in P-M. Chélini & L. Warlouzet, eds., *Calmer les prix/Slowing Down Prices*, Presses de Sciences Po, Paris, pp. 77–94.

Villa, P. (1997), *Séries macro-économiques historiques: méthodologie et analyse économique*, Institut National de la Statistique et des Etudes Economiques, Paris.

Vinen, R. (2002), *Bourgeois Politics in France, 1945–1951*, Cambridge University Press, Cambridge, UK.

Vittas, D. & Cho, Y. J. (1995), "Credit policies: Lessons from East Asia," World Bank Policy Research Working Paper No. 1458.

Von Hagen, J. (1999), "A new approach to monetary policy (1971–1978)," in Deutsche Bundesbank, ed., *Fifty Years of the Deutsche Mark*, Oxford University Press, Oxford, UK, pp. 403–438.

Vonyo, T. (2008), "Postwar reconstruction and the golden age of economic growth," *European Review of Economic History* 12(2), 221–241.

Voth, H. (2003), "Convertibility, currency controls and the cost of capital in Western Europe, 1950–1999," *International Journal of Finance & Economics* 8(3), 255–276.

Wade, R. (1992), *Governing the Market*, Princeton University Press, Princeton, NY.

Warburg, P. M. (1910), *The Discount System in Europe: Monetary Commission*, Vol. 402, US Government Printing Office, Washington, DC.

Warlouzet, L. (2010), *Le choix de la CEE pour la France; l'Europe Économique en débat de Mendès France à de Gaulle (1955–1969)*, CHEFF, Paris.

(2017), *Governing Europe in a Globalizing World: Neoliberalism and its Alternatives Following the 1973 Oil Crisis*, Routledge, London.

Werner, R. A. (2002a), "Monetary policy implementation in Japan: What they say versus what they do," *Asian Economic Journal* 16(2), 111–151.

(2002b), "A reconsideration of the rationale for bank-centered economic systems and the effectiveness of directed credit policies in the light of Japanese evidence," *Japanese Economy* 30(3), 3–45.

Williamson, J. (1985), "On the system in Bretton Woods," *American Economic Review* 75(2), 74–79.

Wilson, J. S. (1957), *French Banking Structure and Credit Policy*, Bell, London.

Wyplosz, C. (1999), "Financial restraints and liberalization in postwar Europe," CEPR discussion papers.

Yates, A. M. (2015), *Selling Paris: Property and Commercial Culture in the Fin-de-Siecle Capital*, Harvard University Press, Cambridge, MA.

Zentz, P. (1951), "Le rôle de la caisse nationale des marchés de l'Etat pour l'octroi de crédits de rééquipement dans le cadre professionnel," *Revue économique* 2(5), 675–681.

Zysman, J. (1983), *Governments, Markets, and Growth: Financial Systems and the Politics of Industrial Change*, Cornell University Press, Ithaca, NY.

Index

STUDIES IN MACROECONOMIC HISTORY (*continued from page ii*)

Larry Neal, *The Rise of Financial Capitalism: International Capital Markets in the Age of Reason* (1993)

S. N. Broadberry and N. F. R. Crafts, Editors, *Britain in the International Economy, 1870–1939* (1992)

Aurel Schubert, *The Credit-Anstalt Crisis of 1931* (1992)

Trevor J. O. Dick and John E. Floyd, *Canada and the Gold Standard: Balance of Payments Adjustment under Fixed Exchange Rates, 1871–1913* (1992)

Kenneth Mouré, *Managing the Franc Poincaré: Economic Understanding and Political Constraint in French Monetary Policy, 1928–1936* (1991)

David C. Wheelock, *The Strategy and Consistency of Federal Reserve Monetary Policy, 1924–1933* (1991)

Printed in the United States
By Bookmasters